Asia and Latin America

T0386212

Until the late 1980s, Japan was the only Asian country with notable political and economic relations. Since then, however, several Asian nations have perceived growing links with the Latin American region as a means of diversifying their political and particularly economic relations while many Latin American decision-makers have increasingly recognized the strategic importance of East Asia in their foreign policy and foreign economic policy designs.

This book analyses the economic, political and socio-cultural relations between Asia and Latin America, and examines their growing importance in international relations. In the first part of the book the contributors look at the policies, interests and strategies of individual Asian and Latin American states, while the second part delves into the analysis of multilateral institution-building in Asia–Latin America relations. As such, *Asia and Latin America* will be of interest to undergraduate and postgraduate students and scholars of comparative politics, international relations, Asian politics and Latin American politics.

Jörn Dosch is Professor of Asia Pacific Studies and Director of the Department of East Asian Studies at the University of Leeds, UK. He was previously a Fulbright Scholar at the Asia/Pacific Research Center, Stanford University, and a Lecturer at the University of Mainz, Germany.

Olaf Jacob works at the Konrad-Adenauer Foundation where he is Director of the Regional Program 'Economic and Social Order in Latin America' in Rio de Janeiro. He is a former professor of Latin American and Asian Economics Studies at the Universidad del Pacifico in Lima, Peru.

Routledge Contemporary Asia Series

Asia and Latin America

Political, economic and
multilateral relations

**Edited by Jörn Dosch
and Olaf Jacob**

LONDON AND NEW YORK

First published 2010
by Routledge
2 Park Square, Milton Park, Abingdon, Oxon OX14 4RN

Simultaneously published in the USA and Canada
by Routledge
52 Vanderbilt Avenue, New York, NY 10017

Routledge is an imprint of the Taylor & Francis Group, an Informa business

© 2010 Jörn Dosch and Olaf Jacob

Typeset in Times New Roman by
Keystroke, Tettenhall, Wolverhampton

First issued in paperback 2013

British Library Cataloguing in Publication Data
A catalogue record for this book is available from the British Library

Library of Congress Cataloging-in-Publication Data
Asia and Latin America: political, economic, and multilateral relations /
edited by Jörn Dosch and Olaf Jacob.
    p. cm. – (Routledge contemporary Asia series)
1. Asia–Relations–Latin America. 2. Latin America–Relations–Asia.
I. Dosch, Jörn. II. Jacob, Olaf.
DS33.4.L29A85 2009
303.48′2508–dc22
2009037428

ISBN13: 978–0–415–55650–7 (hbk)
ISBN13: 978–0–415–85466–5 (pbk)

Contents

Figures

Tables

Contributors

Gracia Abad has been Assistant Professor of International Relations and Regional Integration in Asia and the Pacific and Security and Cooperation at Complutense University (Madrid) where she serves as the UNISCI's (Unidad de Investigación sobre Seguridad y Cooperación) expert on the Asia–Pacific since 2000. She also taught at Nebrija University (Madrid). Dr Abad is currently Visiting Fellow at Royal Holloway (University of London). Dr Abad is author, co-author and contributor to a number of publications on these issues, namely *The Crisis in North Korea* (UNISCI Papers 31, Madrid, 2004); 'China e India: Nuevas superpotencias' (in *Una Mirada al Mundo del Siglo XXI*, Madrid: Ministerio de Defensa, 2007); 'Asia: Una región inestable' (in *La paz y las regiones*) (México: Fondo Editorial de Nueva Leon, 2008) and *Las organizaciones internacionales y la seguridad en Asia Central* (ARI 107, Madrid: Real Instituto Elcano, 2008). She holds a BA in Political Science, an MPhil in International Relations and a PhD in Political Science (Honours) from Complutense University.

Karsten Bechle is a Research Fellow at the GIGA German Institute of Global and Area Studies in Hamburg. Previously he has been a Research Fellow at the Arnold-Bergstraesser-Institute in Freiburg and a Lecturer at the University of Freiburg, Department of Political Science. Bechle studied Political Science, History and Spanish at the University of Freiburg and the University of Buenos Aires. He is currently working in Argentina and Venezuela on a research project about 'Persistence and Change of Neopatrimonialism in Various Non-OECD Regions' and he is writing a PhD thesis on the role of ideas in the regional integration process of MERCOSUR.

Alberto Camarena received a BA in International Relations from the Universidad Iberoamericana in Mexico City and an MA in Chinese studies from the Department of East Asian Studies at the University of Leeds, UK, where he is about to complete a PhD on relations between China and Southeast Asia. In 2008 he was awarded a Banco Santander research grant to investigate relations between China and Mexico. From 1995 to 1998 Camarena worked for the CONABIO (Comision Nacional para el Uso y Conocimiento de la Biodiversidad) which is linked to the Mexican Ministry of the Environment.

Jörn Dosch is Professor of Asia Pacific Studies and Director of the Department of East Asian Studies at the University of Leeds, UK. He was previously a Fulbright Scholar at the Asia/Pacific Research Center, Stanford University, and a Lecturer at the University of Mainz, Germany. Professor Dosch has published some 70 books and academic papers on East and Southeast Asian politics and international relations, including the monograph *The Changing Dynamics of Southeast Asian Politics* (Lynne Rienner, 2006). He earned his PhD in political science from the University of Mainz in 1996.

June A. Gordon is Professor of international and comparative studies in the Department of Education at the University of California–Santa Cruz. She conducts research on marginalized youth in the United States, the United Kingdom, Japan, and China. Her most recent book is entitled *Japan's Outcaste Youth: Education for Liberation* (Paradigm Publishers, 2008). Previous publications include *Beyond the Classroom Walls: Ethnographic Inquiry as Pedagogy* (London: RoutledgeFalmer, 2002) and *The Color of Teaching* (London and New York: RoutledgeFalmer, 2000). She completed a BA from Stanford University in East Asian studies and a PhD in educational policy from the University of Washington.

Olaf Jacob works at the Konrad-Adenauer Foundation where he is Director of the Regional Program 'Economic and Social Order in Latin America' in Rio de Janeiro, Brazil. He is a former professor of Latin American and Asian Economics Studies at the Universidad del Pacífico in Lima, Peru. He studied political science and international relations at the Johannes Gutenberg University in Mainz, Germany.

José Luis León-Manríquez holds a PhD in Political Science from Columbia University and is Professor in the Universidad Autónoma Metropolitana (UAM) in Mexico City. He is a former diplomat and worked as Director of the Academic and Outreach Activities at the Mexican Diplomatic Academy. He has published several articles, essays and books on international affairs in both Spanish and English and is an expert on Asian issues.

Howard Loewen is a Research Fellow in the Asia Division of the German Institute for International and Security Affairs in Berlin. His main research interests focus on the international relations and the international political economy of Southeast Asia and East Asia. He is especially interested in trade and financial agreements, regional cooperation, interregionalism and democratization with a country focus on the Philippines, Indonesia and Singapore.

Manfred Mols is Professor Emeritus of Political Science at the University of Mainz, Germany. He studied political science, public law, philosophy, and history in Freiburg, Munich and Glasgow. He also served as guest professor at Stanford University, California; Universidad Iberoamericana, Mexico; Hebrew University, Jerusalem; and National University of Australia, Canberra. Professor

Mols' areas of research include democracy in Latin America and Asia, regional integration in Latin America, Asia–Pacific cooperation and state and society in a comparative perspective. Professor Mols has published 25 books and some 150 academic papers in English, German, Spanish and Italian.

Melba E. Falck Reyes is Researcher at the Pacific Studies Department of the University of Guadalajara and member of the National System of Researchers of Mexico. Her areas of interest are International Political Economy and International Transpacific Relations. She has done research on the political economy of agricultural policy in Japan and South Korea and Mexico's transpacific relations. She is currently involved in a research project about the Mexico–Japan Economic Partnership Agreement. Professor Falck is the author of *Del Proteccionismo a la liberalización agrícola en Japón, Corea del Sur y Taiwán. Oportunidades para México. Un enfoque de economía política* (2006). (*From Protectionism to Liberalization in Japan, South Korea and Taiwan. Opportunities for Mexico. A Political Economy Approach*).

Caroline Rose is Senior Lecturer in Japanese Studies in the Department of East Asian Studies at the University of Leeds, UK. Her main areas of research are Sino-Japanese relations and Japan's foreign policy in general. She is currently working on a major research project on history and citizenship education in China and Japan, and on Japanese and Chinese foreign policy towards Africa. Dr Rose's publications include *Sino-Japanese Relations: Facing the Past, Looking to the Future?* (RoutledgeCurzon, 2004); 'Reconciliation – the broader context' in Dobson, H. and Kosuge Nobuko (eds) *The UK and Japan at War and Peace* (RoutledgeCurzon, 2009); 'Sino-Japanese relations and the dangers of new era diplomacy' in Dent, C.M. (ed.) *China, Japan and Regional Leadership in East Asia* (Edward Elgar, 2008); and 'The Yasukuni Shrine Problem in Sino-Japanese Relations: Facing a Stalemate' in John Breen (ed) *Yasukuni, the war dead and the struggle for Japan's past* (Hurst & Co, 2007).

Jürgen Rüland is Professor of Political Science at the University of Freiburg, and Director of the Arnold-Bergstraesser-Institute for Social Research, Freiburg (Germany). He has spent more than six years as a researcher and visiting professor in Southeast Asian countries including the Philippines, Thailand, Indonesia, Malaysia, Singapore and Vietnam. He has published widely on the Asia Pacific Region and is co-author of *Parliaments and Political Change in Asia* (ISEAS, 2005) and editor of *Interregionalism in International Politics* (Routledge, 2005).

Amalia Stuhldreher received a Licentiate Degree in International Relations (University del Salvador, Buenos Aires, Argentina) in 1993 followed by a PhD in Political Science (University of Mainz, Germany) in 1999. Until recently she was a Research Fellow at the University of Freiburg, Germany, and a member of the Department for Regional and Economical Politics at the Chamber of Commerce and Industry of the Upper Rhine (Germany). She is currently working as a consultant at the Development Agency of Tacuarembó, Uruguay.

Dr Stuhldreher's recent publications include 'Los biocombustibles en la relación de Brasil con la Unión Europea', in *Revista Comercio Exterior*, Vol. 58, No. 6, Banco de Comercio Exterior de México, June 2008 (pp. 442–50) and 'La Unión Europea y el Tratado de Lisboa: ¿Posibilidades de una nueva dinámica interna con implicancias externas?', in *Revista Estudios Internacionales*, Universidad de Chile, No. 159, January–April 2008 (pp. 33–47).

Charalambos Tsardanidis has been Director of the Institute of International Economic Relations, Athens, since 1993. He received his PhD from the London School of Economics and Political Science and has taught at the Panteion University, University of Piraeus and the Hellenic Open University. He is currently teaching at the Harokopeio University of Athens. Dr Tsardanidis has written extensively on areas relating to international political economy, external relations of EU and foreign policy analysis. He is the author of ten books and co-editor of eight. Articles by Dr Tsardanidis have appeared in the *European Foreign Affairs Review*, *Journal of Common Market Studies*, *Journal of European Integration*, *Journal of Political and Military Sociology*, *Journal of Area Studies, Geopolitics, Ethnopolitics*, and others.

Ta Minh Tuan is currently Deputy Director of the Center for Foreign Policy and Regional Studies, Diplomatic Academy of Vietnam (DAV) in Hanoi, Vietnam. Before he joined DAV, he had worked for Vietnam Union of Friendship Organizations as a desk officer at the Vietnam Peace Committee. Dr Tuan's research interests include US foreign and security policy, Vietnam–US relations, Vietnam's politics and foreign policy, the Asia–Pacific security, and non-proliferation of WMD and nuclear energy. He also teaches MA and BA courses on these subjects at DAV. He is a member of CSCAP Vietnam. Dr Tuan received his BA from Hanoi University, Vietnam; MA with First Class from the School of International Relations, Mahatma Gandhi University, India; and PhD in Political Science from the Institute of Political Studies, Polish Academy of Sciences, Warsaw.

Preface

The story of this book begins with a glass of Cuba Libre and a conversation over China's growing presence in Latin America. It is April 2005 and we are sitting in one of the new and trendy bars that have mushroomed in the historic centre of Cuenca, the marvel among Ecuadorian cities. A few months earlier, in November 2004, Chinese President Hu Jintao's first tour of Latin America marked the beginning of a new phase in China's relationship with the region or, as our Argentine colleague Gonzalo S. Paz famously put it, 'the year 2004 will be remembered as one in which an increasingly confident China jumped into Latin America'. While China did not enter the stage out of the blue and recent events are the result of carefully built relations that date back to the 1960s (involving a good deal of trial and error, though), 2004 was certainly a watershed. What strikes us on that chilly spring evening in Cuenca is not the empirical fact of China's emergence as an important economic and to an extent also political actor in Latin America but the little academic attention that this development has attracted. This is in stark contrast to the strong scholarly focus on, for example, China–Africa relations. And there is a second phenomenon that characterises the mainstream analysis of Latin America's international relations: until very recently East Asia was at best mentioned in passing (see for example – the otherwise excellent – edited volumes *Latin America in a Changing Global Environment*, Roett, Riordan and Guadalupe Paz (eds), Lynne Rienner Publishers, and *Latin American and Caribbean Foreign Policy*, Mora, Frank O. and Jeanne A.K. Hey, Rowman & Littlefield, both of 2003; a notable early exception is Abraham F. Lowenthal's and Gregory F. Treverton's 1994 edited book *Latin America in a New World*, Westview Press, with its superb chapters on Japan and China). Surely, from a Latin American perspective Washington, Madrid, Berlin, Paris and London are traditionally more important partners than Tokyo or Seoul. Yet, Japan's and South Korea's, and more recently also Singapore's, Vietnam's and other Asian states' interests towards Latin America and vice versa have resulted in a diversification of foreign relations on both coasts of the Pacific that are worth a deeper look. We are of course not the first to think like this. Two books in particular – *East Asia and Latin America: The Unlikely Alliance*, edited by Peter H. Smith, Kotaro Horisaka and Shoji Nishijima (Rowman & Littlefield, 2003), and *Latin America and East Asia: Attempts at Diversification*, edited by Jörg Faust, Manfred Mols and Won-ho Kim (Lit, 2005) – have made the terra incognita of Asia–Latin America relations analytically accessible (so to speak). The prestigious journal *México y la Cuenca del Pacífico*, published by the Department of Pacific Studies at the University of Guadalajara, has equally contributed to the investigation of the increasingly obvious encounter between the two continents. However – as we think back in 2005 – there is a need for a comprehensive, multi-level and inter-disciplinary stock-taking of Asia–Latin America relations that goes further than the existing literature by painting a more detailed and multi-faceted picture of the structures, processes and the actors involved; a more holistic account of inter-continental relations that does not just look at the biggest players in the game and the most visible trophies of the transpacific encounter, such as free trade agreements, but also analyses the interests and strategies of fast emerging international actors, such as Vietnam and Peru, and the processes of multilateral institution-building (beyond the obvious case of Asia–Pacific Economic Cooperation (APEC)). Hence, we decide to apply to the British Academy for a 'joint activities grant' with the objective of bringing together some of the leading scholars in the field of Asia–Latin America relations from Europe, Latin America, Asia and the United States.

The application is successful and an international conference on the topic takes place in November 2006 at the Department of East Asian Studies, University of Leeds, in the UK. Based on the results and discussions of the workshop the book gradually takes shape over the next two and a half years. During this process several follow-up activities have a significant input into the drafting of the final manuscript. In November 2008 Olaf Jacob co-organizes an international conference ('Tiger meets Jaguar') on Asia–Latin America relations in Berlin. A visiting fellowship to further investigate the interests of China and other Asian actors in Latin America, funded by the British Economic and Social Research Council (ESRC) and the Social Science Research Council (SSRC) of the United States, enables Jörn Dosch to spend a few weeks at the University of Guadalajara in 2009. We gratefully acknowledge the support of the British Academy and the ESRC/SSRC – without these grants the book would never have materialized. The integration of the project into the activities of the White Rose East Asia Centre (WREAC) – an international Centre of Excellence on China and Japan jointly managed by the Departments of East Asian Studies at the Universities of Leeds and Sheffield – was also very beneficial. We would like to thank Professor Mark Williams, Head of the School of Modern Languages and Cultures at the University of Leeds, and Professor Terry King, Executive Director of WREAC, for their continuous support, Stephanie Rogers and her team at Routledge for the pro-fessional guidance and – as always – patience, and last but not least the two anonymous reviewers for their valuable comments on an earlier draft. It goes without saying that all errors are ours alone.

Jörn Dosch and Olaf Jacob
Leeds and Berlin, July 2009

Abbreviations

ACN	Andean Community of Nations
ACP	countries under the framework of the Cotonu Agreement (African, Caribbean and Pacific Group of States)
AFTA	ASEAN Free Trade Area
ALADI (LAIA)	Asociación Latinoamericana de Integración
APEC	Asia–Pacific Economic Cooperation
ARF	ASEAN Regional Forum
ASEAN	Association of Southeast Asian Nations
ASEAN+3	ASEAN + China, South Korea and Japan
ASEF	Asia–Europe Foundation
ASEM	Asia–Europe Meeting
AU	African Union
BRIC	the cooperation between Brazil, Russia, India and China
CAAREM	Confederacy of Customs Agents of the Mexican Republic
CAFTA	Central America Free Trade Agreement
CAN	Andean Community (Comunidad Andina de Naciones)
CARICOM	Caribbean Community
CBMC	Binational Mexico–China Commission
CCP	Chinese Communist Party
CDM	[Cooperation on the] Clean Development Mechanism
CEO	Chief Executive Officer
CEPAL	UN Commission for Latin America and the Caribbean
CIATE	Center for Information and Support for Workers Abroad
CMC	Common Market Council
CMG	Common Market Group
CONABIO	Comision Nacional para el Uso y Conocimiento de la Biodiversidad
CTC	change in tariff classification

DAV	Diplomatic Academy of Vietnam
DR	Dominican Republic
EALAF	East Asia–Latin America Forum
EAS	East Asian Summit
EC	European Commission
ECLAC	Economic Commission for Latin America and the Caribbean
EFTA	European Free Trade Association
EMP	Euro-Mediterranean Partnership
EPA	Economic Partnership Agreement (AAE in Spanish)
EU	European Union
FDI	foreign direct investment
FEALAC	The Forum for East Asia–Latin America Cooperation
FIPS	Five Interested Parties group or G5
FOCALAE	Spanish acronym (FEALAC)
FTA	Free Trade Agreements
FTAA	Free Trade Area of the Americas
GA	General Assembly
GATS	General Agreement on Trade in Services
GATT	General Agreement on Tariffs and Trade
GDP	gross domestic product
GFCF	Gross Fixed Capital Formation
GNI	gross national income
GSTP	Global System of Trade Preferences among Developing Countries
HS	Harmonized System
IAEA	International Atomic Energy Agency
IBSA	India–Brazil–South Africa cooperation
IDB	Inter-American Development Bank
IMF	International Monetary Fund
INTAL	Institute for the Integration of Latin America and the Caribbean
IPE	International Political Economy
IPR	Intellectual Property Rights
IS	Import Substitution
ISI	Import Substitution Industrialization
IWC	International Whaling Commission
JETRO	the official Japanese foreign trade organisation
KIEP	Korean Institute for International Economic Policy
KORUS-FTA	Korea–United States FTA
KORUS-FTALA	Latin America–Korea–United States FTA
LA	Latin America
LAIA (ALADI)	Asociación Latinoamericana de Integración
LDCs	least developed countries

MAFF	Ministry of Agriculture, Forestry and Fisheries
MercoPress	South Atlantic News Agency, independent online news agency based in Montevideo, Uruguay, which covers the news related to MERCOSUR-member countries
MERCOSUR	Common Market of the Cono Sur, grouping Argentina, Brazil, Paraguay and Uruguay (Southern Common Market)
METI	Ministry of Economy, Trade and Industry
MEXT	Ministry of Education, Science, Culture, Sports and Technology
MFN	Most Favoured Nation
MK21CC	Mexico–Korea 21st Century Commission
MoFA	Ministry of Foreign Affairs
MOFAT	Ministry of Foreign Affairs and Trade
MoU	memorandum of understanding
MTC	MERCOSUR Trade Commission
NAFTA	North American Free Trade Agreement
NAM	Non-Aligned Movement
NDU	National Defence University
NPT	Non Proliferation Treaty
NSG	Nuclear Supplier Group
NTA	New Transatlantic Agenda
OAS	Organization of American States
ODA	Overseas Development Assistance
OECD	Organization for Economic Cooperation and Development
OPP	Ouro Preto Protocol
PBEC	Pacific Basin Economic Council
PDVSA	Petroleos de Venezuela
PECC	Pacific Economic Cooperation Council
PLA	People's Liberation Army
PM	Prime Minister
ppp	purchasing power parity
PRC	People's Republic of China
PTA	Preferential Trade Agreement
PYMES	Pequeñas y Medianas Empresas (small and medium-sized companies)
ROK	Republic of Korea
ROO	Rules of Origin
SAARC	South Asian Association for Regional Cooperation
SACU	Southern Africa Customs Union
SADC	Southern African Development Community
SAFTA	South Asian Free Trade Area
SEAA	Strategic Economic Association Agreement

Secex	Brazilian Foreign Trade Secretariat
SELA	Latin American Economic System
SICA	System of Central American Integration
SINOPEC	China Petroleum and Chemical Corp
SMEs	small and medium enterprises
SOM	Senior Officials' Meeting
SP	specific process [rule]
T-FTA	Trilateral Free Trade Agreement
TICAD	Tokyo International Conference on African Development
TN	Transnational Companies
TRIPS	Trade-Related Aspects of Intellectual Property Rights
UAM	Universidad Autónoma Metropolitana
UFC	Uniting for Consensus
UN	United Nations
Unasur	Union of South American Nations
UNCTAD	United Nations Conference on Trade and Development
UNESCO	United Nations Educational, Scientific and Cultural Organization
UNISCI	Unidad de Investigación sobre Seguridad y Cooperación
UNSC	United Nations Security Council
USSR	Union of Soviet Socialist Republics
VA	Value-Added
WREAC	White Rose East Asia Centre

1 Introduction

The three-phase encounter of two continents

Jörn Dosch

The encounter of Asia and Latin America is the story of globalization. If we accept that European colonialism and imperialism constituted the first phase of the phenomenon for which the term globalization has been coined, it was the Spanish colonization of the Philippines that resulted in the earliest contact between Latin America and Asia in the second half of the sixteenth century as part of a worldwide operation. The enormous increase in output of the silver mines in Spanish America in the 1570s finally had its effect on Asia. Some of the silver was carried directly to Manila from Acapulco, to buy Southeast Asian spices and Chinese goods. This sea trading route existed for more than two centuries before the Spanish Pacific fleet ceased its service in 1815. According to Chinese accounts, contacts between the two continents even pre-date the Spanish empire and go back to Chinese expeditions reaching the American continent as early as the fifth century AD (see Chapter 2 in this book). Legend or fact – there is little doubt that the pre-modern encounter between the two continents was a sporadic one.

Fast forward to the Cold War era and the ideologically motivated and balance of power-driven second phase of the encounter, which is prominently associated with, first, the Non-Aligned Movement (NAM) and, second, the dynamics of Sino-American and Sino-Soviet relations respectively. While it was Argentine President Juan Domingo Perón who pioneered the principles of non-alignment and peaceful co-existence from 1946 within the context of the 'Third Position' ideology, Latin America never quite managed to match the influence of Asia in the NAM. Only in Fidel Castro did the continent have a protagonist of as equal status as Nehru of India or Sukarno of Indonesia within the movement that was de facto inaugurated by the Bandung Conference in 1955 and put on an institutional basis at the Belgrade summit meeting in 1961. But Castro was also Latin America's dilemma: the position of members from the Western Hemisphere – with Bolivia, Brazil and Mexico being the most active in the early 1960s – had been made more difficult by Cuban ambiguity about what was meant by non-alignment and Castro's refusal to renounce the advocacy of revolution (Calvert 1994: 212–13). This position, in turn, and the Cuban revolution in general opened a window of opportunity for Mao's China. In the early 1960s the motivation of the Chinese leadership to include Latin America in its foreign policy, albeit in a distant third position behind Asia and Africa, was mainly linked to Beijing's anti-US stance and the quest to counter Washington's economic blockade and political hostility (Xu 1994: 151). China showed great interest in Castro's rise and hoped to see the emergence of the Cuban Revolution as a model for other parts of the region. However, China's flirtation with other communist parties and movements made only very limited impression in Central and South America (Lawrance 1975: 152); and once the Sino-Soviet split had escalated into full-scale political and military antagonism towards the end of the decade, 'China began to discard political biases, distance itself from radical movements and guerrilla bands, and develop relations with established national governments in Latin America' in an attempt to secure more support for its international position (Xu 1994: 152). The Kissinger and Nixon visits to China in 1971–2 eventually paved the way for pragmatic and issues-oriented relations between Beijing and Latin American capitals, free of any ideological ballast. By the end of the decade China had established diplomatic relations with most major Latin American states, including Argentina, Brazil, Chile, Mexico and Peru. Chinese–Latin American relations in the 1970s and 1980s were predominantly politically motivated and driven by quid pro quo strategies. For example, most Latin American governments voted for China's entry into the United Nations while Beijing supported Latin American claims for 200-mile territorial sea limits in the Law of the Sea Negotiations (ibid). A core strategic issue in this context is the Taiwan factor. The diplomatic isolation of Taiwan has been among the – perhaps even the highest-ranking of the – key political objectives in Latin America where Beijing and Taipei have competed fiercely with each other, mobilizing extensive diplomatic and economic resources to hold their camps together (Teng 2007: 102). Currently, only 23 national governments maintain diplomatic relations with Taiwan, 11 of which are in Latin America, including some small Caribbean nations.[1] The most recent state to switch diplomatic relations from Taiwan to China was Costa Rica in 2007.

While economic incentives have played a part in the competition over diplomatic recognition, bilateral trade and investment in China's relations with most Latin American countries was an insignificant factor until well into the 1990s. It was Japan, not China, that spearheaded the third and current phase in the inter-continental encounter which I call the 'mercantilist plus' era, because it is primarily characterized by a substantial increase in economic links in a globalizing world with political, diplomatic and strategic considerations (the 'plus') still blending in. The eventual failure of import substitution in Latin America and the concurrent success of East Asian economies with outward and more market-oriented policies in the 1980s and 1990s led Latin America to look to East Asia as a source of stimulation if not a model. The so-called Asian Miracle is even said to have contributed to Latin America's shift towards more openness in the late 1980s and throughout the 1990s (Edwards 1995; Tussie 2004; Kay 2002).

By the early 1990s Japan had established itself as the second largest trade partner of most Latin American economies and Tokyo had become the largest lender to Latin America, both bilaterally and through its contributions to international financial institutions (Stallings and Horisaka 1994: 126). Japan did not abruptly emerge in the Western Hemisphere though. The country's first interest in Latin America dates back to the late nineteenth century, when the region became an important destination for Japanese emigrants who escaped poverty, over-population and unemployment at home. At the time of the Second World War some 200,000 Japanese citizens (known as *Nikkei*) were living in Brazil, Peru and Mexico. While emigration flows decreased after the War, Japan rapidly gained importance as a trade partner from the 1950s onwards (ibid: 130). In this process Latin America's importance changed from a supplier of raw materials to a market for Japanese exports and destination of foreign direct investment (FDI) which reached its relative peak in the 1981–5 period, when Latin America absorbed 20.1 per cent of Japanese global FDI (Horisaka 2005; this share declined to 11.6 per cent in 1996–2001). Overseas Development Assistance (ODA) also played an important role, with Peru receiving 10 per cent of the entire Japanese ODA budget in the early 1990s – the Japanese origins of then Peruvian President Fujimori were a contributing factor – and Brazil and Mexico, Bolivia and Paraguay (all countries with large numbers of *Nikkei*) also benefiting from direct aid or low-cost loans (Franke 2004: 70).

However, the more other Asian states took an interest in Latin America, the more was Japan's economic and political status weakened and the country's relations with the region declined from the late 1990s. Japan accounted for 11.4 per cent of Latin America's total trade in 1990. By 2005 this had reduced to 6.5 per cent, whereas other Asian countries showed a rapid increase from 7.6 per cent to 22.5 per cent, as Caroline Rose outlines in Chapter 4. South Korea particularly benefited as Asian firms were looking 'for new frontiers beyond the increasingly conflictive industrial markets of the US and Europe, and needed to think more globally in the era of the new division of labour made possible by new informa-tion and communication technologies. They also, particularly those from the post-democratization Korea, had to move abroad to escape from the high-wage domestic environment with its consequent loss of international competitiveness' (Kim 2004: 5). In the mid-1990s, South Korea's trade volume with Latin America accounted for roughly 4 per cent of the country's total trade – a small figure but nevertheless the highest ratio among Asian countries. This meant that the Latin American market became more important to the South Korean economy than to any other Asian nation, including Japan (ibid: 6). Empirical facts like this one, however, went largely unnoticed beyond a small circle of specialists.

For the past two decades, several Asian nations have perceived growing links with the Latin American region as a means of diversifying their political and particularly economic relations while many Latin American decision-makers have increasingly recognized the strategic importance of Asia in their foreign policy and foreign economic policy designs. The ensuing new strategic outlooks resulted in a substantial increase in interregional trade, investments and institution-building. Free Trade Agreements (FTA) have been signed between Japan and Mexico, Chile and Korea, and Peru and Thailand, respectively; a Preferential Trade Agreement (PTA) has come into effect between India and MERCOSUR (Common Market of the Cono Sur, grouping Argentina, Brazil, Paraguay and Uruguay). A number of bilateral arrangements are also being explored between various Asian countries such as Japan, Korea and Singapore, on the one hand, and Latin American countries such as Brazil, Chile and Mexico, on the other.

Of all these activities it was especially China's charm offensive of the early twenty-first century, which saw a first peak with President Hu Jintao's first tour of Latin America in 2004 (it had made a much stronger impact than the trip of his predecessor Jiang Zemin in 2001) and increasing levels of diplomatic and economic activity since then, that has caught everyone's imagination. Gonzalo S. Paz (2006: 96) noted that 'Hu Jintao has spent more time travelling in Latin America than [then] President Bush, and many Latin American presidents – among them, Brazil's Lula da Silva, Argentina's Nestor Kirchner, and Venezuela's Hugo Chávez – have spent more time in Beijing than in Washington'. The sharp growth of the China–Latin America trade volume from US$13 billion in 2000 to US$102.6 billion in 2007 (Li He 2008a: 3) and the fact that bilateral trade has already exceeded Hu's original benchmark of $100 billion set for 2010 (Xinhua News Agency, 6 November 2008); the frantic and in most cases successful attempts of Chinese state-owned corporations, such as PetroChina and Sinopec, to get their hands on Latin American oil; the establishment of 'strategic partnerships' and 'strategic dialogues' with several states in the region; China's training of increasing numbers of Latin American military personnel; extensive party-to-party ties of the Chinese Communist Party (CCP) with political parties across the continent and other examples for intensifying Sino-Latin American links seemingly support the neo-realist notion of China following a 'containment through surrogates' strategy (Malik 2006). According to this view, Beijing counters the perceived containment of its regional and global aspirations by the United States and Washington's allies and engages in soft balancing of the OECD world through trade, investment and development aid. China, so the argument goes, takes advantage of a power vacuum in the region that had been created by the United States' and also Russia's declining interest in Latin America (Li He 2008b: 195). June Teufel Dreyer (2006: 2) suggests that 'Latin America and the Caribbean are crucial to the evolution of the world order that the Chinese leadership would like to see'. Do Latin American governments concur? According to some analysts China is already being seriously looked at as an '*alternative* diplomatic and economic partner to Washington' (Lanteigne 2009: 139) [emphasis added].

There can be little doubt that particularly some of the left-wing and, as it seems, by default more Washington-critical Latin American governments such as those of Venezuela, Brazil, Ecuador or Bolivia, perceive a partnership with Beijing as a welcome means of soft balancing or at least hedging against traditional US hegemony in Latin America. However, as Paul Schroeder reminded us in one of the most refreshing critiques of neo-realism ever written,

> the [neo-realists'] insistence on the sameness effect and on the unchanging, structurally determined nature of international politics make it unhistorical, perhaps anti-historical . . . Neo-realist theory not only prevents scholars from seeing and explaining the various strategies alternative to balancing, or the different functions and roles of various actors within the system, but

even blocks a genuine historical understanding of balancing conduct and
the balance of power itself as a historical variable, changing over time,
conditioned by historical circumstances, and freighted with ideological
assumptions.

(Schroeder 1994: 148)

Latin American governments may rightly complain about a frequent lack of
serious attention on the part of the United States and Washington's rather narrowly
defined national security interests in its relations with the hemispheric neighbours,
but why should they be interested in replacing a decades-long dependency on the
United States by a new dependency on China? Would there be any convincing
economic reason to play the China card in an attempt to balance against the United
States given that in 2006 US–Latin America trade was ten times larger than
China–Latin America trade and US companies invested US$300 billion compared
to just US$8 billion Chinese FDI in Latin America?

   China is an increasingly important factor in Latin America but it is one actor
among others. David Shambaugh (2008) accurately stresses that Latin American
countries 'embrace China as part of their new multidirectional diplomacy'.
Multidirectional is the key word here. All Latin American governments have
diversified their foreign relations. Their main interest is directed at moderating
US hegemony, not substituting it. As part of this strategy and particularly in
times of economic hardship such as the current global economic crisis, every trade
and investment opportunity is welcome. Modern and post-modern states in the era
of globalization are best described as rational opportunity maximizers. This applies
to Latin America as much as East Asia; it is true for Vietnam or South Korea in
the same way as Peru or Mexico. The result of opportunity maximizing in Asia–
Latin America relations is a growing and fast-tightening (but not yet deeply
institutionalized) transpacific network comprising trade, investment, political
and even security links in both bilateral and increasingly multilateral contexts.
This is the book's red thread, the general argument it wants to make. The following
chapters are not – and cannot – be guided by a narrowly defined comparative
framework. The empirically observable reality of Japan's approach vis-à-vis Latin
America is embedded in a different set of structures, actor interests and policy
processes than Mexico's strategy towards South Korea, to give just one example.
By systematically analysing the specific factors that influence bilateral and
multilateral interregional interactions they provide – as far as possible – a holistic
perspective on the Asian–Latin American encounter at the beginning of the
twenty-first century.

The book's structure

While the first part of the book looks at the policies, interests and strategies of
individual Asian and Latin American states, the second part delves into the
analysis of multilateral institution-building in Asia–Latin America relations, which
has not been widely studied yet – with the exception of the Asia–Pacific Economic

Cooperation forum (APEC) whose membership, however, goes beyond an Asian and Latin American constituency. As the most visible actors of the transcontinental encounter, China, Japan and Mexico are covered in particular detail.

In Chapter 2 of this book Manfred Mols highlights an important difference between China's pre-modern and current aspirations to international pre-eminence. While in the past, proximity and vicinity to the centre (the Middle Kingdom) were the main criteria for collating the sequence and structure of the concentric circles, China nowadays reflects on the importance of the surrounding international world in terms of power and global influence without entering herself into an open global power contest. 'To be a rule-maker, and no longer a rule-taker in the process of globalization, is what really counts.' Mols differentiates three clusters in China's bilateral relations with Latin America: strategic partners (Brazil, Mexico, Argentina, Venezuela), cooperative partners (e.g. Chile, Peru, Cuba) and friendly-cooperative partners (Central America and the Caribbean). He does not fail to mention that China's open flirtation with Latin America, both in terms of political and economic relations, has the potential to challenge the United States. Will the traditional dependency of Latin America on the US sooner or later be replaced by a new dependency on Beijing? In other words, is China poaching in Washington's backyard? Alberto Camarena (Chapter 3) asserts that China has so far not been interested in fully exploiting the potential that closer relations with the socialist-left-wing-oriented regimes, such as particularly those of Venezuela and Bolivia, might have in store in terms of diminishing US power in the region. In Camarena's words, 'China tacitly acquiesces to the Monroe Doctrine'. Beijing's rejection of Hugo Chávez's advances is a point in case. Despite Chávez's high-profile visit to China in August 2006, Beijing has been reluctant to join the Venezuelan bandwagon of anti-American rhetoric. At the same time, the Chinese presence in Latin America has not become a matter of priority for Washington and remained a relatively low-key issue because, as Camarena concludes, Sino-Latin American relations lack sufficient strategic and political importance for the United States. This perception might change rather soon as there are already a number of factors that do concern Washington. The US is mostly interested in the support for liberal and economic orders and the deepening of economic integration between the US and Latin American countries. With regard to these core interests, the US closely observes Sino-Latin American relations as China might be disrupting the existing patterns of bi- and multilateralism. For the time being, however, China is not a firmly established power in Latin America and Beijing's rise on the continent is a relatively recent phenomenon.

What does China's position in Latin America mean for Japan? Following the decline in the relative importance of Japan–Latin America relations in the 1990s, at the start of the twenty-first century Japanese governments have sought to revitalize links with Latin America, and these moves have been stepped up in recent years. Former Prime Minister Koizumi Junichirō's visit to Latin America in 2004, during which he proposed the revitalization of economic links and the need to cooperate on international issues such as the reform of the United Nations Security Council and the environment, is an important marker of this shift in policy. In Chapter 4 Caroline Rose explores the reasons for Japan's 'return' to Latin America by focusing on economic determinants (for example, the attraction of free trade agreements), Japan's interest in creating stronger East Asian regional institutions and, through these, stronger cross-regional links with Latin America (for example, the Forum for East Asian–Latin American Cooperation), and Japan's response to China's growing interest in the region. Rose assesses the progress made since Koizumi set out his vision for the creation of a new Japan–Latin America relationship, and demonstrates that Japan's renewed interest in Latin America is not based on short-term objectives but on the emergence of longer-term strategic planning enunciated by the former Prime Minister. While China's changing position in the region represents a challenge to Japan's interests, Tokyo is not necessarily seeking to catch up with Beijing or other Asian neighbours, but its foreign and foreign economic policy does nonetheless acknowledge the renewed significance of Latin America. Solid foundations for prominent Japanese–Latin American relations exist and some of the strongest links are those formed through migration, with some of Japan's largest overseas communities residing in Latin America. Yet, the transnational aspect of the transpacific relationship is not without its challenges.

After facing the difficulties of a largely illegal influx of 'guest workers' from Asia and the Middle East, the Japanese government in the 1980s offered special visas to descendents of Japanese migrants to South America, the *Nikkei*, assuming common ancestry would guarantee ease of assimilation and control. Forgotten was the transformation that takes place over two to three generations among immi-grants to places as radically different in language and culture from Japan as the nations of Latin America. As June A. Gordon explains in her fascinating account of a crucial cultural dimension of Asia–Latin America relations (Chapter 5), unbound by legal constraints of compulsory attendance or their working parents' watchful eye, *Nikkei* children slip in and out of an educational system unprepared to serve their needs, often ending up in the same menial factory jobs as were held by their parents. Viewing their time in Japan as temporary and unstable, *Nikkeijin* move back and forth between countries, leaving their children and their education in an ambiguous state; a formula of significant concern for the future of Japan.

While Japan and China are the main Asian players in Latin America, bilateral relations between most Asian States (for example Vietnam, Indonesia, Thailand, Singapore, Malaysia, the Philippines and India) and Latin American Countries (for example Peru, Ecuador, Chile, Mexico, Columbia, Costa Rica and Panama) have seen a multiplication of reciprocal state visits and other diplomatic activities.

In Chapter 6 Ta Minh Tuan looks at the example of Southeast Asia and Vietnam in particular. Within the Asia–Pacific area Southeast Asia is the region with the weakest historical links with Latin America. Until the mid-1970s Latin America was one large, unexplored, unknown continent to most governments and peoples of Southeast Asia. Twenty-five years ago only Thailand, Indonesia and the Philippines had diplomatic missions in any of the Latin American states.

In recent years most Southeast Asian states 'discovered' Latin America, and Vietnam has emerged as one of the most pro-active states in the region in their attempts to diversify their foreign policies and foreign economic policies towards the former *terra incognita*. Latin America, as Tuan explains, has provided Vietnam with a variety of raw materials and processed goods at fairly reasonable prices, thus supporting the latter's production of commodities for export and meeting domestic consumption demand, such as sawn timber, paper pulp, leather, soy flour, corns, wheat, cotton, bloom yard, and auto parts. Meanwhile, Vietnam has exported to the Latin American markets manufactured commodities, raw materials, agricultural products and minerals such as textiles and garments, electronics and home appliances with their spare parts, natural rubber, furniture, handicrafts, rice, coffee beans and coal. Some Latin American countries, namely Venezuela, Chile, Peru and Nicaragua have strongly advocated the promotion of economic ties with Vietnam by recognizing it as having a market economy. Cuba, however, has remained Vietnam's closest partner in Latin America, in view of the similarities between the two states' communist-ruled political systems. At the same time the importance of ideological factors has decreased. For example, Mexico has occupied an increasingly important place in Vietnam's foreign and foreign economic policy despite the fact that the two governments 'do not share the same view on various international issues and the developmental path'. Vietnam managed to get Mexico's early support for its (non-permanent) UN Security Council seat.

Mexico was one of Latin America's pioneers in attempting to achieve closer ties with Asia. It was also the first Latin American economy to have assumed the temporary one-year leadership in the Asia–Pacific Economic Cooperation Forum (APEC). Mexico's central role as a partner for Asian economies was confirmed and strengthened when Mexico and Japan concluded a high standard free trade agreement in 2005 that immediately resulted in an increase in bilateral trade of 21.5 per cent in the first ten months after it had come into effect. In their detailed account of Mexico's strategy towards Japan, China and South Korea, Melba E. Falck Reyes and José Luis León-Manríquez (Chapter 7) discuss the reasons for the spectacular growth that economic relations between Mexico and East Asia have undergone in the last decade, with the North American Free Trade Agreement (NAFTA) being the most important factor. The initiation of NAFTA resulted in an increased interest of East Asian firms to invest in Mexico to take advantage of the Mexican access to the US market. In the case of Japan and Korea, increasing FDI in Mexico brought further trade via imports. With regard to China, plenty of consumer goods and inputs for export industries have been brought from the PRC. For Mexico's exports NAFTA has meant an unprecedented degree of concentration in the US market. On the side of imports, however, the increasing presence of East Asian manufactures in Mexico has assisted the diversification of the Mexican economy. While not necessarily the outcome of an explicit strategy of diversification, the increasing presence of East Asian trade and investments in Mexico has relieved Mexican dependence on US imports. In a broader sense, Japan, China and South Korea have become more and more intertwined with the North American market. In this sense East Asia has become 'NAFTA's fourth partner'.

The growing importance of economic relations between the two continents is not necessarily matched with the sufficient reciprocal knowledge base as Olaf Jacob shows in Chapter 8. In the case of Peru, most reports published by governmental and business associations related to the Asia Pacific are characterized by an extreme enthusiasm but also a lack of quality, facts and figures. Peruvian universities have few or sometimes no specialized, Asia-related literature and the academic exchange programmes seldom include universities in Pacific Asia. Governments, media, academia and business sectors of the smaller Pacific countries in Latin America (Colombia, Ecuador and Peru) are increasingly turning their attention towards Pacific Asia but East Asia has still not been included under the top topics of the agenda, neither in business, nor in governmental issues or business relations. At the same time, they have developed a strong interest in transpacific multilateral cooperation fora, particularly with regard to APEC. The APEC CEO summit that took place in November 2008 in Lima has been referred to as 'the most important political and economical event that has taken place in Peru since the independence in 1821'. Ecuador and Colombia, who are members of the Pacific Economic Cooperation Council (PECC) and the Pacific Basin Economic Council (PBEC) are considering becoming candidates for a full APEC membership after the end of the moratorium in 2010. Panama and Costa Rica have indicated an equally strong interest in joining the organization. The possible widening of APEC points to a key development in transpacific diplomacy: the intensification of bilateral political and economic relations between the individual states of the two continents has also triggered multilateral institution-building in relations between the two regions.

The phenomenon of interregionalism – understood as a process through which patterns of relations between geographical regions are institutionalized – as a core element of the post-Cold War debate on multilateralism has attracted growing interest both within the International Relations and Area Studies communities. Examples of well-researched interregional cooperation schemes include relations between Europe and Asia as well as the European Union (EU) and the Southern Mediterranean region. However, the vast majority of studies are Eurocentric as they focus on the external relations of the EU while ignoring the emergence of important matters of interregional cooperation in other parts of the world. The second part of the book is particularly devoted to the analysis of recent trends in institution-building between Asia and Latin America.

Jürgen Rüland and Karsten Bechle's Chapter 9 develops a systemic approach to analyse the India, Brazil and South Africa Dialogue Forum (IBSA) within the emerging multi-layered system of global governance, thereby departing from the reductionist unit-based middle power-perspective prevalent in the limited body of research on IBSA so far. After explaining why this coalition of emerging powers from the South qualifies as a form of interregionalism, albeit a skeletal one, IBSA is conceptualized as an example of what the authors call 'shallow multilateralism', i.e. a form of multilateralism where only the institutional frame remains, but where the cooperative substance gets lost. IBSA is thus considered as an incarnate of a larger trend in international relations, that is, a deepening crisis of norm-based multilateralism. Its members use a seemingly cooperative arrangement to strengthen their institutional power in major global multilateral forums and, in the final consequence, cooperate in order to advance their own status as great powers. Rüland and Bechle corroborate their argument by examining how IBSA members seek to rewrite the rules of major international organisations such as the World Trade Organization (WTO), the International Monetary Fund (IMF) and the United Nations in their favour, concluding that IBSA constitutes another shift towards a more power-driven international order.

The same does not necessarily apply to The Forum for East Asia–Latin America Cooperation (FEALAC) which provides a (weakly) institutionalized framework for increasing dialogue and cooperation on a wide array of economic, political, and social issues without, however, trying to generate major inputs to international order building. FEALAC nevertheless provides an interesting example for a growing trend in international relations that is spearheaded by Asian and Latin American state actors: multilateral cooperation across continental borders outside the Europe–US–East Asia triad. In their Manila Action Plan of 2004 the members of FEALAC stated that, through the process of interregional cooperation, they expected to achieve a more equal distribution of the benefits resulting from globalization as well as prevent the marginalization of any sector of the human society as Gracia Abad explains in Chapter 12. While FEALAC has often been criticized due to its poor outcome-oriented performance, its low profile, the inability to influence the policies of the governments which take part in its meetings and, ultimately, its reduced visibility, Abad believes that FEALAC contributes to the strengthening of regional identities both in Latin America and in East Asia as much as it helps some of the participating states to reduce their peripheral position in the world order and strengthen their negotiation power vis-à-vis the US and the European Union (EU). In his comparison of FEALAC and the Asia–Europe Meeting (ASEM), the model for other interregional dialogues, Charalambos Tsardanidis (Chapter 13) comes to a more critical conclusion: 'Although FEALAC, regarding political cooperation, could serve as an effective forum in exchanging views on security issues, all the gatherings of government officials have failed to advance beyond diplomatic rhetoric, and have not broken down the psychological and mental barriers that still divide the two sides of the Pacific.'

Do institutional arrangements with a longer track record than FEALAC stand a better chance of breaking down the barriers? MERCOSUR, the Southern Common Market grouping Argentina, Brazil, Paraguay and Uruguay (Venezuela signed an accession agreement in 2006 but has not yet been formally admitted), is potentially in a strong position to deepen interregional relations with East Asia. Since its creation in March 1991, MERCOSUR has established the project of regional integration in Latin America which has reached the highest level of consolidation on the long list of integrative experiments carried out within the region. In Chapter 10 Amalia Stuhldreher argues that in spite of MERCOSUR's broad external cooperation agenda, the bloc has not been able to make any significant progress at the various negotiation fronts, with a particularly poor balance vis-à-vis Asia. For the time being there can be little doubt about the fact that the expanding web of interregional relations between the two continents mainly rests on the pillar of bilateral initiatives, particularly in the trade sector. As trade bilateralism in both Latin America and East Asia steadily grows, so do trade agreements between the two regions. The trend is not without its critics, however. One basic argument against FTAs especially in East Asia is that they are not compliant with WTO rules, some introducing new elements, some including exceptions, some lacking dispute settlement procedures. This image of a chaotic 'noodle bowl' is seen as a threatening force not only to free trade in general but also to interregional trade relations between East Asia and Latin America. Yet, empirical evidence discussed by Howard Loewen (Chapter 11) shows that interregional free trade agreements between the two regions are well-structured and even conform to WTO standards. All agreements include trade in goods, services and investments and show the tendency to extend their scope. Small and middle-sized countries are at the forefront of concluding new bilateral FTAs. Beyond bilateralism, multilateral FTAs such as the Trans-Pacific Strategic Economic Partnership have emerged. These could eventually be manifestations of a functional necessity: the multi-lateralization of bilateral trade agreement networks. Loewen concludes that enabling factors (political and economic factors) might be applied to interregional as well as to regional FTAs. However, their effects on trade and global trade negations might not be as negative as is commonly assumed in the regional case.

Note

1   Belize, Dominican Republic, El Salvador, Guatemala, Haiti, Honduras, Nicaragua, Panama, Paraguay, St Christopher and Nevis, and St Vincent and Grenadines.

References

Calvert, Peter (1994) *The International Politics of Latin America*, Manchester and New York: Manchester University Press.
Edwards, Sebastian (1995) *Crisis and Reform in Latin America: From Despair to Hope.* New York: Oxford University Press.
Franke, Uwe (2004) 'In weiter Ferne, so nah? – Die Beziehungen zwischen Japan und Lateinamerika', KAS Auslandsinformationen, no. 8/2004, pp. 68–96.
Horisaka, Kotaro (2005) 'Japan and Latin America – Missing Strategies and Political Will', in Manfred Mols, Jörg Faust and Woh-Ho Kim, eds, *Latin America and East Asia – Attempts at Diversification*, Münster: Lit.
Kay, Cristóbal (2002) 'Why East Asia overtook Latin America: agrarian reform, industrialisation and development', *Third World Quarterly*, vol. 23, no. 6 (December), pp. 1073–102.
Kim, Won-Ho (2004) 'East Asian–Latin American Economic Relations: A Korean Perspective after the International Financial Crisis', Korean Institute for International Economic Policy (KIEP) Working Paper: 00–04.
Lanteigne, Marc (2009) *Chinese Foreign Policy*, London and New York: Routledge.
Lawrance, Alan (1975) *China's Foreign Relations since 1949*, London and Boston: Routledge & Kegan Paul.

12   *Jörn Dosch*

Li He (2008a) 'China's growing influence in Latin America: Challenges and Opportunities', *EAI Background Brief No. 411*, 30 October 2008.
—— (2008b) 'Latin America and China's growing interest', in Quansheng Zhao, Guoli Liu, eds, *Managing the China Challenge. Global Perspectives*, London and New York: Routledge, pp. 195–214.
Malik, Mohan (2006) 'China's Growing Involvement in Latin America', *Power and Interest News Report (PINR)*, 12 June.
Paz, Gonzalo S. (2006) 'Rising China's Offensive in Latin America and the U.S. Reaction', *Asian Perspective*, vol. 30, no. 4, pp. 95–112.
Schroeder, Paul (1994) 'Historical Reality vs. Neo-Realist Theory', *International Security*, vol. 19, no. 1 (Summer), pp. 108–48.
Shambaugh, David (2008) 'China's New Foray Into Latin America', *YaleGlobal*, 17 November, online, http://yaleglobal.yale.edu/display.article?id=11615 (accessed 9 July 2009).
Stallings, Barbara and Kataro Horisaka (1994) 'Japan and Latin America: New Patterns in the 1990s', in Abraham F. Lowenthal and Gregory F. Treverton, eds, *Latin America in a New World*, Boulder et al.: Westview Press, pp. 126–49.
Teng, Chung-chian (2007) 'Hegemony or Partnership: China's Strategy and Diplomacy Toward Latin America' in Joshua Eisenman, Eric Heginbotham and Derek Mitchell, eds, *China and the Developing World. Beijing's Strategy for the Twenty-First Century*, Armonk and London: M.E. Sharpe, pp. 84–112.
Teufel Dreyer, June (2006) 'The China Connection', *China–Latin America Task Force March–June 2006*, Center for Hemispheric Policy, University of Miami.
Tussie, Diane (2004) 'Off the Beaten Track: From the Margins of Globalization', *International Studies Review*, vol. 6, pp. 158–60.
Xu, Feng (1994) 'China and Latin America after the Cold War's End', in Abraham F. Lowenthal and Gregory F. Treverton, eds, *Latin America in a New World*, Boulder, CO: Westview Press, pp.150–66.

Part I

The interests and strategies of states and their actors

2   Is China the avant-garde of East Asia in Latin America?

Manfred Mols

Viewed from our perspective of the twenty-first century, the answer is definitely positive, and it would not be wrong to start with the last decade of the previous century, the 1990s. Yet the relationship between China and East Asia and Latin America is older than a couple of years. It started in the second half of the sixteenth century thanks to the yearly fleet connection between Acapulco and Manila. Does it therefore make sense at all to put China and East Asia at the beginning of this chapter into the same basket? Are we able to verify times of keen competition between China and East Asia as far as Latin America is concerned? Why and when did China enter into a tighter relationship with Latin America than other Asian countries? What are the salient and promising features of the current situation? How is the present situation of the highly visible presence of China perceived in Latin America? And what about its implications for third parties, particularly the US and Europe? These are the questions to be dealt with in this chapter.

Some words on history

The Acapulco–Manila connection existed from 1575 to 1815. It is reported that between 20 and 60 ships sailed every year across the Pacific Ocean (Shixue 2007). It was only officially a connection between the Vice-Kingdom of New Spain (later in larger parts called Mexico) and the Spanish colony in the Far East. Acapulco–Manila meant trade. The Spanish American world exported shoes, hats, wine, olive oil, soap and food to China, whereas the Chinese themselves reciprocated with silk, cotton cloth, arts and crafts, jewellery, gunpowder, food and animals (ibid). The connection became known as the 'silk road of the sea'. For the rest of the nineteenth century half a million Chinese workers ('coolies') went to Latin American countries, and two or three generations later not an insignificant number of them advanced into respectable middle- and even upper-class positions. This was particularly the case in Brazil, Cuba, Mexico, Peru and also in parts of Central America. For quite a while, the Mexican Silver Dollar became in the coastal parts of China and in other places in Southeast Asia a legal tender. When in 1911 the Chinese Republic became established, its political shift was soon diplomatically recognized by Brazil and Peru (April 1913), soon followed by Mexico. In 1915 and 1916, China opened relations with Chile and Bolivia. Nicaragua and Guatemala followed in 1930 and 1933 respectively.[1] The very decisive year for China, 1949 (founding of the People's Republic), witnessed diplomatic interests of Mexico, Argentina, Chile and some other Latin American countries, after some years of more or less open sympathies in some influential intellectual circles behind the political philosophy of Mao's Long March.

All these remarks portray a positive notion of Chinese–Latin American relations for quite some time. It is interesting to note that Latin America appears in official Chinese statements in terms of a sort of legacy, though the historical evidence of older contacts is by far more speculative than professionally certified. Or to put it in a different way: Chinese connections with Latin America demonstrate a mutual familiarity which is intended to legitimize the current Chinese approach. This was for instance the case when the then Foreign Minister of the People's Republic of China Tang Jiaxuan said in his speech in the First Ministerial Meeting of the Forum for East Asia–Latin America Cooperation (FEALAC), organized in Santiago de Chile in March 2001: 'The friendly ties between East Asia and Latin America date back to ancient times. It is said that Chinese monks travelled to Mexico across vast oceans as early as the fifth century.'[2] Jiang Shixue alludes in his scholarly piece to the famous Chinese Admiral Zheng He, who reputedly discovered in the first decades of the fifteenth century the southern parts of what was later called the Americas. The professor is not an optional figure in our context, but the deputy director of Beijing's semi-official Institute of Latin American Studies in the Chinese Academy of Social Sciences. The question is therefore: What is the meaning and purpose of such prepositions exhibited without a sober empirical and/or historical base? The answer is relatively simple: They define a claim for a Chinese–Latin American familiarity, that can at best be underlined by indicators of a restored historical normalcy which sells itself and deviates in given cases from troubling interpretations of the current Chinese role in Latin America. Statements of this kind are possible thanks to the lack of a reliable and respectable work on the relations between East Asia and Latin America which has still to be written.

Do China and East Asia belong to an identical category vis-à-vis Latin America?

Any answer depends upon the chosen historical and analytical perspective. It makes little sense to regard China and East Asia as a historically connected or even integrated group. The Chinese Empire was for centuries fairly influential in larger parts of the East Asian mainland, and Chinese civilization represented until the end of the eighteenth century probably the most advanced technological and spiritual culture of the world. But not all countries belonged to the sphere of Chinese influence. And this is even truer regarding the world of Pacific islands, with Japan playing the most prominent part. Beginning around AD 1500 and continuing until the nineteenth century, substantial parts of what is today called East and Southeast Asia began to be 'protected' by European powers, joined both directly and indirectly in the nineteenth and twentieth centuries by the United States of America and Imperial Japan. Independence came for most countries in the wake of the de-colonization process after the Second World War. In given cases (e.g. Indonesia, Vietnam and the Malayan region inclusive of Singapore) the achievement of national statehood was a long-lasting, burdensome and repeatedly bloody business. Korea was for decades a Japanese colony and is still divided. Japan joined in many aspects of the Western camp or, more precisely, modern-ization patterns, although an identification with Western culture has not yet completely followed (Ishihara 1989). We find today and in the past in East Asia diverging political and economic systems, cultural and religious worlds full of suspense, disputatious ideological camps, digressive natural endowments and self-supporting geopolitical interests, unrelated languages and ethnicities and last, though not least, absolutely divergent levels of development.[3] China is, compared with Singapore or Malaysia or even more so with South Korea, not the most modern East Asian state. But none of the others in the region come close to China in terms of economic growth, population, territory or military capabilities. China is however, if we also bear in mind the extraordinary economic and technological profile of Japan, the other East Asian power with the status of global player and therefore a possible challenge to the United States of America. It does all in all not make much sense to regard the East and Southeast Asian part of the world as a comprehensive unit in the international system. Therefore, to put China and all of East and Southeast Asia together, smacks of a relativization of China's preponderant position in the Asian World. It also distracts from a certain Chinese inclination of an imperialism towards its own in the Far East.

This is not the place to discuss the difficult question of whether and how Latin America regards itself in terms of interfering identities. Former attempts at Latin American integration with respect to unity belong more and more to the past. In relative comparison, however, to the East and Southeast Asian situation and creed, a considerable number of intergovernmental, transnational economic and trans-societal ties remain vigorous. This is true in politics, for instance, of the Rio Group with its meetings of presidents and ministers, through the common membership in the Organization of American States, a significant coming together of Latin American families of political parties in Latin America itself and in the international arena. We find in the economic field the still not obsolete institutions like the Inter-American Development Bank (IDB) and a series of subregional development banks. The UN Commission for Latin America and the Caribbean (CEPAL) means a common asset. At the cultural level, there exist two very closely related main languages, last but not least in the arts a practically common pride in a great and nearly worldwide read literature, and stimulating music, different in each country and yet regarded in nearly all parts of Latin America as a common heritage. Christianity, and particularly Catholicism, provides a still relevant religious connection. In social terms similar and often nearly identical structures prevail, so do norms and patterns of behaviour. All this does not mean, that Latin America appears as an integrated, proper actor in the international field respectively vis-à-vis China or East Asia. And we also find in Latin America as well, fairly divergent political systems and deviating ranks of development in social, economic and cultural terms. Comparisons between East Asia/China and Latin America prove to be difficult, for our analytical instruments as social scientists display too much of what A.B. Shamsul named quite correctly 'colonial knowledge', that is the dependence on concepts and analytical patterns from the Western colonial powers, respectively their theoreticians (Shamsul 2002; see also Derichs 2002). Apart from the fact that Latin America, whose modern existence started in comparison to East Asia (and India and the Islamic states of the Near East and Southern Central Asia) at different times, I would like to propose two central judgements for bringing Latin America and East Asia together analytically: on average, the leading Latin American countries such as Brazil, Mexico, Argentina, Chile, Uruguay, Costa Rica and perhaps even Venezuela can, at least from a view of political science, be classified as more developed in political and social regards than most of their Asian counterparts (China, Indonesia, the Philippines, Malaysia, Laos, Cambodia, Brunei etc.) – which has given indirect credibility to Alain Rouquié's dictum that Latin America is, despite its problems and shortcomings a shareholder of the 'extreme Occident'.[4]

The second point is that neither Latin America nor East Asia behave on the international stage as actors who agree on politics, economics or culture. Sinologists like to stress that China 'returns' to world politics. Such statements are historically meaningless, for China was never an integral part of a world system,[5] whose roots were not planted in the Far East but step by step through Western imperialism, which started in the age of great discoveries. China has to keep up with a process of globalization it did not invent. It has to be acknowledged that it strives – not without successes – to join this process and to influence it, but we are still somewhat far from what is discussed in some international circles as the coming of a 'Chinese Century' (Kim 2000) – a comparable judgement may be allowed with regard to Latin America. Though it joined far earlier than East Asia in politics and economics; basic traits of the Western world (more precisely, it was created by the Western world), neither the Ibero-American region as such nor its more outstanding countries, like Argentina, Mexico, Brazil or temporarily Chile, have yet developed as rule-makers in the international system. So the identical evaluative category for Latin America and East Asia was for a long time the minor quality as international factors and – though with differences – limited potentialities to discuss and design their mutual futures and destinies. 'The capacity to forge its own destiny', 'the conscious action of men dedicated to transform the conditions of their own existence' (Stavenhagen 1981), existed neither for Latin America nor for East Asia (again with the exception of Japan). It was simply restrained and repressed by outside powers imposing themselves upon each of the two regions under consideration. That these negative conditions changed in the last 10 or 15 years and that the mutual approach between Latin America and East Asia nowadays forms a new pattern of international relations, dating back to perhaps only some 15 years, is in a way surprising (Faust and Mols 1998).

This is because China, regarded since the years of the Bandung-philosophy as an authentic part of the 'South' respectively the Third World (though it never joined the big organizations of the 'South'), never hesitated to include Latin America in this new and rising projection of the planet's future. Latin America interpreted China in a similar way. It did not strive for a close relationship with Beijing, because the Ibero-American countries tried to avoid entering too openly into the communist sphere with its internal clashes and to shy away from its special relationship with the West and particularly the United States. Latin America's pronounced *tercermundismo* in the 1970s was never absolutely free from elements of political caution, the more so as substantial parts of the Latin American elites preferred the ongoing connection with the western capitalist world. Notwithstanding this, the two regions had a very basic common interest in diversifying their international political and economic relations. Somewhere looming over the horizon the other side of the Pacific Ocean was a potential of future attention – whenever this future might arrive. However it did not happen for a while, and this is another basic statement, that in the case of our two subject matters clustered regions did not meet or work together. Admittedly, there is a diffuse set of contacts and interrelations between East/Southeast Asia and Latin America. Yet this does not allow us to speak about an interregional connection. East/Southeast Asia and Latin America is a series of bilateral, country-based relations, with China in Asia currently and for years to come the outstanding unit, whereas Latin America presents itself vis-à-vis this as a conglomerate of mainly separate state and societal actors without an undisputed spearhead. It is this structural asymmetry that allows us to regard China as an Asian avant-garde in Latin America.

East Asia's and China's new connections towards Latin America and the twofold Chinese strategies

A concise historical report of the maturing relationship between East Asia (Southeast Asia included) and Latin America has still to be written. But it is not wrong to state that Japan was until the end of the 1980s the leading Asian power in Latin America, particularly in the economic and developmental fields (De la Flor Belaunde 1991). JETRO, the official Japanese foreign trade organisation, began in the late 1950s, with the establishment of offices in a number of Latin American countries. At the same time, the first steps in a high-ranking diplomatic visitor's programme was initiated, which became in later years a regular encounter between East and Southeast Asia and Latin America. The principal Latin American motive was to achieve via diversification of international political and economic relations a substantial degree of independence from the USA, whereas Asia, beyond Japan that had started earlier, began to initiate a proper web of connections in the international system. The adherence of Asian and Latin American states atop the Non-Alignment Movement was a part of this development. Many Latin American decision-makers began to consider in a cautious, but conscious way the strategic significance of the Asia–Pacific for their foreign policy designs (Faust and Mols 2005).

To a lesser, but significant extent East and Southeast Asian nations began to perceive increasing links with Latin America as a means to amplify their political and economic relations (strategies that were put to a halt for a while in the wake of the Asian Crisis of the late 1990s). And both sides of the Pacific Rim completed their hitherto limited diplomatic and consular representations up to internationally normal levels. To shorten a more complicated story: the new international climate, due to the end of the East–West schism and the implosion of the Soviet Empire, made moves from Asia towards Latin America possible that in former times were practically beyond imagination. Japan and the Republic of Korea belong to the member countries of the Inter-American Development Bank and are regarded as partners. Organization of American States (OAS) observer membership was made possible for Asian participation as well. Chile, Mexico and Peru became ordinary members of the Asian Pacific Economic Cooperation (APEC) and, together with other Latin American countries, with other transpacific institutions like PBEC, PECC and PAFTAD.[6]

Due to an initiative of Singapore's Premier Go Chock Tong in 1998 a high-ranking Asian–Latin American Dialogue Forum FEALAC[7] was founded with the idea of replicating the ASEM process as 'the missing link' in world politics. In Asia as well as in Latin America leading officials in foreign ministries (China, Japan, Korea, Singapore, Chile, Argentina, Peru) are, according to personal interviews by the author of this chapter, proud of trying to establish interregional links – without North American participation and/or intervention.

Nowadays it can be disputed whether APEC or FEALAC have so far come up to expectations. They contribute, however, to the fact that at the level of leading politicians and senior officials institutional dialogues and a mutual understanding were initiated. Last but not least, the Association of Southeast Asian Nations (ASEAN) as a collective institution began to enter into contacts (visits, seminars etc.) with Latin American groups of integration and cooperation like the Andean Group, the Latin American Economic System (SELA),[8] MERCOSUR[9] etc. China occupies a number of Latin American institutions and in the OAS has observer status. With SELA cooperation agreements exist. Even new dialogue channels had been established, for instance the China–Caribbean Economy and Trade Cooperation Forum with its first ministerial meeting in 2005. This does not, however, imply that persistent group-to-group relations have settled down.

The international weakness of Latin America is its ongoing fragmentation (Mols 2007), and in almost the same manner East and Southeast Asia cannot be regarded, in spite of all visions and plans, as becoming an authentic Asian Community, as a consolidated bloc perceivable as an authentic integration scheme. Jörn Dosch describes current Latin American–East Asian relations as a sort of 'peripheral interregionalism' (Dosch 2005) whose future has to remain open for the time being. Let us hope that this might develop some day. At present, interregionalism is an anticipated interpretation. The very core of Latin American relations with East and Southeast Asia and even more so with China are bilateral country-to-country dealings. Peter H. Smith, Kotaro Horisaka and Shoji Nishijima (2003) refer in their book *East Asia and Latin America* to an 'unlikely alliance'.

Here, additional remarks about China and Latin America are necessary.

Most academic presentations of the Chinese–Latin American relationship focus upon the growing necessity to enlarge China's economic possibilities – and we will come back to this topic. As a political scientist, I should begin with a fundamental political component, which was amongst others very firmly stressed in recent times by Stefanie Mann.[10] '. . . considering China's self-perception as a global player, the country still needs acceptance and most of all, international partners. Thus, relations with Latin American partners beyond economic gain-seeking . . . fulfil the function of supporting the PRC's [People's Republic of China] objective to strengthen its position in the international system' (Reis 2005: 131). Several internationally respected specialists on China believe that the country is returning to world politics and they acknowledge the high level of Chinese civilization and development up until the beginning of the nenteenth century. This interpretation is more or less meaningless, because the creation, and even more so the structures and norms, of the modern international system, which began at the time of discoveries, is a European legacy and product (later completed by a north American agenda), not something that was designed and introduced by the East.

There is no doubt that the Western setup and texture of an international system is still a dominant feature of world politics. Its basic profile was presented a few years ago by a United Nations Educational, Scientific and Cultural Organization (UNESCO) research commission as the 'late Western Civilization' (Jaguaribe de Mattos 2001). China's turn to the international world began with Deng Hsiao Ping's pragmatic opening of the hitherto nearly closed country, and this relatively soon included an eye upon Latin America – at that time and for quite a while longer as an observed member of the international system rather than as a concrete asset for China. Later, the idea of a political partnership and, in some particular cases, of a strategic partnership became a functional idea in Beijing. Whatever the changes in China's engagement in Latin America with its strong emphasis on economic interests mean today: the interests remain bifocal; none of them reflects for itself a fundamental priority. 'Useful' means in the political context for instance, that Latin America is an adjuvant partner in the voting processes of the United Nations.

In the words of Günther Maihold (2006: 40), 'With China and Latin American states voting identically in UN bodies 80 per cent of the time, it would seem that their positions are very close.' He goes on to write: 'It is plain that China is working to ensure broad Latin American support for its own international role through diplomatic cooperation.' Apart from very concrete interests in the Doha-context and in treating China in the WTO as performing basically as a 'market economy', Latin American support means for China another cornerstone in its strategy to pursue the idea of a multipolar international system. Stating this, one has to give a warning not to overestimate these strategic considerations in an overall evaluation of China's international thinking.

For many centuries, the Chinese saw their position in the world in terms of a 'Middle Kingdom', surrounded by concentric circles of 'the others' – an attitude that stills seems to prevail (Friedrich 2000). While in the past proximity and vicinity to the centre were the main criteria for collating the sequence and structure of the concentric circles, China nowadays reflects on the importance of the surrounding international world in terms of power and global influence without entering into an open global power contest. To be a rule-maker, and no longer a rule-taker in the process of globalization, is what really counts. Knowledgeable personalities in Chinese affairs stress the fact that China's traditional 'Middle Kingdom' orientation still remains as a sort of a living history, in which a network of harmonious relations in the international system remains an official guideline (Schoetttli 2007).

It was Hu Jintao[11] himself who publicly remembered this ancestral line shortly before the 17th party congress in October 2007. That means in other words that the USA and to a somewhat lesser degree Europe are regarded as the most direct dimensions of political interest, and that the 'rest' of the world and its regions are marked according to special utilities for the 'Middle Kingdom'. Latin America belongs, from a strictly political point of view, to this 'rest'.

As for the second motive for China's current regard of Latin America: despite strong underpinning by political concerns, there is, now, on equal terms, the necessity to cope with the needs of obtaining food, minerals and energy. In addition, Latin America seems to offer assured access to a market in the southern part of the Western Hemisphere that comprises more than 500 million people and an abundance of the goods needed in China.

It is of some significance to note that it is perhaps doubtful whether the majority of Latin American countries and their governments and economic leaders believed that they were living in a honeymoon relationship with China for the past ten or fifteen years. Nonetheless the Chinese approach was to a large extent hailed because it offered a chance for a diversification of Latin America's rather unilateral and in many given cases burdensome attachment to the West, particularly to the United States. China's interest in Latin America was seen as a palpable possibility to substantially reduce the cumbrous 'dependencia'. Was this a realistic assumption? – We should turn now a little more precisely to the Chinese–Latin American economic relationship.

A second look at the economic side of the Chinese–Latin American flirtation

Up to now, we have spoken sweepingly of Latin America as a regional entity vis-à-vis China. This does not reflect the real situation, neither in political nor in economic terms. Orwell's famous statement that though all pigs are equal, some of them are more equal than others can easily be applied to Latin America and the treatment of its countries by China. This is particularly true from an economic perspective. The countries that really count for Beijing economically are – in this order – Brazil, Argentina, Mexico, Venezuela, Chile, Peru and Cuba.[12]

The overall evaluation of China's enormously growing economic interest in Latin America is, as has already been mentioned, the pressing need to import food for its immense and still increasing population. The other need is to obtain raw materials and energy because China is less and less likely to achieve self-sufficiency. One guaranty of the Chinese presence in Latin American markets and in structures of production and hauling is secured through a blend of investments and aid in the fields of infrastructure and communications. The exports of the above-mentioned countries to China illustrate in a clear way what China expects respectively where connections flourish and where Chinese investments are located.

Brazil is significant for China because of iron ore and corresponding concentrates and also because of its agricultural capacity (soybeans). Argentina also counts for its soybeans and soybean oil, as well as for meat and leather from cattle. Chile, economically, means copper ore and concentrates in bleached chemical wood pulp. Peru is relatively attractive for its minerals (copper, silver, gold, zinc, lead), fish and fishmeal and also for petroleum and natural gas. Venezuela's attraction for China consists of its enormous crude oil capacity. Cuba disposes of large amounts of bauxite (Kleining 2007).

Some additional comments are necessary. Relations with Venezuela present two sides of a coin. As an energy supplier the country is indispensable for China. President Chávez is a useful gadfly in an overwhelmingly western and slowly moving region (Mols 2007). On the other hand, China is positively interested – also in Latin America – in predictable situations and clear political tranquillity as the basic guarantee of its undisturbed international political and economic involvements. Whether the same ambiguity applies to Cuba is at present more a historical question since the retirement of Fidel Castro. But at least under his regime, Cuba was never an assured political support. Mexico is – more than Brazil – a competitor of China in international markets for manufactured products of a medium-level technical quality (Palacios Lara *et al.* 2006). Mexico features a substantial trade deficit with China. Brazil's case is different since it has a large trade surplus and it is a country or an economy with a remarkable amount of technological cooperation and a renowned capacity for joint ventures. The often mentioned example is the concrete exchange of Chinese technological experience with satellites and in space research versus Brazil's aircraft construction (Embraer). If we take China's foreign trade with Latin America and vice versa, the mutual share of their trade is not substantially significant. China's part in the export-import balances of Latin American countries is about 5 to 6 per cent (Hänni 2008).

The Latin American share in China's foreign trade fluctuates between 3.5 per cent and 3.7 per cent, with a deficit in disadvantage for the 'Middle Kingdom' (with some exceptions like Mexico). The main effect of China's trade presence in Latin America is not the amount of imports and exports as such, but the so far unbroken tendency of its growth. In 1999 for instance, Chinese imports from Latin America added up to US$3 billion. Five years later it came to more than six times as much, namely US$21.7 billion (ibid). As far as investments are concerned, China is so far not a dominant player, yet again a rising trend can be seen. In 2005, just 1 per cent of all foreign investments in Latin America had a Chinese origin (Kleining 2007).

Within all these trade and investment pushes, the Chinese pursue a rising emphasis on bilateral commitments. In the context of Hu Jintao's legendary visit to Latin America (Chile, Brazil, Cuba and Venezuela) in 2004, US$30 billion-worth of investments were signed, and 400 additional accords as well (Latin America–Asia Review 2005). These Chinese activities were repeated by Vice-President Zeng Quinghong's trip to Latin America one year later. It should be mentioned that Hu Jintao met Latin American leaders who were already aware of China's interest in the region. In 2001 the then Chinese President Jiang Zemin had been in Brazil, Cuba, Venezuela, Chile, Argentina and Uruguay. All the visits of these high-ranking Chinese visitors and their delegations were reciprocated by Latin American political leaders and their entourage of officials in charge of the economies, thus forming a vivid network that thrives up to the present day.

China's international relations with Latin America are often classified into three categories: strategic partners (Brazil, Mexico, Argentina, Venezuela), cooperative partners (e.g. Chile, Peru, Cuba) and friendly-cooperative partners when dealing with one another (Central America and the Caribbean) (Kleining 2007: 12). It is in these approaches that in October 2006 the first Chinese–Latin American free trade agreement was signed with Chile, and in May 2007 a feasibility study concerning a free trade agreement with Peru was promoted, and that an investment agreement with Mexico was planned. Several cooperation treaties exist between Brazil and China, and it was the Brazilian President Lula who suggested a free trade agreement between MERCOSUR and China. Incidentally, China and Brazil have worked closely for quite some time in the Group of 20 in order to establish a counterweight to the Western industrial nations.

Reactions and attitude vis-à-vis China's growing presence in Latin America

Both Chinese strategies, the political as well as the economic, have provoked or will provoke some critical considerations in Latin America as well as in the extended international system, particularly in the United States. Nobody can forget the fact that Latin America became since Blaine's Pan-American Conference in Washington in 1889/90, and particularly after the end of the First World War, the strategic and economic backyard of the USA. The other provocation is a rising concern in Latin America about the remarkable and still growing asymmetry between the Latin countries and the Chinese Republic in terms of political and economic clout. A widely spread Latin American concern reads like this: will the traditional dependency of Latin America on the USA sooner or later be replaced by a new dependency on Beijing? And how do the Europeans as well as Asian powers regard China's rising presence in Latin America? Though it is not possible at this time to give final answers to such questions, a cautious approach to them should be feasible.

Without underestimating these preoccupations of the 'Latinos' and without downplaying the long-term effects of the growing Chinese presence, the discussion touches on the advantages of the Chinese and generally the Asian dispersion in

Latin America, because it means the broadening of political ties and, on a growing scale, an access to the enormously prospering and receptive Asian markets, even beyond the People's Republic. But concerned subjects of the Chinese performance and activities in the affected Latin American countries increasingly gauge the pros and cons. Mexico for instance is highly concerned about the decline of its textile industry and the general decrease of its international competition in manufactured goods due to the growing Chinese presence in promising markets in the US, in Europe and in Latin America itself, which means at the same time limits for the sale of comparable Mexican and respectively Latin American goods in those markets. The Mexican 'maquilas' have lost several hundred thousand jobs. Against such preoccupations the Mexicans experience a feeling of belonging more and more with China in the large 'Pacific Family' with its promising possibilities (Palacios Lara 2006).

Similar preoccupations and assertive voices are articulated in Argentina, Brazil and in other Latin American countries. Chinese state-owned companies are active in constructing a modern or at least functioning infrastructure (ports, railways, roads – also technical loading and shipping facilities, new lines of communication) in several countries. This means in fact in given cases a positive contribution to the host country's development, but the Chinese regard their own import necessities from Latin America as taking precedence – this repeating the British attitude in Latin countries in the nineteenth century. At least in economic terms, China offers less in partnership than its self-interests. Consequently for instance, Eduardo Lora (2007) asked 'Should Latin America Fear China?'. His answer is typical for present-day Latin America. One main statement in his deliberations seems to be clear: 'In fact, the growth of China has most certainly been favourable to Latin America' (ibid: 10). Another point in his chapter reads: given the lack of separation between State and economy in China, 'state owned enterprises are structured to respond more to the political and strategic objectives of the Communist Party than to market signals' (ibid: 17). From a liberal market perspective, this comes close to indicating a fundamental Latin American superiority, at least in the long run, but neither Lora nor other Latin American personalities are blind to Latin America's inferiority in 'Research and Development' nor to the fact that nowadays the mainstream of international investments are not directed to Latin America but to China (and on a growing scale also to India).

Finally, Lora stresses a series of common weaknesses of China and Latin America such as limited and unequal education, corruption and the absence of the rule of law, and the underlying fragility of the financial systems etc. So the final conclusion is that 'in several ways the Chinese economy does not differ substantially from that of the typical Latin American country' (ibid: 27). And he adds: 'All of this means that China's supremacy over Latin America is less worrisome and less global than is commonly believed' (ibid: 28). There are of course dissenting opinions. Deborah Cheng (2007) remembers for instance 'an air of caution' in relation to the new partner of Latin American countries.

In a similar way, Gonzalo S. Paz speaks of a 'new dragon', but cautiously says: 'However, for the foreseeable future, the dragon wants to keep the backyard's dog sleeping' (Paz 2006: 112). Returning to the unbalanced interests of their own in Latin America, the 'Latinos' are more and more aware of Chinese disinterest in questions of human rights, good governance, constitutional correctness etc. They become increasingly familiar with the Chinese care for questions of political stability or at least tranquillity in their host countries. The indifference and insensitivity to ecological questions (which might relatively soon put an end to the economic rise of China) is another demonstration of limited Chinese engagement in promoting broadly based modernity and development in Latin America (though the traditional apathy of the Latin Americans in these fields should not remain unnoticed).

We are therefore witness to a remarkable contradiction in China's Latin American strategy. The Chinese idea to contribute via Latin America or some of their most outstanding governments (Brazil, Mexico) to a multipolar world does not meet with even a limited understanding of what development really means, so that we come back to the argument that the Chinese repeat the dependency structures that Latin America was never really able to be free of.

'Hegemony or partnership?' therefore repeats the disputes in Latin American apprehension of China's movement across the Pacific (Teng 2007). A short look at the Chinese–Latin American export-import side underlines the impression of older historical impacts from the outside in Latin America: apart from the establishment of joint ventures and a certain cooperation in technological fields (e.g. with Brazil and to a lesser degree with Mexico and other Latin American countries), the trade between the two units repeats colonial exchange patterns, that is mainly raw materials and foodstuff against more or less elaborate goods. This seems to be a prototype without prospect of change – unless the Latin American countries invest substantially more resources in technical research and development and in vocational training as a norm and for a future-oriented industrial production.

The dependency and perhaps maturating impression of dominating Chinese self-interests are mitigated by the fact that China (as had Japan earlier) tries to introduce, via the establishment of Confucius Institutes in Latin America, the transference of basic tenets of Chinese culture, thus establishing pillars for the overdue construction of a bridge of mutual understanding between the two sides of the Pacific. There are also the progressing deliberations both in Latin America and in China to establish a regular air connection that cannot simply be interpreted as a paradigm of a Chinese drive to superiority, because both sides would benefit. Finally, there is the lack of mutual knowledge and familiarity with the situation, the life and the culture.

After many interviews in China (and in other parts of East and Southeast Asia) and in Latin America as well as contacts with corresponding university institutions and 'think tanks' I gained the impression that in several Latin American countries the efforts to learn about China and Asia in general are by far more visible than a comparable Chinese academic interest in Latin America. We find well-developed Institutes of Asian studies in a number of Mexican universities and scientific colleges, in Peru, in Chile, also increasingly in Argentina (but surprisingly less in

Brazil and Venezuela) whereas a matching tendency in China and in the rest of Asia (with the exception of Japan) appears more modest or is simply nonexistent.

I witnessed at the famous Academy of Latin American Studies in Beijing that many members preferred English to Spanish or Portuguese. In contrast, in Latin American universities – and not only in the previously mentioned four countries – masters programmes in Asian and/or Chinese studies appear more and more on the curricula, including languages. The Mexican scientific periodical *Mexico y la cuenca del pacífico*, edited by the Departamento de Estudios del Pacífico of the University of Guadalajara in Jalisco/Mexico offers without any doubt one of the best scientific reviews of the Pacific situation. One should not forget diverging media situations. In Mexico, Brazil, Chile, Peru or Paraguay(!) the daily and weekly papers are far more internationally oriented than most of their East Asian counterparts with their inherent provincialism and political controls. That means that the Latin American elites are better informed on China and Asia than the Asians are on Latin America.

All in all, the acceptance of the growing presence of China in Latin America is ambivalent. On the one hand, the USA is one of the leading founding members of the 'Pacific Family' in general, e.g. for the APEC and related processes, and this means a cooperative attitude in the whole Pacific Rim with parts of Latin America and China as partners.

On the other hand, the question was raised 'Will the Hegemon Bark?' (Paz 2006: 103) The hegemon here is of course the USA. Gonzalo Paz suggests the following answer: 'To some extent, the Chinese offensive in Latin America, although fuelled by its own rationale, has been taking place with perfect timing, at a moment in which the dog was sleeping' (ibid: 104). This is indeed a major statement about Washington's current level of attention in and with Latin America. Asia, including China, is fully aware of the dominant claims of the Colossus of the North in Latin America, and Asia respects it to a large degree. The Asians (as well as the Latin Americans and the Europeans) came to know since the second part of the Clinton Administration that the basic US policy orientation towards Latin America meant 'benign neglect', continued under Bush Jr as nearly complete neglect. There are reasons for it in Latin America; for instance the resistance of leading South American governments and Mexico against a comprehensive Free Trade Area of the Americas, the appearance of Chávez in Venezuela with his allies in befriended governments, the foundation of a South American Union in Quito in 2004, which found its paradigm in the European example and means in plain English a revitalization of the old ideas of Simon Bolívar . . . Perhaps the fundamental raison d'être of the far-reaching relative neglect of Latin America is simply 'imperial overstretch', to use Paul Kennedy's metaphor as applied to ancient Rome and present-day Washington.

The Economist[13] stressed the enormous loss of strengthening ties with former allies in favour of a nearly unlimited struggle against terrorism, Islamic fundamentalism and rogue states. Pan-Americanism seems to be over or at least nearly over. China is fully aware of this situation of North American weakness. And there is little hope that the Obama administration in Washington will be willing or able to overcome this creeping mixture of neo-isolationism, overconfidence in a worldwide capitalist blessing and overdrawn US militarism with at least an idea of truly cooperative international structures.

Here, China comes in again. The basic theme is less the growing Chinese presence in Latin America but rather the direct impact of China upon the USA in terms of trade, investment, exchange rates of currencies, financial support (of the USA!), the race in armaments and the Chinese impact upon Asia. So far, appearances of the Chinese presence in Latin America cause irritation; for instance the Chinese presence in the peace-establishing process in Haiti or the Chinese possibility of one day closing the Panama Canal to the passage of US vessels, as well as the Chinese strategy to reduce the influence and diplomatic presence of Taiwan in Central America and the Caribbean.

There are articulated concerns about China's engagement in Latin America in the United States Southern Command and even in the US Senate. An official source is quoted to have said within the context of a high-ranking visitor's diplomacy in 2006: 'We want to make sure that we don't get our wires crossed' (cited in Paz 2006: 107).[14]

The Chinese have already caused some misunderstanding but they are still cautious not to provoke a broad North American concern about their activities south of the Rio Grande del Norte. 'For the foreseeable future' – writes Gonzalo Paz – 'the dragon wants to keep the backyard's dog sleeping' (ibid: 111). But he pleads for caution: 'However, China, the rest of East Asia and the Latin American countries will probably use the attention vacuum to continue weaving a more dense network, to increase interaction, to learn more about each other, and to develop shared understandings' (ibid: 110).

Brussels observes these developments with concern. For Europeans, the idea of a less one-sided orientation of Latin America towards the North of the Western Hemisphere bears some attraction. One of our suggestions has been articulated for decades and should be maintained: an effectively pursued Latin American policy of integration would be the best precondition to avoid dependencies on dominant powers. The current political fragmentation of the Latin world is the 'best guaranty' for a long-lasting second-class status.

Notes

1 All these and some following historical hints draw heavily, in parts literally, upon Shixue 2005 and 2007.
2 The speech is quoted in English in Foro de Cooperación América Latina–Esia del Este: Informe des los Presidentes/Forum for East Asia–Latin America Cooperation: Co-Chair's Report (completed and published by the Dirección Asia Pacifico of the Chilean Foreign Office in 2001).
3 Regardless how the phenomenon of development should be gauged and evaluated.
4 For the current political profile of Latin America see Mols 2007.
5 For the self-sufficiency of China during many centuries see Buckley Ebry 1998.
6 PBEC = Pacific Basin Economic Council, founded in 1967; PECC = Pacific Economic Cooperation Council, founded in 1980; PAFTAD = Conferencia de Comercio y

Desarrollo del Pacífico, founded 1969 (a private academic conference series, but supported by governments).
7 Forum for East Asian–Latin American Cooperation.
8 Sistema Ecoomico Latinoamericano.
9 Mercado Comun del Sur (Argentina, Brazil, Paraguay, Uruguay).
10 Stefanie Mann (under her maiden name Stefanie Reis) was a member of the Mainz research group on the relationship between Latin America and East Asia. She published various articles and a book on the subject matter, amongst others: 'China and Latin America' (Reis 2005).
11 For the current perception of Chinese politics see Lam 2006.
12 For a general picture of the economic relations between China and Latin America see Devlin *et al.*, eds, 2006 and Husar 2007.
13 29 March–4 April 2008 (special report).
14 Quoted in Paz 2006, p. 107.

References

Buckley Ebry, Patricia, ed. (1998) *Chinese Civilization: A Sourcebook*, 2nd edition, New York: The Free Press.
Cheng, Deborah (2007) 'China invests in Latin America, Building on Local Ties', in Adrian Hearn, *China's Engagement with Latin America: Economic and Political Implications*, 7 February, http://clas.berkeley.edu/Events/spring2007/02-07-07-hearn/index.html
De la Flor Belaunde, Pablo ed., (1991) *Japon en la escena internacional: Sus relaciones con América Latina y el Peru*, Lima.
Derichs, Claudia (2002) 'Geschichte von gestern – Geschichte von heute: Asiatische Perspektiven', in Peter Birle *et al.*, eds, *Globalisierung und Regionalismus. Herausforderungen für Staat und Demokratie in Asien und Lateinamerika*, Opaden, pp. 19–36.
Devlin, Robert, Antoni Estevadeordal and Andres Rodriguez-Clare, eds, (2006) *The Emergence of China. Opportunities and Challenges for Latin America and the Caribbean*, Washington: Inter-American Development Bank/ David Rockefeller Center for Latin American Studies, Harvard University.
Dosch, Jörn (2005) 'Southeast Asia and Latin America', in Jörg Faust, Manfred Mols, Won-ho Kim, eds, *Latin America and East Asia – Attempts at Diversification. New Patterns of Power, Interest and Cooperation*, Münster: Lit, pp. 183–96.
Faust, Jörg and Manfred Mols (1998) *Latin America and the Asia–Pacific. An Emerging Pattern of International Relations*, Mainz (Institut für Politikwissenschaft, Dokumente und Materialien 28).
—— (2005) 'Latin America and East Asia: Defining the Research Agenda', in Jörg Faust, Manfred Mols, Won-ho Kim, eds, *Latin America and East Asia – Attempts at Diversification. New Patterns of Power, Interest and Cooperation*, Münster: Lit, pp. 1–14.
Friedrich, Stefan (2000) 'Außenpolitik', in Brunhild Staiger, ed., *Länderbericht China. Geschichte, Politik, Wirtschaf, Gesellschaft, Kultur*, Darmstadt, pp. 103–34.
Hänni, Tobias (2008) 'Wirtschaftliche Beziehungen zwischen Lateinamerika und China', online, http://ahusun.blogspot.com/2008/11/wirtschaftliche-beziehungen-zwischen.html (accessed 8 July 2009).
Husar, Jörg (2007) *China's Engagement in Latin America. Rohstoffbedarf, Versorgungssicherheit und Investitionen*, Saarbrücken.
Ishihara, Shintaro (1989) *The Japan That Can Say No*, New York.

Jaguaribe de Mattos, Helio (2001) *Un estudio crítico de la historia*, México (2 vols.)

Kennedy, Paul (1987) *The Rise and Fall of the Great Powers: Economic Change and Military Conflict from 1500 to 2000*, London: Random House.

Kim, Samuel S., ed., (2000) *East Asia and Globalization*, London: Rowman and Littlefield.

Kleining, Jochen (2007) 'China und Lateinamerika: Eine neue transpazifische Partnerschaft', *KAS Auslandsinformationen* 9/07, pp. 6–23.

Lam, Willy Wo-Lap (2006) *Chinese Politics in the Hu Jintao Era. New Leaders, New Challenges*, Armonk, New York and London.

Latin America–Asia Review (2005) 'Hu Jintao's visit to the Americas, September'.

Lora, Eduardo (2007) 'Should Latin America Fear China?' in Javier Santiso, ed., *The Visible Hand of China in Latin America*, Paris: Development Centre of the OECD, pp. 15–44.

Maihold, Günther (2006) 'China and Latin America', in Gudrun Wacker, ed., *China's Rise: the Return of Geopolitics?* Berlin (SWP Research Paper), pp. 37–45.

Mols, Manfred (2007) 'Das politische Lateinamerika: Profil und Entwicklungstendenzen', München: Hans Seidel Stiftung (Akademie für Politik und Zeitgeschehen aktuelle Analysen 45).

Palacios Lara, Juan José (2006) 'La relaciones de México con el Pacífico asiático. Contornes y líneas de estrategia', in Juan José Palacios Lara *et al..*, eds, *Las relaciones económicas–Asia Pacifico en los albores del siglo XXI, Análisis de su dinámica e implicaciones de política*, Colima, pp. 17–44.

Palacios Lara, Juan José *et al.*, eds, (2006) *Las relaciones económicas–Asia Pacifico en los albores del siglo XXI, Análisis de su dinámica e implicaciones de política*, Colima.

Paz, Gonzalo S. (2006) 'Rising China's Offensive in Latin America and the U.S. Reaction', *Asian Perspective*, vol. 30, no. 4, pp. 95–112.

Reis, Stefanie (2005) 'China and Latin America', in Jörg Faust, Manfred Mols, Won-ho Kim, eds., *Latin America and East Asia – Attempts at Diversification. New Patterns of Power, Interest and Cooperation*, Münster: Lit, pp. 129–46.

Schoettli, Urs (2007) *China. Die Neue Weltmacht*, Paderborn: Schoeningh Ferdinand Gmbh.

Shamsul, A. B. (2002) 'The European–Asian Knowledge Complex: A Critical Commentary', in K. S. Nathan, ed., *The European Union, United States and ASEAN: Challenges and Prospects for Cooperative Engagement in the 21st Century*, London, pp. 139–55.

Shixue, Jiang (2007) *South–South Cooperation across the Pacific: Development of the Relations between China and Latin America*, Beijing: Institute of Latin American Studies, Chinese Academy of Social Sciences.

—— (2005) *A New Look at the Chinese Relations with Latin America*, Beijing: Institute of Latin American Studies, Chinese Academy of Social Sciences.

Smith, Peter H., Kotaro Horisaka and Shoji Nishijima, eds, (2003) *East Asia and Latin America: the unlikely alliance*, Lanham, MD: Rowman & Littlefield Publishers.

Stavenhagen, Rodolfo (1981) 'The Future of Latin America Between Underdevelopment and Revolution', in Heraldo Muñoz, ed., *From Dependency to Development: Strategies to Overcome Underdevelopment and Inequality*, Boulder, CO: pp. 207–23.

Teng, Chung chian (2007) 'Hegemony or Partnership: China's Strategy and Diplomacy Towards Latin America', in Joshua Eisenman, *et al.*, eds, *China and the Developing World. Beijing's Strategy for the Twenty-first Century*, Armonk, New York and London: M.E. Sharpe, pp. 84–112.

3 Poaching in the hegemon's backyard?

Relations between China and Latin America and the US response[1]

Alberto Camarena

Introduction

The last few years have witnessed an increasing level of interaction between the regions of East Asia and Latin America.[2] This particular phenomenon has been part of a wider intensification of the demarcation, expansion and overall interactions between different regions in the world. According to Dent (2008: 6), 'regionalism is one of the key defining features of the international system' as 'we live in "a world of regions"; an international system increasingly defined by interactions between regions and regional powers'. Processes of regionalism and regionalization and the consequent interest in studying the expression of such international phenomena have begun to expand since the early 1990s, after the end of the Cold War and the demise of the Soviet Union.

The aftermath of such events allowed for a radical restructuring of the international system, one which opened new possibilities for states to engage for the first time in novel processes of cooperation and/or integration, even when in some cases such states had previously interacted in hostile and antagonistic ways. Ideological confrontation gave way to pragmatism, thus the ideal of the creation of wealth and an improved lifestyle for all national populations became universalized in a way that superseded the previous importance given to which particular socio-political and economic paradigm should be followed. Without a doubt, one of the most important debutantes within the post-Cold War system has been the region of East Asia, and on an individual basis, China. East Asia's current economic prowess and further potential in this field and the political one is already considered by some as enabling East Asia to become one of the fundamental regional actors in the world. In the same vein, China has positioned itself as a regional power and even an emerging global power, not just economically but again, also within the international politics sphere. Summing up, do East Asia and China matter? (Segal 1999). The answer is a clear yes.

On the other hand, the Latin American region has not gained the same level of importance as East Asia. Though from a historical perspective Latin America is more clearly defined and settled than East Asia, Latin America has not been able to 'take off' in the same way that East Asia has done. From a particular viewpoint, Latin America shares some similarities with East Asia: both regions have vast populations, extensive geographies, a generous pool of natural resources and strong cultural inheritances. Nevertheless, Latin America has been unable so far to generate an explosive economic boom with impressive and sustained levels of growth such as Northeast Asia has experienced and even some nations in Southeast Asia. Latin America as a region is home to well-established middle-range economic and even political powers such as Brazil and Mexico, or the more recent economic success, Chile. Nevertheless, most Latin American nations are still submerged in dire poverty and the region's levels of economic and social inequality are widespread and rampant.

Notwithstanding the different levels of global impact and overall prowess of each region, East Asia and Latin America have been interacting much more intensely than in previous decades. As argued before, one of the main reasons has been the presence of new structural underpinnings of the international system. But yet another reason is that some nations within East Asia have been spearheading these intensified interactions, namely the conspicuous interest shown by the People's Republic of China (PRC) in the region. That is not to say it is China which exclusively interacts with Latin America; other countries in the region such as Japan, South Korea and Singapore have engaged Latin America too, but it is currently China which by far engages the region with a yet unmatched interest, intensity and depth. Thus, this chapter focuses on current Sino-Latin American relations, and in particular the effect that such new interactions are having with the traditional hegemonic power in the region: the United States of America (US). Simply put, the US is an inseparable factor when considering the history and current economic, political and in some cases even social developments in the region. Since Latin American nations attained the status of sovereign states, the US has played a close and fundamental role in their history. Thus, both any inner and outer development in Latin America will more than probably involve a keen interest from the US in order for Latin America to assess how much of its own national interest might be affected due to these interactions.

Sino-Latin America relations: a phased relationship

As many academics have noted before, relations between China and Latin America go back a long way. Both China and several Latin American nations are not completely unfamiliar with each other, as since the times of 'La Colonia' both China and Latin America have engaged, mainly in trade relations of some relevance (i.e. the Manila Galleon).[3] However, since the birth of the PRC, and particularly during the Cold War period, relations between China and Latin America had been mostly characterized by minimal engagement. In the words of He Li, 'during the pre-Cuban Revolution period, Beijing had neither the opportunity nor the incentive for involvement in Latin America ... until the Chinese "open door policy" in 1978, however, the political and economic ties between the two regions were very limited' (He Li 1991: 1). China's interactions with Latin America during this period were constrained by a number of factors, namely, geographical remoteness, the dominant presence of the US and its strong bias against communist states, a lack of immediate geopolitical significance and an almost total lack of understanding about the region from a socio-cultural point of view.

Seen from an international politics point of view, Sino-Latin American relations could be roughly divided into four main periods. The first of these periods (1949–late 1950s) characterized relations between the newly born People's Republic of China and Latin America in a way that both actors paid the scantiest attention to each other. This outcome on the other hand, was not a mere coincidence. China was still immersed in consolidating its statehood, which included defining and securing its borders (e.g. the invasion of Tibet and the intention to recover Taiwan from the virtually defeated Kuomintang). China also needed to attend to more pressing issues, such as the fast-deteriorating relations with the US, the Korean War and building its alliance with the Soviet Union. Latin America on the other hand had to deal with its own pressing problems, mostly of a domestic nature, and in most cases viewed the emergence of the PRC as something nearly irrelevant. During the early and mid-1950s, some Latin American countries had embarked on ambitious modernization projects which often implied entering models of import substitutions. During this period, the United States had been the most important external actor with which Latin America interacted. For Latin American nations, China could only play a marginal and indirect role, the latter as part of the American-led policy not to recognize mainland China but Taiwan as the legitimate Chinese nation. The Chinese rhetoric of the 1950s aimed at developing nations and pursuing a non-aligned stance (epitomized in the Bandung Conference) had more active resonance in Asia than Latin America. During this period, China had no pragmatic benefits to offer to Latin America but even if this had been the case, the proximity of the US would have created considerable hurdles for Latin American countries to develop closer links with China running independently from American influence.

The second period (late 1950s–early 1970s) began with the triumph of the Cuban Revolution led by the charismatic revolutionary leader Fidel Castro. As Castro declared Cuba's revolution to be a socialist one, this created an opportunity for both China and the Soviet Union to extend their support and influence in Latin America; for the first time with a true potential. Early relations between Beijing and La Havana developed positively, but the nature of such relations began to deteriorate along with the growing enmity between Beijing and Moscow. Later on, China managed to establish diplomatic relations with Chile's socialist government of Salvador Allende (December 1970). But twenty years after the birth of the PRC, Beijing had only succeeded in establishing two diplomatic relations in the region. The rest of Latin America remained firmly linked to the US policy on China, meaning non-recognition. Moreover, China's characteristic belligerent rhetoric and the Cultural Revolution did little to help improve the country's image within ruling Latin American elites. Until the late 1960s, China had a poor record in terms of establishing formal diplomatic relations in Latin America. Nevertheless, Beijing had been relatively successful in exporting the Mao Zedong revolutionary ethos into the region. Mao's line of thought became popular, particularly amongst Latin American students, and in Peru a Maoist armed peasant movement took form (i.e. Sendero Luminoso).

The third period in Sino-Latin American relations (early 1970s–late 1990s) became a milestone as it was characterized by a clear breakthrough in the relations between the two entities. Two main factors came to reshape the nature of China–Latin America relations. The first one was the Sino-US rapprochement, highlighted by US President Nixon's visit to China in 1972, and the new strategic alliance agreed between Washington and Beijing in order to contain the Union of Soviet Socialist Republics (USSR). These developments paved the way for Latin America to improve relations with China. The Sino-US rapprochement cleared the way for several Latin American countries to begin recognizing China diplomatically, as the US tacitly approved such developments. By the end of 1977, even before the official establishment of diplomatic relations between the PRC and the US, 12 Latin American countries had already established diplomatic relations with China. Also during this period, trade between China and Latin America, if still negligible, experienced a dynamic evolution.

The second factor relates to the ascendance to power of 'the paramount leader' Deng Xiaoping, the father of China's modernizing policies that have permeated pervasively into most aspects of the country's life. Deng's decision to abandon the centrally planned economic model, and to embrace the introduction of a phased market economic system, made him and the rest of the top leadership realize that in order to achieve this goal China would need to restructure its former relations with the rest of the world. China's modernizing project would require at its core significant amounts of foreign investment and technological transfers. The leadership understood that a vital step to be taken was to be perceived by other nations (particularly those in the West) not as a belligerent and unpredictable state, but rather as a responsible nation willing to play along with the established rules governing the international system of states. A gradual transformation of the economic system produced major changes in China's foreign policy and to Beijing's understanding of international institutions. China made pragmatism the source of foreign policy substituting the ideological principles embedded in world revolution, the inevitability of war and the promotion of armed struggle. The idea of peace gained a central position in China's conceptualization of how to engage in world politics, and how other nations should understand China's own development. Thus, Chinese modernization is supposed to be understood as 'the development path to a peaceful rise'. According to Zheng Bijian (2005), a top influential advisor to China's political leadership, 'China does not seek hegemony or predominance in world affairs . . . China's development depends on peace, a peace that its development will in turn reinforce.'

China's efforts to generate a new image abroad divorced from the ideological assertiveness of the past have indeed gone a long way and achieved considerable success. In other words, what China has industriously been working on for the last few decades is the development of its own brand of *soft power*. Particularly since the beginning of the 1990s, China decided to implement a well-orchestrated foreign policy in order to boost its image abroad and also to improve its access to resources of many sorts, so necessary to feed the voracious developmental needs of the nation. Some observers have branded China's diplomatic strategy as the 'charm offensive' (Kurlantzick 2007). Moreover, this diplomatic strategy has left almost no part of the world untouched, including Latin America.

China's diplomatic charm offensive initiated its first comprehensive overture in Southeast Asia during the early 1990s. The charm offensive was partly inspired because China was going through a new period of international isolation after the events of Tiananmen Square. The US and Western Europe, two of the most important external actors to help accelerate China's modernization drive, had condemned the massacre and established sanctions against China. The PRC felt an urgent need to improve its external image at any front possible. But China could also re-engage other parts of the world in a new way because it was now free from the structural constraints of the Cold War. The end of the Cold War and the demise of the Soviet Union offered new possibilities of positive engagement with indifferent and even previously hostile actors. Since then, China has moved progressively towards an effort to reach and cajole other regions in the world such as Africa, Central Asia, the Middle East and the South Pacific, and also individual countries such as the US, Japan, India and Russia amongst others. Latin America has also being targeted as part of China's ambitious charm offensive diplomacy.

Embedded in the logic of Beijing's latest diplomatic manoeuvrings, China and Latin America have entered a fourth period of relations characterized by an increasing mutual interest, in tandem with a significant growth of economic and political interactions.[4] The critical year for this new set of relations was 2004, which from a Chinese perspective could be branded as 'the Latin America year'. Gonzalo Paz (2006: 95) has argued that '2004 will be remembered as the year in which China jumped with energy into a geopolitical and geoeconomic space considered until recently as the American backyard: Latin America.' China's diplomacy in Latin America has followed a similar pattern in the way Beijing has decided to engage other regions of the world. First, high-ranking Chinese political figures have toured Latin American capitals, and top political figures of Latin America have reciprocated by visiting China (this is why the year 2004 became such a landmark between China and Latin America). This strategy is what some have branded as 'visit diplomacy', one upon which China and Latin America had keenly engaged.

Though high-level Chinese state visits to Latin America had also regularly taken place before the turn of the century, the early 2000s witnessed a considerable improvement in the quantity and quality of such visits. On the margins of the Asia–Pacific Economic Cooperation (APEC) meeting in 2004 in Santiago de Chile, Chinese President Hu Jintao visited Argentina, Brazil, Chile and Cuba. President of Brazil Lula da Silva and Argentina's Nestor Kirchner also visited China in May and June 2004 respectively. Furthermore, Venezuela's President Hugo Chávez visited China in December of the same year and Bolivia's President Evo Morales paid a visit in January, before taking office as elected president. Hu also visited Mexico and held discussions with former Mexican President Vicente Fox as part of his North America trip in September 2005. Chile's President

Michelle Bachelet met with Hu in November 2006 when attending the APEC summit meeting in Vietnam. During January and February 2005, China's Vice President Zeng Qinghong visited Mexico, Venezuela and Peru and attended the ministerial meeting of the China–Caribbean Economy and Trade Cooperation. In most cases such visits have become the means to express China's eagerness to establish closer links with Latin America in order to facilitate particular political objectives and broader economic-strategic ones.

Second, China and its counterparts have been able to create regional forums at which the different actors involved can further advance their social learning processes about each other and to follow up the ongoing causeway of their interactions.[5] Several Asian and Latin American states established the Forum for East Asia–Latin America Cooperation (FEALAC) comprising over 30 countries from both East Asia and Latin America (see Chapters 12 and 13 in this book). FEALAC is only in its initial stages and has no intention of sophisticating its institutional *modus operandi*, but rather is meant to serve as a regional medium in order to 'increase mutual understanding, trust, political dialogue and friendly cooperation amongst member states'.[6]

Mutual high-ranking visits brought with them the willingness to sign agreements and cooperation schemes. Hu Jintao's tour to Latin America proposed a framework for relations in order to 'deepen strategic common consensus and enhancing political mutual trust, focusing on tapping cooperation potential in areas such as economics, trade, science and technology, to intensify mutual coordination and multilateral cooperation, and also valuing cultural exchanges and enhancing mutual understanding'.[7] As part of the sophistication of relations between both entities, countries like Brazil and Argentina upgraded their relationships with China to the status of strategic partnerships. Also, Brazil, Argentina and Chile gave China 'market economy status' which should better enable Beijing to deal with claims of unfair economic competition with trade partners. China and Chile signed a Free Trade Agreement (FTA), operational since October 2006, and completed a first round of negotiations to expand the scope of the Treaty to the areas of services and investment (January 2007).[8] Since Hu Jintao visited Latin America he has announced that China will be investing US$100 billion in the region within the next ten years. Most of the investment projected is to be destined to develop infrastructure that directly or indirectly relates to China's imports from the region, such as the development of transport systems (e.g. highways and railways) and the extraction of natural resources such as minerals and oil. Another field in which China is interested to invest is that of telecommunications and space technology. China is very interested in utilizing satellite-launching sites in Brazil and Suriname.

China's objectives in Latin America

As part of China's comprehensive new foreign policy engagements with the rest of the world, Latin America finally became a target of the charm offensive. Undoubtedly, many Latin American countries have developed a keen interest in understanding the current developments in China, but it was the PRC which finally decided to engage the Latin American region pragmatically. It is not a coincidence that Beijing has decided to take the first steps towards engagement as its own inner developments are forcing the Chinese leadership to look elsewhere in order to satisfy a voracious demand for natural resources. China has found in some Latin American countries, such as Brazil, Argentina and Chile, reliable providers of resources such as meat, soybeans and copper; Cuba a provider of nickel and Venezuela might be growing as a provider of crude oil. All of these are very welcome commodities needed to feed the emerging and affluent Chinese middle classes and to further underpin the high-paced economic growth of the country. The provision of oil is yet another critical factor to be considered, as China is currently the second largest consumer of hydrocarbons in the world, behind the US. China also sees Latin America as a viable means for the possibility of gaining access to the North American market via the already established or ongoing processes of trade liberalization between North and Latin America (i.e. NAFTA and FTAA) and also Latin American markets.

The expansion of trade and the need to access natural resources have played a fundamental role in moulding the rationale behind China's desire to engage Latin America. Nevertheless, the reason for this engagement is not based purely on material considerations. A political and strategic dimension is also part of China's calculations. Beijing seeks to benefit from enriched relations with Latin America in order to further isolate Taiwan diplomatically, to promote the concept of multipolarity and to strengthen its position in the international system. Beijing acknowledges that the 'Taiwan issue' in Latin America represents one of the last and strongest bastions of diplomatic recognition for Taipei.[9] For this reason, it is in China's interest to actively engage these Latin American countries so that it might convince Taipei's Latin American allies to cease formal diplomatic relations.

Moreover, the Chinese political leadership and Chinese international politics theorists have advanced the paradigm of multipolarity. Since the early 1990s, China has conceptualized its place in the world as one of a number of evolving poles in a system that is continuously moving towards multipolarity, or as Deng Xiaping once put it: 'in the so-called multipolar world, China will be counted as a pole.'[10] The concept of an evolving international system moving towards a multipolar structure has not subsided in the minds of Chinese decision-makers and international relations analysts, even though there have been strong signals that a prevailing unipolar world headed by the US is in place and may even be settling for some time to come. Therefore, the paradigm of multipolarity and its promotion amongst diplomatic allies and friends becomes of considerable relevance for China, as Beijing has been permanently concerned about its status as an emerging power, and how this condition is being seen and acknowledged by the rest of the world, particularly the US. After all, it was within the US that the 'China Threat theory' (the rise of China signals global power ambitions, hegemonic behaviour and an almost inevitable and eventual clash with American interests worldwide) appeared for the first time and has been keenly embraced by some factions within the American political apparatus. Furthermore, the idea of a threatening China has expanded beyond the US and has been discussed in a serious fashion by other regions and countries in the world. China's leadership is aware of such views about the country and inevitably some have linked the China Threat argument as a revitalized post-Cold War attempt to contain China.[11] In the view of China's decision-makers and political analysts, the promotion of a multipolar world should contribute to diminish the pervasively dominant position of the US in world affairs, one which – according to this perception – could easily turn against China's emergence if ripe conditions for this arise.[12]

Thus, the promotion of multipolarity should also contribute to enhance China's position in the international system for those who, along with China, feel uncomfortable about an international system dominated by the US; but also strengthening China's position within the international system should contribute to enhance the advantages of a multipolar system for these same countries. In this particular sense, China could try to further advance the idea of belonging, along with Latin American nations, to the developing world. The idea of belonging to the developing world could introduce in a veiled manner a mild-tempered opposition to US unilateralism and thus the promotion of a multilateral power front that could balance the so often seen extreme leeway of single hegemonic powers. The usage of such ideas is already present, as when Hu Jintao, addressing the Argentinean parliament said that 'China *will always stand on the side of developing countries* and work together to promote the prosperity and progress of developing countries and push forward for peace and development.'[13]

Sino-Latin American relations: the economic and political dimension

Since the beginning of the twenty-first century China has become an important trading partner to all of Latin America's largest economies. Sino-Latin American trade is mostly complementary in nature as one actor has been able to provide many commodities that the other needs, only there are some exceptions to this rule. For most Latin American economies, the US has remained as the most important trading partner, but China has gained a sudden and impressive status rising to third and second place in less than ten years. According to data from the World Trade Organization (WTO), China has recently figured as one of the five most important export and import partners in merchandise trade with Peru, Chile, Argentina, Brazil and Cuba. In 2006, China figured as the third most important export destination for Peru, the fourth for Chile, Brazil and Cuba, and fifth for Argentina. During the same year, China became a considerable source of imports for countries like Paraguay and Mexico (in first and third place respectively). Other import sources were Colombia in fourth place and Uruguay, Ecuador and Venezuela in fifth place. In Central America, China became the third export partner for Costa Rica and the third and fourth import partner for Nicaragua and Guatemala respectively.[14]

Though China ranks within the first five most important export and/or import markets for these Latin American countries, it is important to note that such figures are not as substantial as their equivalents with other trade partners such as the European Union and the US. Though the volume of bilateral trade remains relatively small and leaves considerable room for expansion, Sino-Latin American trade can be expected to continue to expand as China's growth also continues. As noted earlier, trade relations between China and Latin America have significantly expanded, only not in absolute but rather in relative terms. Up to 2005, China's exports and imports to the region represented only 3 and 4 per cent respectively of its worldwide exports and imports (Hammer and Kilpatrick 2006: 6). China's imports from Latin America grew from near US$3 billion during the late 1990s to US$21.7 billion in 2004. In a similar vein, China's exports to Latin America have also grown considerably for the same period, the late 1990s to 2004, from US$5.3 billion to US$18.3 billion (Dumbaugh and Sullivan 2005). China has been keen to import crucial commodities from some Latin American countries such as ores and minerals, hydrocarbons and food, as the Asian country needs to find stable supplies in order to feed its growing consumption of energy and its need for resources in order to further industrialize and feed its population. In the year 2006, Chile exported over 250 million kilograms of refined copper and copper alloys to China (in the same year Chile exported nearly 17 million kilos to the UK), in 2007 Brazil exported to China slightly over 100 million tons of iron ore.[15] In 2006, Brazil exported 11 million tons of soybeans, nearly double the amount shipped to China in 2004.[16] Argentina is also exporting soybeans to China; in early 2005 Argentina was already providing for one-third of China's soya needs.[17]

While direct investments from Chinese sources have increased too, FDI flows have not reached the same level of importance as trade. The top destinations of Chinese investment are outside Latin America (i.e. Hong Kong, the US and Germany). Nevertheless and considering the scale of China's investment abroad, the figures aimed at Latin America are not negligible. According to some sources, in 2004 Chinese overseas investment in Latin America reached US$1.76 billion,[18] and China's government has pledged a total of US$100 billion investment in the region within the next ten years. Chinese companies have decided to invest in Latin America as a wider strategy in order to ensure steady supplies of raw materials and also to gain access to the US market. Chinese investment in Latin American countries has mainly focused on the extraction and production of raw materials and resources though it has also included such sectors as manufacturing assembly, textiles and telecommunications. Shanghai-based steel maker Baosteel, for example, announced early in 2004 that the company had formally started the establishment of a large-scale iron and steel joint venture in Brazil with Brazilian partner iron ore miner 'Vale do Rio Doce'.[19]

Recently, the Chairman of China's computer manufacturers Lenovo Group declared that the company is very interested in concentrating investment in emerging markets, some of them located in Latin American countries such as Brazil and Mexico.[20] China is also to invest over a billion US dollars in the Cuban–Chinese San Felipe project aiming at exploiting nickel deposits. Investments have not flown exclusively from China towards Latin America. According to the Chinese Ministry of Commerce, by the end of 2005 some 18,000 projects in the PRC were funded by Latin American companies, with a total investment of US$60 billion.[21] The Mexican bakery giant 'Grupo Bimbo' bought Beijing Panrico Food Processing Centre based in China, an investment that, 'has enabled the company to attain important presence and recognition in the cities of Beijing and Tianjin . . . [as] this acquisition represents a solid opportunity to immediately enter one of the fastest growing and dynamic markets in the world'.[22] In a similar vein, Brazil's aircraft manufacturer Embraer established a production unit in Northeast China through a joint venture with the China Aviation Industry Corp where it has been producing tailored aircraft for the Chinese market.

The procurement of energy and energy-related topics has also become a very important factor affecting China–Latin America relations. China has signed energy agreements with Venezuela, and Ecuador is exploring the possibility of investing in Peru, Colombia and Bolivia. China's undertakings have been quite visible in Venezuela and Colombia. In late 2006 China's Sinopec partly acquired Ominex de Colombia for US$850 million. Amongst the agreements signed between the current president of Venezuela Hugo Chávez and his Chinese counterparts during January 2005, Venezuela has agreed to develop plans for Chinese stakes in oil and gas fields. The agreements included the establishment of an investment fund worth US$6 billion (China is to contribute with US$4 billion) with the objective of financing development projects in Venezuela. According to Petroleos de Venezuela (PDVSA), in 2005 Venezuela was sending 350,000 barrels of crude per day and the intention is to raise that number to 1 million barrels per day by 2010–11.[23] PDVSA and Sinopec have agreed to study the existing oil fields of the Orinoco Belt, and their governments to enhance energy cooperation and to supply fuel oil to the Chinese market.

Within the political dimension that links China to Latin America, the region can be broadly divided into two groups. The first group is made up of those countries that have not developed any major antagonisms with the US. The economic models that these countries have applied to their own economies and societies are not opposed in the main to trade liberalization and socio-political democratic practices, in other words, they broadly run in tandem with the US model. Within this group we can find as the most important representatives Chile, Mexico, Colombia, Argentina and Brazil, even though the Brazilian government of Lula da Silva and that of Cristina Fernandez in Argentina have a centre-left orientation. On the other end of the spectrum, there is a group of Latin American countries that has expressed an open opposition to neo-liberal policies and practices, and in general frequent remarks of hostility towards the US. This bloc is represented by Venezuela, Cuba, Nicaragua, Bolivia and Ecuador. Apart from Cuba, the political leaderships of these countries have accessed power relatively recently. In Venezuela, President Hugo Chávez claims to be heading towards a 'Bolivarian socialist revolution', which has been characterized by the nationalization of major industries, a strong personality-based leadership and a deep-seated anti-Americanism. In Nicaragua, Daniel Ortega, the former leader of the Marxist-oriented Sandinista movement and also ex-president (1979–90), became president of the country again in early 2007. In Bolivia, Evo Morales was elected president in early 2006. Morales is a charismatic leader of Indian descent who has also expressed his opposition to neo-liberal economics. The Bolivian president nationalized the energy industry and is a close friend of Hugo Chávez and Fidel Castro. Since 2007 Ecuador's President has been Rafael Correa who maintains close relations with Chávez and Morales.

The leadership characteristics of these Latin American countries could offer China political exploits serving its own interests. Nevertheless, Beijing has been cautious not to foment interactions that could awaken negative responses from the US. Foremost, China has approached Latin American countries seeking to benefit from an abundant source of natural resources and commodities that have become essential needs to advance its own development. For that reason, the Chinese leadership is not so much interested in the type of government it is dealing with but rather, the type of trade and provision agreements they reach with these governments. In spite of the latter and at least theoretically speaking, China could attempt to cajole Latin American regimes with a strong opposition to the US in order to strengthen its own position in the continent. A more influential China in Latin America would also serve the cause to promote multipolarity by means of debilitating the American position in the international system and strengthening China's. Other countries such as Iran and Russia have already attempted to develop closer links with Latin America (Russia with Cuba and Venezuela, and Iran with Venezuela) in order to try to strike back at the US due to actions and policies that have been interpreted by these countries as detrimental to their own interests.

If China was to become interested, it could attempt to forge deeper political relations with anti-US Latin American governments such as Cuba, Venezuela and Nicaragua, but it is most probable that Beijing will not pursue this course of action. The reason is clear: the Sino-American relationship is of much more importance for China than that with any Latin American country. China needs to maintain a sound relationship with the US in order to keep the ongoing investment flows, technology transfers and not least, access to the American market. Sino-Latin American relations are thus framed within Beijing's articulated foreign policy of good-neighbourliness. Deng Xiaoping's pragmatism is still one of the guiding principles in foreign policy to the extent that relations based on ideological similarities have been sacrificed in order to encourage relations promoting beneficial outcomes for China's own development. China has not approached Latin American nations seeking political advantages in order to diminish the US regional and even international influence. China's main interests still lay in economic interactions.[24]

The US reaction to China's presence and activities in Latin America

The United States is well aware of China's growing presence and activities in Latin America, and for that reason Washington has keenly been following the evolution of Sino-Latin American relations. The US Congress has already called for hearings on this particular matter (in April 2005 through the Subcommittee on the Western Hemisphere/Committee on International relations, House of Representatives) and also enacted other related measures.[25] Adding significance to the US's detailed analysis of the PRC's activities in the region, it is important to note that the first Congressional hearing on the matter was entitled 'China's influence in the Western Hemisphere' (Committee on International Relations 2005). Any form of influence exercised by any other power or emerging power in Latin America is something that the US, almost by default, would be reacting against. In order to better understand the reason why the US gives so much consideration to China's growing relations with Latin America, it is necessary to locate US–Latin American relations in a historical perspective.

One particular aspect which stands out about how the US perceives Latin America can be summarized in the Monroe Doctrine enacted by the American government in 1823. The Doctrine originally intended to keep well-established European powers from interfering with already established sovereign states in the Western Hemisphere, thus it euphemistically warned European powers that 'we [the US] should consider any attempt from their part [outside powers] to extend their system to any portion of this hemisphere as dangerous to our peace and safety' (Perkins 1963: 392). Though referring to particular actors and historical regional developments at the time, the Monroe Doctrine was to become a permanent cornerstone of US regional foreign policy. Since the enactment of the Doctrine, it became clear that Latin America was becoming a crucial sphere of interest for the US. Thus, 'America for the Americans'[26] contained a more subtle message hidden within the idea that only sovereign states in the Western Hemisphere had the right to control their own national destinies. The Doctrine also tacitly acknowledged that no other power but the US should have the 'right' to interfere in Latin American affairs, particularly when the interests of the US were directly affected.

Thus, acknowledging that the US perceives Latin America as one of its core regional spheres of influence, what has been the US reaction to China's recent approaches in the region? Overall, Washington has not reacted alarmingly to China's penetration into its 'backyard'. Nevertheless, the US non-alarmist reaction is not tantamount to a blasé attitude towards these events. The US has limited itself to a close observation of the unfolding events accompanied with fact findings and discussions at Congressional level. Instead of proactively reacting against Beijing's charm offensive in Latin America, Washington has decided to 'wait and see' and to react based on further developments. But the latter could shift if the US administration was to consider China has taken any particular action that has 'stepped out of line' with the notion of 'America for the Americans', albeit updated to a twenty-first century version. This is tantamount to saying that the notion of Latin America still being a region which the Americans consider as a sphere of influence is quite in place; and for that same reason, the possibility of debilitating the otherwise prime position of the US in the region by external powers would not be welcomed. On the other hand, the US has also approved China's engagements with Latin America, as these are seen as part of a sound expression of the Asian country's integration with the world economy. These new interactions should further underpin China's willingness to act as a responsible international player and to bring stability to the country and the wider East Asian region. The US also has a keen interest in seeing China align as much as possible with American interests so that it becomes easier to interact both economically and politically. The former US Secretary of State Condoleezza Rice commented that 'so clearly, America has reason to welcome the rise of a confident, peaceful and prosperous China. We want China as a global partner, able and willing to match its growing capabilities to its international responsibilities.'[27]

It is also important to note that China's presence in Latin America does not rank as a priority for the US and for that reason it has remained a relatively low-key issue. Washington is aware that, even if Sino-Latin American relations have been developing a deeper and more direct nature, such relations still lack sufficient strategic and political importance. Within the international sphere, the US is much more concerned with the war on terror, the process of peace in the Middle East and the reduction of nuclear stockpiles.

Furthermore, amongst American legislators and other high-ranking govern-ment officials, it is possible to identify divergent views about how serious the implications are in relation to China's activities in Latin America. Dan Burton, Congressman and Chairman of the Subcommittee on the Western Hemisphere in 2005 expressed that 'we [Americans] should be cautious and view the rise of Chinese power as something to be counterbalanced or contained, and perhaps go so far as to consider China's actions in Latin America as the movement of an hegemonic power into our hemisphere.'[28] Nevertheless, during the same period and in the view of now former Assistant Secretary to the US Bureau of Western Hemisphere Affairs, Roger F. Noriega, 'the implications of China's engagement in the region do not necessarily point towards instability in the region . . . China's growing presence in the region reflects its growing engagement throughout the world. It does not necessarily constitute a threat to US interests.'[29] In spite of such differing views, the position of the US Department of State is that there are two major trends in China's engagement with Latin America. The first is China's attempts to increase its own trade and investment in the region to fuel its domestic development; the second is to try to match these growing economic engagements with political influence. This set of economic and political interactions *per se* are not discouraged by the US, so that the US Department of State has declared that 'we [the US] support China's engagement in the region [of Latin America] in ways that create prosperity and promote transparency, good governance and respect for human rights . . . We need to work with China and our allied friends to ensure that every effort is taken to promote policies that converge with our interests.'[30]

In spite of supporting China's engagement with Latin America, the US has legitimate concerns arising from such relations, which have the potential to run adversely against American interests in the region. Washington would be concerned if closer relations between Beijing and some Latin American countries could debilitate the support for the improvement of democratic practices and the protection of human rights. In other geographical regions, such as Africa and

Southeast Asia, China has been willing to establish close relations with some political regimes regardless of their poor record in democratic practices, abuses in the area of human rights and even genocide. China's keen interest in developing political and economic links with such regimes has given these countries considerable leverage, as governments realize they can rely on China if other doors close.

China is already in contact with regimes in Latin America which Washington finds in breach of the respect of human rights and poor democratic practices (e.g. Cuba). Moreover, Washington is aware that China has been very successful in improving its image and influence in other regions of the world, even at the expense of the US. Thus, another concern for Washington would be that China might increase its popularity with Latin America due to a clever use of soft power and aid. At least in some countries, the US could be relegated to an undesirable second place in terms of influence, particularly if at some point China was to make use of anti-Americanism in the region which has been traditionally present and pervasive. China's presence in Latin America has been on the rise, and larger sections of the population in four out of seven countries in the region acknowledge China's influence has been seen as 'a good thing' (Kohut 2007). The US has to consider Latin American anti-Americanism which to this day is still a present and widespread feature of US–Latin American relations. Even amongst Latin American countries more attuned to US practices and values, and those not so radically pitted against Washington, there have been signs of opposition to a fully committed support to American regional and world views. During the fourth Summit of the Americas in Argentina (November 2005) for example, the American push for a Free Trade Area of the Americas (FTAA) was defeated when amongst others, the MERCOSUR group (Argentina, Brazil, Paraguay and Uruguay) argued that 'the necessary conditions are not yet in place for achieving a balanced and equitable free trade agreement with effective access to markets free from subsidies and trade-distorting practices and that takes into account the needs and sensitivities of all partners'.[31] The risk that the US could face in relation to China is that, in order to gain better access to strategic resources and to improve its overall image in the region, Beijing could eventually propose alternative trade deals reflecting Latin American concerns for market accessibility and distorted trade practices. For example, China has already offered to some Southeast Asian countries early harvest trade clauses and financial assistance in times of trouble. Could China eventually envisage similar schemes with Latin America? How would such interactions affect present relations and perceptions between Latin America and the US?

Furthermore, the US is also concerned about an enhanced level of military interaction between China and Latin America. American politicians do not see China's military activities as a serious threat; nevertheless, it is recognized that 'there is a significant military dimension to China's presence in Latin America, still relatively small but growing' (Committee on International Relations 2005: 46). Thus, the military has been another tool of diplomacy which China has used to engage Latin America. For example, China has made use of the People's

Liberation Army National Defence University (NDU) and its links to foreign military personnel to establish contacts with the region. Since less than ten years ago, senior figures of the PLA have visited and received military delegations from Latin American states (Watson 2007), in some cases large delegations travelling to Brazil, Venezuela, Argentina and even President Uribe's staunch pro-American government in Colombia (Blank 2005). In spite of the latter, the military links that concern the US the most are those between Beijing, Caracas and La Havana. Such concerns are understandable as Venezuela and Cuba have been the most out-spoken anti-American regimes in Latin America, a situation that facilitates these governments to cooperate in military matters with external powers at risk of infuriating the US. There are suspicions China might be operating a number of intelligence signal facilities from Cuba (cyber-warfare and intercepting com-munications), specifically from Russia's Lourdes military base, which target the US. Furthermore, President Chávez has expressed his willingness to acquire weapons from China and other providers for up to US$5 billion (Blank 2005).

On the other hand, China's economic rise has also contributed to create a negative image of the Asian giant in Latin America. Some sectors of Mexican industry for example, see with alarm the rising economic prowess of China and its capacity to enter the US market displacing Mexican products in the process. Even at the level of government, Mexican technocracies seem to fear the ongoing and future competition with China in economic terms. For those Latin American economies that are not complementary to but competitive with that of China, such a sense of concern seems to be shared.[32]

Should the US fear China's growing interest and presence in Latin America?

The US has reasons to follow closely further developments between China and Latin America, but in general, Washington is neither opposed nor is too concerned about the current level of interactions between Beijing and the Latin American capitals, not even when considering the military interactions.

One of the reasons that explains Washington's lack of deep concerns about China's activities in Latin America is the historical background that has characterized US–Latin American relations. First, there is a shared geography between the United States and Latin America, as both entities inhabit the same continent. Regardless of the vastness of the continent, the US has been able to play a significant and permanent role in the history of Latin American nations which at the same time has created a closely knit history. Often such interactions have created a deep-seated distrust and animosity against the US, but what gives an advantage to the Americans is precisely that Latin American countries are familiarized with the United States' interests, values and practices, which facilitates the possibility of further interactions between both actors, even if often surrounded by clashing interests. China might be a new and attractive partner, but there is a cultural unawareness that could prove difficult to deal with when furthering interactions with Latin America. Moreover, most Latin American countries have shared the same democratic political values and practices as the US, and have also embraced a capitalist, free market economic system.

To a larger extent Latin America has inherited the same political values from the American War of Independence and the French Revolution, a fact of which the Americans have always been aware. In 1818, Henry Clay, a member of the US House of Representatives noted that 'we are the Latin Americans' great example. Of us they constantly speak as of brothers having a similar origin. They adopt our principles, copy our institutions, and, in many cases, employ the very language and sentiments of our revolutionary papers' (Perkins 1963: 3). Recently, Roger Noriega has spoken on the very same tenets, arguing that 'The Western Hemisphere is our home by virtue of geography, history, culture, demographics and economics. The United States is linked to our Western Hemispheric partners in ways other countries cannot match.'[33] Noriega's reference to the current inability to match such linkages might well have been directed to China, as the American government understands no other non-Latin American country in the world could match such powerful and pervasive links with the region. As part of such linkages, socio-cultural phenomena have also played a fundamental role in establishing strong interactions between the US and Latin America. A clear and visible aspect of the latter has been the large number of Hispanics living in the US and their constant migration into the country, particularly through the US–Mexican border. In terms of trade and assistance, Washington is also aware how the US exceeds China's initiatives in Latin America, both quantitatively and qualitatively.[34] Since the mid-1990s, US investment in the region has been at least three times more than the projected Chinese US$100 billion of investment within the next ten years. It is also crucial to note that the US remains, by far, the largest market for Latin American exports. Moreover, and in spite of being relatively new, Sino-Latin American relations seem not to be free of potential disappointments, as for example, President Hu Jintao's promise to make sizeable investments in the region has not been kept (McCarthy 2008).[35] Another area of criticism is that the proposed Chinese investment in Latin America tends to focus narrowly on the exploitation of raw materials and other areas which directly relate to the extraction of commodities required to build roads, rail infrastructure and ports. Such types of investment seem to represent a significant gain to China but not to the host countries as it is not directed to other value-added sectors that could report more substantial benefits to the structure of the economic system and society in general. Furthermore, Sino-Latin American trade relations are not exclusively complementary. Along with soaring trade deficits, some countries in the region have expressed their apprehension about China's competition in certain sectors (such as textiles, footwear and apparel) which are limiting the exporting capacity of such countries. During mid-2003 for example, the Argentine government announced a series of restrictions on Chinese imports of products in leather, garments, toys and other products.[36] Finally, the US is also clear that China is not unaware of US sensitivities in the region. When Hu Jintao travelled to the 2004 APEC CEO Summit held in the Chilean capital of Santiago for example, he explicitly avoided going to Caracas knowing that this move would have upset Washington. In relation to military exchanges, it is not China who leads a concerted effort to expand its military relations with Latin America in order to upset the US. The inconspicuous political angle in such relations has been exercised by countries, like Venezuela, which also aim at upsetting Washington by means of establishing closer military links with outside powers.

Conclusions

Relations between China and Latin America have experienced a considerable revamp, particularly since the early 2000s with concerted efforts by China's political leadership to approach and engage the region. The expansion of China's diplomatic charm offensive towards Latin America is part of an overall diplomatic effort which aims to gain access to raw materials and other critical commodities that the PRC greatly needs in order to continue fuelling its own development. In pursuing the latter, China has eyed Latin America but there is also a political dimension to its intentions, namely to promote the concept of international multipolarity and to strengthen China's position within the international system. China is also interested in broadening its relations with Latin America, not least because it is in this region that Taiwan finds one of its last important remnants of diplomatic recognition.

Sino-Latin American relations have produced mutual benefits, mostly as Latin American countries are able to sell commodities to China, and China has been able to find a reliable source of such commodities. In spite of such mutual economic benefits, Latin American economies have also expressed concern about growing trade deficits with China and the growing competition on particular areas of economic production and access to markets abroad. China has also pledged heavy sums of money for investment in Latin America, but the scope of such investments seems to be limited in its potential to generate positive spill-over effects in the local economies. A crucial factor that China needs to consider is the role of the US in Latin America as Washington considers the region as its traditional sphere of influence. The US is not opposed to China's interactions with Latin America, just as long as such interactions are not understood to be undermining the United States' traditional (and undisputed) influence in the region. For that reason, American analysts and decision-makers have been observing the evolution of the Sino-Latin American relationship, and have begun to discuss vigorously the potential impacts, directions and outcomes of such interactions.

China seems to understand the strategic importance that the US gives to Latin America and the historic-psychological factors that make the region so close to American interests. Thus, China tacitly acquiesces to the Monroe Doctrine. It also looks very possible that the Sino-Latin American relationship will grow so that it will become more complex. China's reliance on natural resources and other imports from abroad can only be expected to grow. On the other hand, Latin American people in general, and their political and business elites, increasingly need to understand more about China as they face the development of China-related factors affecting their interests both positively and negatively.

Notes

1 I would like to express my gratitude to the Banco Santander for a generous grant that allowed me to research and write this chapter.
2 East Asia is understood here as Northeast Asia: China, Japan and South Korea, plus the ten members of the Association of Southeast Asian Nations (ASEAN): Thailand, Indonesia, Malaysia, the Philippines, Brunei, Myanmar, Cambodia, Vietnam, Laos and Singapore.
3 'La Colonia' is the term in Spanish used to denote the period between the Spanish conquest of what today comprises Latin America and the successful independence movements of these countries. China or the 'Middle Kingdom' might have interacted from earlier times; as, for example, some scholars have argued Chinese expeditions arrived to the American continent even before the Spaniards. But such contacts are not considered here as having significantly affected the nature of relations between modern China and Latin American countries, thus there is no reference to this in the main text.
4 For the official view see *China's Policy Paper on Latin America and the Caribbean* of November 2008, http://english.people.com.cn/90001/90776/90883/6528385.html (accessed 12 July 2009).
5 Some examples are the ASEAN+3 framework (APT), the Shanghai Cooperation Organization (SCO) and the Forum on China–Africa Cooperation.
6 At www.focalae.org
7 President Hu declared these objectives addressing the Brazilian and Argentinean parliaments. 'Jintao Addresses the Brazilian Parliament' and 'Hu Jinatao holds talks with Argentine President', November 2004, Chinese Ministry of Foreign Affairs, http://www.fmprc.gov.cn/
8 'Republica Popular China y su relacion con Chile', Republica de Chile, Ministerio de Relaciones Exteriores, Direccion de Asia Pacifico, at www.minrel.gov.cl
9 The countries in the region that still recognize Taiwan diplomatically are Paraguay in the South Cone and Panama, El Salvador, Honduras and Guatemala in Central America.
10 Deng Xiaoping, *Selected Works 1982–1992*, vol. 3, Beijing, Foreign Language Press: 341.
11 For a detailed discussion on how China's leadership interprets the China Threat theory see Al-Rhodan (2007).
12 See for example 'Multipolarity Plays Key Role in World Peace', 6 November 2001, *People's Daily* online at http://english.peopledaily.com.cn/, 'China's View on the Development of Multi-polarity', Embassy of the People's Republic of China in Switzerland, June 2004, at http://ch.china-embassy.org/eng/wjzc/t139006.htm, '"China threat" theory rejected', *People's Daily* online: 9 April 2009, at http://english.people daily.com.cn
13 Hu Jintao delivers an important speech to the Upper and Lower Houses of Argentine Parliament, 18 November 2004, at http://chinaebassy.org (emphasis added).
14 Trade profiles, merchandise in trade at http://stat.wto.org
15 United Nations Commodity Trade Statistics at http://comtrade.un.org
16 'China's appetite for meat feeds a Brazilian soybean boom', *The International Herald Tribune*, online edition, 5 April 2007.
17 'China's soya needs lift Argentina', BBC news online, March 2005, at http://news.bbc.co.uk
18 'China and Latin America forge closer links for win-win end', Embassy of the People's Republic of China in the UK, at http://uk.china-embassy.org
19 'Baosteel and CVRD Signs Prophase Contract to Establish Steel Plant in Brazil', 31 January 2004, at http://www.baosteel.com
20 'China's Lenovo eyes emerging markets for investment', Reuters India, 11 March 2008, at http://in.reuters.com

21 'China and Latin America forge closer links for win-win end', Embassy of the People's Republic of China in the UK, at http://uk.china-embassy.org
22 'Grupo Bimbo acquires company in China', 24 March 2006, at http://www.grupo bimbo.com.mx
23 'Venezuela and China build a pluripolar world through socialism', Petroleos de Venezuela website at http://wwwpdvsa.com
24 Personal interview with Luis Enrique Vertiz, Chief of Economic Matters and Promotion, Embassy of Mexico in Singapore, October 2008.
25 In October 2000, the US–China Economic and Security Review Commission was created with the explicit purpose to monitor, investigate and submit to congress an annual report on the national security implications of the bilateral trade and economic relationship between the United States and the People's Republic of China. In spite of the Commission's purpose stating the bilateral nature of its enquiries and findings, the reports go well beyond the direct Sino-US relation and expand towards China's influence and interactions within other regions of the world, due to the extended interests of the US around the world.
26 For Latin Americans, the concept of 'America' does not refer to the United States of America but to the whole continent (i.e. the American continent). For that reason, people in Latin America and even government representatives do not address the US as 'America' but more frequently as 'Los Estados Unidos' (i.e. the United States). Latin American students of international politics and the US summarize the core idea contained in the Monroe Doctrine in the phrase 'America para los americanos' which roughly translates as 'the Western Hemisphere belongs to the nations of this continent (i.e. America for the Americans)'. Moreover, Latin Americans tend to view the origins of the Monroe Doctrine not as an attempt from the US to protect younger and fragile American states from 'predatory' external powers, but rather, as an expression of American imperialism in the continent.
27 Condoleezza Rice interviewed at Sophia University, Tokyo, Japan, March 2005, US Department of State website, www.state.gov
28 Member of the House of Representatives Hon. Dan Burton, opening remarks at the hearing before the Subcommittee on the Western Hemisphere of the Committee on International Relations, House of Representatives, One Hundred Ninth Congress, first session, 6 April 2006: 4–5.
29 Roger Noriega, Hearing before the Subcommittee on the Western Hemisphere of the Committee on International Relations, House of Representatives, One Hundred Ninth Congress, first session, 6 April 2006: 18, 23.
30 'US Official Comments on Chinese Engagement in Latin America', US Department of State, statement by Charles Shapiro, Principal Deputy Assistant Secretary of State for Western Hemisphere Affairs, September 2005, at http://usinfo.state.gov
31 'Creating Jobs to Fight Poverty and Strengthen Democratic Governance', Fourth Summit of the Americas, Declaration of Mar de la Plata, Argentina, 5 November 2005.
32 Personal interview with Luis Enrique Vertiz, Chief of economic matters and promotion, Embassy of Mexico in Singapore, October 2008.
33 Roger Noriega, Hearing before the Subcommittee on the Western Hemisphere of the Committee on International Relations, House of Representatives, One Hundred Ninth Congress, first session, 6 April 2006: 13.
34 The US has signed Free Trade Agreements (FTAs) with Canada and Mexico (NAFTA), with Chile, with Central America and the Dominican Republic (CAFTA–DR) and more recently with Colombia. It has also signed trade promotion agreements with Peru and Panama, and a Bilateral Investment Treaty with Uruguay. The US is active in providing development and financial assistance to Latin America through the Foreign Assistance Act (1961), the Enterprise of the Americas Initiative (1990) and the Millennium Challenge Account (2002). The latter provides resources to seven Latin American countries. The US also assists countries like Colombia and Mexico in the fight against

narcotics. Recently Mexico and the US agreed to the 'Merida Initiative' to combat drug-trafficking flowing from Central America and Mexico into the US. Former President George W. Bush asked Congress for US$550 million in what is expected to become a US$1.4 billion multi-year security cooperation package.
35 'Growing trade ties China to Latin America', Julie McCarthy, May 2008, at http://www.npr.org
36 'China expresses "serious concern" over Argentina restrictions on Chinese exports', Ministry of Foreign Affairs, People's Republic of China, August 2003, at http://www.china-embsy.org

References

Al-Rhodan, Khalid (2007) 'A critique of the China Threat theory: a systematic analysis', *Asian Perspective*, vol. 31 issue 3, pp. 41–66.
Blank, Stephen (2005) 'Will Venezuela send Russian weapons to South American terrorists?' The Jamestown Foundation, *Eurasia Daily Monitor*, vol. 2 issue 34, 17 February, online edition, http://www.jamestown.org/single/?no_cache=1&tx_ttnews%5Btt_news%5D=27560 (accessed 14 July 2009).
Committee on International Relations (2005) 'China's influence in the Western Hemisphere', Hearing before the Subcommittee on the Western Hemisphere of the Committee on International Relations, House of Representatives, One Hundred Ninth Congress, First Session, 6 April, Serial no. 109–63, http://www.foreignaffairs.house.gov/archives/109/20404.pdf (accessed 14 July 2009).
Deng Xiaoping (1994) *Selected Works 1982–1992*, vol. 3, Beijing: Foreign Language Press.
Dent, Christopher (2008) *East Asian Regionalism*, London: Routledge.
Dumbaugh, Kerry and Sullivan, Mark (2005) *CRS Report for Congress: China's growing interest in Latin America*, April.
Hammer, Alexander and Kilpatrick, James (2006) 'Distinctive Patterns and Prospects in China–Latin America Trade, 1999–2005', *Journal of International Commerce and Economics*, September, p. 6, online, http://www.usitc.gov/journal/documents/china_latin_america.pdf (accessed 8 July 2009).
He Li (1991) *Sino-Latin American Economic Relations*, London: Praeger.
Kurlantzick, Joshua (2007) *Charm Offensive: How China's Soft Power is Transforming the World*, New Haven, CT: Yale University Press.
Kohut (2007) 'How the World Sees China', Pew Research Center, December, http://pewresearch.org/pubs/656/how-the-world-sees-china (accessed 14 July 2009).
McCarthy, Julie (2008) 'Growing trade ties China to Latin America', May, http://www.npr.org/templates/story/story.php?storyId=89275971 (accessed 14 July 2009).
Paz, Gonzalo S. (2006) 'Rising China's "Offensive" in Latin America and the US reaction', *Asian Perspective*, vol. 30, no. 4, pp. 95–112.
Perkins, Dexter (1963) *A History of the Monroe Doctrine*, Boston: Little Brown & Company.
Segal, Gerry (1999) 'Does China Matter?', *Foreign Affairs*, vol. 78, issue 5, September/October.
Watson, Cynthia (2007) 'The PLA in Latin America', *China Brief*, vol. 7, issue 20, 31 October.
Zheng Bijian (2005) 'China's "Peaceful Rise" to Great-Power Status', *Foreign Affairs*, September/October, vol. 84, issue 5.

4 Japan and Latin America – can the Koizumi effect last?

Caroline Rose

The aim of this chapter is to consider recent developments in Japan's foreign policy towards Latin America. While Japan was traditionally seen as an important Asian partner for Latin American countries in the 1970s and 1980s, Japan's relations with the region declined in the 1990s. At the start of the twenty-first century, Japanese governments have sought to revitalize links with Latin America, and these moves have been stepped up in recent years. Former Prime Minister Koizumi Junichirō's visit to Latin America in 2004, during which he proposed the revitalization of economic links and the need to cooperate on international issues such as the reform of the United Nations Security Council and the environment, is an important marker of this shift in policy. The chapter explores the reasons behind Japan's renewed interest in the region in the 2000s and suggests that a number of factors have combined to produce a more coherent and long-term foreign policy approach to Latin America which affords greater recognition of the potential economic and political significance of Latin America to Japan's future role in the world. It looks, for example, at Japan's pursuit of such strategic interests as the desire to garner support for a permanent seat on a (reformed) UN Security Council and secure natural resources. It also considers Japan's response to China's rapid advance into Latin America, and explores the reasons behind Japan's signing of free trade agreements with Mexico and Chile. Finally, it considers the achievements of Koizumi's 'vision' enunciated in 2004, and explores whether there is any evidence of it being sustained beyond his premiership.

Introduction

Traditionally, Japan's major relationships in the region have been with Brazil and Mexico with whom Japan enjoys fairly extensive commercial links, followed by Argentina, Chile, Venezuela and Panama where specific industries are of importance (e.g. foodstuffs, minerals and the maritime industry), and smaller nations who are recipients of Japanese aid (Horisaka 2005: 151). The 1980s and 1990s were characterized by debt crises in Latin America and political upheavals. The economic downturn in Japan in the 1990s, marked by the bursting of the bubble, meant that Japanese investment shifted to the more favourable environment of Southeast Asia and China and the economy turned towards a domestic-demand-oriented model (Horisaka 2005: 154). As a result Japan's role in Latin America in terms of its trade and investment ties suffered a certain amount of neglect.[1] By 2003, trade with Latin America accounted for just 3.2 per cent of Japan's overall trade, having fallen from over 8 per cent in the 1960s to 5.2 per cent in the 1980s and 3.7 per cent in the 1990s (*Daily Yomiuri*, 20 September 2004; Tsunekawa 2007: 58). Japan's foreign direct investment (FDI) in Latin America accounted for 14.7 per cent of its total FDI in 1980; small compared to its FDI in the US and Asia, but still greater than its FDI in Europe which stood at 12.1 per cent. The bulk of Japan's FDI (66 per cent) was invested in the manufacturing and mining industries (Tsunekawa 2007: 58). By the 1990s, Japan's FDI accounted for 13 per cent of its total but had moved away from mining and manufacturing towards finance and insurance, with tax havens in the Caribbean attracting much of the FDI.

While trade and investment had declined during what Tsunekawa calls the 'lost 15 years' in Japan–Latin America relations, some links remained in place in the form of cultural and academic exchange (such as the Japan–Mexico student exchange scheme which continued through the 1990s), the establishment in 1991 of the Japan–Mexico 21st Century Commission, the organization in 1993 of the Japan–Latin America–Pacific Ocean 21st Century Committee (of which only the Chilean chapter was active), and in 1999 the establishment of the New Japan Mexico 21st Century Committee (Tsunekawa 2007: 59). In addition, Japan's Overseas Development Assistance (ODA) to certain countries in the region continued throughout the period, increasing from 6 per cent of Japan's total ODA in 1980 to 8.1 per cent in 1990, reaching 12.8 per cent in 1996. After a dip in the late 1990s, the percentage began to climb again in the early 2000s reaching 9.9 per cent in 2001 (Ministry of Foreign Affairs (MoFA) 2006b). The aims of Japan's aid provision in the region are to support basic human needs (that is, education, healthcare and so on), facilitate poverty alleviation, and actively support South–South cooperation. In addition, ODA has been provided 'in consideration of the large number of migrants from Japan and their descendants' (MoFA 2002). In 2005, Japan's ODA to Latin America and the Caribbean constituted just 4 per cent of its total ODA.[2] While this does not compare particularly favourably to Japan's ODA granted to other regions, the region is acknowledged in the ODA White Paper 2006 as strategically important to Japan due to its enormous market and abundant natural resources (pp. 155–8). The bulk of Japan's ODA to the region in recent years has been allocated to Central America under the multilateral 'Partnership for Democracy and Development' to assist in the economic recovery of these countries and the process of democratization. The top five recipients of Japanese bilateral aid are Honduras, Nicaragua, Peru, Bolivia and Guatemala, and activities have included economic and technical assistance and election monitoring and observation. In addition, Japan's assistance has been important in the recovery from natural disasters (for example, El Salvador, and the Caribbean).

Thus, while Japan's relations with Latin America cannot be described as core to Japan's foreign policy strategy in the last two decades, the links have nonetheless had some positive impact on both sides and have taken a number of different forms. Furthermore, bilateral ties developed through the conclusion of commercial treaties and immigration, in many cases with a history of over 100 years, represented an important and useful foundation on which to rebuild and further develop relations in the early 2000s. Japan began to establish diplomatic relations with a number of Latin American countries in the mid-to-late nineteenth century, for example Peru in 1877, Mexico 1888, Brazil 1895 and Chile 1897. The early 2000s were punctuated by celebrations marking key anniversary years, for example Japan and Chile celebrated the 110th anniversary of the signing of the Treaty of Amity, Commerce and Navigation in 2007, an occasion marked, amongst other things, by the visit of Minister of Foreign Affairs, Alejandro Foxley to Japan in March for the signing of the Strategic Economic Partnership agreement, and the summit meeting between President Michelle Bachelet Jeria and Prime Minister Abe in September of the same year.[3]

Some of the strongest links are those formed through migration, with some of Japan's largest overseas communities residing in Latin America. As Kagami notes, Japan–Latin America relations are 'strong in blood, weak in business' (2001: 21). Japanese emigration to Latin American countries started at the end of the nineteenth century and continued, though to a lesser extent after World War Two. The first Japanese emigrants to Mexico arrived in 1897, Peru in 1899 and Brazil in 1908. Brazil has the largest Japanese community (approximately 1.5 million), followed by Peru, Argentina, Mexico, Bolivia and Paraguay. Japanese communities have acted as an important bridge to Japan, and have served as a means by which to revitalize bilateral relations in the 2000s. Thus, in addition to the various anniversary celebrations marking the establishment of Japan–Latin American commercial treaties, various events were held to celebrate Japanese emigration. For example, Prince Akishino visited Paraguay in October 2006 to mark the 70th anniversary of the arrival of Japanese emigrants. The 50th anniversary of Japanese emigration to the Dominican Republic took place in the same year, marked in this case by an apology and compensation package from Prime Minister Koizumi for the hardships suffered by migrants during the 1950s (*Japan Times* 31 July 2006).[4] 2008 was the 100th anniversary of Japanese emigration to Brazil and was designated a year of exchange. As part of the year-long commemorative activities and ceremonies, Crown Prince Naruhito visited Brazil in June.

In attempting to rekindle relationships, the Japanese government and those of Latin American countries have talked a great deal of the traditional friendships and lengthy periods of exchange. The Japanese government appears keen to build upon the fact that Japan is viewed positively in the region and is considered a good partner in international society. The Ministry of Foreign Affairs (MoFA) in particular considers this as a good sign for the future of Japan–Latin America relations (MoFA 2007: 73). An opinion poll on Brazilian images of Japan carried out by MoFA in 2008 to mark the Japan–Brazil year of exchange revealed that the majority of respondents viewed Japan positively, and expected Japan–Brazil relations to strengthen in future. Japan was the second best-known country after the US, and considered to be the most promising Asian country ahead of China (albeit by just 1 per cent). Of those polled, 75 per cent expressed support for Japan's permanent membership of the United Nations Security Council (UNSC).[5] Putting cynicism about opinion polls to one side, the stress placed on the long-standing, friendly nature of Japan's relations with particular Latin American countries represents, as Mols suggests in Chapter 2 with reference to China's friendship offensive in the region, an important device for claiming familiarity and historical normalcy.

Summitry and strategy under Koizumi: Japan and Brazil, Mexico, Chile 2004 and beyond

The rekindling of relationships, however, cannot be ascribed to some altruistic desire on the part of the Japanese government simply to renew old friendships. Latin America has gradually come back into view for the Japanese government and companies seeking a market for goods and services, in return for foodstuffs, natural resources and energy resources.

Changes in the economies of Latin American countries, in particular the food and energy resources they can now offer Japan, have undoubtedly contributed to the revival of interest, given the high levels of mutual benefit. While there is limited potential for the sort of trade flows that Japan enjoys with East Asia, the US or the EU, there are nonetheless opportunities for individual sectors such as cars and machinery. In the case of Brazil, the development of offshore oil fields has turned Brazil into an exporter, rather than importer, of crude oil; sugar cane-based ethanol production is being explored, and the redevelopment of agricultural land has yielded soybean production. Factoring in Japan's large ethnic population in Brazil – what former Foreign Minister Aso Tarō (2007) referred to as Japan's 'latent assets' – Kosaka concludes that Brazil 'arguably outranks China and India as an ideal partner for complementary ties with Japan' (Kosaka 2007: 51). Other countries are of interest to Japan too. Twenty per cent of Japan's imports from Mexico are agricultural produce, mainly pork, orange juice, vegetables and fruit; in return Japanese companies are looking to enhance exports of machinery, in addition to developing new activities in an economy ranked tenth in the world (Watanabe 2004: 61). Chile can offer Japan important agricultural foodstuffs and minerals, and Japanese companies wish to develop links with Chilean mining and pulp-making industries (Okamoto 2006: 23).

At governmental level, there were some attempts by Prime Minister Hashimoto in the mid-1990s to breathe some life into Japan–Latin America relations. These came to little however, and despite the emergence of 'new phenomena' in the early 2000s, such as revived corporate interest in Japan–Latin America relations, Horisaka lamented the sluggishness of economic relations in addition to the lack of a clearly delineated 'future vision' in Japan's Latin America policy (2005: 162). This, however, appeared to change under Prime Minister Koizumi's watch, amidst an active programme of summit diplomacy, and a flurry of visits between Japanese and Latin American/Caribbean heads of state which, by the late 2000s, appear to be yielding more than just rhetoric.

The first clear formulation of Japan's new policy towards Latin America was enunciated by Prime Minister Koizumi during his visits to the region in 2004, starting with Brazil and Mexico in September, and followed by Chile in November. This was the first visit to the region by a Japanese prime minister for eight years, and was prompted by the positive changes that had taken place, politically and economically, in the region. The MoFA 2005 *Diplomatic Bluebook* summed these up as economic liberalization and moves towards regional economic integration, which, combined with the region's plentiful natural resources and the potential for economic growth, represented an attractive market. In addition to democratization (almost) across the region, Latin America's positive efforts in international politics, and activities relating to regional political integration further enhanced the prospects for Japan to develop its Latin America policy.

Entitled 'Framework for a New Partnership between Japan and Central and South America', Koizumi's 'vision' set out areas in which Japan's relationship with Latin America, building on traditional friendly links, could be revitalized and expanded. Two types of activity would form the core of the new relationship – namely, cooperation and exchange. Cooperation referred to the resurrection of economic relations, and joint action on international issues. In terms of economic relations, levels of trade and investment would be increased, and Japan would cooperate in the development of infrastructure industries and energy resources. In terms of international issues, Koizumi hoped that Japan and Latin America would work together to promote peace and security in the world. Of particular note, is the reference to the importance of United Nations Security Council (UNSC) reform, in addition to the need to maintain support for and strengthen other multilateral organizations (such as the World Trade Organization (WTO)), and work towards sustainable development and environmental protection. Exchange would be strengthened through the promotion of greater mutual understanding and people exchange, for example with an invitation extended to 4,000 young people from across Latin America to visit Japan. Koizumi also stressed Japan's commitment and leadership role in the Forum on East Asia–Latin America Cooperation (FEALAC) as a means of promoting broad cross-regional relations, and indicated his intention to arrange a FEALAC Foreign Ministers meeting in Japan in due course (Manabe 2004; MoFA 2005).[6]

The Japan–Brazil visit resulted in a joint communiqué which reaffirmed both leaders' commitment to the strengthening of political, economic and cultural ties between the two countries.[7] While it dealt mainly with general aims rather than specific goals, one of the more significant outcomes was the agreement by both sides to support each other's bids to become permanent members of the UNSC. Global environmental concerns were also discussed; Japan gained Brazil's support for its '3R Initiative Ministerial Meeting'[8] planned for the following April, and both sides expressed satisfaction with ongoing bilateral activities on climate change. Discussions of trade and investment tended to be couched within the language of multilateralism, with reference to WTO mechanisms and a desire to expand trade using these channels. These three areas remained firmly on the agenda during the return visit to Japan of President Luis Inacio Lula da Silva in

May 2005. The joint statements issued as a result of this summit reiterated Japan's and Brazil's commitment to UN reform, WTO and global environment issues, in addition to a brief statement on support for disarmament and non-proliferation (presumably connected to the North Korea issue).[9] In addition, the summit meeting produced a slew of memoranda and notes on joint programmes and projects across a range of areas (sustainable development, technical cooperation, cultural and educational exchange, the establishment of the Japan–Brazil Council for the 21st Century, cooperation in science and technology and so on), and MoFA points in particular to the agreement to cooperate in the sphere of bio-fuels.

Koizumi's visit to Mexico was no less productive. The focal point was the signing of the Japan–Mexico Economic Partnership Agreement (EPA), which came into force in April 2005. In contrast to Mexico's 11 free trade agreements involving 32 countries (Watanabe 2004: 54), this was only Japan's second free trade agreement, the first having been signed with Singapore in 2002. For MoFA, the EPA was significant since it would provide a level playing field for Japanese companies hitherto competing with companies of other nations with whom Mexico had already signed free trade agreements. The EPA would also give Japanese companies a foothold in the region, advantageous should they wish to break into American markets (MoFA 2005: 86). The joint statement issued by PM Koizumi and President Fox referred to the potential of the EPA and also contained a statement about the necessity for reform of the United Nations. The role of cultural exchange as a basis to develop friendly relations between the two countries was emphasized, in addition to the development of tourism between the two countries. The summit achieved its aims of consolidating the 'strategic partnership', the label attached to the relationship in the joint declaration announced during President Fox's October 2003 visit to Japan (MoFA 2005: 86).[10]

Prime Minister Koizumi's third major summit in the region took place with Chilean President Ricardo Lagos in November after the APEC meeting. Relations between Japan and Chile seem to have enjoyed slightly more activity than Japan's relationships with other countries in the region, the two having signed a Framework Document for the Japan–Chile Partnership Programme in July 1999 aimed at promoting South–South cooperation in Latin America and the Caribbean. Chile had also been keen to discuss the possibility of a free trade agreement with Japan since the late 1990s, an initiative greeted with some reluctance on the Japanese side. Koizumi argued in 2003, for example, that FTA negotiations with other countries and negotiations by the WTO meant that a Japan–Chile FTA 'could not be realized soon' (MoFA 2003).[11] Echoing the nature of Koizumi's summits with Brazil and Mexico, the talks with the Chilean government in 2004 followed similar lines in terms of the acknowledgement by both sides of the need to improve economic and cultural relations. In this case, and in contrast to Koizumi's stance during his meeting with President Lagos the previous year however, the two leaders agreed on the possibility of concluding a free trade agreement (though it took until November 2005 for Japan to give the go-ahead on negotiations, prompted perhaps by the conclusion of the China–Chile FTA in the same year). The Japan–Chile EPA came into force in September 2007. On cultural exchange, it was agreed to revitalize the Japan–Chile 21st Century Committee by establishing the Permanent Forum for Japan–Chile Relations. Japan's technical assistance (for example, in maths education and IT) and cooperation on environmental matters were highlighted as areas for further collaboration between the two countries. Finally, continuing the theme of Japan's enthusiasm to raise awareness and garner support for UN reform, both leaders shared the view that UN reform was essential and President Lagos expressed support for Japan's accession to a permanent seat on the UNSC (MoFA 2005: 87).[12]

While developments in Japan's bilateral relations with its key partners in Latin America have attracted the most attention, Japan's relations with other countries in the region, and with regional and interregional organizations, have also enjoyed a boost since the early 2000s. Various Latin American and Caribbean heads of state visited Japan in 2005, including the presidents of Colombia, Brazil, Nevis and Paraguay. To mark the 70th anniversary of the establishment of diplomatic relations with Central America, 2005 was named Japan–Central America Year and the heads of state of the seven countries paid a visit to Japan for a summit meeting in August. At this summit Koizumi's main theme centred on the concept of 'friends facing the future together' and the Tokyo Declaration and accompanying Action Plan set out the Japanese government's mid-to-long-term policy. Specifically, the Declaration referred to the need to strengthen dialogue and cooperation, consolidate peace and democracy, cooperate on the economy, environment, tourism and disaster reduction, promote youth, cultural and sports exchange, and cooperate in the international arena.[13] Representatives of the Japan–Central America Forum for Dialogue and Cooperation (established in 1995) continue to meet annually to discuss ways in which to facilitate the exchange and cooperation set out in the Tokyo Declaration and other agreements.

At the regional level, Japanese governments have frequently reiterated a desire to be closely involved in the major regional and cross-regional organizations. Joining FEALAC at its inception in 1999, the Japanese government (or at least MoFA) saw its role as central, and as contributing constructively and positively to the deepening of ties between East Asia and Latin America. One of Japan's initiatives in FEALAC has been to head up, since 2002, the 'Young Leaders Invitation Program' which brings together East Asian and Latin American young professionals to discuss key issues such as sustainable development and environmental problems.[14] Japanese representatives proposed the establishment of working groups in FEALAC to focus on specific projects, and were actively involved (as co-chair with Peru) in the working group on 'Economy and Society' which considered the four areas of institution and governance, economic development and poverty, entrepreneurship and small and medium-sized enterprises, and the IT revolution and developing countries.[15] Finally, since August 2007 Japan has been the Asian regional coordinator for FEALAC (Tsunekawa 2007: 61).

In other spheres, in July 2006 Japan became the first Asian country to be officially affiliated to the UN's Economic Commission for Latin America and the Caribbean (ECLAC), the aim being to expand its contribution to the region's peaceful development and to promote economic and technical cooperation with

Latin America (MoFA 2007: 72). In September 2006 Japan strengthened its credentials with the Caribbean Community (CARICOM) by appointing Japan's first ambassador to the community (attached to Trinidad and Tobago). MoFA states quite clearly that through such routes as the Japan CARICOM office level talks, Japan builds links and promotes cooperation in such institutions as the International Whaling Commission (IWC) (MoFA 2007: 73). While it would be unwise to describe these activities as representative of Japan taking a strong leadership role in regional and interregional organizations, they nonetheless symbolize a more coherent and long-term approach by Japan to involve itself in the key institutions.

Japan's strategy – a case of (trying to) catch-up diplomacy?

What lies behind Japan's return to the region? Clearly there are economic drivers – the attraction of new or restored markets, the pull of natural resources and energy, and the appeal of a stable, friendly trading and investment environment facilitated by the presence of Japanese communities and established business links. But viewed from a more strategic perspective, other factors can also help to explain Japan's drive to revitalize relations in the early 2000s which go beyond pure economics. After all, the percentage of Japan's trade with any investment in Latin America counts for very little in overall terms. A closer look at the changes that have been taking place in Japan's overall foreign policy strategy and economic diplomacy may therefore help to explain Japan's recent activity in Latin America. The first change has been Japan's increasingly assertive stance in international relations since the end of the Cold War, represented most forcefully by the actions of Prime Minister Koizumi, but set in motion by previous Japanese governments in the late 1990s, and continued by his successors. Developments such as the strengthening of the alliance between the US and Japan, particularly since the revision of the US–Japan Defense Guidelines in 1997, and the support offered to the US by the Japanese government in the wake of the September 11 attacks symbolize one of the core features of Japan's foreign policy – the move towards 'normal nation' status. While Japan's closer alliance with the US has prompted one leading Japan scholar to consider Japan a 'client state' of the US (McCormack 2007), there is, however, considerable evidence that Japan has been trying to find a more independent voice for itself in the post-Cold War order. It has tried to achieve this in a number of ways, for example, by adopting a stronger position on its China policy in light of China's 'rise', raising its profile as a responsible, peace-building or peace-fostering nation, and acting as a major player in the movement for global environmental protection and development goals as exemplified in 2008 with Japan's hosting of the G8 Summit, the Cool Earth 50 initiative and the fourth meeting of the Tokyo International Conference on African Development (TICAD IV). It has sought to consolidate its peace-building credentials whilst simultaneously stepping up to the mark as a normal nation by, for example, pushing for greater influence in the UN through reform of the UNSC and other institutions. Japan's initiatives in Latin America should, therefore, be seen against this backdrop of an evolving foreign policy strategy in the twenty-first century. Three aspects of Japan's 'new' foreign policy are worth exploring in more detail in relation to Japan's Latin America initiatives: Japan's drive for support for the UNSC reform proposal; its increasing awareness, and in some circles, alarm at China's increased presence in Latin America (as elsewhere); and the use of Latin America as a test bed for the development of further free trade agreements, symbolizing a change in Japan's foreign economic diplomacy.

UNSC and Japan's quest for permanent membership

Nakatani asserts that the clause written into the Japan–Central America Tokyo Declaration[16] which states that the System of Central American Integration (SICA) 'supports Japan's entry into the UNSC, and that when (if) an election takes place for a new UNSC, then SICA will vote for Japan' represented the centrepiece of the agreement (2005: 3). It is notable that the various joint declarations and communiqués announced in the wake of summit meetings between Japan and Latin American countries in the mid-2000s also contained, almost without exception, some reference to the issue of UN reform in general, and expressions of support for Japan's permanent membership of the UNSC in particular. This is not coincidental but part of Japan's concerted push at the same time for UNSC reform.

Japan has been a keen advocate of UN reform since the early 1990s. Japan takes issue with the composition of the UNSC and the wording of the UN Charter (with its reference to enemy states), and considers that its consistent commitment to world peace since the end of World War II, in addition to its considerable financial contribution to the UN, qualify it for permanent membership. The subject of reform has been discussed in UN circles since the late 1970s, but no substantive progress was made until 2003 when reform re-appeared on the UN's agenda with the establishment by former Secretary General Kofi Annan of the 'High Level Panel on Threats, Challenges and Change' (hereafter the Panel). The Panel was tasked with identifying the nature of new and existing threats to world security and considering what changes would need to be made within the UN in order to deal with the new challenges. While the Panel was deliberating, Japan initiated a campaign, as part of the Group of Four (Japan, Brazil, India and Germany), for the expansion of both permanent and non-permanent seats on the UNSC. The G4 attracted the support of 120 countries in the open debate held at the General Assembly (GA) in September 2004, and Koizumi's speech to the GA emphasized Japan's long-standing contribution to 'post-conflict consolidation of peace worldwide' and its will and capability to become a permanent member (*Daily Yomiuri*, 18 September 2004).

The Panel's report was published in December, and it set out two possible models for reform of the UNSC.[17] The report was followed up in March 2005 with Kofi Annan's address to the GA entitled 'In larger freedom: towards development security and human rights for all'.[18] Annan's address laid out the 'agenda of highest priorities' (p. 3) for the World Summit in September 2005, an important milestone in UN history marking the 60th anniversary of its founding. With regard to UN reform, Annan reiterated the Panel's recommendations and urged member states to take this 'vital decision', preferably by consensus, before the World Summit (Annan 2005: 43).

This provided further impetus to Japan's pro-UN reform activities and in the months leading up to the Summit, the G4 drafted a resolution suggesting its own model for reform (along the lines of the Panel's model A). At the same time, two other groups, the 'Uniting for Consensus' (UFC) group led by Italy and Pakistan, and the 'African group' formulated their own draft resolutions. By June 2005 it seemed that Japan's plans were to be scuppered not merely by the 'Unifying Consensus' group but by its main ally, the US, which announced that the permanent membership should be increased by two, not six as the G4 resolution suggested (*Daily Yomiuri*, 19 June 2005). Despite the fact that the US intended that Japan would be one of those achieving permanent status, its rejection of the G4 proposal essentially dashed Japan's hopes. In addition, China, a long-standing opponent of Japan's acquisition of a permanent seat, stepped up its own campaign. China expressed its disapproval of the G4's proposed resolution, along with other members of the UFC group (*Daily Yomiuri*, 11 June 2005), and the anti-Japanese protests that had taken place in major Chinese cities in April 2005 demonstrated Chinese popular antipathy to permanent Japanese membership. In June the Chinese government reiterated its 'resolute opposition' after the G4 revealed their draft resolution at the UN (*Daily Yomiuri*, 11 June 2005). In the subsequent deliberations in the GA in 2005 none of the proposals received sufficient support, and the question of UN reform continues to be hotly debated today.[19]

The developments of 2004–5 are nonetheless important for understanding the Japanese government's enthusiasm to place the issue of UN reform high on the agenda of summit meetings with Latin American leaders. Japan's efforts can be seen as a means of gathering support for the G4 resolution. In (re-)building economic, cultural, and aid relations with the region, Japan was aiming to boost its credentials as a peace-building nation dedicated to nuclear disarmament and non-proliferation, human security, the environment and so on, and at the same time secure the votes of the Latin American contingent in the GA. Japan had to contend, however, with China and its opposition to the G4 resolution. The Japanese press accused China of 'staging diplomatic wars at the UN and in capitals of UN member countries' and of pressuring Asian and African countries to oppose the G4 plan (*Daily Yomiuri*, 11 June 2005). It is likely that Latin American countries were also lobbied by China on this issue, particularly since China has been able to rely on the support of Latin American states in UN votes in the past.

Warily watching China

Another possible explanation for Japan's revived interest in Latin America stems from China's activities in the region, not least the rapid increase in trade, but also its political and cultural diplomacy. The visits to Latin America of Prime Minister Koizumi and President Hu Jintao in 2004 highlight the similarities in their approaches to Latin America but also symbolize Latin America's position as a potential new battleground for Sino-Japanese rivalry over resources, investment opportunities, and support for wider diplomatic agendas. Both leaders pledged greater trade and investment, in addition to, on the Japanese side, cultural exchange and cooperation on international issues, and on the Chinese side, designation of Argentina and Brazil as official tourist destinations. But Hu's visits, in contrast to Koizumi's, seemed to be accompanied by much greater fanfare and attracted more widespread interest, described for example by *The Economist* as 'a series of spectacular displays of Sino-Latin American solidarity' (29 December 2004).

While Japan was traditionally seen as an important Asian partner for Latin American countries in the 1970s and 1980s, China's economic rise has been of great interest (albeit mixed with concern[20]) to Latin America, with a rapid increase in two-way trade since 1990. This is not lost on Japanese officials, journalists and academics, and represents a recurring theme in the discussions of Asia–Latin America relations. Of particular attention, or concern, is China's resource diplomacy and the fact that Latin America has the potential to provide China with the minerals and energy sources its flourishing economy requires. MoFA comments for the first time in its 2007 *Diplomatic Bluebook* upon the remarkable increase in China's overall trade with Latin America starting in 2004, noting that China's advance is aimed mainly at securing resources and market share (2007: 70). While the share of Latin America's trade with Asia (excluding Japan) increased from 6 per cent to 11 per cent between 1999 and 2005, Japan's share remained more or less the same at 3 per cent suggesting that the bulk of the growth is attributed to Chinese (and South Korean) trade (MoFA 2007: 70).

Nishijima considers China's heightened presence in Latin America as potentially having a huge influence on Japan's own relationship with the region (2005: 54–5). Charting China's movements in the region, he notes in particular China's energy diplomacy with the resource-rich region, but also its attempts to expand its political influence (particularly on the issue of Taiwan). He compares China's imports from the region in 2000, running at $50 billion, with that of 2004, running at $220 billion, and notes the various agreements reached between the Chinese government and those of Brazil, Argentina and Chile during Hu Jintao's visit in November 2004. Specifically he refers to the establishment of the so-called 'all-weather strategic partnership' with Brazil which agreed on Chinese investment in Brazil of $100 billion over two years, and trade over three years of $200 billion. The plan to expand Chinese imports from Brazil beyond beans and coal to (other) energy sources revealed China's plans to secure energy resources from Brazil. Further agreements were reached on previously banned exports from China to Brazil of beef and chicken, and joint development of ethanol (needed for the launching of satellites). In Hu's visits to Argentina and Chile, similar agreements were reached, which further revealed China's interest in securing energy through joint development or investment in infrastructure.

Kai also notes, with some alarm, the pace at which China has moved into Latin American markets in search of oil. He considers the implications for China's actions both for the US and Japan remarking upon China's insatiable appetite for oil, and the rapid increase in China's trade with and investment in the region.

Venezuela is seen as a particularly important partner for China due to its oil reserves. Kai describes Koizumi's diplomacy towards Latin America since 2002 in terms of Japan's direct response to China's own initiatives since the late 1990s, but is critical of the failure to adopt a long-term strategic approach to Latin America when compared with China (2006: 15). Kai also notes the lack of interest shown in Latin America at the highest levels of Japanese government, despite the numerous attempts of the Latin American bureau in MoFA to advise on policy. The result of this inaction, according to Kai, has been Japan's loss of Latin America to China. As a means of correcting the problem, Kai suggests that summit diplomacy should be stepped up and Japan's ODA policy vis-à-vis Latin America should be adjusted (2006: 15).

Okamoto also recommends the adoption of a long-term strategy in order to maintain Japan's presence in Latin America in the face of growing competition from South Korea and China. For Okamoto, it is no longer an option for Japan to take a passive stance, particularly given Japan's own concerns about food and energy security. Offering the Japan–Chile EPA as an example, she suggests that benefits accruing to Japan stem not just from the ability to secure important resources, but also from the fact that it would level the playing field with its East Asian neighbours (2006: 23). Koizumi's 'vision' and activities in Latin America in the mid-2000s represent an indirect response to these sorts of critiques.

FTAs – joining the global rush

The third explanation for Japan's more active diplomacy in Latin America since the early 2000s is related to a change in its overall foreign economic diplomacy. As noted, since 2005 Japan has established EPAs[21] with Mexico and Chile. There have also been some discussions about the possibility of a Japan–Brazil agreement, and the first round of negotiations for a Japan–Peru economic agreement were held in early 2009. The rationale for each agreement has been slightly different and cannot necessarily be explained merely by a desire to enhance trade and investment, particularly where these do not represent a significant share of overall figures. Japan's trade with Chile for example represented just 0.17 per cent of its overall trade, and Japan's exports to Mexico represented approximately 1 per cent of its total exports.[22] As Solís and Katada point out, however, with regard to the Japan–Mexico agreement, the stakes were very high, and the success of the FTA would 'exert powerful influence over the future evolution of Japan's turn towards economic regionalism' (2007: 279).

Japan's FTA with Mexico represented its first with a Latin American country and was seen as a test case for Japan's future FTAs. While the Japan–Singapore EPA had already come into force in 2002, this had been a relatively easy agreement to conclude given the equity between the two countries in terms of economic development, Singapore's openness to free trade, and, perhaps most importantly, the relative absence of disputes over agricultural products.[23] By contrast, negotiations between the Japanese and Mexican negotiators were lengthy and difficult, hinging mainly on the reluctance of some in the Japanese government to liberalize the highly protected agricultural market. The negotiations having stalled somewhat, it took Koizumi's (and President Vincente Fox Quesada's) intervention on the occasion of the APEC summit in Bangkok in November 2003 to move the talks forward (Solís and Katada 2007: 296–97).[24]

The Japan–Mexico EPA came into effect in April 2005. One of the chief negotiators on the Japanese side considered it a 'landmark event' in Japan's overall trade policy, since it forced Japan to deal with the sensitive issue of liberalization of its agricultural markets (Watanabe 2004: 54). Solís and Katada argue that the significance of the agreement also lies in the 'need to defend substantial interests of Japanese industries and to consolidate domestic support in Japan in favour of FTA diplomacy' (2007: 284). The benefits of the EPA were soon demonstrated by an increase in overall trade between the two countries of 38 per cent over the course of the following year. Similarly in 2005, the volume of investment had increased 3.4 times over the previous year (MoFA 2007: 71). The car industry benefited in particular, with Toyota and Bridgestone expanding production capacity and other companies setting up new operations. In addition, the broader provisions of the EPA were addressed through the establishment of the 'Committee for the Improvement of the Business Environment' which exchanges ideas on such issues as protection of Intellectual Property Rights (IPR) and immigration (Masaki 2006: 56). The success of the Japan–Mexico EPA led the way for Japan to embark on a series of similar agreements with some of its East Asian neighbours, including Malaysia, the Philippines, Thailand, Brunei and the Association of Southeast Asian Nations (ASEAN) etc., though with the notable exceptions of South Korea (under negotiation) and China.

The Japan–Mexico EPA was also significant because it marked a shift away from Japan's adherence to a GATT/WTO-style (General Agreement on Tariffs and Trade/World Trade Organization) multilateral approach to foreign trade in favour of a more balanced two-level approach embracing FTAs. The change in attitude was particularly noticeable in the gradual change in the wording of communiqués and agreements signed between Japan and Latin American countries in the early 2000s, from a reticence to discuss FTA negotiations to a positive embracing of the idea. The change in policy was perceived as an absolute necessity for Japan given the 'global trend toward regional economic arrangements' (Watanabe 2004: 55). Japan's desire to press ahead with other FTA negotiations in the mid-2000s was therefore prompted by a growing unease amongst some in the Japanese government that Japan would simply be left behind in the stampede of FTA negotiations between Latin American countries, Europe, America and, significantly, the emergence of China in the region. According to the *Daily Yomiuri*, by September 2004 there was 'real concern among Japanese officials that Japan could be left behind in the global rush to sign FTAs. Tokyo [was] thus expected to hasten negotiations with countries such as Brazil' (*Daily Yomiuri*, 20 September 2004; *Japan Times*, 10 September 2004). For Okamoto, in relation to Chile for example, the signing of an EPA was essential if Japan was not to be outdone by its closest Asian neighbours. China and South Korea signed FTAs with Chile (in 2005 and 2003 respectively) and reaped the benefits of access to markets while Japanese exports (especially cars) still attracted a 6 per cent tax surcharge (Okamoto 2006: 23).

The move towards greater promotion of EPAs was formalized by the Japanese government in late 2004 in the form of the 'Basic Policy towards further promotion of Economic Partnership Agreements' approved by the Council of Ministers on the Promotion of Economic Partnership. Amongst its aims, the policy outlined the ability of EPAs to contribute to Japan's overall political and diplomatic strategy by 'contributing to the creation of an international environment that will benefit Japan by, among other effects, fostering the establishment of an East Asian community' (Masaki 2006: 55). Thus for the Japanese, the benefits of EPAs, apart from the obvious economic ones, are the reinforcement of partnerships deemed to be of political and diplomatic significance (Masaki 2006: 56).

Has the 'vision' become a reality?

This chapter has suggested that Japan's renewed interest in Latin America is not based on short-term objectives but on the emergence of longer-term strategic planning enunciated by PM Koizumi. If this is the case, what evidence is there that Koizumi's framework has been sustained beyond his premiership? The core elements of Koizumi's vision, that is, cooperation and exchange, have been continued, and indeed expanded, under subsequent Japanese leaders. The MoFA *Diplomatic Bluebook* of 2007 suggests that a momentum has built up in the areas for development highlighted by Koizumi. The increasing emphasis placed on the region's significance and importance to Japan is of particular interest, and the *Bluebook* stresses the ways in which Japan's strategic needs can be met by the region (2007: 70). For example, in the preamble to the section on Japan's diplomatic strategy towards Latin America, the *Bluebook* notes that Latin America is one of Japan's important trade partners, with Japan relying on the region for 52 per cent of its silver imports, 50 per cent of its copper, 17 per cent of its iron ore, 68 per cent of its molybdenum and 18 per cent of its soybean imports. The volume of trade in 2005 exceeded 4.5 trillion yen. There is reference to the large number of *Nikkeijin* residing in Latin America, particularly Brazil, in addition to the supportive stance of Latin American countries regarding Japan's quest for a permanent seat on the UNSC and Japan's position on the North Korea problem. For these reasons, the *Bluebook* describes the relationship between Japan and Latin America as unwavering and reliable. In addition to noting the increase in trade and investment figures, the *Bluebook* outlines activities in new areas such as Brazil's decision to adopt Japanese-style digital TV broadcasts which, it is envisaged, would promote the expansion of demand for communications technology from Japan. The Cooperation on the Clean Development Mechanism (CDM) outlined in the Kyoto Protocol also made advances with the Japanese and Brazilian governments establishing the first Biomass Working Group in April 2006.

In an important speech made in advance of his departure for the FEALAC Third Foreign Ministers' meeting in summer 2007, then Foreign Minister Aso Tarō noted the opportunities that Latin America and the Caribbean offered Japan in terms of markets, a manufacturing base and resources. He commented on the way in which Japan, through aid, humanitarian assistance and volunteerism has also brought benefits to the region. Finally he stressed the importance of Japan's 'latent assets' in the region and commented on the way in which Japan had built up 'a relationship abundant in trust and gratitude'.[25] Aso identified were three areas in which Japan and Latin America could cooperate in the future, namely 'the strengthening of economic relations, support for efforts to resolve the regional issues of poverty and gaps in society, and joint engagement in addressing issues in international society'. In terms of the latter, he made specific reference to the support already shown by some countries in the region for Japan's efforts to combat climate change (for example, via the Cool Earth 50 initiative), an important element of Japan's foreign policy strategy, particularly in the run-up to the G8 summit hosted by Japan in 2008.

The three areas defined by Aso have subsequently become the 'three pillars' underpinning Japan–Latin America/Caribbean relations and represent the consolidation of a mid-long-term strategic policy on the region. The relatively high level (when compared with the 1990s) of regular diplomatic and business activity in the form of summits, sideline meetings, ministerial visits, trade delegations and so on, certainly suggest a serious commitment on the Japanese side to the strengthening of existing partnerships and development of new initiatives. In July 2007, former Prime Minister Abe proposed a strengthening of economic relations with Brazil through greater cooperation on infrastructure, mining and biofuels (MoFA 2008: 67). The importance of Mexico's position as Japan's main trading partner in the region was underscored by visits from the Japanese Vice-Minister for Foreign Affairs Matsushima Midori in spring 2007, followed by a visit by former Foreign Minister Aso in August during which discussions were held on the need to jointly nurture small and medium-sized enterprises and the components industry. In the meantime, visits to Japan during 2007 were made by Chilean president Michelle Bachelet Jeria on the occasion of the entry into force of the Japan–Chile EPA, Bolivian President Morales and Guyanan President Bharrat Jagdeo (MoFA 2008: 67). By 2008 there was a qualitative change in the language used to describe Japan–Latin America relations in the *Diplomatic Bluebook*, which referred to the fact that Japan and Latin America have become important partners in international society given their shared values. Furthermore, the *Bluebook* emphasises the opportunities for greater cooperation in the future in areas important to Japan such as climate change, human security and reform of the UNSC (MoFA 2009: 65).

The 'golden age' of Japan as a leading East Asian power enjoying a more or less exclusive relationship with the countries of Latin America is over, and Japan is now having to compete with the presence, and more aggressive policies, of China and South Korea and a changing international economic environment. While Japan took 11.4 per cent of Latin America's total trade in 1990, by 2005 this had reduced to 6.5 per cent, whereas other Asian countries showed a rapid increase from 7.6 per cent to 22.5 per cent, with China's rise being particularly notable (Tsunekawa 2007: 60). Japan is not necessarily seeking to catch up with its Asian neighbours (it would clearly struggle to do so with the sustained 'onslaught' from China), but it does nonetheless acknowledge the renewed significance of Latin America and has formulated a policy which has been sustained beyond Koizumi's premiership and, moreover, looks to be sustainable at least for the foreseeable future. Japan's Latin America policy has been integrated into a more coherent and cohesive long-term strategy than was previously the case. The strategy identifies the region as an important trading partner, a valuable source of natural resources and, perhaps most significantly, a region with long-standing pro-Japan sensibilities that can, for now at least, be called upon for support in the pursuit of Japan's broader foreign policy agenda.

Notes

1   See Horisaka for a succinct overview of Japan–Latin America relations since the end of World War Two. Horisaka suggests four stages in Japan–Latin America economic relations: immigration and trading (up to the late 1950s); direct investment (up to the early 1970s); private bank loans to the early 1980s; reverse migration since the end of the 1980s (2005: 153).
2   Africa received 10.8 per cent, Central Asia 1.6 per cent, South Asia 5.4 per cent. The lion's share of Japan's aid continues to go to East Asia and the Middle East (24.3 per cent and 33.2 per cent respectively) (MoFA 2006b).
3   Joint Press Statement on the Occasion of the Summit Meeting between Japan and the Republic of Chile, available at http://www.mofa.go.jp/region/latin/chile/joint0709–1. html
4   'Dominican emigrants mark 50th anniversary' *Japan Times* 31 July 2006, available at http://search.japantimes.co.jp/cgi-bin/nn20060731f2.html
5   Opinion Poll: 2008 Brazil Image of Japan (Summary), available at http://www3.mofa. go.jp/k/news/2008/04/11b.html
6   For the wording of Koizumi's address on Japan's new Latin America/Caribbean policies made during his visit to Brazil in September see http://www.mofa.go.jp/region/latin/pmv0409/adress.html
7   For the full text of the communiqué see http://www.mofa.go.jp/region/latin/brazil/joint0409.html
8   The three 'R's' stand for reduce, re-use, and recycle. For further information on Japan's activities in this regard go to http://www.env.go.jp/recycle/3r/en/index.html
9   See for example 'Joint Statement concerning Cooperation between Japan and the Federative Republic of Brazil on International Affairs', 26 May 2005, available at http://www.mofa.go.jp/region/latin/brazil/pv0505/joint-2.html; and 'Joint Statement concerning Cooperation between Japan and the Federative Republic of Brazil on United Nations Reform', 26 May 2005, available at http://www.mofa.go.jp/region/latin/brazil/pv0505/joint-1.html
10 The full wording of the 'Joint Statement on the occasion of the Signing of the Agreement between Japan and the United Mexican States for the Strengthening of the Economic Partnership' can be found at http://www.mofa.go.jp/region/latin/mexico/agreement/joint.html
11 Japan–Chile Summit Meeting (Overview), 13 February 2003, available at http://www.mofa.go.jp/region/latin/chile/pv0302/overview.html. It was not until November 2005 that both sides agreed that negotiations for a Japan–Chile free trade agreement could begin.
12 See also 'Official Visit by Prime Minister Junichiro Koizumi to the Republic of Chile,

22 November 2004', available at http://www.mofa.go.jp/policy/economy/apec/ 2004/chile.html

13 For the full wording in English see 'Tokyo Declaration. Japan and Central America: Friends United towards the Future', available at http://www.mofa.go.jp/region/ latin/summit/tokyo0508.html

14 For information on the 2007 Young Leaders Program see 'FEALAC Young Leaders Invitation Program on Sustainable Development' at http://www.mofa.go.jp/region/latin/ fealac/program0512/index.html

15 'Policies of the Japanese Government Regarding the Forum for East Asia–Latin America Cooperation' available at http://www.mofa.go.jp/region/latin/fealac/policy.html. The Final Report of the Economy and Society Working Group was published in September 2006 and is available at http://www.mofa.go.jp/region/latin/fealac/report0606.pdf

16 The full text in English of the 'Tokyo Declaration Japan and Central America: Friends United towards a Future' signed in August 2005 is available at http://www.mofa.go.jp/ region/latin/summit/tokyo0508.html. With regard to SICA's support for a permanent Japanese seat on a reformed UNSC, the declaration states 'the SICA countries announced that they support Japan's candidature to become a permanent member of the Security Council, and that when a vote for electing new permanent members of the Security Council is held following a resolution adopted in the General Assembly, they would vote for Japan. In return Japan has expressed its deep appreciation.'

17 The report was entitled 'A more secure world: Our shared responsibility'. It is available at http://www.un.org/secureworld. The first model was to increase the number of permanent seats by 6 and non-permanent seats by 3; the second model was to set up eight quasi-permanent seats with four-year terms, plus one additional non-permanent seat. The first model was favoured by the G4, but only gained the support of 60 countries in the GA general debate in late 2004 (Kitaoka 2005: 12).

18 Available at http://www.un.org/largerfreedom

19 The difficulties of UN reform cannot be underestimated. Adoption of a draft resolution would require revision of the UN Charter which in turn needs the support of two-thirds of UN member countries.

20 See for example Santiso (2007) and Devlin, Estevadeordal and Rodriguez-Clare (2006) for discussion of the challenges China poses to the region.

21 Japan's preferred term, economic partnership agreement (EPA), covers the traditional conventions of FTAs such as the removal of tariffs, but also encompasses more comprehensive types of economic activities such as investment, competition and the movement of natural persons (Watanabe 2004: 55).

22 Mexico does represent a major market for certain Japanese industries, for example, cars, electronics and steel (Solís and Katada 2007: 284).

23 Agricultural trade between Japan and Singapore accounts for just 2 per cent of overall trade. In overall trade between Japan and Mexico it accounts for 7 per cent (Watanabe 2004: 57).

24 Koizumi's support for, and leadership role, in the negotiations are identified by Solís and Katada as one of the main reasons for its ultimate success, in particular his ability to deal with the bureaucratic wrangling between the Ministry of Economy, Trade and Industry and the Ministry of Agriculture, Forestry and Fisheries (2007: 292–5).

25 For the full text of the speech see 'Examining Latin America and the Caribbean from Japan's perspective: Fostering partnerships for a new age', available at http://www.mofa.go.jp/region/latin/speech0707.html. Tsunekawa notes that the address is particularly noteworthy since it focuses solely on Japan–Latin America relations, indicating the importance with which the Foreign Minister viewed this particular relationship (2007: 61).

68   *Caroline Rose*

References

Annan, Kofi (2005) 'In larger freedom: towards development security and human rights for all', available at http://www.un.org/largerfreedom

Aso Tarō (2007) 'Examining Latin America and the Caribbean from Japan's perspective: Fostering partnerships for a new age', available at http://www.mofa.go.jp/region/latin/speech0707.html

Daily Yomiuri, 18 September 2004, 'Koizumi to press for permanent UNSC seat'.

—— 20 September 2004, 'Mexico FTA to shape up farm sector'.

—— 11 June 2005, '3 hurdles remain for G4'.

—— 19 June 2005, 'Japan's UNSC bid crumbling'.

Devlin, Robert, Antoni Estevadeordal and Andres Rodriguez-Clare, eds (2006) *The Emergence of China: Opportunities and Challenges for Latin America and the Caribbean*, Washington DC: Inter-American Development Bank.

The Economist (2004) 'Magic or Realism', 29 December.

Horisaka Kōtarō (2005) 'Japan and Latin America: Policy Goals and Constraints', in Jorg Faust, Manfred Mols and Won-Ho Kim, eds, *Latin America and East Asia – Attempts at Diversification*, Munster: Lit Verlag, pp. 147–62.

—— (2007) 'Haipā infure kara sotsugyō shita Burajiru', *Gaikō Foramu*, March, pp. 42–5.

Japan Times, 10 September 2004, 'Fear of losing out to China prompts FTA stampede'.

Kagami Mitsuhiro (2001) 'Japan and Latin America', *The Japanese Economy*, Vol 29, No. 3, pp. 21–47.

Kai Noritake (2006) 'Chūgoku no Chūnanbei ni taisuru shigen kakutoku gaikō to waga kuni no tai'ō', *Raten Amerika Jiho*, January, pp. 12–16.

Kitaoka Shin'ichi (2005) 'Answering China's Japan Bashers', in *Japan Echo*, Vol. 23, pp. 12–17.

Kosaka Setsuzo (2007) 'Toward a Revival in Japan–Brazil Economic Relations', *Gaikō Forum*, Spring, pp. 45–52.

Manabe Takashi (2004) 'Koizumi sōri no Chūnanbei hōmon', *Raten Amerika Jiho*, November, pp. 2–6.

Masaki Yasushi (2006) 'Economic Partnership Agreements and Japanese Strategy', in *Gaikō Forum*, Fall, pp. 53–63.

McCormack, Gavan (2007) *Client State: Japan in America's Embrace*, Verso.

Ministry of Foreign Affairs (MoFA) (2002) *Japan's Official Development Assistance White Paper*, Tokyo: Economic Cooperation Bureau, Ministry of Foreign Affairs.

—— (2005) *Gaikō Seisho (Diplomatic Bluebook)*, Tokyo: Zaimushō Insatsukyoku.

—— (2006a) *Gaikō Seisho (Diplomatic Bluebook)*, Tokyo: Zaimushō Insatsukyoku.

—— (2006b) *Japan's Official Development Assistance White Paper*, Tokyo: Economic Cooperation Bureau, Ministry of Foreign Affairs.

—— (2007) *Gaikō Seisho (Diplomatic Bluebook)*, Tokyo: Zaimushō Insatsukyoku.

—— (2008) *Gaikō Seisho (Diplomatic Bluebook)*, Tokyo: Zaimushō Insatsukyoku.

—— (2009) *Gaikō Seisho (Diplomatic Bluebook)*, Tokyo: Zaimushō Insatsukyoku.

Nakatani Yoshio (2005) 'Nihon Chūbei shunō kaidan no jisshi', *Raten Amerika Jiho*, October, pp. 2–5.

Nishijima Shoji (2005) 'Raten Amerika de purezensu takameru Chūgoku', *Sekai Shūbō*, March 8, pp. 54–5.

Okamoto Yumiko (2006) 'Kappatsuka suru Chiri no tai Ajia Taiheiyō chiiki keizai gaikō', *Raten Amerika Repōto*, Vol. 23, No. 1, pp. 17–25.

Santiso, Javier, ed. (2007) *The Visible Hand of China in Latin America*, Paris: Development Centre of the OECD.

Solís, Mireya and Saori N. Katada (2007) 'The Japan–Mexico FTA: A Cross-Regional Step in the Path towards Asian Regionalism', *Pacific Affairs*, Vol. 80, No. 2, pp. 279–301.

Tsunekawa Keichi (2007) 'Nihon to Chūnanbei no arata no deai', *Gaikō Foramu*, October, pp. 58–61.

Watanabe Yorizumi (2004) 'Japan's FTA Strategy and the Japan–Mexico EPA', in *Gaiko Forum*, Summer, pp. 54–63.

5   Transnational migration and identity

Brazil and Japan share a workforce

June A. Gordon

Creation of a transnational identity: Japan and Brazil exchange patterns of migration

As Brazil is transformed from a nation of immigrants to one of emigrants, Japan provides a partnership – a nation of emigrants now welcoming a flow of immigrants, albeit with some ambivalence (Befu 2002, Reis 2002). The approximately 300,000 Japanese residents who have arrived from the nations of Latin America are today's human evidence of a global economy at work. After facing the difficulties of a largely illegal influx of 'guest workers' from Asia and the Middle East (Shipper 2002), the Japanese government in the 1980s offered special visas to descendents of Japanese migrants to South America, the *Nikkei*, assuming common ancestry would guarantee ease of assimilation and control (De Carvalho 2003b). Forgotten was the transformation that takes place over two to three generations among immigrants to places as radically different in language and culture from Japan as Brazil and Peru (Tsuda 2003b, Takenaka 2003). Viewing their time in Japan as an opportunity to quickly acquire funds sufficient for a better life in their homeland, the new migrants lacked emotional preparation for the reality of a Japan that matches neither the images of their ancestors nor the blandishments of brokers and immigration officers desirous to provide needed labour for Japan's economic machine.

Unlike provisions made for other groups of guest workers, the *Nikkei* were allowed after 1990 to bring their spouses and children (Reis 2002). However, the instability of their lives in Japan, compounded by frequent trips back to South America, has left the education of their children in an ambiguous state, providing fertile ground for their exploitation and a growing engagement with Japan's underclass. Unbound by legal constraints of compulsory attendance or their working parents' watchful eye, immigrant children slip in and out of a Japanese educational system unprepared to serve their needs. Movement into the same menial factory jobs as were held by their parents – jobs unknown to their middle-class lives 'back home' in Latin America – becomes inevitable.

Process

The research for this chapter is part of an extended study of the historical and economic context of marginalized youth in Japan. The work specifically on South Americans of Japanese descent, or *Nikkei*, began in 2002 and continued for four years with annual visits to Japan. Access to a variety of *Nikkei* communities and schools in the cities of Kanagawa prefecture was provided through a network of community activists and scholars who work with immigrant youth and their families. After two years the research flowed to the shores of Okinawa and on to Brazil due to invitations of *Nikkei* families and/or contacts made in Japan and in response to my interest in the push and pull of the migrating process.

In Okinawa, in addition to meeting with scholars and researchers, I stayed with one of the traditional families on the islands in which three generations of perspective were shared regarding views not only of the occupation of the US but also the brutality of pre-war Japanese who drove many Okinawans to penury, suicide or to the shores of Latin America and beyond. In Brazil the research took place in both the urban context of Sao Paolo and the rural agricultural *colonias* among three generations of *Nikkei*. Throughout the four-year period over one hundred interviews were conducted by the author with teachers, social workers, psychologists, psychiatrists, administrators, priests, professors, museum archivists, government officials and ordinary people who were themselves part of the ebb and flow of Japanese migration. The author is grateful for the gracious introductions and openness of those who granted access to an outsider in the hope that, by providing a fuller understanding of the complexity of their plight and the impact this has had on the schooling and identity of their children, changes might be possible to avoid another generation of ignorance and avoidance.

From Kobe to Santos: the *dekasegi* of Japan become the *Nikkei* of Brazil

The term *dekasegi* in Japan refers to those who for centuries have travelled from their homes to distant places for work and survival, usually to other parts of the Japanese islands. *Nikkei* literally means 'sun line' or is more effectively translated as those who are part of the Japanese blood line. However, the term has more recently come to refer to individuals and their descendants who left Japan as *dekasegi*, migrant workers, as that nation rebuilt itself from 1867 to 1941, following centuries of isolation imposed by the Tokugawa Shogunate. While Japan's isolation was never complete, the transition to a modern nation state and industrial economy led to new levels of poverty and displacement among Japan's growing population. The Meiji government looked to emigration as one solution to its dilemma. Negotiations with the Philippines and Hawai'i were eventually rewarded and then followed by agreements with several Latin American nations as well as the United States. With the signing of the 'Gentlemen's Agreement' between the US and Japan in 1907–8, a steady flow of Japanese immigrants to Hawaii and the US slowed and was finally halted by a new immigration law in

1924 (Masterson and Funada-Classen 2004, Lone 2001). Subsequently, and with the active encouragement of their government, Japanese citizens turned for economic survival to Brazil and Peru as well as to many other Latin American countries, peaking in the 1920s and early 1930s, and resuming after WWII until the early 1970s (Reis 2002). As many as 800,000 individuals left Japan for other nations by 1941. Aside from these migrations, many thousands more were recruited to colonize Japan's expanding empire, most notably in Manchuria, Taiwan and Korea.

Those who left Japan prior to the Asian Pacific War did not necessarily choose to do so; rather, many were pushed out due to the Japanese government's inability to feed its own people, especially those confined to stigmatized communities (Endoh 2002). Overpopulation combined with poverty and draconian taxes left many Japanese on the brink of starvation, leading to the rice riots of the 1920s and a government and its increasingly military leadership searching for ways to pacify the unrest (Lone 2001). The largest single source of emigrants was the prefecture of Okinawa (Arakaki 2002) with significant numbers leaving from other southern and western areas of Japan suffering serious economic dislocation as well as the home for numerous *Burakumin*, the historically outcaste population of ethnic Japanese (Murakoshi and Yoshino 1977). Fed on false images of their soon-to-be adopted countries, the poor and marginalized left Japan with a vision of building a new life outside the constraints of the old society. After having suffered discrimination within Japan's highly stratified society, the immigrants believed life would not only be better but that their prior status as lower-class Japanese might be forgotten (De Carvalho 2003). Unaware of the type of work expected of them, the nature of their servitude, or the vastness of Brazil, Japanese immigrants arrived in boatloads to tame the Brazilian wilderness and work on the coffee plantations in the state of Sao Paulo (Reis 2002). Here they joined European immigrants, especially Portuguese and Italians, along with thousands of internal migrants from the largely African and Indian communities of northern Brazil.

Having come to a life worse than that which they left in Japan enabled first-generation Japanese immigrants, the *Issei*, to hold on to images of life in Japan that were quickly being outdated as both militarism and deprivation increased 'back home'. It is ironic, but not surprising, that the *Issei*, who for the most part had left Japan due to discrimination against them based on their class and/or ethnic status as Okinawans or *Burakumin*, would attempt to recreate themselves as 'real Japanese' complete with the importation of prejudices and hierarchy that had constrained them 'back home'. Part of this social construction entailed the projection of an image of themselves as being different and/or 'better' than other immigrants. Their successful move up the social and economic ladder played on this image, as mostly positive attributes were gradually ascribed to them as Japanese, an ascription applied even to those from Okinawa or the *Burakumin* (Amemiya 1993, Lesser, 2003, Mori 2003).

Interestingly, one negative image the *Issei* had to overcome was that of being unreliable and untrustworthy. This impression resulted from their abandonment of the work they had been contracted to perform in their new country. Unable to endure the brutal life on the plantations, many *Nikkei* fled when possible in an attempt to set up independent communities, often living in isolation from other immigrants, but remaining a part of a larger *Nikkei* network within their respective nation. While many died of malaria and other diseases of the rural labourer, those who survived became skilled workers with strong business acumen and set about to develop agricultural cooperatives and related rural enterprises. Increased diversification of crops, especially cotton, combined with innovative intensive farming techniques for fruit and vegetables, positioned *Nikkei* as economically successful and significant in the supply of crucial food supplies to industrial Sao Paulo (Reis 2002, Masterson and Funada-Classen 2004).

Desiring to recreate the values they perceived as true Japanese, the *Nikkei* set about developing associations, schools and cultural organizations that paralleled those back in Japan. Both Japanese and Brazilian schools assisted in the education of the second and third generation of *Nikkei* youth. Those who could afford it were sent off to the city for boarding schools, growing fluent in Portuguese and melding into Brazilian life. Many of these children were able to take advantage of what opportunities an often chaotic society offered for professional life. During these initial pre-war years, both urban and rural life proved a struggle for survival, resulting in the gradual diminishing of many aspects of Japanese culture and language. However, a strong loyalty to Japan persisted among many *Nikkei*, causing at times a nationalistic fanaticism that verged on terrorism. Japan's increased aggression in other parts of Asia as well as entrance into WWII left many *Nikkei* confused over their role in supporting such actions. It also created unease and suspicion among the larger Brazilian community as the *Nikkei* community divided between those who remained in denial of Japan's eventual defeat and those who accepted it (De Carvalho 2003).

In the 1970s, as Japanese companies gained increased access to national markets, a new type of immigrant arrived in Sao Paulo fresh from Japan. Many of them had been technically trained in the post-war industrial era and were accustomed to urban life. They did not join their compatriots in the countryside but rather, along with the *Nikkei* who had moved to the city for education, jobs and professional opportunities, entered urban Brazil through the old district of Liberdade. Ironically, what had once been a centre for the liberation of African slaves more than a century before, now served as a place of respite for the *Nikkei*. These individuals, arriving with white skin, speaking a modernized form of Japanese, and using a simplified written version (*katakana*), found themselves set apart from their darker-skinned Japanese brethren who not only retained an antiquated style of speaking Japanese but had also acquired a new language, Portuguese, though in most cases it was rendered in its pidgin form. Accusations of contamination and pollution went in both directions, the old comers had become too Latin and the newcomers too American (De Carvalho 2003).

From Sao Paulo to Yokohama: the *Nikkei* return home as *dekasegi*

When Japan decided in the late 1980s to address its labour shortage by allowing immigration of workers with Japanese ancestry, the Brazilian government co-operated, providing the legal and financial means for large-scale migration of *Nikkei* to Japan (Reis 2002, Tsuda 2003b). The journey was facilitated by the Japanese government's desire to replace foreign day labourers from other countries, who could not claim Japanese blood, with individuals whom they thought, due to their 'Japanese heritage', would accept the constrained and hierarchical work life of Japan (Shipper 2002). They presumed that *Nikkei*, having maintained their Japanese identity abroad, would fit in (Roth 2002). During the first decade many of those who left Brazil were single, young men sent by their families to seek their fortune, send back remittances and return wealthier than when they had left.

As the economic and political situation continued to deteriorate in Brazil, rural communities joined their urban brethren in sending thousands of *Nikkei*, adding to those from Peru and other South American nations, to Japan in an attempt to gain from the fabled prosperity of the world's most successful post-war economy. In 1990 a new law enabled intact families to make the move, supposedly as a form of reuniting these *Nikkei* with their long-lost families back in Japan, often out of touch for several decades (Usui 2006). The reality, however, was that urban Honshu had never been home for the majority (Reis 2002) and while welcomed for family visits, the newcomers were required to build new social networks amidst Japan's often ignored labouring and immigrant neighbourhoods. Although welcomed with special visas and work contracts, most 'newcomers' of Japanese descent are relegated to some of the most vulnerable jobs while often living in substandard conditions (Roberts 2003).

Aware of the potential loss of their children to the factories and glitz of Japan, combined with their own memories of an immigrant past, older *Nikkei* have been hesitant to allow their young to make the journey. But when cast as only a temporary sojourn with insured rewards for everyone, including the promise of increased wealth and status for the family back in Brazil, best wishes are granted. Moreover, for a government in economic chaos, the remittances to Brazil are invaluable and, depending on whether the source is official or not, can amount to from two to four billion US dollars each year (Reis 2002, Mori 2002). Remittances to the home country and/or the expectation of them have played a major role in the South American *Nikkei* saga. When the Brazilian government finally agreed to accept Japanese immigrants in the early 1900s, the expectation held that money would be sent back to Japan to ease the economic crisis at that time.

The reality was quite different due to the level of servitude on the plantations during the first few decades in Latin America prohibiting the possibility of saving, not to mention remittances. Ironically the tragedy has now gone full circle. As Japan's economy declined in the late 1990s, many *Nikkei* either lost their jobs or were placed in the untenable position of temporary workers. Remittances declined. The *Nikkei*, unable to face their families back home or return with needed funds, attempt to 'save face' by remaining in a nether world caught between two cultures that in many ways seem incompatible (Yamanaka 2003). Still, many thousands of young *Nikkei* are convinced that a few years of work in Japan will solve their financial problems, caused by the deterioration of the Brazilian economy, and enable them to return to Brazil for a better life. Stories abound of the dentist who needed an extra $5,000 to build on an addition to his office or the numerous teachers who, desiring to assist their families in old age, ventured out, fully intending to return to their profession. Knowing that factory work awaited them, they convinced themselves that they could put up with the cramped housing projects and the ignorance of their fellow Japanese, as long as they could maintain the hope that this trial, this adventure, would soon be over (Linger 2001).

A further incentive to leave Brazil, or the push part of the equation, lies in the fact that schooling in Brazil is an uncertain venture. Private schooling is usually necessary for successful advancement to university attendance and university degrees are no guarantee of professional life. The *Nikkei* have a remarkably high degree of educational success but unemployment in Brazil is staggering and opportunities for *Nikkei* professionals uncertain. Facing such a dubious relationship between education and work caused one government worker in Brazil to comment that 'The *Nikkei* [in Brazil] who are not going to university and leave school early are creating a new underclass. The people who ask for help by CIATE (Center for Information and Support for Workers Abroad) are those who have no future. Going to Japan is a way of giving up on their life in Brazil.' These are not the people whom Japan expects or wants. As I think on this, I am reminded of conversations with social psychologists and *Nikkei* cultural liaison workers who despair that, while those who came in the 1980s and 1990s were professionals, over the last ten years the most desperate are arriving in Japan, giving a negative image to the *Nikkei* community overall.

Sitting in the Sao Paolo Immigration office with about forty *Nikkei* waiting to receive information on immigration, I hear nothing about the problems of cramped housing, back-breaking work, language barriers or possible discrimination, not to mention difficulties their children will face in school. The room is filled with *Nikkei* who I know would not pass for Japanese in Japan. From this vantage point I realize how narrow is the band of conformity, of what it means to 'look' Japanese, even though when in Japan I am struck by the variation in physiognomy. Most of the people in this room, by Japanese standards, are 'overweight', their skin is darker, and their facial features more pronounced. They would clearly stick out in a crowd in an urban Japanese train station, not to mention a village, something few Japanese would ever want, particularly if they were trying to 'pass'. But what I am most bewildered by is their age. More than half of the group is over forty and it is common knowledge that *dekasegis* will not be hired after the age of forty. How can these Japanese government officers blatantly lead these people on about their prospects in Japan? Are the kickbacks so significant in terms of broker fees and remittances that they are willing to ship these people off, not caring about their life chances on the other side?

Thanks to the deception of both governments and their private agents, the lucrative nature of transnational migration, the discrepancy in cost of living between Japan and Brazil, and the false pride of the *Nikkei* themselves, most have not returned to Latin America to remain once they have tasted life in Japan, as desperate and dysfunctional as it is. Ironically, many have found a kind of free abandonment in their constructed life in Japan. Regardless of the prejudice, coldness, ostracization and difficult work conditions, there is a certain excitement, for men in particular, that goes with the urban, fast-paced anonymity they could not have as easily back in the more traditional *Nikkei* community of South America (Linger 2001).

The image most frequently brought to mind when thinking of *dekasegis* in Japan is that of a *Nikkei* worker in a Toyota factory (Roth 2002, Tsuda 2003b). Much has been written on this topic but according to my informants, the reality is quite different. Most *Nikkei* actually work for small companies or businesses, often employing twenty to thirty workers. One of them playfully asks me one day, 'How many people do you think work for Toyota?' Shaking my head in bewilderment, wondering what she is getting at, she laughs and says 'Zero', but then modifies it to a few, and continues to explain how Toyota and other companies work via brokers so that the employees do not show up on payrolls and do not receive direct payment from the company; they are subcontracted out. I ask if the *Nikkei* pay the broker, 'No they [*Nikkei* workers] just receive less from the company and the broker gets part of their salary. At Toyota everything is organized, like a pyramid. If you want to work in a particular part of the company, make a certain thing, then you have to talk to a certain person. In Gifu it is all done through an agency.'

Labour brokers, both legal and illegal, in the two countries engage in flagrant recruitment and financing of the process (Reis 2002). These middlemen, who are usually *Nikkei* themselves, continue to extract huge profits through their success in luring rural *Nikkei*, in particular, to boring and dangerous factory work in urban Japan. While the financial cost is high, two million yen (approximately US\$20,000) for a plane ticket, a job contact and minimal accommodation, the emotional and psychological toll is often horrendous (Tsuda 2003a). My wonderment as to why these issues have not gained the attention of Human Rights advocates leads one of my informants (who has made the journey himself) to explain not only the fact that *Nikkei* receive far better treatment and wages than other immigrants but also the nature of the interdependence: 'Brokers are essential for those who do not speak Japanese as it is difficult to get hired by a Japanese company; you need a broker who will organize it all.' Interviewing social workers as well as pastors whose congregations are filled with *Nikkei* every Sunday, I find out that one of the main reasons for the use of brokers is so that companies do not have to come into direct contact with the workers. As part of the growing number of non-regular temporary employees, their precarious position enables companies the 'flexibility' to 'manage' their workforce, laying off workers if there is a downturn in the economy, if the worker turns forty, or if there are accidents (Nishitani 2003, Terasawa 2003).

Housing is the other 'benefit' provided for *Nikkei* by brokers. Stories abound among both teachers and community members of multiple families living in a small apartment. A common first step in the immigration process is for people to live in the factory's dormitory but I am told that these spaces are too small for a family. From here they attempt to rent an apartment. However, it is very difficult for them to do so, due to discrimination, not only to *Nikkei* but to all foreigners. Estate agents tend to require a Japanese person as security as well as a very high non-refundable 'key fee', which is the expectation for all Japanese people, regardless of background. Having little access to the world beyond the factory or business, *Nikkei* tend not to socialize with other Japanese and, as a result, are limited in opportunities to find a sponsor or to learn the host language.

According to a study conducted by the Kanagawa prefectural office (International Policy Research Group 2001), some *Nikkei*, due to their inability to read Japanese, enter into contracts without full knowledge of the conditions and content of their work. This leaves them at the mercy of their employers to decide on wages, hours and type of work (Terasawa 2003). In general, benefits of holidays and bonuses are provided only to regular workers, not temporary workers. While insurance and pension systems do exist, few foreigners pay the high premiums. Some think they would rather have the money available for immediate disposal, others assume retirement means a return to South America. The broker inadvertently becomes the conduit through which the *Nikkei* survive, or don't.

Clearly the preparation provided to *Nikkei* prior to migration is less than basic (Reis 2002). For the most part it covers the legal and financial aspects, with little attention to the cultural difficulties any Brazilian would face in Japan. Ironically, the situation for many Japanese Brazilians is far worse than that of their fellow countrymen. Due to the presumed shared culture and heritage, they are subject to a higher standard than other foreigners for knowing the language and customs of their ancestral homeland. It is perhaps no surprise that such expectations can lead not only to resistance to a system that demands conformity yet rejects assimilation, but also to a situation where non-*Nikkei* South Americans are learning the language faster and more effectively than are *Nikkei* whose grandparents spoke Japanese as their first language. Similarly, many non-*Nikkei* accept customs as quaint, rather than constraining, enabling greater flexibility, fluidity and freedom for those not enmeshed in the mask of commonality.

Schooling and life in Japan for Nikkei *youth*

With the collapse of the Japanese economic bubble in the early 1990s, the *Nikkei* have found themselves working in factories and shops earning unreliable wages and dubious benefits in one of the most expensive urban societies in the world. Less able to send money back to South America or to save for their own return trip, the reality of permanent residency has dawned on the *Nikkei* just as the first generation of their children emerge from schools where their education has been less than adequate. Realizing that their children will be doomed to work in the same factories that sap the self-esteem of their mostly middle-class, well-educated parents, a new imperative for educating *Nikkei* youth has hit the system as figures for drop-outs and crime increase (Yasuda 2003, Kondo 2005). Without knowledge of the Japanese language and ways of operating in modern Japanese culture, *Nikkei* youth will have little recourse but to join their relatives on the assembly lines (Ninomiya 2002). As relayed to me by one such worker, 'There are many Brazilians who are in trouble. Mostly those under twenty years of age but it is not all their fault. If you come to Japan at age fifteen or over, you cannot go to school, you cannot speak the language so you can't get a job. What do you do? You get into trouble.'

Schooling beyond the compulsory middle-school years in Japan is the crucial link to employment beyond the unskilled and/or illegal labour markets (Okano and Tsuchiya 1999, Yasuda 2003). Even as access to high school has become easier due to population decline among school-age youth, the need to keep schools open and tenured teachers employed, and a more flexible admissions process that includes interviews as well as exam scores (Takeuchi 2007), many *Nikkei* youth still do not enter high school or else they drop out soon after they make a start. One social worker shares with me in dismay, 'Some even drop out in elementary school.' There are a variety of reasons for staying out of the system. Students who have never attended school in their home country arrive in Japan at the age of eight or nine without the knowledge, skills or language to 'do school'. Often from rural areas, these young people are at a loss in the regimented schooling of urban Japan and many decide the effort is not worth the sacrifice, particularly if they are bullied (*ijime*). These are the children left in the streets to fend for themselves. While not so evident in Kanagawa, the site of my research, a Brazilian translator at one of the schools tells me that, 'In the city of Toyoto, forty per cent of South American children are not in school. In Gumma you will see kids everywhere during the day, playing in the streets. This is why some people began to set up Brazilian schools, but the kids would enter and then drop out.' But Brazilian schools are not the answer for most families. The costs are prohibitive and there is no articulation with the Japanese educational system as such private schools are not accredited by MEXT, the Ministry of Education, Science, Culture, Sports and Technology. In many ways, I am told, these are not real schools as understood in Japan. 'They are located in a factory building; there is no playground.' With a fee of 60,000 yen [approximately US$600] a month, these schools are beyond the reach of the average labourer. What keeps them alive is the illusion of a quick return to Brazil.

Knowing that the chances of their children entering university or even high school in Japan are slim, some *Nikkei* parents cling to the hope that if their children can graduate from a Brazilian school, they will be able to transfer the credit back to Brazil and continue their education. Few do so. As a result, children and their parents are trapped in a time warp. If they want to go to high school in Brazil, they have to leave Japan at a specific time in their educational experience, otherwise they have to sit for entrance exams at the end of junior high school. These national exams, given in the Japanese language, prove extremely difficult for *Nikkei* to pass. If they do, it is usually to only the very lowest level of schooling, which ill prepares them for higher education or middle-class jobs. Lacking adequate high school preparation, *Nikkei* children remain on the outer edge. Those who leave school can justify it in terms of the material needs of the family. Once in the factories earning wages beyond their wildest dreams, many become hooked on the money and it is difficult to conceive of returning to Brazil, especially since they have no credentials.

In discussing the situation of *Nikkei* youth with social workers, translators and other cultural intermediaries designated as the official links to school, community, NGOs, social services, government legalities and beyond, I am amazed at their candour about the problems within the *Nikkei* community itself and how these were exacerbated by the host society (Shipper 2006, Yamanaka 2006). The blame was seldom left solely on the shoulders of any one party. Maybe this was due to the fact that all of these people had family members who had made the journeys back and forth, often more than once, and knew of the confusion and disillusion resulting in perpetuating the myths that either Japan could solve their problems or that it was the cause of them. It is the interaction of these multiple variables that tends to be forgotten or masked in discussions of immigration, regardless of the countries involved.

As is true in many immigrant stories, and certainly here in Japan, single men, most of the early arrivals, long for their families and, when they are unable to join them, take up new partners, beginning a new, though attenuated, life. If and when the spouse arrives, infidelity is claimed and often both parties agree to go their separate ways, often leaving children in the breach, both from the families back home and those newly created in Japan. If the male stays in Japan and deserts his wife and family, he is held liable for support if he returns to Brazil. The term 'dysfunctionality' was used repeatedly by social workers, immigrant community workers, and foreign liaison officers to describe many *Nikkei* families, although rarely openly discussed among school teachers. Whether dysfunctionality is due to the circumstances extant in their Latin homelands or whether developed upon arrival in Japan due to cultural shock, loss of status, and degrading work conditions is difficult to document. What is clear is that the community is in crisis. One social worker who has worked with *Nikkei* for decades and is *Nikkei* herself states:

> Japanese Brazilians who return to Japan come from broken families; they are disappointed and unsuccessful people. They are youngsters looking for cash for university or business start-ups in Brazil; they are not those who were doing well in Brazil. I have been working with Brazilian children in Japan for ten years. Those who come from Brazil to Japan are not stable. They have had problems emotionally or financially in Brazil and have not been able to survive so they come to Japan and think that their problems will go away but they do not. People bring their problems with them. The children are the results of these problems. There is no cooperation from parents. People who are doing well in Brazil do not leave, why would they?

This portrayal of the destitute arriving on the shores of the motherland to reclaim their rightful place in a first-world country in need of their labour contrasts radically from the interviews I held with many *Nikkei* in Japan. These people spoke of themselves as middle-class professionals, university educated, who held professional jobs in Brazil, Peru, Mexico and Cuba but due to the political upheaval and economic conditions of those countries felt their talents could not be used to the fullest extent.

(Higuchi and Tanno 2003)

The picture of hardworking, moralistic, family-centred Japanese in South America, encountering modern Japan and its rejection of them as real Japanese, provides grist for the potential for significant psychological disequilibrium. Instability within homes, including a high divorce rate among the *Nikkei*, as well as the return of parents back to South America, leave immigrant youth to fend for themselves, taking on adult responsibilities at an early age, including working long hours and becoming parents themselves. Such levels of uncertainty bring some social workers to conclude that parents' apparent lack of engagement with schooling in Japan has more to do with their own confusion about the system, their role in it and the demands it makes upon them. In the words of a *Nikkei* social worker, 'They say education is important but they don't know what to do.'

Young people, angered and frustrated by the betrayal of their future for their parents' illusion of gain, and by their inability to function effectively within the host country, are said to take on a defiant attitude towards their parents and society in general. It is difficult to imagine a future for oneself when thwarted by conditions beyond one's control. Newcomer children did not choose to return to Japan; most were born here and live in daily disillusionment with the frustrations of a language, culture and an educational system restricted, if not closed, to most of them (Shimizu 2000). But some of the problems newcomer youth face reside neither within the educational system nor within the immigrant communities from which they come. Rather, they are located in that mystical space that few speak of: the communities of low-income Japanese themselves. Many of these areas are home to people having great difficulty in life, including a large proportion of single-parent households. In a society where employer discrimination against women exceeds that of any other group, a woman with children but without a husband seldom fares well (Roberts 2003). While *danchi*, housing projects or estates, can vary greatly throughout Japan, the low-income subsidized high rises that loom in many of these communities are small, cramped, noisy and barren. Granted this could describe a great deal of urban housing in Japan, but when stigma of location is added, the term *danchi* takes on a very different meaning. Schools in these areas, which serve mostly Japanese, tend to be ranked near or at the bottom. One principal explained that the schools would be around level three to four (on a scale of one to ten, with ten the highest). When asked what schools would be ranked one or two, he just smiled and noted that usually three is as low as the ranking goes. While one might be able to understand employment limitations on foreign-born children due to possible language constraints, and, perhaps, the inability to access higher-ranked secondary schools, I am told repeatedly that it is equally limiting for those foreigners born and educated in Japan. Regardless of the success of exams, or the hoops that may have been passed through, teachers, cultural intermediaries and government officials all felt that many companies simply refuse to hire students just because they have a foreign nationality.

Nikkei *who return to South America after working in Japan* *as* dekasegi

Interviews with *Nikkei* who, after working in Japan as *dekasegi*, returned to Brazil, as well as with those who are in Japan for their second and third attempt, create a complex picture of family loyalties tested by the financial demands of Brazilian life. A pastor at one of the many revivalist churches springing up around Brazil, as well as in *Nikkei* communities in Japan, told me that there are two types of *Nikkei* who return to Brazil: 'One are those whose economic options are closed; the other are those who are psychologically or socially ruined.' He elaborates on this assumption in explaining that while there was a time in the 1990s when *dekasegi* could make as much or more than a Japanese worker, times have changed: 'The average wage in Japan was 1800 yen (approx. US$15) an hour; now it is down to 920 (US$7.40). You can't live on this.' Due to the high cost of living in urban Japan, which is where the jobs are, 'they usually do not find or keep a job after age thirty-five; they are misplaced, they are slaves to work.'

The paradox, according to several informants in Brazil, is that when these people return, they are often seen as successful by those who were too afraid to make the journey, even though the costs are well known. This creates a complex identity issue as few returnees are able to re-establish themselves back into the Brazilian economy. Once they leave, *Nikkei* lose their place in the job market and can never get it back because there are hundreds, if not thousands, waiting for the opportunity. An example provided to me from a situation that had occurred just a few weeks prior to my visit illustrates this dilemma. A job announcement went out for an official employment position that required extensive experience and strong recommendations. My informant tells me that 'the pay was comparable to US$60–70 a month, which is about the same as the level for food welfare in Brazil.' Once the word got out, '5,000 people showed up the next day to wait in line for the same job. Out these 10 per cent had graduated from university.' One *Nikkei* cultural worker refers to the work of Kiyoto Tanno from Hitotsubashi University, an economist who has researched workplaces of *Nikkei*, in noting that there's no place for *Nikkei* to go back to due to rapid structural changes in Brazilian society. As in many countries, small businesses and shops are being taken over by wholesale supermarkets and shopping malls.

Complicating financial and emotional issues further is that *Nikkei* returning to Brazil tend to refuse to accept work perceived as lower status and/or which pays less than what they received either in Japan, or in Brazil before they left. Perceiving themselves as middle-class and expecting a comparable lifestyle a social worker in Sao Paolo relates, 'They will not descend to do lower level work.' This creates an almost impossible situation given that, 'Wages in Japan are twenty times what they are in Brazil.' The irony is powerful and painful for *Nikkei* who left middle-class jobs in Brazil to go to work in the factories of Japan, supposedly to increase their income and status back home, returning unemployed and unemployable. The logical response is pretence. Some buy large homes, cars and all the trappings of success but soon find themselves unable to make the monthly payments. Facing humiliation, many return to Japan yet again, some in hope of work, others for escape (Yamanaka 2003).

The *Nikkei* who return after having lived in Japan as *dekasegi* are often mute about the hardships they faced as labourers in Japan, wanting to appear that the sacrifice was worth it, that their brash decision to leave Brazil for work and money was not in vain. But the evidence is clear that *Nikkei* in Brazil share a view of contemporary Japanese life – a life that is emotionally chilling and overly demanding of one's labour and social behaviour (Linger 2001). According to a psychiatrist who works with returning *Nikkei*, the human degradation faced by these individuals is devastating. Once back home some returned *Nikkei* claim that life in Brazil is indeed far better than that in Japan and that the work overseas had been a temporary necessity. Others, however, remember life in Japan as a reprieve from the oppressive demands of financial and family constraints as held within the traditional *Nikkei* enclaves of South America. Stories of male camaraderie, wild flings and liberation abound. The instant wealth that arrived with the first few pay slips, the sense of abandonment in urban Japan, which seemed to be open 24/7. Women appreciated the modern conveniences, if they lacked them back home; the fashion, the wealth, the ability to recreate oneself, the thrill of it all . . . at first. And there are exceptions to these examples; those who have succeeded in negotiating new lives in a foreign space and capitalized on their biculturalism opening businesses that cater to the needs of newcomers. These few claim to have found a level of self-confidence that eluded them back home. They have no need or desire to return permanently to Brazil.

Conclusion

Lost in a confusion of identity and torn between two cultures, the *Nikkei* sojourners have been called a bridge (Reis 2002) but all indicators point to a more accurate metaphor of a ladder with wide rungs on which many, far too many, fail to climb or simply fall (Tsuda 2002a). The surprise shared throughout the *Nikkei* community is that their Japanese identity has little to do with the demands of life in Japan and that, in fact, immigrants and fellow workers of non-Japanese ancestry and appearance seem to have an easier time adjusting to Japanese culture (Kondo 2005). While this wisdom is widely shared among the *Nikkei* community, the economic needs are still compelling enough for a continuing flow of young Brazilians to try their hand, sometimes at the risk of permanent injury, labouring in the factories of their ancestral homeland (Higuchi and Tanno 2003).

Japan's cultural, political, and economic patterns have led to an effort to meet labour needs with a selective and racially based immigration policy (Befu 2001, Lie 2003, Clark 2005). That policy relied on reversing Japan's long history of emigration but the results have tested a national distrust and intolerance for foreigners, even those who share the outward appearance of commonality with those of the homeland (Sekiguchi 2002). Whether the long-term outcomes will meet the goals of an immigrant population that can be assimilated or lead to the creation of separate immigrant enclaves is the question that must haunt Japan's policy-makers and will surely fuel further research (Douglass and Roberts 2003, Lie 2003). On the other side of the Pacific, Brazil faces the threat of emigration, largely to the US and Europe but also to Japan, of several hundred thousand of its educated and professional young citizens who seek to avoid the uncertainties of life in Brazil. Remittances are a welcome contribution to the Brazilian economy but come with substantial malaise among the families and communities of the emigrants. Brazil and Japan need to coordinate their immigration and educational policies if the lives of their shared citizenry are to survive and thrive as they cross and re-cross the Pacific (Reis 2002).

References

Amemiya, K. K. (1993) Being 'Japanese' in Brazil and Okinawa, *JPRI Occasional Paper No. 13*, Japan Policy Research Institute.
Arakaki, M. (2002) The Uchinanchu Diaspora and the Boundary of 'Nikkei', in L. R. Hirabayashi, A. Kikumura-Yano, and J. A. Hirabayashi, eds, *New Worlds, New Lives: Globalization and People of Japanese Descent in the Americas and from Latin America in Japan*, Stanford, CA: Stanford University Press, pp. 296–309.
Befu, H. (2001) *Hegemony of Homogeneity: An Anthropological Analysis of Nihonjinron*, Melbourne, AU: Trans Pacific Press.
—— (2002) Globalization as Human Dispersal: Nikkei in the World, in L. R. Hirabayashi, A. Kikumura-Yano, and J. A. Hirabayashi, eds, *New Worlds, New Lives: Globalization and People of Japanese Descent in the Americas and from Latin America in Japan*, Stanford, CA: Stanford University Press, pp. 5–18.
Clark, G. (2005) Japan's Migration Conundrum, *Japan Focus*, May.
De Carvalho, D. (2003) *Migrants and Identity in Japan and Brazil: The Nikkeijin*, London and New York: RoutledgeCurzon.
Douglass, M. and Roberts, G. S. (2003) Japan in a Global Era of Migration, in M. Douglass and G. S. Roberts, eds, *Japan and Global Migration: Foreign Workers and the Advent of a Multicultural Society*, Honolulu: University of Hawai'i Press, pp. 3–37.
Endoh, T. (2002) Shedding the Unwanted: Japan's Emigration Policy, *JPRI Working Paper No. 72*, Japan Policy Research Institute.
Higuchi, N. and Tanno, K. (2003) What's Driving Brazil–Japan Migration? The Making and Re-making of the Brazilian Niche in Japan, *International Journal of Japanese Sociology*, 12, 33–47.
International Policy Research Group in Kanagawa (2001) *Study on Foreigners in Kanagawa*, Yokohama: Kanagawa Prefecture.
Kondo, M. (2005) Japan's New Misfits, *Japan Echo*, 32, 1.
Lesser, J. (2003) Japanese, Brazilians, Nikkei: A Short History of Identity Building and Homemaking, in Lesser, J., ed., *Search for Home Abroad: Japanese Brazilians and Transnationalism*, Durham, NC and London: Duke University Press, pp. 5–19.
Lie, J. (2003) The discourse of Japaneseness, in M. Douglass and G. S. Roberts, eds, *Japan and Global Migration: Foreign Workers and the Advent of a Multicultural Society*, Honolulu: University of Hawai'i Press, pp. 70–90.
Linger, D. T. (2001) *No One Home: Brazilian Selves Remade in Japan*, Stanford, CA: Stanford University Press.
Lone, Stewart (2001) *The Japanese Community in Brazil, 1908–1940: Between Samurai and Carnival*, New York: Palgrave.

Masterson, D. M., and Funada-Classen, S. (2004) *The Japanese in Latin America*. Urbana and Chicago: University of Illinois Press.

Mori, E. (2002) The Japanese–Brazilian Dekasegi Phenomenon: An Economic Perspective, in L. R. Hirabayashi, A. Kikumura-Yano, and J. A. Hirabayashi, eds, *New Worlds, New Lives: Globalization and People of Japanese Descent in the Americas and from Latin America in Japan*, Stanford, CA: Stanford University Press, pp. 237–48.

Mori, K. (2003) Identity Transformations among Okinawans and Their Descendants in Brazil, in J. Lesser, ed., *Searching for Home Abroad: Japanese Brazilians and Transnationalism*, Durham, NC and London: Duke University Press, pp. 47–66.

Murakoshi, S. and Yoshino, I. R. (1977) *The Invisible Visible Minority*, Japan: Osaka City University Center for the Study of Anti-discrimination Education.

Ninomiya, M. (2002) The Dekassegui Phenomenon and the Education of Japanese Brazilian Children in Japanese Schools, in L. R. Hirabayashi, A. Kikumura-Yano, and J. A. Hirabayashi, eds, *New Worlds, New Lives: Globalization and People of Japanese Descent in the Americas and from Latin America in Japan*, Stanford, CA: Stanford University Press, pp. 249–60.

Nishitani, S. (2003) Assessing the Growth in Nonregular Employment, *Japan Echo*, 30, 2, April, pp. 63–7.

Okano, K., and Tsuchiya, M. (1999) *Education in Contemporary Japan: Inequality and Diversity*, Cambridge, UK: Cambridge University Press.

Reis, M. E. F. (2002) *Brazilians in Japan: The Human Tie in the Bilateral Relationship*, Sao Paulo: Kaleidus-Primus.

Roberts, G. S. (2003) NGO Support for Migrant Labor in Japan, in M. Douglass and G. S. Roberts, eds, *Japan and Global Migration: Foreign Workers and the Advent of a Multicultural Society*, Honolulu: University of Hawai'i Press, pp. 275–300.

Roth, J. H. (2002) *Brokered Homeland: Japanese Brazilian Migrants in Japan*, Ithaca, NY and London: Cornell University Press.

Sekiguchi, T. (2002) Nikkei Brazilians in Japan: The Ideology and Symbolic Content Faced by this New Ethnic Minority, in R. T. Donahue, ed., *Exploring Japaneseness: On Japanese Enactments of Culture and Consciousness*, Westport, CT and London: Alex Publishing, pp. 197–224.

Shimizu, K. (2000) The Reverse Side of 'Nippon': 'Dekassegui' South Americans of Japanese Descent and Japanese Schools, *Sociology of Education Research Seminar*, 66, 21–39.

Shipper, A. W. (2002) The Political Construction of Foreign Workers in Japan, *Critical Asian Studies*, 34, 1, 41–68.

Shipper, A. W. (2006) Foreigners and Civil Society in Japan, *Pacific Affairs*, 79, 2, 269–89.

Takenaka, A. (2003) Paradoxes of Ethnicity-based Immigration: Peruvian and Japanese-Peruvian Migrants in Japan, in R. Goodman, C. Peach, A. Takenaka, and P. White, eds, *Global Japan: The Experience of Japan's New Immigrant and Overseas Communities*, London and New York: RoutledgeCurzon, pp. 222–36.

Takeuchi, K. (2007) The Dumbing Down of College Culture, *Japan Echo*, 34, 2, 16–19.

Terasawa, K. (2003) Labor Law, Civil Law, Immigration Law and the Reality of Immigrants and Their Children, in M. Douglass and G. S. Roberts, eds, *Japan and Global Migration: Foreign Workers and the Advent of a Multicultural Society*, Honolulu: University of Hawai'i Press, pp. 219–43.

Tsuda, T. (2003a) Homeland-less Abroad: Transnational Liminality, Social Alienation, and Personal Malaise, in J. Lesser, ed., *Search for Home Abroad: Japanese Brazilians and Transnationalism*, Durham, NC and London: Duke University Press, pp. 121–61.

—— (2003b) *Strangers in the Ethnic Homeland*, New York: Columbia University Press.

Usui, C. (2006) Japan's Demographic Future and the Challenge of Foreign Workers, in T. Tsuda, *Local Citizenship in Recent Countries of Immigration: Japan in Comparative Perspective*, Lanham, MD and Oxford: Lexington Books, pp. 37–62.

Yamanaka, K. (2003) 'I will go home, but when?': Labor Migration and Circular Diaspora Formation by Japanese Brazilians in Japan, in M. Douglass, and G. S. Roberts, eds, *Japan and Global Migration: Foreign Workers and the Advent of a Multicultural Society*, Honolulu: University of Hawai'i Press, pp. 123–52.

—— (2006) Immigrant Incorporation and Women's Community Activities in Japan: Local NGOs and Public Education for Immigrant Children, in T. Tsuda, *Local Citizenship in Recent Countries of Immigration: Japan in Comparative Perspective*, Lanham, MD and Oxford: Lexington Books, pp. 97–122.

Yasuda, Y. (2003) High School Graduates Who Cannot Find Work, *Japan Echo*, 30, 2, April.

6   Vietnam's policy towards Latin America after the Cold War

Ta Minh Tuan

Changes in Vietnam's foreign policy

As the Cold War was coming to an end in the late 1980s, Vietnam had to change its foreign policy in order to adapt to the fast-changing international environment. At the Sixth National Congress of the Communist Party of Vietnam in 1986, Vietnam officially announced the *doi moi* policy, which gave priority to a comprehensive economic reform, gradual opening and integration into the outside world. Hanoi adopted a strategy of 'diversification and multilateralization of foreign relations' and proclaimed 'Vietnam wishes to befriend all countries in the world community, striving for peace, national independence and development' (Communist Party of Vietnam 1991: 43). Vietnam survived as one of the few remaining communist countries since the communist regimes collapsed in Eastern Europe and the Soviet Union. What has drawn attention is the fact that Vietnam did not fall, but it has quickly undergone substantial changes to overcome the tide of history and surge ahead with rather successful economic transformation. As a result, its international standing has been heightened in recent years.

The fundamental change in Vietnam's foreign policy stemmed from the 'emancipation of mind' in its conduct of diplomacy. Between 1976 and 1988 Vietnam saw the world as divided into two blocs, i.e. the socialist headed by the Soviet Union and the capitalist headed by the United States. Being a member of the socialist bloc, Vietnam leaned completely on the Soviet Union against the United States and her Western allies – as observers later named it a 'one-sided tilt' policy. In so doing, Vietnam made a clear distinction between friends and foes, which meant practically that those who followed the Soviet camp were friends, and those on the US side were foes. The Soviet Union received Vietnam's patronage. In this period, ideology played a leading role in the making of Vietnam's foreign policy, which limited Vietnam's foreign relations mostly with the socialist camp. Its diplomatic relationships with other countries, therefore, were ignored or taken lightly. Moreover, the Cambodian episode further strained Vietnam's foreign relations. In fact Vietnam found itself isolated for a decade.

Towards the end of the 1980s, Vietnam's economic assistance from socialist countries was sharply reduced and eventually cut off in 1991. In an instant, Vietnam lost its major markets (more than 80 per cent of Vietnam's trade was with the Soviet Union and socialist countries), foreign borrowing declined to almost zero, price subsidies and compensation ended, overdue foreign debt increased annually. In addition, the political support that Vietnam had been used to receiving from these countries also evaporated. Vietnam had no choice but to find a way of standing on its own feet, forcing it to adopt a more impartial world view. Now, Vietnam concluded that ideology no longer guided international relations and socialism was driven into temporary regression (Dang Cong San Viet Nam 1996: 76). The United States became the only superpower and the process of globalization, regionalization and international integration was gaining great momentum. Promoting economic development has become the priority of many countries. Against this backdrop, Vietnam had to go along with these trends in order to survive by means of opening itself up to international economic co-operation and integration. In other words, Vietnam has marginalized the major factor of ideology in its foreign policy and accepted new languages popular in the age of globalization.

With this emancipation, Vietnam has laid emphasis on economic development as the main goal, striving to lift the country out of acute socio-economic crisis and to elevate itself to the level of an industrialized country by 2020 (Communist Party of Vietnam 2001: 35). Vietnam's foreign policy has, therefore, to serve these objectives. Vietnam needs to maintain a peaceful and stable international and regional environment and to improve its relations with countries around the world so as to attract foreign direct investment (FDI), seek new markets for Vietnam's exports and push for the transfer of advanced technology and managerial skills. Vietnam sets out the policy of equal and mutually beneficial cooperation with all countries, regardless of the politico-social system differences and based on the principles of peaceful co-existence (Dang Cong San Viet Nam 1991: 88). To this end, Vietnam quickly normalized its relations with China in 1991, joined the Association of Southeast Asian Nations (ASEAN) in 1995, established diplomatic relations with the United States and signed a cooperation framework agreement with the European Union in 1995. At the same time, relationships with other important partners such as Japan, South Korea, Australia, France, Germany and Canada have also been enhanced. Vietnam has proactively worked at international and multilateral mechanisms such as World Trade Organization (WTO), Asia–Europe Meeting (ASEM), Asia Pacific Economic Cooperation Forum (APEC), ASEAN Regional Forum (ARF) and ASEAN Free Trade Area (AFTA). In October 2007 Vietnam was elected to become a non-permanent member of the UN Security Council with a near unanimous vote. In addition to a strong econ-omy and a fairly strong national defence, expanded foreign relations have not only helped heighten Vietnam's standing, but created entwined interests and secured greater foreign presence in Vietnam as well, which, in turn, better served Vietnam's national security.

In the *doi moi* period, Vietnam paid more attention to developing its relations with countries possessing great potentials and advantages. However, it is the new direction of foreign policy that has redefined Vietnam's relationships with some 'traditional friends', hitherto sidelined for some time during the 1980s. Russia and other former communist countries in Eastern Europe have again been highlighted on Vietnam's diplomatic map and so has Latin America.

Latin American foreign policies

The post-Cold War world has opened up new opportunities for Vietnam to reach out. In this same period Latin America has undergone changes in its internal politics and foreign policies. The right-wing parties have gradually lost their positions in elections and given way to the left-wing parties to form governments. Most of these leftist governments, except Venezuela, have conducted pragmatic and moderate reform policies within the existing systems, not abolished them in order to create new ones. Their priority is to keep political stability and promote freedom and democracy; make all efforts to revive and develop the economy; solve pressing social issues such as inequality, poverty, unemployment and corruption; and improve workers' living conditions, particularly those of poor people.

A number of Latin American countries have attached importance to regional integration based on criteria to

(i)   identify a common model of transnational linkages that accommodates unity in diversity and respects a political stand on the democratic system of all member countries; commit to the building of a region with even, harmonized and all-round development; value unity among nations, cooperation and efforts to eliminate hunger and alleviate poverty; respect human rights and narrow the gap of development;
(ii) seek cooperation in the energy sector, construction of infrastructure, an appropriate financial mechanism given each member's circumstances; establish a transparent and fair trading system aimed at fully tapping individual comparative strengths.

In the foreign policy of most Latin American countries, the United States continues to occupy a crucial place. However, in the current context, policy towards the US is manifested in different ways. The countries with right-wing governments such as Mexico, Colombia and some other nations in Central America and the Caribbean consider the US their strategic ally and thus lean on her for the protection of their interests. For instance, in the last few years the US has provided Colombia with US$4.7 billion in economic and military aid, meanwhile 90 per cent of Mexico's total export turnover has been done with the US. Whereas, the moderate leftist governments in Brazil, Argentina and Chile have maintained their friendly relations with the US on the one hand, especially with regard to the economic realm, on the other hand they have tried to become more independent of the US. They have lent their support to the US war on terrorism, but differed on the US campaigns in Afghanistan and Iraq. They also objected to the resumption of negotiation on the Free Trade Area of the Americas (FTAA) unless the US made some concession on agriculture subsidies and opening of the US market to their agricultural produce. Other radical leftist governments such as Cuba, Venezuela and Bolivia have seen the US as an imperialist and shown their political stance against her, although their economic ties have been kept. For example, Venezuela's export to the US in 2008 recorded US$51.423 billion, an increase of US$11.527 billion as compared to the 2007 figure (US Census Bureau 2008a), while Cuba imported US$711.5 million in goods from the US, almost double the US$447 million of 2007 (US Census Bureau 2008b). The left-wing Latin American countries have also tried to expand their economic cooperation beyond their region to include the EU, Russia and Asia–Pacific, particularly Japan and China. There are currently some multilateral fora in which Latin America play an active role, for instance the summit meeting between Latin America and the EU, and the Forum for East Asia–Latin America Cooperation (Vu Chau My 2007).

Vietnam's policy towards Latin America

Changes in the foreign policy of Vietnam and the Latin American countries have brought about favourable conditions for the advancement of their bilateral relations. In Vietnam's foreign policy priorities, relations with the neighbouring countries and big powers constitute the most important aspect; relations with Latin America are ranked in the group of 'traditional friends'. Two dimensions of this idea can be explained. First, traditional friends are interpreted as being the countries that have maintained relationships with Vietnam for a long time and been regarded as Vietnam's friends. They supported Vietnam in its fights for freedom and national independence against foreign invasions in the twentieth century. The invaluable assistance of the Latin American people, among others, formed the 'third battle front', making important contributions to Vietnam's ultimate victory. As part of their cultural heritage, the Vietnamese always take note of and remember the support their friends render them when they are in need. Hence, when and where possible, Vietnam is willing to continue building and nurturing close relations with its traditional friends. One could argue that this idea is similar to the meaning of allies in international relations. Nevertheless, it differs, in fact, in that the Vietnamese term refers much more to the emotional and moral ground of a relationship than the popular basis of national interest or *realpolitik*.

Second, Vietnam's perception of friends, however, has changed since the end of the Cold War. Friends are now understood broadly, that is, 'anyone who is ready to cooperate with and help us [Vietnam] to alleviate poverty and backwardness' (Tran Quang Co 1995: 108) and who 'does not nurture an intention to interfere in Vietnam's internal affairs and territorial sovereignty' (Tran Bach Dang 2000: 8). Vietnam no longer expects its friends wholeheartedly and unconditionally to support it or side with it. Friends have become equal partners in international affairs. This change has opened the door for Vietnam to forge better relations with countries otherwise easily marginalized in its policy such as those in Scandinavia, Australia and the Middle East. Latin America as a traditional friend falls into this categorization in Vietnam's policy. But it is hard to pinpoint the real substance of

Vietnam's policy towards Latin America since it has not yet framed concrete and comprehensive policy guidelines for this region of the world. In fact, it is easier to study Vietnam's policy through its actual conduct of diplomacy and economic relations. If one starts from this approach, one could argue that Vietnam has maintained multi-faceted ties with Latin America.

In the political area, Vietnam has established diplomatic relations with 26 countries in Latin America, of which 12 countries have had official ties since the Cold War ended (Bo Ngoai Giao 2007a). This clearly demonstrates Vietnam's willingness to reach out and downplay the ideological element. Vietnam and the Latin American countries basically do not have conflicting interests, making it easier for the two to share common understanding and perception about international and regional issues of concern. Vietnam has exchanged with the Latin American countries high-level visits by heads of State, Presidents of the Parliament, Deputy Prime Ministers and Foreign Ministers. These visits have reaffirmed their commitments to strengthen political ties. Vietnam has also had annual political consultative meetings with some of Latin America's foreign ministries such as Chile, Mexico and Cuba in order to support each other in international fora and organizations. People-to-people exchanges have been enhanced too, particularly between young people, union and women's organizations. The Communist Party of Vietnam has forged good relations with 115 parties, including the ruling parties and other leftist parties in this region. Being an important member of ASEAN, Vietnam has opened multilateral channels to strengthen its relations with Latin America, such as the Forum for East Asia–Latin America Cooperation (FEALAC) and the ASEAN–MERCOSUR Ministerial Meeting. If one studies Vietnam's politics, one can discover that political will, concensus and common understanding constitute watchwords in Vietnam's relations with the outside world. Thus, it is believed that once Vietnam's political ties with Latin America are good, other areas of cooperation can be promoted.

Both Vietnam and the Latin American countries have paid great attention to economic development. The need for expanding markets to supply raw materials and sell finished products has resulted in the enhancement of their economic relations. Since 2001 trade between Vietnam and Latin America has increased around 41 per cent a year. The total trade value in 2006 was US$1.2 billion (Mexico excluded), and the figure in 2007 was approximately US$1.5 billion (Thong Tan Xa Viet Nam 2008). Latin America has provided Vietnam with a variety of raw materials and processed goods at fairly reasonable prices, hence supporting the latter's production of commodities for export and meeting domestic consumption demand, such as sawn timber, paper pulp, leather, soy flour, corn, wheat, cotton, bloom yard, and auto parts. Meanwhile, Vietnam has exported to the Latin American markets manufactured commodities, raw materials, agricultural products and minerals, such as textiles and garments, electronics and home appliances with their spare parts, natural rubber, furniture, handicrafts, rice, coffee beans and coal. Some Latin American countries, namely Venezuela, Chile, Peru and Nicaragua have strongly advocated the promotion of economic ties with Vietnam by recognizing it as having a market economy.

Although Vietnam maintains a good partnership with most Latin American countries, it has forged closer relations with Brazil, Cuba, Chile, Argentina, Mexico and Venezuela. To cite some examples: Brazil became the first nation in South America to open an embassy in Hanoi in September 1994. Vietnam opened its embassy in Brasilia in August 2000. Vietnam has sent high-ranking delegations to visit Brazil led by President Le Duc Anh in October 1995, President Tran Duc Luong in November 2004, Chairman of the National Assembly Nguyen Van An in March 2006 and the party chief Nong Duc Manh in May 2007. Vietnam signed an agreement with Brazil on political consultation between the two foreign ministries in October 1995 and other agreements on cultural cooperation in October 2003, on the conclusion of Vietnam's WTO negotiation in November 2004, and on healthcare and health science in May 2007. In 2008, during President Lula Da Silva's visit to Vietnam, a memorandum of understanding (MoU) on the establishment of the Vietnam–Brazil Joint Governmental Committee was signed. Vietnam also voiced its support for Brazil's candidacy for non-permanent membership of the UN Security Council in the 2010–11 term and for extended permanent membership of the UN Security Council (Bo Ngoai Giao 2008a).

Vietnam's trade with Brazil has increased in recent years but remained fairly modest in absolute terms. Two-way trade was valued at US$75 million in 2004, US$204 million in 2006 and US$323 million in 2007. Vietnam's main exports include coal, rice, garments, footwear, bicycles and motorbikes, furniture, electronics and handicrafts. Vietnam imported from Brazil flour, soy oil, desiccated soybeans, cattle, rolled steel and leather. In 2008 animal and plant products alone accounted for 85 per cent of Brazil's exports to Vietnam, worth US$285.14 million. Vietnam currently ranks 44th among importers of Brazil's animal and plant products and 35th among exporters of these products to Brazil (Bo Ngoai Giao 2008b). The current friendly relationships have made it possible for Vietnam and Brazil to step up cooperation in areas where they possess great potential, such as agriculture, energy, bio-technology and healthcare.

Cuba is Vietnam's closest partner in Latin America, particularly in view of the similarities between their communist-ruled systems. The two leaderships have shared the conviction that the two countries should further enhance their relations of cooperation, friendship and solidarity, and improve the effectiveness of these ties on a par with each country's strength and potential. Since the end of the Cold War, almost all Vietnamese Prime Ministers, Presidents and Secretary Generals have visited Cuba. In return, President Fidel Castro and other high Cuban officials have paid visits to Vietnam. It is possible to take Cuba as a telling example of Vietnam's policy towards 'traditional friends'. When discussing Vietnam–Cuba political affinity, the Ministry of Foreign Affairs of Vietnam notes:

> Since the establishment of diplomatic relations (2 December 1960), in spite of the ups and downs that happen around the world, the relationship between Vietnam and Cuba has been maintained and developed, reflecting the sincere feelings, the faithful and consistent positions of the two Parties, Governments and Peoples towards the Revolutionary process taking place in each country.

Cuba has always been in the vanguard of the popular movements that supported Vietnam's struggle for independence and freedom as well as for nation building.

(Bo Ngoai Giao 2007b)

In this case, ideology seems to continue to play its guiding role.

Economic relations between Vietnam and Cuba in the last decade remain rather modest as compared with the political ties. The total trade in 2001 was only US$45.6 million, and the figure for 2006 was US$300 million (Minh Thu 2007). Vietnam has exported to Cuba rice, coal, electronics, home appliances, garments and footwear. Vietnam has imported from Cuba pharmaceuticals and raw materials for pharmaceutical production. Vietnam has become Cuba's sixth largest trading partner and constantly runs a trade surplus (Bo Ngoai Giao 2008c). In other areas Vietnam and Cuba have implemented some cooperative projects and programmes on science and technology, such as exchanges of scientists in agriculture, construction, healthcare, bio-technology, aquaculture, oil exploration and exploitation in the Gulf of Mexico, finance and sport. Cuba has trained about 2,000 Vietnamese cadres with graduate and postgraduate degrees. On its part, Vietnam has offered scholarships for Cuban students to study the Vietnamese language, Vietnamese culture and some other subjects. Since 2007 Vietnam has set aside ten scholarships a year for Cubans. These limited economic relationships and rather small mutual benefits could signal that bilateral ties would possibly be strained if the generation of the old revolutionary vanguard in either country was to retreat from the political scene.

Vietnam has maintained good relations with Argentina for many years. Vietnam's embassy was established in Buenos Aires in 1995. The two countries have exchanged high-ranking visits, including at presidential level. A number of bilateral agreements have been signed, such as agreements on investment stimulation and protection, economic cooperation, culture and education, and MoU on the Mechanism of Political Consultation between the two Ministries of Foreign Affairs. In particular, Vietnam signed an agreement with Argentina on the application of nuclear energy for peaceful purposes. Argentina strongly supported Vietnam's bid for WTO and UN Security Council membership.

Economic ties have been expanded with the total trade value of 2008 reaching US$424 million, an increase 13 times that of ten years previously (Bo Ngoai Giao 2009a). Argentina has overtaken Brazil to become Vietnam's largest trading partner in South America. Vietnam exports to Argentina garments, footwear, rubber, electronic equipment, furniture, auto and bicycle parts, bags, handicrafts, steamer clams and mechanical tools. Vietnam imports cooking oil, tobacco, raw materials, pharmaceuticals, chemicals, plastics, fibre, textile materials, machinery, automobile and auto parts, milk and milk products, timber and feedstuffs.

Mexico has occupied an increasingly important place in Vietnam's policy. More regular high-level visits have been conducted to consolidate political ties despite the fact that the two do not share the same views on various international issues and the developmental path. Like other Latin American countries, Vietnam managed to get Mexico's early support for its UN Security Council seat. Vietnamese Prime Minister Phan Van Khai was the highest-ranking leader to come to Mexico in 2002 when he attended the APEC Summit Meeting. The closer political relationship has paved the way for Vietnam to open the Mexican market for its exports.

Economic ties have developed rather quickly with total trade worth approximately US$600 million in 2008, an increase of 15 per cent a year, of which Vietnam ran a surplus (Bo Ngoai Giao 2009b). Vietnam exports to Mexico garments, footwear and handicrafts while it imports cotton, plastics and wood products. Mexico has also provided Vietnam with various high-yielding plants and cattle, and helped to improve the contingent of technicians and specialists in the area of oil and minerals exploration and exploitation, and farming. Vietnam has sent agricultural experts to assist Mexico's paddy cultivation. Mexico was one of the countries that concluded the WTO accession agreement with Vietnam early in 2006.

Since Hugo Chávez took office as Venezuela's president, Vietnam has quickly enhanced its political relationship with this country. President Chávez visited Vietnam in 2006. The General Secretary of the Communist Party of Vietnam Nong Duc Manh and Vietnam's President Nguyen Minh Triet paid reciprocal visits to Venezuela in 2007 and 2008 respectively. The leaders of the two countries seem to share many concerns in ideological terms. They affirmed their determination to further develop the comprehensive partnership between the two countries. President Chávez proposed the formation of a Joint Government Committee to promote bilateral relations in all fields. At the first session of this Committee, held in August 2008, Vietnam and Venezuela identified areas where they can work together, particularly in energy, oil and gas, industry and agriculture, and lay a legal foundation for promoting bilateral social and economic relations in the future. However, trade between the two remains very small – only US$20 million in 2006, US$11.7 million in 2007 and US$10.1 million in the first six months of 2008 (Quoc Hoi Nuoc Cong Hoa Xa Hoi Chu Nghia Viet Nam 2008). Vietnam and Venezuela do have a great potential for cooperation in the energy sector, particularly oil exploitation and processing, agriculture and consumer goods production, but trade figures indicate that Venezuela is far from being an important economic partner of Vietnam.

There are a number of ways to explain Vietnam's policy of promoting closer relations with Latin America. Vietnam and the Latin American countries – being small and medium-size with the exception of Mexico, Brazil and Argentina – share many things in common in terms of world view and development path. They both advocate stability, peace building and peace making, and strive for a fairer world order. These create favourable conditions for international integration, socio-economic development and improvement of people's living standards. In the international fora, Latin America has strongly supported Vietnam, particularly its bid for a non-permanent seat at the UN Security Council. This is an important perceptual foundation for further expanding Vietnam's relations with Latin America. Today, when Vietnam concludes that ideology has been marginalized in international relations, it no longer considers Latin America 'the US backyard' and therefore does not harbour a Cold War mentality in promoting its relationships with this region. Moreover, Vietnam and the Latin American countries basically do not have conflicting interests. This has made it possible for them to expand their ties without mutual suspicion, which Vietnam has to face in its relations with some neighbours.

While Vietnam opens its door and integrates into the world in order to develop its economy, it has laid great emphasis on foreign trade and diversification of markets for exports. Vietnam has tried to avoid concentrating too much on major markets such as the US, China, the EU and Japan. As some main export products such as frozen shrimps, shoes, garments and textiles have been confronted with mounting pressure of competition and lawsuits for anti-dumping in these countries, it seems natural for Vietnam to look to potential markets further afield. With more than 500 million people, Latin America constitutes a new market for Vietnam and does not discriminate against Vietnam's goods as some other markets do. At the same time, Vietnam needs to import from Latin America a large quantity of reasonably priced raw materials for domestic consumption and production.

For Latin American countries, promoting relations with Vietnam forms a part of their overall policy towards Asia–Pacific. Nevertheless, Vietnam's stand in their policy differs sharply. At one end of the political spectrum, the leftist governments such as in Cuba, Venezuela and Bolivia tend to gear their ties partly to ideological foundation and they all have, to a certain degree, conflicting interests with the United States. Therefore, they have been seeking support from countries that share their leftist ideals, and obviously Vietnam can be a targeted partner. At the other end, Mexico, Argentina and Brazil do not expect political benefits from their relationships with Vietnam; rather, they prefer better economic gains. Vietnam has become a fast-growing economy with a fairly large market of 85 million people, bringing more business opportunities to Latin America's big companies. However, it remains true that Latin America's level of economic development is yet to catch up with that of developed countries, and people in this region enjoy only a moderate income, making them more likely to accept consumer goods of a fair quality and price, which Vietnam can supply.

The relationships between Vietnam and Latin America also face some constraints. First, Vietnam's policy has not paid substantial attention to this part of the world as a whole. It has stressed the promotion of relations with Cuba, Argentina and Brazil and recently with Venezuela. Diverse political orientations in Latin America, including the differences among the leftist governments, have made it difficult for Vietnam to determine an appropriate policy. It is worth noting that the rising leftist movement, which led to the high office of some leftist parties in Latin America, has reopened the debate and with it a perception of a possible resurrection of the left, arousing much enthusiasm in Vietnam, particularly among the ideologues. If studying the way Vietnam has undertaken its propaganda and the exchange of high-ranking visits with Cuba and Venezuela, one can reasonably argue that ideology seems to continue to play a certain role in Vietnam's policy towards Latin America. Elsewhere, Vietnam has conducted a fairly pragmatic policy, but in the case of Latin America, it appears that *realpolitik* takes a back seat. This has somehow distorted Vietnam's expectation that it can benefit more from closer ties with countries where the leftists are in power. In reality, it is hard for Vietnam to claim 'socialist affinity' as most Latin American regimes came to power by democratic election; therefore they do not embrace the orthodox 'communist' ideology that Vietnam has been following.

Second, expanding the economic ties constitutes a priority in Vietnam's overall foreign policy. In recent years, economic diplomacy has become a new vocabulary that all leaders, diplomats and economists favour. As a result, Vietnam has also accelerated its economic ties with Latin America. However, at present, Vietnamese enterprises remain reluctant to do business with this region as the markets there are far from Vietnam, communication and means of transportation are limited, and Vietnam does not possess a strong fleet of containerships capable of reaching the region. These are all reasons that put more constraints on Vietnam's trading capacity. Moreover, Vietnamese enterprises' standing and prestige in the Latin American markets are modest; some have even been detrimental to Vietnam's image. Vietnamese businesspeople are not accustomed to Latin Amerian culture, business norms and languages. They find it hard to choose the right partner. It becomes obvious that an appropriate economic promotion policy cannot be conducted effectively and successfully without the backing of a strong business community. Moreover, perhaps Vietnam's market is not attractive to Latin American enterprises and/or their own capacity is limited. Neither side can invest in the other as each has to compete for investments from developed countries. Some economic agreements have been reached, but they are not specific enough to be operational. Some others prove unfeasible. This explains why the total trade between Vietnam and Latin America remains far less than that of Vietnam's other economic partners, such as Singapore.

In conclusion, Vietnam's policy towards Latin America has been transformed to meet the new requirements of the country's development since the end of the Cold War. Although this policy has not yet put Vietnam's relations with Latin America on a par with that of big powers and partners, it clearly reflects Vietnam's grand strategy of 'diversification and multilateralization'. In this region new large powers will emerge, such as Brazil, Argentina and Mexico, and therefore the fact that Vietnam pays more attention to forging closer relations with them will lay a solid foundation for raising its standing and projecting its image there. The ideological factor in Vietnam's policy needs to be considered on a reasonable basis in order to avoid unintended consequences when different political parties take power in Latin America. This will certainly serve Vietnam's national interests better and more effectively.

References

Bo Ngoai Giao Viet Nam (2007a) *Danh Sach Cac Nuoc Co Quan He Ngoai Giao Voi CHXHCN Viet Nam*, http://www.mofa.gov.vn/vi/cn_vakv/ (accessed 28 December 2007).
—— (2007b) 'Vietnam–Cuba Relations', http://www.mofa.gov.vn/en/cn_vakv/america/nr040819113922/ns071219092719/view (accessed 19 May 2009).

—— (2008a) 'Vietnamese, Brazilian Presidents Hold Talks', http://www.mofa.gov.vn/en/nr 040807104143/nr040807105001/ns080711085753 (accessed 19 May 2009).

—— (2008b) 'Vietnam–Brazil Trade Turnover on the Rise', http://www.mofa.gov.vn/en/nr 040807104143/nr040807105001/ns090305092443 (accessed 19 May 2009).

—— (2008c) 'Vietnam Becomes One of Cuba's Top Trading Partners', http://www.mofa. gov.vn/en/nr040807104143/nr040807105039/ns081110145108 (accessed 19 May 2009).

—— (2009a) 'Thuc Day Hop Tac Nhieu Mat Viet Nam–Achentina', http://mofa.gov. vn/vi/nr040807104143/nr040807105001/ns090520091819 (accessed 29 May 2009).

—— (2009b) 'Viet Nam Muon Thuc Day Thuong Mai Voi Mexico', http://mofa.gov.vn/ vi/nr040807104143/nr040807105001/ns090512153635 (accessed 29 May 2009).

Communist Party of Vietnam (2001) *Ninth National Congress: Documents*, Hanoi: The Gioi Publishers, 35.

—— (1991) *Seventh National Congress: Documents*, Hanoi: The Gioi Publishers, 43.

Dang Cong San Viet Nam (1996) *Van Kien Dai Hoi Dai Bieu Toan Quoc Lan Thu VIII*, Ha Noi: Nha Xuat Ban Chinh Tri Quoc Gia, 76.

—— (1991) *Van Kien Dai Hoi Dai Bieu Toan Quoc Lan Thu VII*, Ha Noi: Nha Xuat Ban Su That, 88.

Minh Thu (2007) 'Nhin Lai Quan He Kinh Te-Thuong Mai Viet Nam–Cuba', *VnEconomy*, http://vneconomy.vn/69441P10C1002/nhin-lai-quan-he-kinh-te-thuong-mai-viet-nam-cuba.htm (accessed 19 May 2009).

Quoc Hoi Nuoc Cong Hoa Xa Hoi Chu Nghia Viet Nam (2008) 'Promoting Vietnam–Venezuela Relations', http://www.na.gov.vn/htx/Vietnamese/Default.asp?Newid=%27 24429%27 (accessed 17 June 2009).

Thong Tan Xa Viet Nam (2008) *Van Phong Dai Dien Tai*, Buenos Aires, Argentina.

Tran Bach Dang (2000) 'Vai Suy Nghi Ve Ngoai Giao Viet Nam Buoc Vao The Ky Moi', *Quoc Te*, 8.

Tran Quang Co (1995) 'Tuong Lai Cua Cac Quan He Giua Viet Nam Va Cac Nuoc Chau A-Thai Dinh Duong: Tac Dong Den Phat Trien Kinh Te Cua Viet Nam', In Bo Ngoai Giao, *Hoi Nhap Quoc Te Va Giu Vung Ban Sac*, Ha Noi: Nha Xuat Ban Chinh Tri Quoc Gia, 108.

US Census Bureau (2008a) *Trade with Venezuela: 2008*, http://www.census.gov/foreign-trade/balance/c3070.html#2008 (accessed 19 May 2009).

—— (2008b) *Trade with Cuba: 2008*, http://www.census.gov/foreign-trade/balance/c2390. html#2008 (accessed 19 May 2009).

Vu Chau My (2007) *Tinh Hinh Moi O My-La Tinh Va Trien Vong Quan He Voi Viet Nam Trong 5–10 Nam Toi*, Ha Noi: Bo Ngoai Giao.

7 Mexico's East Asia strategy

Melba E. Falck Reyes and
José Luis León-Manríquez

In recent years the economic relations of Latin America (LA) and Asia have strengthened in an international framework in which Asia has become one of the most dynamic regions in the world, both because of the highs in its economic growth as well as for its greater participation in the international flow of goods and capital. Asia poses serious challenges and opportunities for Latin America that differ depending on the resource endowment and the productive structure of each subregion. In the case of South America, the wide variety of natural resources it possesses and the nature of its productive structure, concentrated on the production of goods based on natural resources, has rendered the relationship with the Asian countries as mainly complementary, turning the Southern Cone into an important provider of these goods for Asia, especially to China, and an attracting pole to investment projects that tend to exploit these resources. In the case of Mexico and Central America, the relationship with countries of similar resource endowments (Southeast Asia and China) is rather one of competition, especially in the production of goods intensive in the use of labour; a competition that goes beyond the domestic markets to the destination markets of their exports.

For the purposes of this chapter, we will concentrate our attention on the relationship between Mexico and East Asia, including in this region Japan, South Korea and China, for they are the countries with which Mexico holds closer economic relations in the Asia–Pacific area. With Japan, Mexico presents greater complementarity than with South Korea and China. Mexico competes directly with China both for international markets of goods and for the international flow of investment. This competition has intensified in the last few years not only because of Chinese penetration into the international markets but also because Mexico has been losing competitiveness in its exporting sector.

Notwithstanding the importance of the historical, political and cultural relations between Mexico and East Asia, we will concentrate in this chapter on their economic relations, making especial emphasis on trade and investment in the period in which Mexico liberalized its economy, that is to say, since the mid-1980s. Thus, in the first section we analyse the most general environment of the process of liberalization undergone by Mexico, and the following three sections will cover trade and investment relations with Japan, the Republic of Korea and China during that period. Some general conclusions round up the chapter.

Mexico's liberalization process

After the financial crisis of 1982 Mexico abandoned the model of Import Substitution (IS) implemented since the 1950s, and encouraged a new strategy of development based on the state's withdrawal from economic activities, transferring its assigning functions to the market and taking a turn to finance its development with emphasis on foreign direct investment (FDI) that replaced external indebtedness. Thus the sources and destination of financing investment concentrated on the private sector. Transnational Companies (TN) became the main source of external saving, and export investment projects became the recipients of this financing (Ibarra 2005). The new model's pillars were the liberalization of the economy, both in terms of the trade of goods as well as FDI. It also presupposed the sale of public companies to the domestic and foreign private sector and the deregulation of the economy. All these aspects were relevant for the insertion of East Asia's relations with Mexico although it was belated and it represented a strong imbalance for Mexico.

The liberalization of Mexico's foreign trade started with its joining the General Agreement on Tariffs and Trade (GATT) in 1986. Two stages can be distinguished in this process. The first one started in the mid-1980s, when Mexico applied a unilateral liberalization by diminishing and eliminating tariffs and dismantling the quantitative barriers to trade, the main protection instrument used in the IS period. During the second phase, which began in the 1990s, Mexico undertook an active programme of reciprocal liberalization by signing multiple free trade agreements (FTA) and/or Economic Partnership Agreements (EPAs). Under this new scheme, Mexico was seeking to obtain greater benefits with the bilateral opening to its products.

So far Mexico has signed 12 FTA with 44 countries. The most important of them has been the North American Free Trade Agreement (NAFTA) with Canada and the United States (US) that came into force in 1994. NAFTA has had a very important impact in the transformation of Mexico's trade structure due to the magnitude of the North American market and the geographical proximity to its partners. With the European Union (EU), Mexico's second most important regional partner, the FTA came into force in 2000. The last of the EPAs signed by Mexico (in 2004) was with Japan, the other world economic pole (Secretaría de Economía 2004a). That is to say, the strengthening of economic relations between Mexico and East Asia took place 14 years after the beginning of the reciprocal liberalization phase. Currently, the government is in the process of negotiating an EPA with South Korea but its conclusion has been delayed because of opposition from the private sector. In the case of China, trade tensions and also a negative perception from the Mexican business community have hindered the possibility of signing an EPA.

Under the framework of bilateral liberalization the partners of the agreements have been granted preferences generating a deviation of trade that affects third parties that are charged with Most Favoured Nation (MFN) tariffs that are even higher than the average for the Organization for Economic Cooperation and Development (OECD) countries. This has had a negative impact on the import of

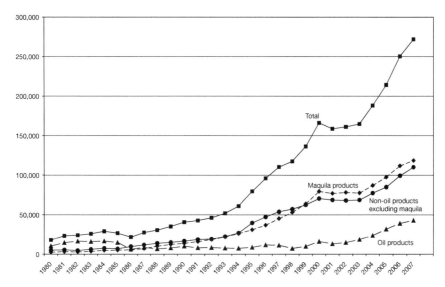

Figure 7.1 Mexico: evolution of exports by type, 1980–2007 (US$m)
Source: Bank of Mexico.

the cheapest inputs from other sources affecting the costs of the exporting industry. That was the case for Japanese companies established in Mexico that import their inputs from Asia because their competitive capacity was affected, compared to that of companies that stock up with their inputs from the North American region under NAFTA. In 2001, with the elimination of the fiscal preferential treatment to imports of inputs granted to the 'in bond industry', most commonly known as the *maquiladora* system, the Japanese *maquiladoras* established in Mexico, felt a greater pressure to compete and that was partially the reason for Japan to start an EPA negotiation with Mexico. Though the Mexican government established sector support programmes granting tax exemptions to reduce the impact on trade deviation brought about by the FTA/EPA, they have not yielded the results expected since they have been subjected to a discretional policy that introduced high levels of uncertainty among the economic agents (OECD 2007).

The liberalization of trade in its two forms (unilateral and bilateral) partially achieved the results expected from a policy of this nature. Mexico's foreign trade showed, especially in the 1990s, an unprecedented heyday. Both exports and imports showed two-digit growth rates. Total trade went from representing 20 per cent of the GDP in the 1980s to 64 per cent at present. Exports which had concentrated, since the 1950s until the mid-1970s, on a few agricultural products and that became petrolized until the mid-1980s, are now comprised mostly (85 per cent) of manufactured goods. Two sectors stand out: the automotive and electronics and electric appliances sectors. The pillars of these exports have been the cross-border assembly plants, which were established in 1964 but had their boom

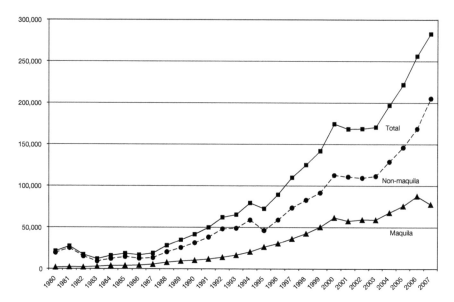

Figure 7.2 Mexico: evolution of imports by type of industry, 1980–2007 (US$m)
Source: Bank of Mexico.

during liberalization, contributing at present with 45 per cent of total exports. Oil exports, in turn, have at present (2007) a participation of 15 per cent, diminishing their share from 76 per cent during the mid-1980s (Figure 7.1). Imports, on the other hand, have also shown two-digit growth rates and they mostly comprise intermediate products (73 per cent) and capital goods (13 per cent). *Maquiladoras* participate with 46 per cent in the import of intermediate goods although they contribute with a surplus to the trade balance that mostly compensates the deficit incurred by the rest of the export companies. Imports of consumer goods have also shown high growth rates and currently they represent 15 per cent of total imports, having quadrupled between 1997 and 2007. However, the bulk of Mexican imports continues to be the inputs used by the exporting industry (Figure 7.2).

East Asia, especially Japan and to a lesser degree South Korea, has shared the Mexican exporting boom with the participation of its transnational companies established in Mexico in the sales of automobiles, automotive parts and components, and electronic products for the North American market. Mexico has had an increasing deficit with East Asia that denotes on the one hand Mexico's low participation in the dynamic markets of East Asia, and on the other the high dependency of Asian TN on the imports of inputs.

Notwithstanding the outstanding performance of the Mexican export sector during the 1990s, since the beginning of the twenty-first century the accelerated expansion of Mexican exports was interrupted. There seem to be three main factors responsible for this outcome: the deceleration of the United States (US) economy,

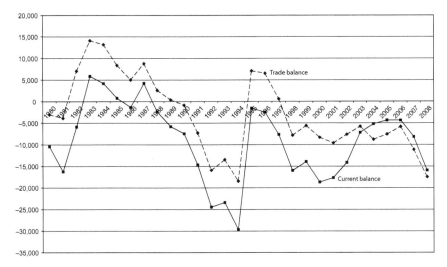

Figure 7.3 Mexico: evolution of balance of payments, 1980–2008 (US$m)
Source: Bank of Mexico, Informe Annual 2008.

the main market for Mexican exports; the loss of competitiveness of the Mexican economy; and the participation in the US market of competitors with a relative resource endowment similar to Mexico's. The main important factor is China, who after joining the World Trade Organization (WTO) in 2001 has displaced Mexico in the United States' import of manufactured goods with a current participation of 20 per cent as opposed to Mexico's 11 per cent. The sectors that have been affected most by this competition are textiles and garments, wood products, paper and printing products, chemical products, non-metallic mineral products, metallic products, computer and electronic products, and furniture. Mexico still keeps a greater participation in food, machinery, equipment, electric appliances and components, and transportation equipment. The biggest advantage lies in the last category and in food, drinks and tobacco. According to some empirical studies on Mexico's 'revealed comparative advantage' as opposed to that of its main competitors with similar resource endowment, in some sectors such as textile and garments, Mexico was enjoying an advantage because entering to the US market was still restricted for other countries. But once China joined the WTO and penetrated the North American market, Mexico was easily displaced in such sectors where it was not showing a strong comparative advantage (Chiquiar, Fragoso and Ramos-Francia, 2007).

The result of the pattern shown by exports and imports has been a chronic but manageable trade deficit that has been in the order of $5–10 billion since 1999, although from 2004 to 2007 it showed a reducing tendency favoured in part by the higher prices of oil and also by the recovery of some *maquiladora* sectors (Figure 7.3). The current balance on the other hand started its recovery much earlier because of the positive impact of Mexican migrants' remittances. However, despite these positive developments, both deficits have increased since 2007 as a result of the impact of the global crisis.

With regard to the destination of Mexican exports, the tendency prior to the period of liberalization has been accentuated. The United States continues to be the main market for exports (83 per cent) and this position has been intensified by NAFTA. That is to say, in spite of the fact that the signing of EPAs with the other 43 countries has accelerated Mexican exports, sales to the United States have shown more accelerated rates than those of other partners. It is indisputable that geographical proximity has played an important role in strengthening these relations, accentuated by the high relative participation of the United Sates TN in the foreign direct investment (FDI) flows towards Mexico. Regarding imports, the United States has been losing its relevance as the principal supplier and has been displaced by Asia, especially East Asia. In the case of Japan, the imports of parts and components of its companies established in Mexico have been a determining factor and, to a lesser degree, that has been the case with South Korea as well. China seems to be participating more in the Mexican consumer goods market. As a result, Mexico holds a very favourable balance with the United States, which partly compensates for the deficit generated with Asia and Europe, although the overall trade balance keeps on being in deficit (Figure 7.4 and Table 7.1).

What impact has this dynamism in trade and investment flows brought about on the Mexican economy? Though there is plenty of empirical evidence confirming that trade growth is positively related to the general economic growth of an econ-omy, the Mexican case seems to contradict these remarks. In effect, the Mexican

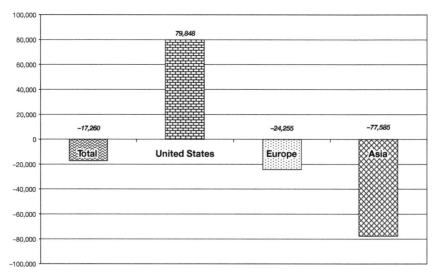

Figure 7.4 Mexico: trade balance by regions, 2008 (US$m)

Source: Bank of Mexico, *Informe Annual 2008*.

Table 7.1 Mexico's balance of trade with East Asia and the United States, 1993–2008* (US$m)

Year	Japan	South Korea**	China**	Total East Asia	USA	World
1993	−2,852	−680	−261	−3,793	−2,444	−13,481
1994	−3,437	−709	−406	−4,552	−3,145	−18,464
1995	−2,459	−463	−326	−3,248	11,361	7,088
1996	−2,241	−651	−463	−3,355	12,244	6,531
1997	−2,717	−1,241	−1,063	−5,021	10,929	624
1998	−3,313	−1,632	−1,470	−6,415	8,692	−7,834
1999	−3,431	−2,488	−1,762	−7,681	13,365	−5,613
2000	−4,070	−3,312	−2,392	−9,773	18,680	−8,337
2001	−6,068	−3,264	−3,266	−12,598	22,680	−9,617
2002	−7,564	−3,614	−5,159	−16,337	35,341	−7,633
2003	−5,853	−3,778	−7,724	−17,355	38,933	−5,779
2004	−8,454	−4,816	−12,234	−25,504	53,695	−8,811
2005	−10,527	−6,035	−15,468	−32,030	65,016	−7,587
2006	−12,472	−9,823	−21,831	−44,127	81,488	−5,838
2007	−13,191	−11,646	−26,516	−51,353	82,697	−11,136
2008	−12,538	−13,050	−32,707	−58,295	81,942	−17,496

Sources: Secretaría de Economía, México; Annual Yearbook of Korea Customs Administration; Japan External Trade Organization, JETRO-México; International Monetary Fund (IMF) Direction of Trade Statistics; United Nations Commodity Trade Statistics Database, COMTRADE.

Notes
*The sources for Mexico's exports are each partner imports.
** Due to data availability, in 2008 the figures of exports for South Korea and China were obtained from the Ministry of Economy (Secretaria de Economía), and not from each partner imports.

economy, which grew at an average rate of 6.5 per cent when the IS model was in place during the liberalization period, has shown a meagre economic growth of 3.5 per cent annually, while exports were growing five times faster. Recent studies on the Mexican external sector indicate three important factors for such results:

a) that Mexico has lacked a package of governmental accompanying actions in order for liberalization to bring about the expected effects, such as improvements in the quality of the human capital and of infrastructure; deeper penetration of the financial system and greater competition and flexibility on the labour market, among others (OECD 2007);
b) that the Mexican exporting model has not established productive chains with small and medium-sized companies (PYMES) and therefore the exporting dynamism has concentrated on a small sector of companies (300) dissociated from the rest of the economy. This has had to do with the cross-border assembly plant scheme of exportation, the strong presence of the TN and the intra-industrial trade that they have generated (Ibarra 2005; Moreno-Brid, Rivas Valdivia and Santamaría 2005);
c) that the exporting Mexican model has not been renewing itself, but rather it has remained stuck in exports of low added value, mostly of assembly-type

with an intensive use of unskilled labour. Therefore, the diffusion of outsourcing by the exporting activities has been limited in terms of the dissemination of leading-edge technology and the improvement of the human capital.

Notwithstanding that it is generally accepted that these factors have hindered the links between the exporting sector and the rest of the Mexican economy, a recent, profound study on the border *maquiladoras* in the electronic and automotive sectors points out a reversing tendency in some niches of the in-bond industry. This study, carried out in 2002 (in the middle of the crisis of the *maquila* industry), has found interesting results that point to the evolution and heterogeneity of the *maquiladora* enterprises, some of them upgrading their processes as well as forming clusters with close links with Mexican suppliers and with strong local government support. The automotive sector has shown the best performance in this sense and is the one that boasts the best advantage at present (Carrillo and Barajas 2007). In the mid-1990s the establishment by a TN of the first centre of research and development, the Delphi centre, at the border city Ciudad Juárez, to serve the automotive industry stands out; this centre was followed by the ones established by the French TN, Valeo and Visteon. In the electronic industry, Thompson, Philips, Samsung and Sony opened up engineering and design departments at their respective plants (Carrillo and Gomis 2007).

As to the effects of the liberalization process on employment and salaries, in general it has had a positive impact, with some qualification. Although employment in the exporting sector, especially in the *maquiladora* branch, increased substantially in the 1990s (Almaraz 2007), it lost its dynamism since 2000 when many companies closed their businesses, affected mainly by lower US demand, a relatively strong peso, fiscal uncertainty, lack of infrastructure and security and Chinese competition (Carrillo and Gomis 2007: 39). Salaries in the cross-border assembly sector have shown a tendency to rise, but they have had a greater impact on the income of unskilled labour than in the technicians' and the administrative staff segment; a reflection of the type of goods produced, more intensive in the use of unskilled labour. Once again, the automotive industry seems to be the exception. On the other hand, the FDI geographical concentration has affected this result. It is in the US border area, where numerous cross-border exporting assembly plants have been set up, where this phenomenon has been most evident. The participation of employment in manufacture in this area went from 20 to 35 per cent between 1970 and 1998; while it was diminishing in the area influenced by Mexico City (Chiquiar 2004).

With regard to the liberalization of FDI, as already mentioned, it began by the mid-1980s when the sources and uses of development financing became private. The theory points out that capital moves towards other geographical locations motivated by profit differentials. Nevertheless, recent tendencies on technology advancement and more flexible production processes have induced TN enterprises to make their production and location plans on the basis of global considerations. In this sense geographical proximity plays an important role, as well as the size of the domestic market and its dynamism, the integration of the transnational networks, the security environment and the capacity for technology absorption, among other factors (Ibarra 2005).

In Mexico, the flows of FDI increased considerably with the implementation of NAFTA. In the 1999–2008 period, the overall FDI accumulated was $216 billion, which amounts to an average annual flow of $21.5 billion (Table 7.2). Out of this flow, nearly half of it was channelled into the manufacturing sector and one-third went to services, including financing services (Table 7.3). That is to say, the FDI at present is also targeting sectors of non-tradable goods such as the financial and distribution sector. The Mexican financial sector is already practically in the hands of foreign entities (both Spanish and US) and in the distribution sector the big commercial chains have been displacing the retail distributors. According to the new methodology used by Banco de Mexico to calculate FDI flows, that includes new investments, reinvested earnings and intra-firm transactions, of the inward FDI flows accumulated between 2000 and 2006 ($140 billion), 53 per cent comprised new investments, 32 per cent transactions among firms and 15 per cent reinvested from earnings by TN.

According to official figures, FDI in Mexico comes mainly from US companies. In the 1999–2008 period, East Asia barely participated, with 1.2 per cent of the accumulated FDI flow and about 2,000 companies representing 5.4 per cent of the companies with FDI established in Mexico (Tables 7.2, 7.3 and 7.4). Half the companies from East Asia are concentrated on commercial activities (most of them Chinese and Korean) and one-quarter on the manufacturing industry (Japanese and Korean). However, the official data doesn't take into account the FDI made by Asian subsidiaries (especially Japanese) established in the US that invest in Mexico.

In sum, the liberalization policy undertaken by Mexico since the mid-1980s has been partially successful. On the one hand, it has yielded the results expected in terms of trade expansion and in attracting foreign investment. Nevertheless, by the beginning of the first decade of the twenty-first century its dynamism diminished. This has been the result of a passive government policy which was accommodating to the new liberalizing environment without implementing actions that would promote the benefits of trade and which would 'guide' the FDI flows towards uses more in accordance to the national interests. On the other hand, the increasing participation of competitors with comparative advantages similar to those of Mexico in other markets, especially with China's joining the WTO, has posed a challenge for Mexico, not only because of these economies' dynamism but also because the Mexican economy has been losing its competitiveness in the last few years. Lastly, East Asian participation in the Mexican trade boom has been mainly on the import side, provoked by the intra-firm relationship of the Asian companies established in Mexico. Investment by the latter was attracted by the network of EPAs that Mexico promoted since the mid-1990s, especially by NAFTA. Asian flows came from two sources: directly from their countries of origin and from their subsidiaries in the US market. Notwithstanding, Asian FDI participation in inward flows of investment in Mexico is still low and is competing with countries in Asia,

Table 7.2 Mexico: flows of foreign direct investment from East Asia and the United States, 1999–2008** (US$m)

Year	Japan		South Korea		China		United States		Total East Asia	Total world	East Asia participation in total FDI in Mexico %
	Value	Participation %*	Value	Participation %*	Value	Participation %*	Value	Participation %*			
1999	1,232.7	8.9	46.2	0.3	5.0	0.04	7,485	54.07	1,284	13,844	9.3
2000	419.1	2.3	30.2	0.2	10.7	0.06	12,920	71.67	460	18,028	2.6
2001	187.8	0.6	50.2	0.2	2.4	0.01	21,411	71.84	240	29,802	0.8
2002	166.3	0.7	31.8	0.1	-1.7	-0.01	13,013	54.86	196	23,722	0.8
2003	121.9	0.7	57.1	0.3	25.6	0.16	9,190	55.78	205	16,475	1.2
2004	368.2	1.6	47.5	0.2	11.9	0.05	8,618	36.43	428	23,659	1.8
2005	123.6	0.6	96.3	0.4	4.6	0.02	11,638	53.09	225	21,922	1.0
2006	-1,459.7	-7.6	71.2	0.4	4.3	0.02	12,431	64.36	-1,384	19,316	-7.2
2007	376.1	1.4	40.4	0.0	8.3	1.3	11577	42.44	231.0	27,278	1.2
2008p*	159.3	0.7	345.4	0.0	-2.0	0.6	8939	40.73	419.5	21,949	2.7
Accumulated FDI 1999–2008	1,695		816		69		117,222		2,304	215,995	
Period's average	169.5	1.0	81.6	0.2	6.9	0.2	11,722.2	54.5	230.4	21,599.5	1.4

Source: Dirección General de Inversión Extranjera, Secretaría de Economía.

Notes
* Of total Foreign Direct Investment in Mexico p = preliminary data. FDI includes amount realized and notified to the National Register of Foreign Investment (RNIE), plus an estimation of amounts of investment realized but not yet notified to the RNIE.
** Since 1999 the Ministry of Economy and the Bank of Mexico have adopted a new methodology to calculate FDI following the recommendations from the International Monetary Fund (IMF) and the Organization for Economic Cooperation and Development (OECD). From 1999 on, FDI includes three main items: a) equity capital: foreign direct investor's purchase of shares of an enterprise; b) transactions between companies (i.e. loans between subsidiaries and their parent corportation) and c) reinvested earnings.

Table 7.3 Foreign direct investment in Mexico from East Asia and the US by main sectors, accumulated in the period 1999–2008 (US$m)

Sector	Japan			South Korea			China			United States			Total FDI Inflows Mexico	
	Value	%	Country's share on total FDI %	Value	%	Country's share on total FDI %	Value	%	Country's share on total FDI %	Value	%	Country's share on total FDI %	Value	%
Total	1,695	100.0	0.78	816	100.0	0.38	69	100.0	0.03	117,222	100.0	54.27	215,995	100.0
Manufacture	1,117	69.4	1.26	438	53.7	0.47	27	39.1	0.03	53,505	45.6	57.20	93,548	43.3
Commerce	170	10.0	1.31	153	18.8	1.18	16	23.6	0.13	13,048	11.1	100.33	13,005	6.0
Services*	30	1.8	0.04	9	1.1	0.01	24	35.4	0.03	35,357	30.2	45.99	76,875	35.6
Others	319	18.8	0.98	216	26.4	0.66	1.3	1.9	0.00	15,312	13.1	47.01	32,567	15.1

Source: Dirección General de Inversión Extranjera, Secretaría de Economía.

Note: * Including Financial Services.

Table 7.4 Mexico: foreign investment enterprises by main sectors and countries, 2008 (by no. of enterprises)

	Total in Mexico	From China		From Japan		From South Korea		From USA		From East Asia	
	Number	Number	Share in total %	Number	Share in total %	Number	Share in total %	Number	Share in total %	Number	Share in total %
Total number of enterprises	39,782	495	1.2	345	0.9	1,295	3.3	20,716	52.1	2,135	5.4
Manufacture	9,801	86	0.9	118	1.2	365	3.7	5,492	56.0	569	5.8
Commerce	9,561	316	3.3	90	0.9	771	8.1	4,018	42.0	1,177	12.3
Services*	17,445	84	0.5	102	0.6	135	0.8	9,774	56.0	321	1.8
Others	2,975	9	0.3	35	1.2	24	0.8	1,432	48.1	68	2.3

Source: Dirección General de Inversion Extranjera, Secretaría de Economia.

Note: * Including financial services.

especially with China. Moreover, Mexico's chronic deficit with East Asia has its roots in this country's trade policy of high interdependence with the US market, overlooking the potential offered by the growing and rich Asian markets. Now, we turn to the relations of Mexico with each East Asian country.

Economic relations between Mexico and Japan

Mexico and Japan have maintained a longstanding relationship that dates back to the sixteenth century when the earliest contacts between the Japanese and the sailors and missionaries from New Spain took place, which was intensified by the voyages of the China vessel (*Nao de la China*) between Acapulco and Manila in the mid-1500s. Nevertheless, it was not until 1888, with the signature of the Agreement of Friendship, Commerce and Navigation, that the two countries began their formal links. At the time, Mexico was the first country outside Asia that recognized Japan in conditions of equality, in contrast to other unequal agreements that were imposed on Japan by the Western powers of the time. Since then the diplomatic relations between the two countries strengthened though they were interrupted in 1941 by the unleashing of the Pacific Ocean War; a decade later (1952), these relations were resumed by the reinstillation of the Diplomatic Mission to Mexico, an activity of which the Mexican Nobel Laureate, Octavio Paz, was in charge.

Since then and until 2006, both countries' heads of state have exchanged 18 visits in order to consolidate their relationship, strengthening them by signing six agreements related to cultural issues, student exchange, technical cooperation and facilitating commerce and investment. Nevertheless, it was not until 2004 when the legal framework to deepen their relationship was established with the signature of the Economic Partnership Agreement (EPA) between Mexico and Japan, the first agreement that Mexico signed with an Asian country and the first in which Japan included the agricultural sector.

In spite of the dynamic diplomatic activity between the two countries in the post-war period, it must be pointed out that Mexico did not include Asia in its strategy for reciprocal liberalization until a decade after the latter had begun. NAFTA's success in promoting foreign trade and in attracting investment flow had eclipsed relations with Mexico's other commercial associates, including Japan.

This section aims to analyse the economic relationship between Mexico and Japan during the period of reciprocal liberalization undertaken by Mexico since NAFTA was signed, especially emphasizing the trade and investment flow, and the conditions that propitiated the EPA signature with Japan. It was the changing international environment for both countries that propitiated their belated approach. The stagnant conditions prevailing in the Japanese economy in the 1990s (Bailey 2003; Kingston 2004) led Japan to seek bilateral agreements in contrast to its traditional position in favour of multilateralism (Krauss 2003). Mexico, which had started the bilateral liberalization process much earlier, was also seeking a strategic position on the global markets and thus turned its attention to the other side of the Pacific. Japan was the best choice because of the longstanding relations between the two countries.

The complementary nature of Japan's and Mexico's economies

Considering their respective availability of resources, Japan's and Mexico's economies complement one another: Japan with a relative abundance of capital and Mexico with a relative abundance of labour and natural resources. Japan's economy is 4.2 times larger (in purchasing power parity (ppp)) than Mexico's and the Japanese per capita gross national income (GNI) of $37,790 ppp is 4 times larger than that of the Mexicans (Table 7.5). According to the World Bank, Mexico is considered to be a country whose development is medium-high, while Japan belongs to the group of countries whose economies are the most developed.

Mexico, with its two million square kilometre surface has 20 million hectares of cultivable land, four times more than Japan, a country whose population is 128 million, 23 million more than that of Mexico. According to its employment structure, Mexico's is still an economy where agriculture and livestock employ

Table 7.5 Mexico and East Asia: key economic indicators, 2007

	Mexico	*Japan*	*Korea*	*China*
Factor endowments				
Surface area (thousand sq. km)	1,964	378	99	9,598
Agricultural land (% of land area)*	55.3	12.9	19.1	59.6
Population (millions)	105.2	127.7	484.5	1,318.3
Life expectancy at birth, total (years)	75	83	79	73
Economy				
GDP (million US$)	1,022,815	4,384,254	9,697,945	3,205,506
GNI per capita, (current US$)	9,400	37,790	19,730	2,370
GNI, ppp (million US$)	1,464,416	4,440,208	1,203,573	7,150,544
Agriculture (% of GDP)	4	1	3	11
Industry (% of GDP)	36	30	39	49
Services (% of GDP)	60	68	58	40
Exports of goods (billion dollars)	272	712.3	371.5	1217.8
Imports of goods (billion dollars)	296.3	621.1	356.8	956
Exports of goods and services (% of GDP)	28	16	46	42
Imports of goods and services (% of GDP)	30	15	45	32
Gross capital formation (% of GDP)	26	24	29	43
State and market				
Electric power consumption (kWh per capita)*	2,003	8,220	8,063	2,041
Time required to start a business (days)	27	23	17	35
Fixed line and mobile phone subscribers (per 1,000 people)*	74	121	139	63
Internet users (per 100 people)	23	69	76	16

Source: World Bank, World Development Indicators database, revised May 2009.

Note: * 2006 data for the selected indicator.

22 per cent of its workforce, although its contribution to the gross domestic product (GDP) is only 4 per cent, while these indicators are at 6 and 1 per cent respectively for Japan. These economies also differ in terms of income distribution: Japan's development model propitiated greater equality while inequality has been an ever-present phenomenon in Mexico's economic growth. And although relative poverty has diminished in the last few years, a very unequal distribution of income persists.

In terms of their economies' sheer size, the level of trade is much higher for Japan than for Mexico. In 2007 the Japanese exports of $713 billion were more than twice as many as those of Mexico; while in terms of imports the difference is less; 2.1 times ($621 billion for Japan), denoting a greater degree of protectionism on the part of Japan (Table 7.5). As for the openness of their economies, as measured by the participation of trade in their GDP, Mexico's exhibits a greater degree of openness with a GDP participation of exports and imports of 58 per cent while for Japan this indicator is just 31 per cent (Table 7.5). The low participation of exports in the Japanese GDP (16 per cent) does not reflect their strategic importance for the Japanese economy. In fact, because of its scarcity of natural resources, Japan has to import most of the raw materials and fuel that its industry uses.

The two countries' exports and imports structure by main categories of product are a reflection of their economy's degree of development and their availability of productive resources. Mexico, as was already pointed out in the first part of this chapter, imports in most cases intermediate goods and those of medium and high technology capital (61 per cent) while Japan concentrates its imports (60 per cent) on three categories: primary products, manufactured products based on natural resources, and low technology manufactured products (Table 7.6). As for the exports, 77 per cent of Japan's are manufactured products of medium and high technology; while for Mexico, the same categories represent 60 per cent, the remaining 40 per cent are made up of primary products, manufactured goods based on natural resources, and low technology manufactured goods (Table 7.7).

Growing trade between Japan and Mexico

Until it was displaced by China in 2003, Japan was traditionally Mexico's most important partner in the Asia Pacific region. Mexico's relative importance as Japan's partner was and still is very little. In 2001, the year when negotiations for an EPA started, Japan's exports to Mexico represented scarcely 1.1 per cent of its total exports and Mexico occupied twenty-first place as a trade partner; Mexican imports represented scarcely 0.5 per cent of the total of Japanese imports, which placed Mexico thirty-sixth among its partners. As for Mexico's participation in the flow of Japanese FDI, in 2001 it represented 0.5 per cent of the $31.5 billion that Japanese companies invested throughout the world (Secretaría de Economía 2002).

In spite of this relative low intensity in the relationship, when considering Japan's and Mexico's other partners, in the period between 1993 and 2008 the

Table 7.6 Mexico and East Asia: imports composition by product category, 1990–2006*

Pariticipation % of total

	1990	1995	2000	2004	2005	2006
Mexico						
Value million dollars	*29,560*	*72,453*	*174,412*	*196,809*	*221,819*	*256,086*
Total	100%	100%	100%	100%	100%	100%
Primary products	13.1	6.3	5.5	7.2	7.0	6.6
Manufactures based in natural resources	18.7	12.9	11.4	13.2	14.6	15.4
Low technology manufactures	12.1	18.7	17.7	16.0	15.4	14.8
Medium technology manufactures	31.0	34.6	37.4	37.2	37.8	36.9
High technology manufactures	13.4	19.7	24.4	24.6	23.5	24.3
Others	11.6	7.9	3.6	1.7	1.7	2.0
Japan						
Value million dollars	*234,799*	*336,094*	*379,663*	*455,254*	*515,866*	*579,064*
Total	100%	100%	100%	100%	100%	100%
Primary products	37.5	31.0	30.8	30.9	34.0	35.8
Manufactures based in natural resources	22.9	20.0	16.6	16.4	15.6	15.9
Low technology manufactures	11.4	15.0	13.8	13.6	13.2	12.5
Medium technology manufactures	13.3	14.7	14.5	16.7	16.3	15.7
High technology manufactures	10.2	16.8	22.3	20.2	18.9	18.1
Others	4.7	2.6	2.0	2.1	2.1	1.9

China

Value million dollars	53,345	132,083	225,094	561,229	659,953	791,461
Total	100%	100%	100%	100%	100%	100%
Primary products	10.8	10.3	13.7	14.5	16.4	17.4
Manufactures based in natural resources	11.9	13.9	15.2	13.2	12.6	13.0
Low technology manufactures	17.0	14.9	11.6	8.2	7.8	6.7
Medium technology manufactures	45.9	42.0	30.4	29.4	27.0	25.8
High technology manufactures	13.4	17.4	28.0	34.2	35.7	36.6
Others	1.0	1.0	1.1	0.5	0.6	0.5

South Korea

Value million dollars	69,840	135,113	160,479	224,461	261,236	309,379
Total	100%	100%	100%	100%	100%	100%
Primary products	22.9	19.1	26.9	25.3	28.8	31.3
Manufactures based in natural resources	20.4	18.6	15.1	16.2	15.5	15.8
Low technology manufactures	8.4	9.2	7.1	8.5	8.7	8.7
Medium technology manufactures	29.8	29.8	20.7	23.5	23.3	22.0
High technology manufactures	17.7	20.9	28.5	24.7	23.2	21.5
Others	0.7	2.4	1.7	1.9	0.6	0.7

Source: CEPAL, International Commerce and Integration Division (www.cepal.org/comercio).

Note: * Data for 2006 is the latest available in CEPAL for the selected countries.

Table 7.7 Mexico and East Asia: exports composition by product category, 1990–2006*

Pariticipation % of total

	1990	1995	2000	2004	2006
Mexico					
Value million dollars	*26,345*	*79,541*	*166,192*	*187,980*	*249,961*
Total	100%	100%	100%	100%	100%
Primary products	46.8	16.4	12.6	15.2	17.6
Manufactures based in natural resources	13.0	8.3	5.9	6.7	8.0
Low technology manufactures	7.1	14.1	15.3	14.0	11.3
Medium technology manufactures	27.8	39.9	37.7	37.1	36.6
High technology manufactures	4.5	20.6	28.2	26.5	25.4
Others	0.9	0.7	0.3	0.4	1.1
Japan					
Value million dollars	*286,947*	*442,937*	*479,248*	*565,761*	*646,725*
Total	100%	100%	100%	100%	100%
Primary products	0.4	0.3	0.3	0.4	0.4
Manufactures based in natural resources	6.7	7.2	6.9	7.7	8.9
Low technology manufactures	9.2	8.1	7.1	7.3	7.5
Medium technology manufactures	54.9	50.9	50.6	54.3	55.0
High technology manufactures	27.0	31.3	31.2	25.7	22.8
Others	1.8	2.3	3.9	4.6	5.4

China

Value million dollars	62,091	148,779	249,203	593,326	968,936
Total	100%	100%	100%	100%	100%
Primary products	20.2	9.0	6.2	3.5	2.6
Manufactures based in natural resources	11.4	12.0	9.9	9.3	9.6
Low technology manufactures	40.2	46.3	41.2	32.5	31.3
Medium technology manufactures	20.8	18.8	19.6	21.7	22.2
High technology manufactures	5.3	13.0	22.4	32.1	33.7
Others	2.1	0.7	0.7	0.5	0.5

South Korea

Value million dollars	65,016	125,056	172,267	253,845	325,457
Total	100%	100%	100%	100%	100%
Primary products	2.9	1.7	1.2	0.7	0.6
Manufactures based in natural resources	7.3	8.5	12.4	11.5	14.5
Low technology manufactures	38.2	20.9	16.4	11.8	10.2
Medium technology manufactures	30.3	36.0	33.2	38.5	39.8
High technology manufactures	20.7	30.7	35.8	36.1	34.4
Others	0.6	2.2	1.1	1.4	0.6

Source: CEPAL, International Commerce and Integration Division (www.cepal.org/comercio).

Note: * Data for 2006 is the latest available in CEPAL for the selected countries.

trade between the two nations more than quadrupled when it went from US$5 billion to US$20 billion; although Japan's relative participation in Mexico's total trade dropped from 4.3 to 3.3 per cent in that period (Table 7.8). On the other hand, the increase in the level of trade between the two nations was largely determined by the growth of Mexican imports coming from Japan, that rose from US$4 billion to US$16 billion at a rate of 11 per cent annually, which has accelerated since 2000 (Table 7.9). Mexican exports to Japan[1] also exhibited an important dynamism when they grew at a mean annual rate of 10 per cent, although it was much more variable than that of the imports, and it allowed the former to more than triple to US$3,788 billion in 2008. Nevertheless, since it began from a more modest base, the exported level represents scarcely 23 per cent of the value of the imports (Tables 7.9 and 7.10). The result has been a chronic, increasing deficit trade balance for Mexico, which went from US$2,852 billion to US$12,538 billion in the period analysed (Table 7.1).

It must be pointed out that the statistics presented do not reflect the true nature of the economic relations between Mexico and Japan. Two considerations are in order. On the one hand, most of the deficit is explained by the intra-industrial and intra-company relations that take place among the Japanese companies established in Mexico and their counterparts in Japan. The Japanese companies that operate in Mexico import most of the inputs that they need (see below the characteristics of the Japanese FDI in Mexico) from Japanese providers. On the other hand, a high percentage of Japanese companies established in Mexico devote themselves to exporting products manufactured in the country to other trade partners of Mexico's, especially to the United States. Consequently, the Japanese-producing sector residing in Mexico helps to a great extent to generate the surplus that Mexico has with its northern neighbouring country and to generate employment due to the high concentration of Japanese investment in manufacturing. Therefore, if the temporary imports of inputs on the part of the Japanese assembly plant industry in Mexico are taken into account, the deficit between the two countries diminishes considerably.

Analysing more thoroughly the composition of the trade between the two countries, it may be observed that Mexican exports to Japan are concentrated on three groups of products: food (20 per cent), raw materials (20 per cent) and manufactured products (60 per cent). In these three groups of products, Mexico participates in the total of Japan's imports of 1.1, 1.3 and 0.5 per cent respectively. In the Japanese food market, Mexico's main competitors in order of importance are the United States, China and Australia; in the raw materials category Australia, the United States and Chile; and in manufactured products, China, the United States and South Korea (JETRO–México 2006). In the case of Japan, its exports to Mexico are concentrated on intermediate and capital goods with a high technological content, which include electric machinery, non-electric machinery and transport equipment, and as it was already pointed out it largely corresponds to the temporary import of the Japanese assembly plant industry in Mexico. For details of the 15 main products exported and imported by Mexico to and from Japan see Table 7.11.

Table 7.8 Mexico's trade with East Asia and United States, total trade*, 1993–2008 (US$m)

Year	Japan	South Korea	China	Total East Asia	USA	World	Share in total trade % East Asia	Share in total trade % USA
1993	5,005	995	511	6,511	88,145	117,253	5.6	75.2
1994	6,123	1,167	594	7,883	106,435	140,228	5.6	75.9
1995	5,445	1,077	716	7,237	119,018	151,995	4.8	78.3
1996	6,023	1,467	1,057	8,547	147,316	185,469	4.6	79.4
1997	5,951	1,928	1,431	9,310	174,933	220,239	4.2	79.4
1998	5,761	2,014	1,764	9,538	195,209	242,912	3.9	80.4
1999	6,735	3,072	2,080	11,887	223,899	278,337	4.3	80.4
2000	8,862	4,068	3,368	16,297	273,748	340,579	4.8	80.4
2001	10,104	3,798	4,788	18,690	250,213	327,176	5.7	76.5
2002	11,134	4,204	7,389	22,727	248,454	329,725	6.9	75.4
2003	9,393	4,446	11,078	24,916	249,654	335,312	7.4	74.5
2004	12,794	5,638	16,514	34,946	275,348	384,808	9.1	71.6
2005	15,629	6,955	19,924	42,508	302,110	436,052	9.7	69.3
2006	18,118	11,419	27,045	56,582	342,254	506,423	11.2	67.6
2007	19,497	13,670	33,040	66,207	446,266	554,850	11.9	80.4
2008	20,114	14,132	36,801	71,047	387,172	602,768	11.8	64.2
Period's average	10,418	5,003	10,506	25,927	239,386	322,133	7.0	75.5

Sources: Secretaría de Economía, México; Annual Yearbook of Korea Customs Administration; Japan External Trade Organization, JETRO–México; International Monetary Fund (IMF) Direction of Trade Statistics; United Nations Commodity Trade Statistics Database, COMTRADE.

Note: * The sources for Mexico's exports are each partner imports.

Table 7.9 Mexico's trade with East Asia, evolution of imports, 1993–2008 (US$m)

Year	Japan		South Korea		China		Total East Asia		World		East Asia share in total imports
	Value	Growth %	Value	Growth %	Value	Growth %	Value	Growth %	Value	Growth %	%
1993	3,929		837		386		5,152		65,367		7.9
1994	4,780	21.7	938	12.1	500	29.3	6,218	20.7	79,346	21.4	7.8
1995	3,952	–17.3	770	–17.9	521	4.2	5,243	–15.7	72,453	–8.7	7.2
1996	4,132	4.6	1,059	37.5	760	45.9	5,951	13.5	89,469	23.5	6.7
1997	4,334	4.9	1,584	49.6	1,247	64.2	7,165	20.4	109,808	22.7	6.5
1998	4,537	4.7	1,823	15.1	1,617	29.6	7,977	11.3	125,373	14.2	6.4
1999	5,083	12.0	2,780	52.5	1,921	18.8	9,784	22.7	141,975	13.2	6.9
2000	6,466	27.2	3,690	32.7	2,880	49.9	13,035	33.2	174,458	22.9	7.5
2001	8,086	25.1	3,531	–4.3	4,027	39.9	15,644	20.0	168,396	–3.5	9.3
2002	9,349	15.6	3,909	10.7	6,274	55.8	19,532	24.9	168,679	0.2	11.6
2003	7,623	–18.5	4,112	5.2	9,401	49.8	21,135	8.2	170,546	1.1	12.4
2004	10,624	39.4	5,227	27.1	14,374	52.9	30,225	43.0	196,810	15.4	15.4
2005	13,078	23.1	6,495	24.3	17,696	23.1	37,269	23.3	221,820	12.7	16.8
2006	15,295	17.0	10,621	63.5	24,438	38.1	50,354	35.1	256,130	15.5	19.7
2007	16,344	6.9	12,658	19.2	29,778	21.8	58,780	16.7	282,975	10.5	20.8
2008	16,326	–0.1	13,591	7.4	34,754	16.7	64,671	10.0	310,132	9.6	20.9
Period's average	8,371	11.1	4,602	22.3	9,411	36.0	22,383	19.2	164,608	11.4	11.5

Source: Secretaria de Economia de México, (www.economia.gob.mx/).

Table 7.10 Mexico's trade with East Asia, evolution of exports*, 1993–2008 (US$m)

Year	Japan		South Korea**		China**		Total East Asia		World		East Asia share in total exports %
	Value	Growth %	Value	Growth %	Value	Growth %	Value	Growth %	Value	Growth %	%
1993	1,077		158		125		1,234		51,886		2.4
1994	1,343	24.7	229	45.1	94	−24.8	1,571	27.3	60,882	17.3	2.6
1995	1,493	11.2	307	34.2	195	107.4	1,800	14.5	79,542	30.6	2.3
1996	1,891	26.7	408	33.1	297	52.3	2,299	27.8	96,000	20.7	2.4
1997	1,617	−14.5	344	−15.9	184	−38.0	1,961	−14.7	110,431	15.0	1.8
1998	1,224	−24.3	191	−44.5	147	−20.1	1,415	−27.8	117,539	6.4	1.2
1999	1,652	35.0	292	53.0	159	8.2	1,944	37.4	136,362	16.0	1.4
2000	2,396	45.0	378	29.6	488	206.9	2,774	42.7	166,121	21.8	1.7
2001	2,018	−15.8	267	−29.3	761	55.9	2,285	−17.6	158,780	−4.4	1.4
2002	1,785	−11.5	295	10.5	1,115	46.5	2,080	−9.0	161,046	1.4	1.3
2003	1,770	−0.8	334	13.1	1,677	50.4	2,104	1.1	164,766	2.3	1.3
2004	2,170	22.6	411	23.3	2,140	27.6	2,581	22.7	187,999	14.1	1.4
2005	2,551	17.6	460	11.8	2,228	4.1	3,011	16.6	214,233	14.0	1.4
2006	2,823	10.7	798	73.5	2,607	17.0	3,621	20.3	250,292	16.8	1.4
2007	3,153	11.7	1,012	26.9	3,262	25.1	7,427	105.1	271,875	8.6	2.7
2008	3,788	20.1	541	−46.5	2,047	−37.2	6,376	−14.2	292,636	7.6	2.2
Period's average	2,047	10.6	401	14.5	1,095	32.1	2,780	15.5	157,524	12.6	1.8

Sources: Secretaría de Economía, México; Annual Yearbook of Korea Customs Administration; Japan External Trade Organization, JETRO–México; International Monetary Fund (IMF) Direction of Trade Statistics; United Nations Commodity Trade Statistics Database, COMTRADE.

Notes: *The sources for Mexico's exports are each partner imports.
**Due to data availability the exports in 2008, to the selected countries, were obtained from the Economy Secretary (Secretaria de Economía), and not as each partner imports.

Table 7.11 Mexico: top 15 products imported and exported to Japan, 2007 (US$m)

	Exports				Imports			
	HS	Products	Value	Share in total (%)	HS	Product	Value	Share in total (%)
Total			**3,153**				**16,344**	
Total value of top 15 products			*1,776.9*	*56.4*			*6,075.8*	*37.2*
1	940190	Parts of seats	248.8	7.9	852990	Transmission devices, parts	1,887.9	11.6
2	261310	Molybdenum ores and concentrates	239.9	7.6	870323	Motor car, gasoline eng, 1500<cap<=3000cc	1,117.6	6.8
3	250100	Salt	189.8	6.0	870840	Gear boxes	896.2	5.5
4	710691	Unwrought silver	163.3	5.2	0.00000	Re-export goods	547.0	3.3
5	020329	Swine meat	152.0	4.8	870899	Other parts of motor vehicles	242.8	1.5
6	870323	Motor car, gasoline eng, 1500<cap<=3000cc	131.3	4.2	870829	Accessories of car bodies	186.2	1.1
7	901890	Surgical instruments	128.9	4.1	870324	Motor car, gasoline eng, cap>3000cc	185.9	1.1
8	851762	Recept/conversion telephone machines	101.4	3.2	844399	Printer accessories	159.1	1.0
9	260800	Zinc ores and concentrates	68.9	2.2	870324	Motor car, gasoline eng, 1000<cap<=1500cc	152.0	0.9
10	020319	Swine ham, boneless	66.9	2.1	271019	Petroleum	141.9	0.9
11	080440	Avocado	62.2	2.0	850730	Nickel and cadmium storage cells	137.3	0.8
12	851770	Parts of telephone sets	61.8	2.0	721049	Iron, non-elec. zinc-plated	123.5	0.8
13	847170	Storage units, for computers	54.1	1.7	840991	Parts for other gasoline engines	107.9	0.7
14	870895	Safety airbags	53.8	1.7	870431	Goods wagon	96.9	0.6
15	847150	Processing units	53.8	1.7	854140	Photosensitive semiconductor devices	93.8	0.6

Source: Japan External Trade Organization, JETRO (www.jetro.go.jp/).

From the analysis of the previous figures, four aspects stand out:

i)   the trade between Mexico and Japan – although it has increased significantly in absolute terms, in relative terms it has tended to diminish since Mexico's trade with other partners, especially those with which it has trade agreements, has increased more rapidly;

ii) Mexico's participation in three groups of products where Mexican exports concentrate on the Japanese market is quite low;

iii) the strong growth of imports coming from Japan may be explained by the absence of a suitable offer of national supplies that would cope with the demand of Japanese companies established in Mexico;

iv) there is a strong potential for exportation that Mexico has not taken advantage of in the Japanese market, especially in the food market, considering Mexico's comparative advantages.

This last aspect has been the result of the fact that both the Mexican government and the exporting sector concentrated most of their efforts on making use of the advantages that NAFTA offered, neglecting other regions such as the European Union and the Asia–Pacific area. In the latter area, Japan offered attractive opportunities due both to the income level reached by its population and the consequent change in their consumption patterns, as well as to the gradual sectorial liberalization undertaken by Japan in the 1990s, which along with the globalization of its companies, pushed the country to a foreign policy that is active in signing bilateral agreements.

The Japanese food market deserves special attention, since Japan has become the world's biggest net importer of food products, with a total of US$46 billion, which represent 60 per cent of the food consumption measured in terms of calories. Japan is, among industrialized economies, the country that has the least degree of food self-sufficiency. This growth of the Japanese food market has been the result of the gap between production and increasing internal demand. Japanese agricultural production has stagnated, not only due to the scarcity of cultivable land and labour; but also because the protectionist agricultural policy that had prevailed until the end of the 1980s, especially with regard to rice, provoked strong distortions in the efficient use of productive factors, which were already scarce (Falck 2006). On the other hand, people's increasing revenue induced modifications in their consumption habits, replacing cereals for meat, fruit and vegetables. The demand for imported products was also encouraged by women's greater participation in the labour market, which, with the economy's stagnation during the 1990s, became the second source of family income. Now Japanese families consume more processed and frozen food than in the past when fresh food was preferred, and food prepared outside the home is also consumed more frequently now. The change in food demand by Japanese families and the deregulation of the food distribution system in the 1990s propitiated the proliferation of large retailers and convenience stores in the food sector as well as the entry of foreign suppliers, all of them with a strong importer component in their food offer to the local market.

Considering its availability of resources, Mexico has comparative advantages as opposed to Japan, especially in those intensive products in the use of labour, such as fruit, vegetables and processed meat. This advantage became partially apparent in the period between 1993 and 2006 when Mexico increased its food exports to Japan from US$155 million to US$525 million; nevertheless, during this period it only represented, as an average, 4.5 per cent of the total Mexican food and agriculture exports.[2] In spite of the fact that in some products Mexico achieved an important penetration into Japanese imports, such as avocado, melon, tuna, mango, asparagus, salt, beer, vegetables, lemon and pork ham, its participation in this market is still very low (Falck 2006). With the EPA, Mexico got Japan to agree to include the agricultural sector. In fact, this was the first agreement in which Japan included the sector. The EPA will be dealt with later in the chapter.

In short, Mexico's business relationship with Japan until the late 1990s was characterized by a very low penetration of Mexican products in the Japanese market, whereas the imports coming from Japan were strongly linked to the Japanese investment established in Mexico. On the exports side, the absence of a long-term strategy to penetrate the Japanese market caused Mexico to overlook the opportunities that had begun to open in this market during the 1990s with the deregulation and gradual liberalization undertaken by Japan. NAFTA was absorbing all of Mexico's attention. On the imports side, the absence of an industrial strategy with an emphasis on the development of the Mexican role as supplier in the PYMES sector also determined the strong dependency on inputs imported by the Japanese assembly-plant sector. It was not until the beginning of the first decade of the 2000s, when both Japan and Mexico were losing competitiveness in the global markets, that both became interested in encouraging the relationship by promoting the signature of the EPA.

The Japanese investment in Mexico

Japan has turned into an important source of investment flow, especially since the 1990s, with outward investment flow averaging US$42 billion since the 1990s (Table 7.12). Its more than 4,000 transnational companies (TN) represent 8 per cent of all the transnationals from developed countries and 9 out of the 100 major transnational companies are Japanese (Dussel Peters 2007). The Japanese multi-nationals have 16,000 subsidiary companies abroad, which have increased their exports substantially to US$686 billion in 2005 generating 4.4 million jobs in the host countries (UNCTAD 2008). For Mexico, both the TN based in Japan and the subsidiary companies established in the United States are an important source of investment.

The flow of direct foreign investment to Mexico increased significantly since NAFTA was signed in 1994. As was already mentioned in the first part of this chapter, the FDI came to replace foreign savings captured by Mexico in previous decades via foreign debt. As a percentage of the Gross Fixed Capital Formation (GFCF), the FDI more than doubled its participation when it went from representing 4 per cent as an average in the 1970s to an average of 10 per cent from

Table 7.12 Mexico and East Asia: FDI flows 1990–2007*, selected periods and years (US$m)

Period	Mexico		China		South Korea		Japan	
	Outward	Inward	Outward	Inward	Outward	Inward	Outward	Inward
Periods' annual average								
1990–2000	591	9,328	2,195	30,104	3,101	3,060	25,409	3,149
2003–2006	4,479	19,191	10,444	64,814	5,127	6,324	38,950	2,602
1990–2007	4,463	18,567	10,983	62,528	6,288	5,330	41,958	5,530
Year								
2003	1,253	15,340	2,855	53,505	3,426	4,384	28,800	6,324
2004	4,432	22,396	5,498	60,630	4,658	8,980	30,951	7,816
2005	6,474	19,736	12,261	72,406	4,298	7,050	45,781	2,775
2006	5,758	19,291	21,160	72,715	8,127	4,881	50,266	–6,506
2007	8,256	24,686	22,469	83,521	15,276	2,628	73,549	22,549

Source: UNCTAD; FDI statistics and World Investment Report (www.unctad.org/).

Note: * Data for 2007 is the latest available at UNCTAD.

1987 onwards (UNCTAD 2006). According to the statistics provided by the Ministry of Economy, which from 1999 adopted a new methodology for calculating the FDI that is not comparable with the calculations of the previous years, between 1999 and 2008 the investment flow averaged annually US$21 billion, and US$216 billion were accumulated in this period (Table 7.2). Of this sum total, the transnational companies established in the United States contributed 54 per cent, whereas the Japanese FDI reported by this source participated with scarcely 0.8 per cent (Table 7.3). Nevertheless, as is the case in trade, these numbers do not reflect the whole story with regard to the Japanese FDI in Mexico, since they do not include investments that the Japanese subsidiary companies, established in the United States, make in Mexico. According to Almaraz, in the last few years Asian investment has acquired greater importance and in the border states of Mexico the FDI coming from Japanese TN had a participation of 11 per cent in 2002 (Almaraz 2007) concentrating on electronic and auto parts industries. Moreover, Carrillo and Hualde point to the transplanting of Japanese subsidiaries to Mexico, which invested in the establishment of a TV cluster in the city of Tijuana, close to the Long Beach port at California, for the production of television sets, thus facilitating imports of inputs from Asia (Carrillo and Hualde 2007).

As stated in the first section of this chapter, foreign TN established in Mexico concentrate on the services sector as being the manufacturing sector next in importance followed by trade and other activities. Japan's case contrasts with the general tendency since out of the 345 Japanese companies established in Mexico, 33 per cent is concentrated on the manufacturing sector, 29 per cent on services and 26 per cent on commercial activities (Table 7.4).

From the total sum invested, one of the main characteristics of the Japanese FDI in Mexico is its high concentration on the manufacturing sector (69 per cent) with a positive impact on employment, exports and technical training (Table 7.3). According to studies carried out by JETRO (the official Japanese foreign trade organization), Japanese companies established in Mexico contribute 3 out of every 100 formal jobs in the manufacturing industry for a total of 132,137 jobs in 1999 (JETRO–México 2004). In this sector, the automotive and electronic sub-sectors are the ones that have received the largest flow of Japanese investment. On the other hand, also according to JETRO information coming from the Confederacy of Customs Agents of the Mexican Republic (CAAREM), among the 100 largest exporting companies, 13 Japanese companies contribute US$8 billion to exports.[3] Most of these exports go to the North American market, contributing in this way to the surplus that Mexico maintains with this country. It is also a reflection of the interest the Japanese FDI show in making use of Mexico as a platform for exportation to the United States. Therefore, the most recent tendency indicates that the border states of Baja California and Nuevo León are important concentrators of Japanese FDI. Aguascalientes in the centre has been gaining in importance, especially due to the Nissan investment, whereas the Distrito Federal zone has been losing relative importance (Dussel Peters 2007; Almaraz 2007).

To sum up, although they are important due to their impact on exports and on the creation of jobs in the manufacturing sectors, the flow of Japanese FDI is still low in relation to both the inward flow to Mexico and the outward flow from Japan. One of the most important objectives of the EPA is to attract this investment, as will become apparent in the following section.

The Economic Partnership Agreement between Mexico and Japan

Two years after the Japan–Singapore EPA was signed, Japan signed with Mexico the second agreement of this kind, which was in turn the first transpacific agreement for both countries. Mexico was already widely experienced in this matter.[4] By 2001 Mexico had become the eighth trade power in the world and the first in Latin America, and had managed to double its participation in the North American market, from 6.4 to 11.2 per cent between the years 1991 and 2000 (Secretaría de Economía 2004a).

In a context of economic slowdown in Mexico and Japan, an agreement of economic association offered an opportunity to improve their strategic position and competitiveness on the global markets. The negotiation process of the agreement was carried out in two stages.[5] In the first phase, the Ministry of Economy commissioned an independent study to evaluate the possibilities of strengthening its relations with Japan. The second stage presupposed the formation of a study group made up by the academic, governmental and business sectors of both countries, in order to analyse the viable alternatives for strengthening the relations between Mexico and Japan. This group met on seven occasions between July 2001 and July 2002. By that time the two ministries in charge of foreign and economic policy of Japan, the Ministry of Foreign Affairs (MoFA) and the Ministry of Economy, Trade and Industry (METI), had already come to the conclusion that it was convenient to promote the bilateral agreements.

Nevertheless, for the Ministry of Agriculture, Forestry and Fisheries (MAFF) the Mexican case presented greater problems with regard to the Singapore EPA, since Mexico enjoyed clear comparative advantages in the agricultural sector when compared to Japan. Initially, the MAFF proposal was to take the Singapore EPA as a model;[6] but for Mexico it was not a viable option due to the advantages the food and agriculture sector had when it came to penetrating the Japanese market. The Mexican stance was that the agreement should include all the sectors.

In addition, the Japanese transnational companies, which were already operating in North America, had to cope with competition from the regional companies when in 2001 the rules of the game changed; article 303 of NAFTA was set in motion, as was contemplated in the original trade agreement. According to the agreement, companies operating in the North American region would pay tariffs for the parts and components imported from outside the region, in this way losing the preferential treatment that they had under the *maquiladora* system.

The results found by the study group were presented in July 2002 (Secretaría de Economía 2002). First, the study indicated that the potential benefits of a strong relationship between Japan and Mexico had not been taken advantage of. It was emphasized that although the trade and investment between the two countries had increased in absolute terms, the relative weight of their economic relations had decreased. The relative importance of Japan as Mexico's partner had diminished. In this context, the study emphasized that, due to the relative abundance of natural resources and labour force in Mexico and of capital in Japan, the complementary nature of the two economies would contribute to the economic development of both countries:

a)   With the network of bilateral agreements that Mexico had, the strengthening of economic relations would be an important element in the Japanese companies' strategy for a greater international development in business.

b)   Japan is a very important FDI source and a great market for Mexican exports. Its investment flow and the transfer of technology would contribute to the growth of production, employment and competitiveness in Mexico.

c)   The strengthening of economic relations between the two countries would contribute to market diversification in Mexico.

d)   The economic ties between the two nations would allow both countries' competitive position in the context of global competition to be strengthened; it would reinforce the position of Japanese companies in Mexico and, at the same time, it would strengthen Mexico's competitive and geopolitical advantage by, among other things, reinforcing productive chains.

Another aspect about the benefits pointed out by the study is the high degree of development of Japanese technology, which, along with high levels of investment abroad, offers a magnificent opportunity for countries that, like Mexico, are seeking to attract foreign savings to complement the low levels of domestic savings. In sum, the opportunities pointed out in the agricultural sector and in the transference of technology were two aspects of the potential between Mexico and Japan that called for strengthening their economic relations.

In October 2002, after the Study Group presented its results and in the framework of the Asia Pacific Economic Cooperation Council (APEC) leaders meeting at Los Cabos, Mexico, President Fox and Prime Minister Koizumi agreed to start formal negotiations for an EPA. After two years of negotiations, in September 2004, both dignitaries signed the EPA in Mexico City. The Japanese Diet approved it in November of the same year and one month later the Mexican Senate did the same. The agreement came into force in April 2005 (Secretaría de Economía 2004b).

As with Singapore, the agreement signed by Japan and Mexico was a second-generation agreement, since it went beyond the liberalization of trade and investment when it included the area of cooperation. In general, the asymmetry in the economic development of the two countries was recognized in the EPA. Hence, Japan offered immediate access to 91 per cent of its tariff lines and Mexico did the same for 44 per cent. Mexico granted immediate access to high-tech products and inputs necessary for industry. For chemical, photographic and textile products the opening will come in 2010 and for those products that represent a greater competition for the national industry, the term for tax relief will be the year 2020 (Secretaría de Economía 2004b).

On the subject of investment, it was agreed to implement the principles of national treatment and the Most Favoured Nation (MFN). In bilateral cooperation, it is necessary to stress the agreements to promote the support industry in Mexico as well as the small and medium-sized companies, considering Japan's experience in this matter. Careful consideration was also given to cooperation in science and technology, education and labour training in tourism, the environment, agriculture and copyright.

With regard to the agricultural sector, Japan granted preferential access to 99.8 per cent of the tariff lines, whereas 0.2 per cent of the lines were not included; and even though the latter were reviewed in April 2009, no agreement was reached to liberalize them. In five products sensitive to Japan – pork meat, beef, chicken, orange juice and oranges – Mexico obtained access by means of quotas, which will be reviewed in 2010. On the other hand, Mexico achieved immediate liberalization in a number of food and agricultural products of interest for the country.

As to the results in the negotiations about the agricultural sector in the Mexico–Japan EPA, it is necessary to highlight that the MAFF finally made its original position of taking the Singapore Agreement as a model more flexible, and in the end the agricultural chapter was broader and more comprehensive in the EPA with Mexico. This was due to the internal pressure exerted by METI and MoFA with the Japanese foreign policy new orientation towards bilateral agreements and to the MAFF actions, which were influenced by international pressure before the commitments acquired by Japan at the WTO (which imply that trade agreements must be comprehensive and include all the sectors). This way, Mexico was able to obtain exclusive preferential treatment for most of its food and agriculture exports to Japan. It would now depend on Mexico to take advantage of this window of opportunity before other countries obtain similar profits through commercial agreements.

What will have been achieved after the Agreement has been in effect for three years? On the subject of trade, the flow has increased, and exports have done so at a more accelerated rate than imports. In fact, total trade increased by 30 per cent to a level of US$20 billion in 2008 (Table 7.8). On the one hand, imports continue to be impelled by the need of Japanese enterprises operating in Mexico to get parts and components from Japanese suppliers (Table 7.9). On the other hand, imports have been favoured by the gradual reduction of the Mexican average tariff rate (16 per cent) an impact that has been felt especially in the automotive sector. Currently with the EPA it is possible to import Japanese vehicles free of tariffs in a quantity equivalent to 5 per cent of the units sold on the Mexican market in the previous year. Moreover, the general tariff that was previously 50 per cent was diminished to 20–30 per cent (Ministry of Economy, Trade and Industry 2007). Enterprises like Isuzu, Hino Motors of Toyota Group and Mazda have taken advantage of this situation. Nowadays Japanese enterprises have one-third of the Mexican automotive market (Secretaría de Economía 2004b).

On the export side, sales to Japan increased in the post-agreement period by 48 per cent to a level, in 2008, of US$3.9 billion (Table 7.10). On the positive side, the diversification of main products exported to Japan is evident. Manufactured goods now constitute 30 per cent of main products exported, especially parts and components of the automotive industry, which denotes the more intensified intra-industry trade. Agro-food products have also made an important inroad in the Japanese market (Table 7.11). On the negative side, the free quotas of tariff in textiles, footwear and agricultural products have not been fully used. In accordance with the JETRO–México information in the period between April 2006 and March 2007 (that corresponds to the Japanese fiscal year) in the following products, only partial use of the quotas was made (the percentages of use are indicated in parentheses): footwear (35), pork (56), beef (20), bananas (30), frozen orange juice (64) and natural honey (3). Even more serious, results showed that in the following products quotas were not even requested: garments, chicken, fresh orange juice, tomato juice, tomato sauce and paste, sorbitol and dextrin. No doubt, this is the result of a lack of promotion of what has been achieved with the Agreement, a lack of knowledge of the Japanese market on the part of the Mexican exporters and the lack of a policy that facilitates the benefits obtained with the EPAs that Mexico has signed.

With regard to the Japanese FDI, upon receiving national treatment just like its American and European counterparts, it has exhibited a boost since 2005, particularly in the automotive sector, since the North American market is attractive for Japanese companies. According to the daily reports of the Representative Office of the Ministry of Economy, Trade and Industry in Japan, between 2005 and 2008, 42 Japanese companies announced a US\$3.5 billion planned investment, most of it directed to the automotive and electronic sectors.

Finally, in the field of cooperation, JETRO has been working actively with the Ministry of Economy to promote support programmes for the Mexican PYMES supplying Japanese transnational companies in the automobile sector. Within the framework of the Agreement, the Committee for Improving the Business Atmosphere was established, which meets every year. The Japanese party has proposed an agenda that includes an improvement in safety, protection of copyright and progress in the transportation infrastructure, to which the Mexican government has responded favourably.

In conclusion, Mexico's strategy towards strengthening economic relations with Japan came late during the second phase of bilateral liberalization. Notwithstanding, the EPA is a powerful instrument to deepen those relations for the benefit of the people of both nations.

Mexico–China

Chinese–Mexican trade: a trajectory of competition

While most of the South American countries have benefited from the Chinese boom through the export of commodities, the case of Mexico differs substantially. Mexico was one of the first Latin American countries to establish diplomatic relations with the People's Republic of China, in 1972. Initially, the relationship was much more political and cultural than economic. At that point, the search for alternative positions in the Cold War environment and their supportive attitude towards the so-called 'Third World' were the main binding factors between the two countries. In the 1980s, China backed up Mexican attempts to reach a negotiated agreement to the Central American conflict via the Contadora Group, while Mexico refrained from having diplomatic relations with Taiwan, tacitly supporting the 'one China' policy. In the last 15 years, the emphasis of the relationship took a notable turn from culture and politics towards economic affairs.

Mexico has become the second trading partner of the People's Republic of China in Latin America, while China has rapidly transformed as Mexico's top trading partner from Asia, surpassing even Japan, which had held this position until 2002. In spite of this dynamism, the relationship is characterized by a remarkable trade imbalance where Mexico has a considerable and continued deficit. According to Table 7.8, Mexico's total trade with China climbed from US$511 million in 1993 to US$3.36 billion in 2000 to US$36.8 billion in 2008. Notwithstanding this impressive performance, the lion's share of trade benefits China. The export-import ratio for Mexico is 1 to 15.5. It is true, however, that an important part of Mexico's exports to China go through Panama or the United States. This is why they appear statistically as transactions with those countries, and not with the People's Republic of China (PRC).

The economic discrepancies between China and Mexico are natural. Unlike the Japanese case, China and Mexico are not complementary economies. Instead, they participate in world markets with a similar offer. Mexico sends to China integrated circuits, beer, mechanical implements, copper, leather and furs, cellulose and paper. It imports computer equipment, telephony, photography and video. As opposed to South America, it is worth noting the scarce participation of agri-cultural products and raw materials in the bilateral trade.

China and Mexico are indeed competing in the sectors of intermediate and light manufactured goods. It is predictable that this concurrence will subsist both in the bilateral relationship and in the US market because of the progressive maturation of the Chinese economy. In past years the bulk of Chinese exports was agricultural products and low-technology manufactured goods, but as time has passed, China's exports feature increasing added value. In 1990, 51.9 per cent of Chinese exports to the world took place in the low technological density sector, and only 13 per cent in the high technology sectors. By 2000 China went from 0.7 per cent to 4.1 per cent of high technology exports in the world (Lall and Albadalejo 2003). And in 2006 China's exports of high technology manufactured goods represented 37 per cent of China's total exports (Table 7.6).

The coming years will witness a growing competitiveness of China in sectors like computers, precision machinery, electronics, cars and petrochemical products. If this trend remains, it is predictable that China will continue to displace not only Mexican exports, but also those of countries like South Korea, which have been greatly benefited by China's economic boom (León-Manríquez 2005).

Another conflict is added to the problem of trade imbalance. In recent years there has been a plethora of complaints from Mexican business groups regarding the smuggling of Chinese products that are easily distributed through the huge networks of informal trade in Mexico. These illegal imports affect many sectors of the country's production system. According to these business groups, more than half the clothing and shoes consumed in the country are made in China. These goods include pyjamas, trousers and footwear. A particular concern is that competition with China takes place precisely in labour-intensive manufacturing sectors – a fact that would have contributed to the loss of almost one million jobs in Mexico since 2000.

The business community, as well as the bulk of Mexican public opinion, is vocal about their concerns that China has begun to export to Mexico indigenous handicrafts that were previously elaborated within Mexico, and even religious figures such as the Virgin of Guadalupe (Martínez 2003). The unequal trade relationship has also provoked trade tensions: of the 24 antidumping procedures that The People's Republic of China (PRC) had faced up to September 2005, 40 per cent had been set by Mexico. At the same time, China had 26 compensatory charges in effect in Mexico (Reforma 2005).

Chinese competitiveness in the US market: another source of conflict

Besides the Mexican trade deficit, there are tensions that result from competition in third countries' markets. For example, Mexican exports in the US market began to diminish steadily in 2002, while those from China grew rapidly, thus displacing Mexico as the second highest exporter to the US. In July 2005, exports from the PRC to the US also surpassed those of the leading country at that point: Canada. In the case of Mexico, 12 out of the 20 main exports are in open competition with Chinese products. Key among them are textiles, cotton products, industrial machinery, televisions and video recorders. According to a short-term study made by the National Bank of Mexico, in the January–May period of 2005, the five main Mexican branches and products of export to the US suffered losses of its share in that market. With the same products, China increased its exports 155 per cent, and gained the market share in all of them. In the case of clothing and shoes, Chinese sales in the US grew almost 33 per cent, while those from Mexico shrank 4 per cent. In the automotive sector, one of the most competitive, Mexico lost 6.3 per cent of its exports, while China's grew 155.9 per cent (Banamex 2005).

Given this situation, it is not surprising that Mexico was very reluctant about the incorporation of the PRC to the World Trade Organization (WTO) and was the last country to sign the bilateral treaties necessary for the incorporation of China to this multilateral organism. Once more, and contrary to the South American countries, Mexico has repeatedly refused to recognize China as a market economy. Mexico argues that, while China is a centrally planned economy, it is impossible to hand over the blank cheque that would mean acknowledging such a trait. Mexico also fears that low wages in China might accelerate a process of diversion of foreign direct investment (FDI). In case this was not enough, in the last few years, the strictly diplomatic relationship, previously characterized by its cordiality, has experienced different incidents that have somehow strained it.

Notwithstanding such tensions, room for cooperation is still open, especially through the reciprocal visits from high-level officers. Thus, Prime Minister Wen Jiabao visited Mexico in December 2003 when an agreement was reached to create the Binational Mexico–China Commission (CBMC). Through this mechanism, whose meetings have been taking place every 18 months, the objective is to build an institutional space in which to strengthen cooperation and repair disagreements in the bilateral relationship. This is a similar instance to that which was established between Mexico and the US in the 1990s in order to mend the most conflictive effects of their relationship and promote closer cooperation.

Lately, and particularly due to the State visit of President Hu Jintao to Mexico in September 2005, the Mexican part has sought to push the concept of 'strategic association', which would allow both countries to reach alliances to increase the bonds between Chinese and Mexican business communities. Additionally, the Mexican discourse has somehow changed, and China is starting to be seen as a potential source of investment in Mexico as well as a potential ally in the conquest of other countries' markets. So far, China's FDI in Mexico has been meagre (Tables 7.2 and 7.3), although China's outward investment has increased from an average of US$2 billion in the 1990s to US$22 billion in 2007 (Table 7.12).

For China, the attraction of Mexico not only dwells in the size of its inner market, but, as we have shown, in its proximity with the United States, the highest quality market in the world. Notwithstanding the mutual interest to repair the relationship, the subscription of a Free Trade Agreement (FTA) between the two countries, which was considered a possibility a few years ago, appears now to be quite remote. This is because of trade tensions and the negative vision that a good part of the business community and Mexican society in general have of China.

Mexico–Korea

From increasing trade to a frustrated FTA

The upsurge of trade and investment between Mexico and the Republic of Korea has to do with market factors, as well as strategies of diversification in both countries. Let us analyse first the Korean case. In the 1960s and 1970s, during the swift expansion of Korean exports, South Korean strategists defined big markets, chiefly Japan and the United Sates, as their main targets. Although successful, by the early 1970s this strategy was generating serious concern among policymakers; they feared that the increasing concentration of Korean trade with these two partners could reduce any room for manoeuvre in case of external shocks. This potential risk made trade-diversification an urgent goal for both Korean officers and businessmen. The high degree of collaboration between them paved the road for the design and implementation of a common strategy.

Korea's diversification efforts in the 1970s were mostly oriented towards Europe, the Middle East and Southeast Asia's markets. The diversification policy was a sound accomplishment, as long as Korea expanded its exports to the European Economic Community from 3 to 16 per cent of total exports between

1970 and 1979. The share of exports to developing countries rose from 13 per cent to 25 per cent for the same period, and the dependence of American and Japanese markets was sharply (although not completely) reduced (Haggard and Moon 1983: 165). Since the 1980s Africa and Latin America would become major targets for Korean exports. As a matter of fact, Latin America had emerged as the most dynamic trade partner for Korea before the East Asian economic crisis. As a pointer of the increasing relevance of Latin America for Korea, in 1996 President Kim Young-Sam undertook the first trip of a Korean president throughout the region (Kim 1996; Kwack 2004).

Not surprisingly, trade with Mexico grew rapidly from the early 1990s, thus becoming a cornerstone of the bilateral relationship. On the Mexican side, the initiation of NAFTA in 1994 further encouraged Korean trade and FDI. Although Mexican policymakers foresaw increasing FDI thanks to NAFTA, this treaty entailed, at least initially, a discriminatory treatment for third countries. As in the case of Japan, concerns about losing competitiveness in the US markets was one of the main factors that led Korean firms to open facilities in Mexico. In turn, these companies, which usually carry out intra-firm trade, boosted trade, mostly through the imports of industrial components from the Republic of Korea (ROK).

As can be seen on Table 7.8, total trade between Mexico and the ROK rose from US$955 million in 1993 to US$4.06 billion in 2000, to US$14.13 billion in 2008. Trade balance was favourable to Mexico until 1987, but the tables turned in 1988. Since then, Mexico's trade deficit with Korea has been soaring. In 2008, for instance, for every dollar that Mexico exported to Korea, it imported 25. While the main Mexican exports to Korea are mostly minerals such as copper and zinc, its main imports are parts and accessories for mechanical machinery and electric and electronic equipment. The bulk of these components is employed in the assembling process of articles which, once finished, are exported to other countries. As the report of the Mexico–Korea 21st Century Commission (MK21CC) states, 'an increase in Korea's investment in Mexico concomitantly brings increases in imports while boosting Mexico's overall export performance' (MK21CC 2005: 54). In sum, in the case of Mexico and South Korea, the link between FDI and increasing trade resembles pretty much the case of Japan, addressed earlier in this chapter.

Having in mind the dynamism of trade and investment, the ROK and Mexico agreed, in 2002, to explore the possibilities of signing a FTA. The timing seemed highly propitious for this initiative. On the Korean side, the intention coincided with the views of the most internationalized sectors of government, business and academia. It is worth remembering that, since the end of the Cold War, these sectors had been pushing for a more assertive participation of the ROK in the increasingly liberal order. Although they reckoned that South Korea was a tiny country from a territorial viewpoint, they also argued that the country had become a major player in the international economy. This way of thinking is epitomized by the words of a well-known scholar and former Minister of Finance, who argued: 'A critical new challenge for Korea is reconciling demands for responsibility-sharing with domestic particular resistance to market opening and sensitivities to necessary but difficult structural adjustments in agriculture and finance' (Sakong 1993: 145).

The juncture for deepening this project would come with the onset of the Asian economic crisis in 1997. Besides a comprehensive restructuring of the bureaucratic apparatus and the attempt to reduce the power of *chaebols* (South Korean big industrial conglomerates) in the domestic market, Korea's response to such a crisis entailed further economic openness, a welcoming attitude towards FDI, and an explicit desire to take advantage of globalization's opportunities. In the Korean view, free trade agreements became a powerful tool with which to carry on this endeavour. Like the rest of the East Asian countries, Seoul had been reluctant to embrace the FTAs fever that had swept over Latin America and many other developing areas in the early 1990s. This defensive position of the ROK underwent a radical transformation in the current decade, as dozens of FTAs are under negotiation or have been concluded in Asia Pacific and the Pacific Rim.

Fearing that South Korea could become a sort of 'international orphan' if it did not sign FTAs, both businessmen and officers in the Korean bureaucracy began looking for potential trade partners. This mindset is embodied, among others, in Chung Hae-kwan, a top officer of the Ministry of Foreign Affairs and Trade (MOFAT). Chung has pointed out that 'the pursuit of FTAs is not a matter of choice for Korea, but rather a necessity for future economic growth' (*Bridges Weekly* 2004). In accordance with this view, in April 2004, a FTA Chile–South Korea took effect, after three delays in its ratification process due to the protests of Korean farmers. This was both the first FTA that the ROK entered into and the first transpacific FTA. After the FTA with Chile, the ROK has signed further treaties with Singapore, the Association of Southeast Asian Nations (ASEAN) excluding Thailand, and the European Free Trade Association (EFTA). On 30 June 2007 the Korea–United States FTA (KORUS–FTA) was signed, thus becoming the largest FTA for the US since NAFTA.

In the case of Mexico, interest in FTAs started since the early 1990s, with the negotiation of NAFTA. Pressed by the imperatives of diversifying foreign trade and paying service to their pro-free trade ideology, by April 2005 Mexican policymakers had managed to enforce 12 FTAs with 43 countries. What has stopped, then, the negotiation of an FTA with Korea? The explanation is to be found in Mexico's internal factors. First of all, the administration of Vicente Fox (2000–6) was very cautious in signing new FTAs, and decreed a moratorium of FTA negotiations, with the exception of the Free Trade Areas of the Americas and Japan.

It is very likely that the scepticism of the government towards new FTAs has a lot to do with increasing doubts of Mexican public opinion about free trade instruments. While Mexican public opinion was pretty confident in the benefits of FTAs in the early 1990s, it has become somewhat sceptical on this subject. For instance, 52 per cent of those interviewed in a recent opinion poll believe that the country should re-negotiate the agriculture chapter of NAFTA, even if this move affects other achievements of the treaty. Regarding other trade treaties, 53 per cent of Mexicans think that the country should stop the negotiation of new FTAs, wanting to take advantage of those pacts already signed (CIDE/COMEXI 2006: 53–4). In the specific case of the FTA with Korea, the Mexican private sector has exerted intense pressures on the government for not signing a FTA. Hence, the scenario of a Mexico–Korea FTA remains highly difficult, albeit not impossible.

The FDI connection

In any case, the future of the economic link between both countries still looks robust. One of the main reasons for this relative optimism has to do with the dynamics of foreign direct investment (FDI). Mexican flow to Korea is virtually nonexistent. Conversely, Korean investments in Mexico rose since the early 1990s, moving from a total accumulated of US$12.4 million in 1993 to US$816 million in 2008 (Tables 7.2, 7.3 and 7.4). However, in the last few years there has been a process of diminishing investments in Mexico (MK21CC 2005: 56–7).

What are the reasons for the sprouting Korean investment? The change of the Mexican economic model from Import Substitution Industrialization (ISI) to a strategy based on export promotion, started by the mid-1980s, also meant decreasing barriers for FDI. As we have argued before, this trend reached a turning point with the beginning of NAFTA. At the same time, the maturation of Korea's economy, the assertiveness of some conglomerates and the liberalization of regulations for FDI facilitated an increasing flow of investments abroad (Table 7.12). Although Korean firms had previously invested in Southeast Asia and the Middle East, these investments were still relatively meagre. After 1986 Korean FDI underwent a two-digit increase and a diversification of targeted countries. By the early 1990s, Korean investments in manufacturing were mostly settled in North America and Southeast Asia, but were swiftly expanding to Latin America (Sakong 1993: 151).

The presence of South Korean investments in Mexico can be understood in this broader context. In 1988 Samsung established a TV assembling plant in the city of Tijuana, while other firms such as LG and Daewoo began showing a keen interest to invest in Central and Northern Mexico. With these moves, South Korean firms were seeking, on the one hand, to take advantage of the geographical proximity of Mexico to the United States. On the other hand, Korea had been losing its initial comparative advantage in low-wage labour; thus, investing in Mexican labour-intensive manufacturing sectors, where wages were relatively lower, allowed both *chaebols* and medium-sized firms to reduce their costs of production.

As can be seen on Table 7.3, the bulk of Korean investments in Mexico have taken place in manufacturing and commerce. In the current decade, however, Korean companies have been more reluctant to invest in Mexico. According to the UN Economic Commission for Latin America and the Caribbean (ECLAC 2006: Ch. 3) the explanations of this behaviour could be, among others, the diversion of Korean investment to China; the reluctance of Korean firms to transform their Mexican assembly plants into manufacturing centres; and the hesitancy of automobile firms such as Hyundai to establish facilities in Mexico. It remains to be seen whether the negotiation of KORUS–FTA will further erode Korean investment in Mexico, as long as Korean companies might ensure a direct access to the US market. Or it may be that Korean subsidiaries in the US take the same path as their Japanese counterparts and take advantage of the clusters in electronics and automotive sectors already established at Mexican border states. In that case, Korean FDI in Mexico may show an upsurge.

Conclusions

Although usually neglected by Mexican media and academia, economic relations between Mexico and East Asia have undergone a spectacular growth in the last decade. Undoubtedly, the initiation of NAFTA also meant an increased interest of East Asian firms to invest in Mexico, in order to take advantage of the Mexican access to the US market. In the case of Japan and Korea, increasing FDI in Mexico brought further trade via imports. In the case of China, plenty of consumer goods and inputs for export industries have been brought from the RPC. For Mexico's exports, NAFTA has meant an unprecedented degree of concentration in the US market. On the side of imports, however, the increasing presence of East Asian manufactured goods in Mexico has assisted the diversification of the Mexican economy. While not necessarily the outcome of an explicit strategy of diversification, the increasing presence of East Asian trade and investments in Mexico has somehow relieved Mexican dependence on US imports. In a broader sense, Japan, China and South Korea have become more and more intertwined with the North American market. In this sense it would not be an exaggeration to state that East Asia has become a sort of 'NAFTAS's 4th partner'.

Another common feature of the Mexican relations with Japan, China and the ROK is the weak penetration of Mexican goods in these markets; Mexican exports to them might grow in absolute terms, but are either stagnant or decreasing in relative terms. While each case has its own specificity, the weakness of Mexican exports to East Asia has its roots in at least a couple of factors. On the one hand, the enlarged access of Mexican goods to the US and Canada has encouraged a concomitant specialization of exports in North American markets. On the other hand, Mexican enthusiasm for free trade has not been accompanied by industrial or strategic trade policies. Mexico's public policies have been limited to reduce barriers for imports and to negotiating several FTAs (including agreements with such attractive economies such as the US, the European Union and Japan), but has not sought to generate a greater exportable offer through incentives to productive agents.

In this sense, Mexico would need a rigorous detection of those market niches that, in current conditions, could be open to Mexican products in East Asia. Once this task is carried out, the government should disseminate this information among Mexican businesses (especially small and medium enterprises) and provide infrastructure as well as tax breaks and credit incentives for those national producers willing to explore East Asian markets. The Mexican failure to take further advantage of its trade agreement with Japan is just an indicator of the limits of its current strategy for foreign trade. It seems clear that Mexican producers in the agricultural sector would have plenty of opportunities to benefit from East Asia.

Acknowledgement

The authors wish to thank Laura Navarro for her support in preparing the statistical data included in this chapter.

Notes

1 In the case of Mexico's exports to Asia, the figures that we use were reported by the Asian source, since the official numbers reported by Mexico do not include the exports that are sent to Asia through North American harbours and they are therefore undervalued.
2 Between 1993 and 2006 Mexican exports of food products to the world went from 3,964 to 13,921 million dollars, most of it (95 per cent) towards the United States of America (Falck 2006).
3 Nissan Mexicana (11), Matsushita TV (15), Sony Tijuana (24), Alcoa Fujikura (31), Pims (Mitsubishi) (44), Sony de Mexicali (45), Hitachi Consumer Products (61), JVC Industrial (66), Sharp Electronica (67), Sony Nuevo Laredo (74), Honda de México (88), Toshiba Eletromex (96) and Sanyo Energy (100). The number in parenthesis indicates the place occupied by the company (JETRO–México 2004).
4 This is the format used by the Mexican government in the agreements' most recent negotiations.
5 By that time, the Ministry of Agriculture, Forestry and Fisheries (MAFF) had yet not defined its position with respect to the agricultural sector in the framework of the EPA negotiations. It was not until November 2004 when it established its strategy regarding the Asian Agreements (MAFF 2004).
6 Mexico obtained a footwear duty quota of 250,000 pairs the first year, with a 20 per cent yearly increase until reaching an unlimited access in the tenth year. In garments – another important sector for Mexico – its market access was US$200,000 duty free and immediate regional access to thread and fabric.

References

Almaraz, Araceli (2007) 'La relevancia económica y el perfil de las maquiladoras electrónicas y de autopartes en tres ciudades del norte deMéxico (1990–2003)', in Carrillo, Jorge and Barajas, María del Rosio, eds, *Maquiladoras fronterizas. Evolución y heterogeneidad en los sectores electrónico y automotriz*, Mexico: El Colegio de la Frontera Norte and Miguel Angel Porrua, Ch. 2.
Bailey, David (2003) 'Explaining Japan's Kudoka [hollowing out]: A Case of Government and Strategic Failure', in *Asia Pacific Business Review*, vol. 10, no. 1, autumn.
Banamex (Banco Nacional de México) (2005) *Examen de la situación económica de México*, vol. LXXXI, no. 954, August.
Banco de México *Informe Annual*, Several years.
—— *Estadísticas*. Available online at www.banxico.org.mx/tipo/estadisticas/index.html
Bridges Weekly (2004) 'Chile–South Korea FTA in Force Despite Korean Concerns', in *Bridges Weekly Trade News Digest*, vol. 8, no. 13, 8 April.
CEPAL: International Commerce and Integration Division. Available online at www.cepal.org/comercio
Carrillo, Jorge and Barajas, María del Rosio, eds, (2007) *Maquiladoras fronterizas. Evolución y heterogeneidad en los sectores electrónico y automotriz*, Mexico: El Colegio de la Frontera Norte and Miguel Angel Porrua.

—— and Gomis, Redi (2007) 'La maquila evoluciona? Podrá evolucionar en el contexto?', in Carrillo, Jorge and Barajas, María del Rosio, eds, *Maquiladoras fronterizas. Evolución y heterogeneidad en los sectores electrónico y automotriz*, Mexico: El Colegio de la Frontera Norte and Miguel Angel Porrua, Ch. 1.

—— and Hualde, Alfredo (2007) 'Presente y futuro de la manufactura de televisores en la frontera norte de México: de la tecnología análoga a la digital', in Carrillo, Jorge and Barajas, María del Rosio, eds, *Maquiladoras fronterizas. Evolución y heterogeneidad en los sectores electrónico y automotriz*, Mexico: El Colegio de la Frontera Norte and Miguel Angel Porrua, Ch. 3.

Chiquiar, Daniel (2004) 'Globalization, Regional Wage Differentials and the Stolper-Samuelson Theorem: Evidence from Mexico', Working Paper No. 2004–06, Mexico: Banco de Mexico.

Chiquiar, Daniel, Fragoso, Edna and Ramos-Francia, Manuel (2007) 'La Ventaja Comparativa y el Desempeño de las Exportaciones Manufactureras Mexicanas en el Periodo 1996–2005', Working Papers no. 12, México: Banco de México.

CIDE/COMEXI (Centro de Investigación y Docencia Económicas/ Consejo Mexicano de Asuntos Internacionales) (2006) *México y el mundo 2006*, Mexico City: CIDE/COMEXI. Available at http://mexicoyelmundo.cide.edu

Dussel Peters, Enrique (Coordinator) (2007) *La Inversión Extranjera Directa en México: Desempeño y Potencial. Una perspectiva macro, meso, micro y territorial*, México: Siglo XXI Editores, UNAM, Secretaría de Economía.

ECLAC (Economic Commisssion for Latin America and the Caribbean) (2006) *Foreign Investment in Latin America*, Santiago: ECLAC.

Falck, Melba (2006) *Del proteccionismo a la liberalización agrícola en Japón, Corea del Sur y Taiwan. Oportunidades para México. Un enfoque de economía política*, México, D.F.: Instituto Matías Romero.

Haggard, Stephan and Chung-In Moon (1983) 'The South Korean State in the International Economy: liberal, dependent or mercantile?', in John G. Ruggie, ed., *The Antinomies of Interdependence: National Welfare and the International Division of Labor*, New York: Columbia University Press.

Ibarra, David (2005) *Ensayos sobre Economía Mexicana*, México: Fondo de Cultura Económica.

JETRO–México (2006) 'Relaciones Económicas México–Japón', Mexico City: JETRO.

—— (2004) 'Relaciones Económicas México–Japón', Mexico City: JETRO.

Kim, Won-Ho (1996) 'Korean–Latin American Relations: Trends and Prospects', in *Asian Journal of Latin American Studies*, Special Issue.

Kingston, Jeff (2004) *Japan's Quiet Transformation. Social Change and Civil Society in the Twenty-first Century*, New York: Routledge Curzon.

Krauss, Ellis S. (2003) 'The US, Japan, and trade liberalization: from bilateralism to regional multilateralism to regionalism', in *The Pacific Review*, vol. 16, no. 3, Routledge.

Kwack, Jae-Sung (2004) 'Galvanizing Inter-Pacific Relations: Korea's Role in Asia–Latin American Cooperation', in *East Asian Review*, vol. 16, no. 4, Winter.

Lall, Sanjaya and Manuel Albadalejo (2003) 'China's Competitive Performance: A Threat to East Asian Manufactured Exports?', in *QEH Working Papers Series*, no. 110, October, University of Oxford.

León-Manríquez, José Luis (2005) 'China y Corea del Sur: ¿amistad, competencia o hegemonía?', in José Luis Estrada, José Luis León and Ricardo Buzo, eds, *China en el siglo XXI, Economía, política y sociedad de una potencia emergente*, Mexico City: Universidad Autónoma Metropolitana-Miguel Ángel Porrúa.

Martínez, Mariana (2003) 'China gana la pulseada a México', in *BBCMundo*, 31 December.

Ministry of Economy, Trade and Industry (METI) (2007) *White Paper on International Economy and Trade. Japan*, Tokyo: Ministry of Economy, Trade and Industry.

Ministry of Agriculture, Forestry and Fisheries (MAFF) (2004) 'Annual Report on Food, Agriculture and Rural Areas in Japan, FY 2004', Tokyo: MAFF. Available at www. maff.go.jp/e/index.html

MK21CC (Mexico–Korea 21st Century Commission) (2005) *Building a Strategic Partnership between Mexico and Korea for the 21st Century*, Mexico City: Secretaría de Relaciones Exteriores.

Moreno-Brid, Juan Carlos, Rivas Valdivia, Juan Carlos and Santamaría, Jesús (2005) 'Mexico: Economic growth, exports and industrial performance after NAFTA', *Serie Estudios y Perspectivas 42*, México: CEPAL.

OECD (2007) *Estudios Económicos de la OCDE. México*, México: OCDE-edebé.

OMC (2004) *Examen de Políticas Comerciales, Japón*, 17 December.

Reforma (2005) 'Critican política comercial mexicana.' In *Reforma*, Mexico City, 13 September.

Sakong, Il (1993) *Korea in the World Economy*, Washington, DC: Institute for International Economics.

Secretaría de Economía (2004a) 'México: negociaciones comerciales internacionales', México City: Secretaría de Economía, May.

—— (2004b) *Acuerdo para el Fortalecimiento de la Asociación Económica México–Japón*, Mexico, Mexico City: Secretaría de Economía.

—— (2002) *Japan–Mexico Joint Study Group on the Strengthening of Bilateral Economic Relations, Final Report*, Mexico and Japan, Mexico City: Secretaría de Economía, July.

—— Estadísticas de Comercio e Inversión. Available at http://www.economia.gob.mx

World Bank, 'World Development Indicators database'. Available online at web.world bank.org

UNCTAD (2006) *World Investment Report 2006*. Available at http://www.unctad.org/ en//docs/wir2006_en.pdf (accessed 1 March 2008).

—— (2008) *World Investment Report 2008*, Transnational Corporations and the Infrastructure Challenge. Available at http://www.unctad.org/en/docs/wir2008en.pdf

8   Peru and Chile

The challenge of playing a determinant role in multilateral Pacific fora

Olaf Jacob

In 2008, Peru, a small actor on the international scene, hosted two major international meetings that placed the country for at least two or three days at the top of the international agenda.[1] These events also represented a unique opportunity to show the world the economic development that has taken place in Peru in the last ten years and it offered the country the chance to boost its tourism-related industry as well, especially towards Asia.

However, independent of the media impact and the surely interesting indirect positive inputs for tourism and economy: Has the Asia Pacific Economic Cooperation Forum (APEC) CEO Summit, regardless of the worldwide short-term media interest towards Peru, offered a possibility to guarantee a sustained economic development? Has the APEC CEO Summit represented a chance to deepen or widen the commercial ties with its partners in the Pacific Community?

What role does APEC really play today and what is the perception of APEC in Peru, in Chile and in other Latin American member economies and candidates for full APEC membership? What are the challenges and objectives of Chile and especially Peru vis-à-vis APEC during the next ten years? Are most Latin American countries following an articulated and logically well-designed policy towards Pacific Asia? Are Chile, Peru and also Mexico following the same, common interest vis-à-vis their Asian partners and are their policies towards Asia coordinated?

This chapter discusses the aspirations of Latin American countries, especially Peru, participating in Pacific multilateral fora, exploring their visions regarding the development of transpacific cooperation and, on the other hand, analysing the content behind the façades of governmental institutions and numerous enthusiastic speeches of governmental and business representatives.

The situation of weak 'brain power'

In 2006, two years before the APEC CEO Summit in Peru, neither the Peruvian Foreign Ministry through the Sub-Secretariat 'Asia Pacific' nor the Diplomatic Academy or the Ministry of Foreign Trade and Commerce or any other governmental institution had issued or presented a plan for the organization of the Summit (only ephemeral statements were given regarding the possible agenda that should include the possible candidature of some Latin American economies to full membership in APEC). This diffident behaviour by the representatives of the Peruvian government changed abruptly at the end of 2007, one year before the APEC CEO Summit in Lima. In an effort to generate general interest in APEC, the few Peruvian representatives in politics, media and from the academic and business communities that are related with Asian Pacific matters, began the challenge of creating interest in civil society and the general public about the possible advantages for Peru in deepening and widening economic and commercial relations with the region.[2]

However, civil society and most members of business associations still have minimal knowledge about Asia and APEC. A survey carried out in 2007 by Peru's leading economic consultancy 'Grupo Apoyo' showed that 92 per cent of all Peruvians did not even know what APEC meant.[3] This hardly seemed to contrast with the real interest of the civil society and representatives of the business sector vis-à-vis the Pacific Asian region. Most Peruvian and Latin American newspapers and business reviews inform their audiences regularly in detailed articles and abstracts about the possibilities and opportunities regarding trade with the countries of East Asia, especially the People's Republic of China.[4] TV programmes and newspapers (especially business magazines) present Asia as an interesting market for Latin American exports, and students in most of the prestigious universities and institutes show a real interest in learning about the region (language institutes teaching Mandarin Chinese are crowded, the seminars of 'Asian economy' and 'Asian development paradigm' are always well booked).

This general interest contrasts with an inability to satisfy the enormous demand for information about Pacific Asia. Peruvian public and private universities have few or sometimes no specialized, Asia-related literature and the academic exchange programmes seldom include universities in Pacific Asia. Any source of knowledge given to students is usually based on the literature that the professor, teacher or lecturer can offer from their personal private library. This situation can be explained as the result of the fact that the academic, political, economic and social interest of Latin America towards East Asia is quite new. Independent of historical ties between the two regions, with a tradition of more than 250 years,[5] it is only since the late 1980s and the early 1990s that a group of Latin American scholars began publishing papers on the possibility of cooperation between Pacific Asia and Latin America (Beckinschtein and Maizal 1994, Orrego Vicuña 1989, Torres 1992). Most of these publications did not aim at any deep investigation of the ties and possible commercial, political, social and cultural links between Pacific Asia and Latin America. The main intention of those early academic contributions was to present an institutional approach to the structure of Pacific Asian institutions related to subregional and transnational cooperation.

A similar situation exists regarding governmental and business institutions. Due to a lack of knowledge, information is often not available. The quality of speeches and reports published by most of the experts in governmental and business associations related to Pacific Asia show an extreme enthusiasm but also a lack of quality, facts and figures.

On the one hand, countries such as Peru (a full member of APEC since 1998) and Ecuador and Colombia (members of the Pacific Economic Cooperation Council (PECC) and the Pacific Basin Economic Council (PBEC)) that are considering becoming candidates for a full APEC membership after the end of the moratorium in 2010, show an increasing interest in Pacific Asia. This is reflected by the quantity of articles and essays published in the local media. On the other hand, there is a lack of 'brain power' to respond to the new challenges regarding the increase of interest vis-à-vis Pacific Asia. This knowledge and 'brain power' is concentrated in just a handful of highly specialized business and trade experts and academics who do not have the infrastructure and capability to satisfy the demands of the civil society regarding Pacific matters. Manfred Wilhelmy and Stefanie Mann (2005: 33–4) have described this group of pioneers as 'pathfinders'. They play a crucial role, creating interest in the media and attracting interest towards the Asia Pacific region. With a minimum of available information, these 'path-finders' represent their countries in Trans Pacific fora, teach at universities and deal with their business and trade partners in Pacific Asia. Many of them have Asian heritage – it is not a coincidence that Peru's main negotiators of the Ministry of Foreign Trade and Commerce regarding the Free Trade Agreements (FTAs) with Thailand, Singapore, the People's Republic of China, the Republic of Korea and in the near future with Japan were Mr Chang and Mr Kuriyama. These experts know each other well and share information and knowledge. Overall, however, the Latin American 'brain power' in Asian–Pacific political, economical, social and cultural affairs lack 'critical mass' (Wilhelmy 2002: 6–7).

The situation in Chile and Mexico is slightly different. In 1994, Chile founded the 'Fundación Chilena del Pacífico', a coordination platform for Chilean interests in the Pacific region that involves not only governmental institutions but also the business and academic sector (Gutiérrez 2005: 88). Six years earlier, in 1988, Mexico created the 'Mexican Commission for the Pacific', a pioneer organization in Latin America that was surely the inspiration for the Chilean 'Fundación' (Faust and Franke 2005: 101).

These facts led to the conclusion that the governments, media, academia and business sectors of the smaller Pacific countries in Latin America (Colombia, Ecuador and Peru) are increasingly turning their attention towards Pacific Asia but East Asia has still not been included under the top topics of the agenda, neither in business, nor in governmental issues or business relations. The APEC CEO meeting in Lima has boosted interest in the Pacific Asian region. However, while the Summit has been described as Peru's most important event since independence from Spain in 1821, it is not clear whether the event will have long-term positive effects on areas beyond merely pragmatic commercial ties.[6] There might be an articulated interest in the development of the relationship, but there is a gap between the desire to increase and deepen the links and the capacity and infrastructure for this challenge.

Multilateralism: The magic key to bilateralism? The role of foreign commerce

There are three main questions that should be answered in order to understand the motivations of Latin American countries in making the enormous effort to become part of a Trans-Pacific network of economies, connected to each other via Free Trade Agreements. Those three main questions are:

- What do Latin American member economies try to achieve when they articulate interest in being a part of the Trans-Pacific community?
- Do they follow neo-realist thoughts, trying to balance the power and influence of the hegemon in North America?
- Or do they look for complementary and compatible economies in Pacific Asia, following simply a purely pragmatic strategy?

For most of the Latin American economies the US market is still the main partner of business and trade. All three Latin American APEC member economies, Mexico, Chile and Peru, have signed Free Trade Agreements (FTAs) with the United States. According to the Economic Commission for Latin America (CEPAL), Chile's top export market during 2006 was the United States with US$8.947 billion (16.01 per cent of total exports), followed by Japan in second place with US$6.038 billion (10.81 per cent of total exports) and China in third place with US$4.942 billion (8.84 per cent of total exports). In fifth place was the Republic of Korea with US$3.405 billion (6.09 per cent of total exports). In 2006, Chile imported mainly from Argentina. The USA ranked in second place (US$4.708 billion, 15.77 per cent of total imports), China in fourth (US$2.540 billion, 8.51 per cent of total imports), and the Republic of Korea ranked in eighth place (US$1.076 billion, 3.6 per cent of total imports). While Chile's trade with Pacific Asia is mostly centred on the export of primary goods, Mexico's situation is different. Mexico has the same main trade partner as Chile, but is much more dependent on the United States for both imports and exports. Mexico's top export market during 2006 was the United States with US$212.131 billion and 84.87 per cent of total exports. China ranked in seventh position, Japan in eighth position; both countries under 1 per cent of the total exports. Regarding imports, the USA ranked first with US$130.085 billion (51.08 per cent of total imports), followed by China with US$24.443 billion (9.55 per cent of total imports), Japan with US$15.293 billion (5.97 per cent of total imports), and the Republic of Korea with US$10.617 billion (4.14 per cent of total imports). Peru, on the other hand, showed a much more diversified group of trade partners. The United States in 2006 ranked first as Peru's most important trade partner in exports and imports. Exports from Peru to the USA in 2006 reached US$5.707 billion (24.02 per cent of total exports), followed by China with US$2.268 billion (9.55 per cent of total exports). Japan ranked in sixth position with US$1.230 billion, and the Republic of Korea ranked twelfth with US$0.548 billion (2.31 per cent of total exports). Peru's main supplier of goods and services in 2006 was the USA with US$2.515 billion (16.43

per cent of total imports). China ranked in third position with US$1.583 billion (10.34 per cent of total imports), Japan in eighth position with US$0.563 billion (3.68 per cent of total imports) and the Republic of Korea in twelfth position with US$0.391 billion (2.56 per cent of total imports) (CEPAL).

Mexico shows a dramatic dependence on the US, being vulnerable to the normal cycle of ups and downs of the US economy. Being aware that this development increases the dependency on US economic and business cycles, Chile and Peru have realized that only through diversification of economic and commercial partnership will a steady growth of their own economies be guaranteed.

From the point of view of the South American APEC member economies (Chile and Peru), the APEC forum gives them a chance to negotiate Free Trade Agreements with other member economies with the goal of reducing their dependency on the North American economy while at the same time it opens the possibility of trading with economies whose main export products are perfectly complementary to the mainly primary goods produced in the Latin American region. Chile and Peru have both understood this situation and have begun rerouting their trade towards Asia.[7] A study published in March 2008 by Peru's most important economic consultant, Grupo Apoyo, shows that, for example, Peru is reducing its dependency on the United States regarding total participation in trade. In the first half of 2007, only 20 per cent of total exports went to the US in comparison to the peak in 2005, when 30 per cent of Peruvian exports were directed to the US (Grupo Apoyo 2008).

East Asia, especially China, has become an important importer of raw materials and primary goods which can be offered by countries like Chile and Peru (Kleinig 2007). On the other hand, Latin American countries tied with Asian Pacific economies through Free Trade Agreements or through multilateral links like APEC, PBEC or the Pacific Economic Cooperation Council (PECC), especially Chile and Peru, understand the improved commercial relationship with Pacific Asia as a win-win situation. While the increase in commerce boosts the economy of both Latin American countries and offers the chance of diversification of commerce, reducing dependency on trade with the USA, Asian Pacific countries benefit from the actual booming economic situation of the Latin American region, gaining new markets and positioning their investments in the growing economies and emerging markets of Latin America. In this sense, Latin American policy towards Pacific Asia is dictated by pure pragmatism, with the main goal of seeking new commercial partners to promote economic growth. And this approach fits perfectly with the approach of most of the partners in Pacific Asia, especially China.[8]

China's growth over the past few decades has important implications for global trade. As a leading importer of raw materials to boost its production for domestic consumption and for export, China played an important role in the increase of raw material prices until the beginning of the economic world crisis in 2008. Latin America, as an excellent provider of primary goods, plays a key role in the Chinese economy (Husar and Lehmann 2007: 245). Some 80 per cent of Chinese imports from Latin America are raw materials: minerals and fish (Peru and Chile), oil

(Argentina, Venezuela and Ecuador), steel (Brazil), and agricultural products (Brazil, Chile, Argentina and Peru) (Tanan 2007: 196). The elevation of raw material prices together with the rise in demand due to the increase of Chinese internal consumption has been an important factor in the improvement of the Latin American trade balance, in the expansion of exports and the significant gross domestic product (GDP) growth of most countries of the region.[9]

Since 2001 China has widened and improved its economic, commercial and political ties. As a new key and predominant player on the international scene, China is showing its power politically, economically and commercially, offering Free Trade Agreements, special economic treatment, investments and economic assistance – and Latin America seems to be an interesting partner for this Chinese strategy.[10] The Chinese strategy towards Latin America is focused on three areas: diversification of international trade relations, support of exports, and Chinese direct investment in projects regarding raw material extraction and production worldwide; this third area being the main priority (Husar and Lehmann 1997: 254). In this sense and following the *go-out-strategy* directed by Chinese diplomacy, China is trying to create globally different Free Trade Areas, based on bilateral Free Trade Agreements. The strategy of the Chinese government also includes the creation of a net of bilateral Free Trade Agreements in Latin America. The first bilateral Free Trade Agreement in the region was signed with Chile in 2006 (Zhang 2007), followed by the signature of a Free Trade Agreement with Peru in April 2009[11] after only one year of negotiations and as a result of the bilateral meetings between Peru's President Alan García and China's President Hu Jintao during the APEC CEO Summit in November 2008 in Lima, Peru.[12] The signing of the Free Trade Agreement between Chile and China had an immediate effect. Between January and June 2007, bilateral trade between Chile and China increased by 79 per cent. Chilean exports to China grew by 104 per cent in the same period of time, increasing the participation of China in total Chilean exports to 15 per cent.[13] A similar effect is expected in Peru after the signing of the Free Trade Agreement with China.[14]

It is clear that Latin America, as a supplier of raw materials, represents a good partner for China; a partner that is becoming indispensable for China's further growth. But China's special commercial relations with Chile and Peru are not free of political conditions clearly set by China. For China, two subjects play a major role in deepening commercial ties and opening the chance to negotiate bilateral FTAs: the recognition of China as a market economy and the acceptance of China's 'One-China-Policy' towards Taiwan.

China became a World Trade Organization (WTO) member in 2001. The accession of China to the WTO was tied to special conditions: as the WTO understands that the central government in China still fixes numerous prices of sensitive products, China is not yet regarded as a completely free market economy according to WTO interpretation. In this sense, WTO members can still apply for discriminatory measures to block the entrance of Chinese subsidized products, following clauses 15 (Price Compatibility in Determining Subsidies and Dumping) and 16 (Transnational Product-Specific Safeguard Mechanism) of the Protocol of Accession of China to the WTO and paragraph 242 of the Report of the Working Party on the Accession of China of the WTO (clause related to Chinese textiles).

The recognition of China as a market economy by other WTO members implies the renouncement of discriminatory measures towards China regarded in the Protocol of Accession of China to the WTO. This renouncement can have serious consequences on economies that produce similar goods to China. Chinese products may overflow these markets, destroying the domestic industry. For these countries China is not a partner but a strong competitor. China often produces more cheaply and faster and especially threatens the *maquila* industry in Mexico and Central America (Mützenich 2007: 379). For this reason, countries with a complementary production structure as compared to Chinese production tend to fully recognize China as a market economy while countries with a similar production structure prefer to maintain the possibility of applying to the WTO discriminatory measures regarding China. Peru, for instance, has mainly a complementary production structure in comparison to China. But it is also an important producer and exporter of textiles. The Peruvian government had to confront strong resistance from the textile industry regarding the recognition of China as a full market economy.[15] The textile industry feared an increase in the import of subsidized Chinese textiles with the consequence of the destruction of the domestic textile industry (Del Castillo Cebreros 2006). For this reason, Peru's government delayed full recognition of China as a market economy until 2007. This recognition by the Peruvian government opened the possibility of negotiations for a Free Trade Agreement between both countries that began in early 2008 and finished with the signature of the Free Trade Agreement in April 2009. Of the 64 countries that have recognized China as a market economy, five are from Latin America: Argentina, Brazil, Chile, Peru and Venezuela (Zhang 2007: 236).

The second condition for deepening commercial, economic and political co-operation is linked to the acceptance of the 'One-China-Policy'. The Tiananmen Square massacre in 1989, 'which intensified diplomatic contestation between the two Chinas, augmented the People's Republic's efforts to secure its relations across the Pacific' (Mann 2005: 130). This was linked to deeper economic and commercial cooperation by China, conditional on the recognition of the People's Republic of China as the sole representative government of the Chinese people and the rejection of Taiwan as a sovereign state. The statement of Peru's President Alan García during his visit to China and Japan in March 2008 shows that Peru is following exactly the conditions expressed by China: he underlined the status of China as a market economy, severely criticized the referendum in Taiwan in March 2008 and accused the Tibetan monks of separatism that follow interests of a western political establishment that does not want to accept China as a new global player.[16] This fact shows that China still needs the support of close partners to fortify its role as a global player. Stefanie Mann underlines this fact as follows: 'Even considering China's self-perception as a global player, the country still needs acceptance and most of all, international partners. Thus, relations with Latin American countries beyond economic gain-seeking and the China–Taiwan contestation also fulfill the function of supporting the People's Republic of China's objective to strengthen its position in the international system' (Mann 2005: 131).

The interest of Peru in the full application of the Free Trade Agreement with the People's Republic of China signed in April 2009, is based on the fact that bilateral trade with China had increased significantly even before the signature of a Free Trade Agreement and has therefore the potential to grow even faster after the full application of the Free Trade Agreement. The trade volume between both countries grew by 48.5 per cent between January and November 1997 in comparison with the same period in 2006, reaching a total trade volume of US$4,972 million.[17] In 1999 Peru's exports to China stood at approximately 4 per cent of Peru's total exports and rose sharply to 11 per cent in 2005 (Santiso 2007). In March and May 2007, for the first time in Peruvian history, China overtook the USA as the main importer of Peruvian goods.[18] Immediately after the signing of the Free Trade Agreement between China and Peru in April 2009 and in spite of the reduction of investments due to the global economic crisis, Chinese enterprises announced investments of nearly US$2.5 billion in the Peruvian mining sector. Companies like Chinalco, Minmetals, Shougang and Zijin also decided to intensify their engagement in Peru.[19]

However, it is not only China in the Pacific basin region that represents an important market for Latin American exports with potential to grow. Asian countries such as Japan, the Republic of Korea, Singapore, Thailand, Malaysia and Indonesia; Australia and New Zealand in Oceania and surely Canada and the United States are interesting trade partners for Latin American economies. Following the logic that augmenting trade is an indispensable step in generating welfare and that tariff and non-tariff barriers are seldom not a major obstacle for increasing trade, Latin American countries, especially Chile and since 2006 Peru, are making important steps to reach bilateral Free Trade Agreements with their Pacific Basin partners. It is not only the failure of the Doha Round to systemati- cally open world markets via multilateral agreements that have been an incentive to widen and deepen trade negotiations with the Pacific partners. The strategic vision that further growth will be generated in the Pacific, and that diversification of trade is important to counterweight the risks if one region falls into recession, plays a considerable role in the fact that Chile and Peru are diversifying their trade and leading a position inside APEC that focuses on the creation of a Free Trade Area of the Pacific if the Doha Round eventually fails completely.[20] Interestingly, the proposition of Peru and Chile to create a Pacific-wide Free Trade Area shows that these member economies are trying to play a key role as main actors inside APEC, bringing back to the discussion the core idea of a Pacific Free Trade Area, initially discussed in the APEC Summit of Bogor in 1994 and nearly forgotten in the last decade. As a first step towards this goal, the Chilean Foreign Ministry proposed a coordinated strategy between Chile and Peru to negotiate further Free Trade Agreements[21] in the region, and in September 2007 Peru's President Alan García proposed the creation of the 'Pacific Arc', a bloc of APEC member economies of the western Pacific rim with common goals regarding free trade, composed of Peru, Chile, Mexico, Canada and the APEC membership candidates

Panama and Colombia.[22] The 'Pacific Arc' will coordinate common member propositions vis-à-vis APEC, meeting every year before the APEC CEO summits.[23] Latin America follows in an exemplary manner the global trend to open its markets through bilateral Free Trade Agreements, making Pacific Asia especially interesting due to the complementary and compatible structure of its economies towards Latin American exports.

All experts interviewed by the author have clearly underlined the fact that the main interest of Latin American countries in Pacific Asia lies in the subscription of bilateral FTAs with as many economies as possible from the region. This strategy produces an increase in trade, opens new markets and reduces the dependency of traditional export partners. The three main Latin American actors in the region are weaving a net of commercial relation, the elder APEC members, Mexico and Chile, being the most advanced, followed by Peru that has already begun with an aggressive policy towards opening its market. Regarding the Pacific region, Mexico has already signed FTAs with Chile, Japan, Canada and the USA (North American Free Trade Agreement (NAFTA)) and Mexico is actually negotiating FTAs with Peru, Singapore and the Republic of Korea. Chile has signed FTAs with the Republic of Korea, the People's Republic of China, Japan,[24] Canada, the United States of America and Mexico. Chile is also a member of the 'Trans-Pacific Strategic Economic Partnership Agreement' also known as Pacific 4 (P-4), a Free Trade Agreement with deep intraregional cooperation implications that includes Singapore, Brunei and New Zealand. Chile is negotiating FTAs with Peru, Australia and Malaysia.

Peru has already signed FTAs with the USA, Singapore, Canada[25] and recently with the People's Republic of China. An 'Early Harvest' Agreement (previous to a FTA) with Thailand has also been signed. Peru is already negotiating FTAs with the Republic of Korea,[26] Mexico, Chile[27] and Japan.[28] During an APEC CEO Summit in Sydney 2007, Peru initiated preliminary talks with Japan. Peru has also been invited by New Zealand and Chile to participate in P-4.[29] The Peruvian Ministry of Foreign Trade and the Ministry of Foreign Relations are currently analysing the proposition.[30] The possibility of establishing a P-7 (P-4 plus Australia, the United States of America and Peru) was first discussed in 2008 during the APEC CEO Summit in Lima.[31]

Observing this new web of bilateral and 'encapsulated' intraregional multilateral agreements (such as P-4), the question to be asked is what role do multilateral fora like APEC play for Latin American economies in this vast network of bilateral connections? There seems to be a close relationship between membership in Trans-Pacific multilateral agreements (especially APEC) and the proliferation of FTAs between Asian Pacific and Latin American economies. In this sense, APEC membership allows participation in APEC summits, which are seen by Latin American leaders as a 'magic key' that opens the possibility of more intense cooperation with Pacific Asia and therefore prepares the path for FTAs with other member economies of the region.

The main objective of an active participation in APEC lies in the fact that being a full member allows the leaders of Latin American economies to be part of a 'select club' of actors in the world economy, giving the heads of state of Latin American members the opportunity to interact during APEC summits with their colleagues from many of the most important economies of the world. For this reason, the APEC Summit is seen as a kind of 'English Club', open only for a select group of prestigious members, whose membership is a sign of status and perfect for informal contacts and lobbyism that could (and should) lead to a formal form of cooperation, e.g. in the form of bilateral Free Trade Agreements.[32]

APEC CEO Summit 2008: widening the Latin American presence or deepening the relationship with Asian Pacific member economies?

During the 2007 APEC CEO Summit in Sydney, the APEC Secretariat announced that the ten-year moratorium for the inclusion of new economy members to APEC, which was agreed during the Summit of Kuala Lumpur 1998 after the acceptance of full membership of Russia, Papua New Guinea and Peru, was extended for a further three years until the end of 2010. It is highly improbable that the moratorium will be maintained for a longer period of time. For this reason, Latin American candidates for full membership in APEC are lobbying to be taken into account. Peru, as host of the APEC CEO Summit in 2008, had the chance to set the agenda for this Summit and include possible candidacies for 2010.

Colombia, Ecuador, Panama and Costa Rica have all shown interest in being full members of APEC, with Colombia having the best chance of becoming a full new member.[33] Colombia has shown a steady, market-oriented economic policy and a real interest in participating in APEC, coordinating its policy towards full membership with the United States of America and other Latin American APEC members, especially with Chile (Friedrich Ebert Stiftung Colombia 2005: 5). In September 2006, Peru's Foreign Minister Antonio García Belaúnde announced the full support of Peru in relation to the candidature of Ecuador towards APEC, agreeing to include this issue in the agenda for the Summit in 2008.[34] Regarding the actual policy of Ecuador in relation to free trade and the general economic policy of Ecuador's government, it is improbable that Peru, Chile, Mexico and the United States will still support Ecuador's eventual application for full APEC membership. The inclusion of Panama and Colombia as members of the Peruvian project of the 'Pacific Arc' is also a sign that Peru will support the membership in APEC of Latin American economies that are comprised of liberal, market-friendly economic polities.

A widening of APEC with more Latin American economies would surely give more presence and weight to Latin America inside APEC. With Colombia and eventually Ecuador, Panama and Costa Rica as possible full APEC members, the power of negotiation and the impact of Latin American proposals would gain more strength. The United States of America will surely support any attempt at widening APEC with Latin American economies that are aligned to Washington – in this sense, Colombia will be the preferred candidate, the acceptance of Ecuador will probably be dependent on the economic and social development of the actual policy of Ecuador's government and on President Correa's 'special relationship' with Venezuela – strengthening the 'western position' inside APEC.

It is no coincidence that in June 2006, Mexico's Secretary of Foreign Relations Luis Ernesto Derbez called for the creation of a 'Pacific Community of Latin American Nations' that should include all Latin American countries that share a Pacific coast (Mexico, Central America, Colombia, Ecuador, Peru and Chile).[35] This project could be interpreted as a predecessor of the Peruvian proposal of the creation of the 'Pacific Arc' as a bloc of emerging economies with a friendly approach towards free trade, excluding Ecuador. It is equally no coincidence that Mexico's offer of membership of the proposed 'Pacific Community of Latin American Nations' is tied to the previous condition that the candidacy for a membership is linked with a previous signature of an FTA with the USA. This makes it clear that Mexico's proposal includes an intraregional alignment with Washington vis-à-vis Pacific Asia, building a liberal, free trade-friendly bloc as a counterweight to the more protectionist group of Latin American nations led by Venezuela's President Hugo Chávez.

At the same time, national and domestic interest prevail in most Latin American countries over an intraregional and interregional perspective. During numerous meetings with negotiators and advisors of the Ministry of Foreign Trade and Commerce of Peru, the most generalized approach towards the inclusion of other Latin American economies to APEC showed a clear tendency against widening APEC, not including in the agenda for the next APEC CEO Summits the proposal for membership of Colombia, Ecuador, Panama and Costa Rica.

The membership of Colombia is viewed with particular caution. The main argument is that more Latin American members in APEC will lead to tougher intraregional competition between Latin American economies for bilateral FTAs with Asian Pacific economies. Peruvian advisors and authorities of the Ministry of Foreign Trade and Commerce see Colombia as a strong competitor that could divert the interest of the main Asian economies towards Colombia, losing interest in signing FTAs with Peru. Regarding this situation, there are no signs of co-ordination between the Ministry of Foreign Affairs that has openly supported the process of widening APEC with new Latin American economies and the Ministry of Foreign Trade and Commerce, whose position tends to secure and deepen Peru's position in APEC (allowing the further development of the process of systematic signing of FTAs with Asian economies) instead of widening the forum with new Latin American members and trying to influence the character of APEC as a select club of members.

Conclusion

Professor Fernando Gonzalez Vigil, one of the few East Asia experts in Peru, has called the APEC CEO Summit in Lima: 'the most important political and economical event that has taken place in Peru since the independence in 1821'. The APEC Summit 2008 in Lima also represented a great chance for Peru to project an image of an emerging economy that is considered open and catching up with the economies of its neighbours. But an important percentage of Peruvian people still do not comprehend the role that Pacific Asia plays in the international context – politically and commercially. It will depend on the capability of the government, business associations and academic circles to feed the media with information, permitting the public to access information about the opportunities and challenges to do with Pacific Asia.

For Latin American member economies within APEC the main challenge after the APEC CEO Summit 2008 is to set a common agenda, focusing on regional interests over national and domestic issues. The main goal towards the APEC forum should be the deepening of cooperation with Asian Pacific emerging economies with a common and well-articulated Latin American position and proposal. Nowadays, such a 'Latin American common policy' is still missing. Some first steps have been taken in the sense of Mexico's 'Pacific Community of Latin American Nations' and Peru's proposition of the 'Pacific Arc'. On a plurilateral level, there is the forum for consultation, cooperation and dialogue, 'Forum of East Asian–Latin American Cooperation (FEALAC)' that unites most of the Latin American countries – also those countries which do not belong to the Pacific community – and Asian Pacific countries plus Australia and New Zealand, excluding the United States of America and Canada. The initiative of establishing FEALAC was articulated by Singapore's Prime Minister Goh Chok Tong, together with Chile's President Eduardo Frei in 1998 (Wilhelmy 2002: 3). FEALAC was conceived as the Latin American counterpart of ASEM, the system of East Asian–European dialogue (Wilhelmy and Mann 2005: 42). But in contrast to the Asia–Europe Meeting (ASEM), FEALAC has not been perceived by its members, until now, as an instrument for coordination of common proposals and interests and is still widely unknown in both East Asia and Latin America.

The question regarding the new membership of Colombia, Ecuador, Costa Rica and Panama is still being negotiated on a bilateral basis and there is no sign of an articulated position of Peru, Chile and Mexico vis-à-vis the question of presenting these candidacies as a common Latin American proposal. The participation of Latin America in Pacific fora is still characterized by volubility and a lack of coordination. There is enthusiasm and willingness to coordinate at least a common Latin American position, but in the last instance, Pacific Asia is still not at the top of the agenda for most Latin American countries. Chile is possibly the most advanced country regarding a strategic presence in Asian Pacific fora, while Peru's approach towards Pacific Asia has improved in recent years – vis-à-vis the APEC CEO Summit in Lima in 2008 – supported by a huge effort to create consciousness in civil society, business associations, academic circles and governmental institutions about the importance of Pacific Asia as a region characterized by important development. Only after 2008 will Peru see if an improvement related to the perception of Pacific Asia has been reached or if the year 2008 was an exception in terms of enthusiasm and 'Pacific-mania', and the Peruvian eclectic and in some cases inconsistent policy towards East Asia persists.

The APEC CEO Summit in 2008 offered Peru the chance to improve its presence and to optimize its projections towards Pacific Asia. It provides both input and the opportunity to create a Peruvian institution, similar to Chile's 'Fundación Chilena del Pacífico' or Mexico's 'Commission for the Pacific' that should independently focus on Pacific issues, involving representatives of government, academia and business associations. This institution should be enabled to elaborate national policy towards the Pacific region and to coordinate Peru's Pacific policy with other Latin American national Pacific institutions, elaborating a common Latin American agenda of propositions vis-à-vis APEC and the other Pacific institutions and enhancing the Latin American position within the Pacific community.

Notes

1 In May 2008 Peru hosted the European Union–Latin American Summit; in November the APEC CEO Summit.
2 Cultural, social or the building of epistemic communities still play a subordinated role for the Peruvian discussion regarding the Asian Pacific region. The interest is centred on the question of how to maximize the chances of improving commercial ties to accelerate economic growth.
3 *El Comercio*, 27 September 2007: El Perú se prepara para ser sede de foro Asia Pacífico.
4 During the APEC CEO Summit, most Peruvian newspaper and political magazines issued special editions focusing on China (*Caretas*, Edición Extraordinaria 19 November 2008: Cumbre: Rayos y Sueños; *El Comercio*, 17 November 2008: APEC Día 1; *El Comercio*, 24 November 2008: APEC Día 1).
5 For a general overview of Latin American historical ties with East Asia see: Faust and Mols (2005); for relations between Peru and East Asia: De la Flor Belaúnde (1991), González Vigil (1994), De la Puente (1990), Berríos (2005).
6 Peru's President Alan García comments on the APEC CEO Summit in Lima as 'the entry of Peru in the 21st century' (*El Comercio*, 20 November 2008: La entrada del Perú al siglo XXI).
7 *El Comercio*, 31 January 2008: Exportaciones peruanas comienzan a virar hacia los países asiáticos.
8 A wide perspective of the relations between China and Latin America can be found in Albiez *et al.*, eds, (2007).
9 Peru is probably the best example of growth in the Latin American Pacific region with a GDP growth of 8.99 per cent during 2007 and 9.84 per cent during 2008. See *Instituto Peruano de Economía* (March 2008), 'Boletín Económico Número 14' p. 2; Andina – Agencia Peruana de Noticias, 15 February 2009: Perú registró record extraordinario de crecimiento de 9.84 per cent en 2008, anuncia Presidente Alan García.
10 Shortly after Chile signed a Free Trade Agreement with the People's Republic of China in 2006, Peru initiated conversations with the People's Republic of China to begin negotiations towards a bilateral Free Trade Agreement. See *El Comercio*, 23 January 2008: Perú y China avanzan en primera ronda; *El Comercio*, 19 January 2008: Perú y China inician mañana el camino hacia un nuevo TLC; *El Comercio*, 19 September 2007: El Perú firmará un TLC con la UE y China el próximo año; *El Comercio*, 7 September 2007: Alan García estima que TLC con China se firmará en noviembre del 2008. Radioprogramas del Perú, 5 September 2007: Perú y China oficializarán esta semana inicio de negociaciones para un TLC.
11 The Free Trade Agreement was signed on 29 April 2009 in Beijing, China. See: *El Comercio*, 29 April 2009; Perú y China suscriben TLC y logran una visión estratégica.
12 See: *El Comercio*, 20 November 2008; TLC con China abre un mercado de 1.315 millones de personas; *El Comercio*, 20 November 2008; China y Perú culminaron sus negociaciones y se acercan al TLC.

13 See: *El Mercurio*, 18 July 2007: Envíos a China crecen 104% en primer semestre.

14 See: *El Comercio*, 28 May 2009: El TLC con China incrementará las inversiones de ese país en el Perú; *El Comercio*, 23 March 2009: Exportaciones no tradicionales a China crecerán tras el TLC.

15 *Perú Exporta*, May/June 2005: Declaración de China como economía de mercado debe basarse en condiciones de inversion.

16 *El Comercio*, 27 March 2008: China olímpica y sus adversarios.

17 *El Comercio*, 21 January 2008: Buscan que el TLC del Perú y China se firme en noviembre.

18 *Expreso*, 2 July 2007: Milagro chino en Perú.

19 *El Comercio*, 30 April 2009: Inversionistas chinos interesados en el Perú.

20 *El Comercio*, 17 November 2006: APEC formaría area de libre comercio si fracas Ronda Doha; *El Comercio*, 31 January 2008: Empresarios estudian un TLC entre los miembros de APEC.

21 *El Comercio*, 19 June 2006: Chile plantea alianza con el Perú para TLC con Asia.

22 For Panama, the membership in the 'Pacific Arc' means a first step towards a future full APEC membership, while Colombia is already a member of PECC and PBEC.

23 See: *El Comercio*, 10 September 2007: García impulsa creación de Arco del Pacífico; *El Comercio*, 10 September 2007: García: La democracia en lo politico y en lo económico sí es eficaz; *El Comercio*, 11 September 2007: Ven el Arco del Pacífico como puerta al comercio; *El Comercio*, 11 September 2007: El Arco del Pacífico y el blindaje que busca.

24 The FTA with Japan targets the elimination of 92 per cent of bilateral trade between both countries, excluding some agricultural products that have been declared 'sensible' by the Japanese negotiators. See: *El Comercio*, 2 September 2007: Entra en vigor TLC entre Japón y Chile que elimina arancel a 92% del comercio.

25 *El Comercio*, 26 January 2008: El Perú y Canadá firman TLC, anunció el presidente Alán García.

26 *El Comercio*, 10 September 2007: El Perú planteó a Corea del Sur emprender tratado de libre comercio; *El Comercio*, 25 September 2007: Corea del Sur y el Perú evalúan un possible TLC; Radioprogramas del Perú: Perú y Corea iniciarán negociaciones para TLC en segundo semester 2008; *El Comercio*, 16 March 2009: Perú y Corea del Sur inician primera ronda de negociaciones de TLC; *El Comercio*, 15 May 2009: TLC entre el Perú y Corea ya tiene un avance del 30 per cent.

27 www.bilaterals.org

28 *El Comercio*, 13 April 2009: Perú y Japón anunciarán inicio de negociaciones de tratado de libre comercio.

29 *El Peruano*, 4 September 2006: A la conquista del Asia.

30 *El Comercio*, 28 October 2006: Ingreso al P-4 podría tener dificultades.

31 *El Comercio*, 21 November 2008: Perfilan en Lima las bases de pacto comercial Asia–Pacífico.

32 Mann (2006: 57) sees Peru's interest in APEC in a similar way.

33 Colombia and Ecuador are full members of PECC. Ecuador's actual unfriendly policy towards foreign investments and President Correa's 'anti-imperialistic policy' towards the United States of America and his friendly relationship with Venezuela's President Chávez, opens the possibility that the US will veto the application of Ecuador to a full membership of APEC. It is actually also highly improbable that Ecuador will present a formal candidacy for an APEC membership in 2010.

34 *El Comercio*, 7 September 2006: El Perú anuncia apoyo para ingreso de Ecuador al foro de APEC.

35 *Radio Cooperativa*, 27 July 2006: México quiere a Chile para crear una Comunidad del Pacífico.

References

Albiez, Sarah, Philipp Kauppert and Sophie Müller, eds, (2007) *China und Lateinamerika. Ein transpazifischer Brückenschlag*, Berlin: wvb Verlag.

Beckinschtein, José A. and Maizal, Nélida (1994) 'La integración regional en Asia Pacífico: vías de participación', *Integración Latinoamericana*, Vol. 19, No. 197.

Berríos, Rubén (2005) 'Peru and Pacific Asia', in Jörg Faust, Manfred Mols, Won-Ho Kim, eds, *Latin America and East Asia – Attempts at Diversification*, Münster, Seoul: LIT.

CEPA (Division de Comercio Internacional e Integración) Comtrade, United Nations Commodity Trade Statistics Database, DESA/UNSD, www.cepal.org

De la Flor Belaúnde, Pablo (1991) *Japón en la escena internacional. Sus relaciones con América Latina y el Perú*. Lima.

De la Puente, José (1990) 'El Desafío del Pacífico', in Alfredo Barnechea, ed., *El Perú de los 90*, Lima, pp. 47–65.

Del Castillo Cebreros, Sergio Alonso (2006) *Implicancias para el Perú del reconociento a China como economía de Mercado*. Unpublished manuscript presented at the Peruvian Diplomatic Academy.

Faust, Jörg and Manfred Mols (2005) 'Latin America and East Asia: Defining the Research Agenda', in Jörg Faust, Manfred Mols, Won-Ho Kim, eds, *Latin America and East Asia – Attempts at Diversification*, Münster, Seoul: LIT.

Faust, Jörg and Uwe Franke (2005) 'Relations between Mexico and East Asia', in Jörg Faust, Manfred Mols, Won-Ho Kim, eds., *Latin America and East Asia – Attempts at Diversification*, Münster, Seoul: LIT.

Friedrich Ebert Stiftung Colombia (FESCOL) (2005) ¿Es deseable el ingreso de Colombia a APEC? *Policy Paper 17*, Bogota, http://www.colombiainternacional.org/Asia-pacifico-pp.htm (accessed 16 July 2009).

González Vigil, Fernando (1994) 'Relaciones del Perú con los países del Asia–Pacífico', *Análisis Internacional*.

Grupo Apoyo (2008) *Perú: Panorama Político-Económico 2008–2009*, Lima, March.

Gutiérrez, Hernán (2005) 'Chile and Asia Pacific: The Economic Connection', in Jörg Faust, Manfred Mols, Won-Ho Kim, eds, *Latin America and East Asia – Attempts at Diversification*, Münster, Seoul: LIT.

Husar, Jörg and Vera Lehmann (2007) 'Ziele, Strategien und Instrumente der chinesischen lateinamerikapolitik', in Albiez, Sarah, Philipp Kauppert and Sophie Müller, eds, *China und Lateinamerika. Ein transpazifischer Brückenschlag*, Berlin: wvb Verlag.

Kleinig, Jochen (2007) 'China und Lateinamerika: Eine neue transpazifische Partnerschaft, *KAS Auslandsinformationen*, September.

Mann, Stefanie (2006) *Peru's Relations with Pacific Asia: Democracy and Foreign Policy under Alan García, Alberto Fujimori and Alejandro Toledo*, Münster: LIT.

——— (2005). 'China and Latin America', in Jörg Faust, Manfred Mols, Won-Ho Kim, eds, *Latin America and East Asia – Attempts at Diversification*, Münster, Seoul: LIT.

Mützenich, Rolf (2007) 'China und Lateinamerika – Brückenschlag zwischen ungleichen Handelspartnern', in Albiez, Sarah, Philipp Kauppert and Sophie Müller, eds, *China und Lateinamerika. Ein transpazifischer Brückenschlag*, Berlin: wvb Verlag.

Orrego Vicuña, Francisco (1989), 'La cooperación en el Pacífico: Una perspectiva desde América Latina', *Estudios Internacionales*, Vol. 21, No. 86.

Santiso, Javier (2007) *The visible hand of China in Latin America. Opportunities, Challenges and Risks*. Presentation at Deutsche Bank Research Conference, Berlin, 13 September.

Tanan, Costa (2007) 'Die Au ßenpolitik Chinas unter Hu Jintao und das neue Konzept des "Friedlichen Aufstiegs", Chancen und Gefahren für Lateinamerika', in Albiez, Sarah, Philipp Kauppert and Sophie Müller, eds, *China und Lateinamerika. Ein transpazifischer Brückenschlag*, Berlin: wvb Verlag.

Torres, Víctor (1992) 'El Perú y la Cuenca del Pacífico', *Política Internacional*, April–June.

Wilhelmy, Manfred (2002) 'La cooperación económica entre América Latina y Asia', www.casaasia.org/esp/pdf/Wilhelmy.pdf (assessed 30 May 2009).

Wilhelmy, Manfred and Mann, Stefanie (2005) 'Multilateral Co-operation between Latin America and East Asia, in Jörg Faust, Manfred Mols, Won-Ho Kim, eds, *Latin America and East Asia – Attempts at Diversification*, Münster, Seoul: LIT, pp. 33–4.

Zhang, Junhua (2007) 'Chinas go-out strategy und ihre Auswirkungen auf Lateinamerika', in Albiez, Sarah, Philipp Kauppert and Sophie Müller, eds, *China und Lateinamerika. Ein transpazifischer Brückenschlag*, Berlin: wvb Verlag.

Part II

Multilateral and interregional relations

9 Interregionalism without regions

IBSA as a form of shallow multilateralism

Jürgen Rüland and Karsten Bechle

The ups and downs of interregionalism

Globalization has had a twofold effect on international relations: it has, on the one hand, facilitated a process of fragmentation, as exemplified by ethno-religious violence, failing states and international terrorism and, on the other, an unprecedented growth of cooperative arrangements. The latter are the result of a growing interdependence which has given rise to an institutionally increasingly dense system of global governance. With it went the expectation that institutional growth would mitigate or even overcome the anarchical character of international relations. Accordingly, universally accepted norms would make state behaviour more predictable, lower transaction costs, engage revisionist powers and socialize them into the existing international order through political learning. As institutions grow in strength and legitimacy, international relations would become more rule-based and, hence, more peaceful.

An offshoot of this seemingly emergent multi-layered system of global governance is interregionalism. Interregionalism is part of an increasing vertical differentiation of international institutions ranging from the global to the local level. A driving force in this process has been the proliferation of new regional organizations in all parts of the world since the mid-1980s. This 'new regionalism' has given rise to the emergence of new intermediary institutions linking the regional level 'upstream' with the global level (interregionalism) and 'downstream' (trans-border or subregional institutions) with the national level of decision-making. Interregionalism thrived on the fact that regionalism added a new chess board to policymakers, and that thus it was only natural that regions would begin to interact and cooperate with each other, either to position themselves against other regions or to influence in their favour decision-making in global multilateral institutions (Roloff 1998, 2001, 2006).

Hand in hand with vertical differentiation went a horizontal differentiation of international institutitions. Horizontal differentiation denotes regime-building in specific policy areas such as security, trade, monetary issues, migration, environment, natural resource management, maritime law and outer space, to name just a few examples. Although many nation states and, here, especially former colonies, still have great misgivings about sacrificing sovereignty and foreign policy-making autonomy, their governments increasingly realize that without a modicum of collective action many border-crossing issues can no longer be solved by them.

In this process of an increasingly densifying network of international institutions (Reinecke 1998), political scientists ascribe to interregional dialogue forums a potential for performing important nodal functions. Interregional institutions may integrate vertical and horizontal institution-building and contribute to institutional 'nesting' (Aggarwal 1998; Aggarwal and Fogerty 2004) if they function as 'multilateral utilities' (Dent 2003, 2006). As multilateral utilities, interregional dialogues perform 'subsidiary' clearing house and agenda-setting functions for global multilateral forums. These functions respond to the fact that global multilateral institutions have become increasingly unwieldy due to both a growing number of actors and an increasing complexity and technicality of policy issues. Interregional forums may thus help to broker agreements or agendas between regions, bringing down markedly the number of players at the global level. This, at least theoretically, helps in striking compromise solutions, facilitating and accelerating decisions and thus improving the efficiency and enhancing the 'output' legitimacy of global multilateral institutions (Rüland 1999, 2001, 2006; Hänggi, Roloff and Rüland 2006).

In practice, however, interregional forums have so far largely failed to function as 'multilateral utilities' (Bersick 2003; Yeo 2003; Loewen 2004, 2005; Doidge 2004, 2008; Robles 2008; Rüland and Storz 2008). This would have presupposed an institutional strengthening and a trend towards binding and more precise decisions; in other words a progressive legalization of global governance processes (Messner and Nuscheler 2006) and the increasing production of 'hard law' (Abbott and Snidal 2000). Yet, neither has occurred. By contrast, what we witness currently is an atrophy of global governance institutions, their retreat into configurations of 'shallow' multilateralism, a resurgence of sovereignty and a proliferation of numerous forms of low-intensity cooperation. Examples are the coalitions of the willing in the field of security cooperation, the free trade bi- and minilateralism in the economic domain and the emergence of a 'new bilateralism' in the form of numerous strategic partnerships formed by major and minor powers around the world.

The India–Brazil–South Africa cooperation (IBSA) is one of these relationships typical for the emerging web of global strategic partnerships under the framework of 'shallow' multilateralism. It stands for a strategic partnership in which three regional hegemons claim to be not only pursuing their own national interests but also speaking as advocates for their respective regions. The subsequent parts of this chapter will thus try to portray the IBSA as a skeletal form of interregionalism and an embodiment of a weakening, in other words 'shallow', global multilateral architecture. We will show that while IBSA retains certain formal elements of multilateralism and institutional politics, it also reflects the heightened significance of power and national interest in the conduct of foreign affairs. In a first step we will thus show why IBSA may be categorized as a hollowed-out sub-type of interregionalism and an incarnate of 'shallow' multilateralism. Subsequent parts of the chapter will then explore which objectives IBSA pursues, what means of cooperation it applies and against whom its policies are directed.

Towards an era of 'shallow' multilateralism

Not unexpectedly, recent changes in the international order are beginning to make inroads into theoretical debates. With them goes a rediscovery of the concept of power in international relations (Hurrell 2004, 2006; Barnett and Duvall 2005; Mayntz 2005). This leads to a downgrading of both: the institutionalist belief in a progressive legalization of international relations and the constructivist emphasis on the discursive processes of social learning, norm diffusion and the constitutive capacity of institutions as driving forces of a constantly deepening multi-layered system of global governance. Replacing the network perspective of 'multistakeholder governance' (Martens 2003, 2007; Forman and Segaar 2006) is a growing trend to perceive the international system as hierarchical or, more sophisticated, by taking into account the varying distribution of power in different issue areas, a set of hierarchies. Already years ago, though arguing from a cultural perspective, Kang portrayed East Asia's international order in positional terms, with China at the apex and bandwagoned by the smaller countries of the region (Kang 2003; for a critique, see Acharya 2003/2004). More recently, the international system has been subdivided into the sole remaining superpower, that is, the United States, emerging powers, leading regional powers (Nolte 2006), anchor states, middle powers, and so on (Stamm 2004).

While some of these studies rightfully criticize the neglect of power in the global governance debate, there is certainly a danger of throwing out the baby with the bath water. The new emphasis on 'bringing power back in' tends to obscure the cooperative dimension of international relations (Hurrell 2004: 48). In fact, more recent empirical analyses have amply shown that states neither exclusively act as power maximizers, nor primarily pursue cooperative strategies, not even the so-called civilian powers (Maull 1990, 1992; Kirste and Maull 1996). Foreign policy is thus much better described as shifting back and forth on a continuum where (hard) power-based politics is one pole and supranational cooperation the other extreme. The precise place of a state on this continuum is determined by the extent on which it relies on military 'hard' power and forms of 'soft' power such as institutional, structural or ideological power (Barnett and Duvall 2005). The mixture between 'hard' and 'soft' power greatly depends on cognitive factors as embodied in the role concept foreign policy-making elites have defined for their countries. The role concept denotes the collective identity of states which is the result of mental representations of historical experience, past social interactions, political culture and the institutional arrangements in which it is embedded. This means that in political practice, power, national self-interest and cooperation are often inextricably intertwined. This ambiguity is well captured in Link's terms of 'cooperative competition' and 'competitive cooperation' (Link 1998) or, more recently, in the concepts of 'hedging' and 'soft balancing' (Chwee 2008; He and Feng 2008).

Moreover, despite doctrinal changes in US foreign policy under the Bush administration, the overwhelming majority of states still regard the use of force as an extremely costly option of pursuing national interest. The Iraq War has disproved the belief of the neoconservatives in the Bush administration that with superior military power wars can be won in a short period of time, with minimal troop strength and few casualties and that military force is able to influence outcomes in other policy fields. Most governments keen to revise the international distribution of power thus prefer to change the distribution of institutional power. This, however, has greatly changed the nature of international institutions. Institutions thus become less a place in which to solve common policy problems through collective action, which would invariably mean sacrificing national sovereignty and decision-making autonomy. To a much greater extent, albeit by no means exclusively, they become arenas where states are pursuing their national interests without proclivity to give up sovereignty.

The changing nature and function of international institutions must be attributed to at least two major factors. One is the rise or resurgence of powers such as China, India, Brazil, South Africa and Russia, which due to internal reforms have been among the beneficiaries of economic globalization and which due to their size and/or previous grandeur claim for themselves great power status and a global political role. They are dissatisfied with the existing distribution of institutional power which, they criticize, is largely the result of decisions made at the end and in the aftermath of the Second World War. As colonies, semi-colonies, post-colonial structurally dependent nations or states pre-occupied with the process of nation-building they had then little or no leverage to influence the post-war international institutional architecture that in their view disproportionately benefits the US and other developed countries of the global North. Closely related is the second factor, that is, the reluctance of Northern developed countries to agree to adjustments of the international institutional architecture, so that it would cease reflecting the power equation at the end of the Second World War and become more responsive to the changes that have taken place since then. Particularly irritating for many rising powers is the seemingly declining willingness of the US to make concessions for accommodating dissent and divergent interests of other nations. Under the Bush administration, the US has become increasingly intolerant towards countries diverting from its security outlook, working for an economic order beyond the Washington Consensus and disagreeing with American designs for reforming the rules and decision-making procedures of international institutions. Rising new powers thus vocally strive for revisions of the norms, rules and decision-making procedures under which current international institutions operate. Foremost among these institutions are the United Nations and the international financial institutions. In other institutions, which respond to global trans-boundary problems and where agreed rules of cooperation do not yet exist, they try to create a level playing field right from the start. We expect these intra-institutional power struggles to intensify further as, under the impact of globalization, many new policy fields need international regulation and, as a result, international institutions produce a rapidly growing number of behind-the-border rules which markedly curtail national policy-making autonomy, especially of economically less advanced countries.

Where institutions have become arenas for power struggles over norms, rules, decision-making and membership issues balancing moves tend to dominate. This means that states form institutional alignments or coalitions in order to prevent other states or state coalitions from realizing their policy objectives. Such institutional or 'soft balancing' signifies reactions to changes of the global or regional distribution of power. 'Soft balancing' – in contrast to military or 'hard balancing' – is usually pursued by smaller actors which in recognition of the superior military might of a hegemon use institutional means to balance hegemonic power (Pape 2005; Flemes 2007; Sequeira 2008) by diluting, slowing down, modifying or even obstructing the latter's policies. As power configurations are usually dynamic and change frequently, states are not much interested in investing in institutional strengthening. Instead of investing in the governance costs of institutions, states are more prepared to beef up those power resources that make them attractive as coalition partners. This is the international environment where 'shallow multi-lateralism' thrives.

'Shallow multilateralism' is a form of multilateralism where only the institutional shell remains, but where the normative substance was lost. It does not rest on durable institutions, and, consequently, it does not create the actor predictability, transparency and mutual trust that multilateral frameworks are expected to provide. This includes a decline of 'hard law' and the simultaneous ubiquitous rise of 'soft law'. With the rising stakes of bargaining, a growing number of actors and the complexity of policy matters, it becomes increasingly difficult to reach binding, precise and enforceable agreements. 'Soft law' suits the interests of many actors in multilateral institutions as it keeps commitment low and thus allows for swift and opportunistic responses to changing power equations and new policy issues. The flexibility inherent in 'soft law' serves hegemonic powers such as the US, as much as rising powers. It permits the hegemon to divest itself of commitments and costs constraining its autonomy, while it makes it easier for rising powers to reshape the power asymmetries within institutions and the rules supporting it. They also appreciate flexibility because their interests change quickly as they rise. Moreover, as 'soft law' does not entail sanctions for non-complying states, opportunity, governance and legitimacy costs are limited and peer pressure for compliance is low.

Cultural factors add to the widespread preferences for 'soft law' and forms of 'shallow' multilateralism. Old civilizations such as China and India have their own deeply entrenched traditions of political thought which are strongly informed by the spirit of political realism. A case in point is the Kautilya's Arthashastra which up to the present is well known to virtually every Indian policymaker. The lessons these ancient prescriptions for successful rulers provide have been deeply inculcated in the minds of policymakers by humiliating experiences with Western colonialism and imperialism, and adverse experiences with Western institutionalism. Rules made by Western-dominated institutions have often been of a double-standard nature, applied only as long as they served the interests of their creators.

The foregoing paragraphs have briefly sketched the institutional environment in which strategic alliances such as IBSA operate. IBSA thus fits very well within the structures of shallow multilateralism. With three members it fits Keohane's minimalist nominal definition of multilateralism (Keohane 1990: 731). Beyond this formal criterion, IBSA clearly pursues strategic interests which envisage enhancing the international stature of the three powers. All three members of IBSA have repeatedly declared their intention to transform globalization into a process with a human face. Their thrust for a socially more equitable process of globalization entails a vocal opposition against the neo-liberal agenda of the US and other Western powers. The redistribution of economic gains of globalization can however only be achieved if the power distribution within global institutions changes. Foremost in their mind here are the global economic organizations such as the World Trade Organization (WTO), and the International Monetary Fund (IMF), which are regarded as the strongholds buttressing the economic power of developed countries. IBSA is thus a cooperative arrangement of three major regional powers with the objective of strengthening their national power, of consolidating power in their respective region and to enhance their power in global international institutions. With their combined strength, they seek to rewrite the rules of the international institutional order, which they would like to transform from a unipolar into a genuinely multipolar international system. What they demand is, in other words, a new power-sharing formula in global multilateral forums, or to put it even more succinctly, a democratization of international relations.

While as a strategic partnership IBSA fits very well the concept of shallow multilateralism, it can also be depicted as a skeletal form of interregionalism. Following Hänggi's distinction between interregionalism in a 'narrower' sense and a 'wider' sense (Hänggi 2006), IBSA must undoubtedly be categorized as interregionalism in a 'wider' sense. While interregionalism in a narrower sense basically includes what elsewhere has been designated as bi-regional interregionalism and transregionalism (Rüland 2001, 2006), interregionalism in a wider sense includes many continental dialogues; dialogues between a regional group and countries belonging to a region without being members of a regional organization and dialogues between regional groupings and large powers. All forms of interregionalism in the 'wider' sense are marginal forms of interregionalism which are even less institutionalized than interregionalism in a 'narrower' sense.

But IBSA conforms to none of the types of interregionalism in the 'wider' sense named by Hänggi. This raises the question why then IBSA may qualify as an interregional arrangement at all? First, very simply, the arrangement links three global regions, which seemed to have been a deliberate choice in the formation of the forum. Second, all three member countries, being hegemons in their respective region, consider themselves as speakers for their region, claiming to work for the latter's benefit. One example is, as discussed in greater detail below, that Brazil and South Africa promoted and eventually reached the conclusion of interregional preferential trade agreements. But even if the self-declared advocacy function is by no means shared by their regional partners, the shadow and the political weight of their respective region is behind them. Third, more than being a mere coalition, they have formed with the Trilateral Commission a joint institution, albeit a rather shallow one. Fourth, and finally, IBSA constitutes some sort of 'reflexive interregionalism' due to the importance and the role concept of regional leaders attached to them by others.[1]

IBSA members' strategy to create an interregional forum without regions is the ultimate form of the flexibility inherent in the institutions created under the auspices of the 'new regionalism'. Cooperating without their regional partners highlights their hegemonial claim, but, more importantly, substantially increases their autonomy of action. It relieves them from the hedging, double-binding and engagement by which the smaller members of regional organizations normally seek to curtail regional hegemons. This is particularly the case, where regional organizations are divided, such as the South Asian Association for Regional Cooperation (SAARC) in South Asia because of the Indian–Pakistani conflict. Due to its small number of members, IBSA is thus able to make much faster decisions on objectives, strategies and policies than fully fledged interregional dialogues. Moreover, the paternalism inherent in this form of interregionalism also strengthens the regional leadership of the three powers, as they are the ones who can claim to bring benefits to their regions (such as in the case of interregional free trade agreements or better deals in the WTO). Skeletal interregionalism ultimately premiums short-term efficiency which also reflects a trend in more established interregional dialogues. The proposal, for instance, of reducing the Asia–Europe Meeting (ASEM) to a dialogue between the *troikas* representing the Asian and the European side, clearly points to this direction (University of Helsinki 2006).

IBSA – A shallow institution

Ever since IBSA was officially launched by the heads of state of its member countries at the 50th General Assembly of the United Nations (UN) in September 2003, it deployed a wide range of activities to lend substance to the trilateral cooperation. Already in June, the three foreign ministers had agreed upon the Brasilia Declaration that foresees 'regular political consultations on international agenda items, as well as to exchange information on areas of mutual cooperation in order to coordinate their positions on issues of common interest'.[2]

Since then, the IBSA Forum held regular consultations at the senior official (Focal Point) and the ministerial (Trilateral Joint Commission) levels. In September 2006 Manmohan Singh (India), Lula da Silva (Brazil) and Thabo Mbeki (South Africa) met in Brazil for the first Presidential Summit. South Africa hosted the second summit meeting in October 2007 and India followed in 2008. The national business communities were also involved from the beginning. State visits have been regularly accompanied by large groups of business leaders. To formalize these relations in March 2005, the IBSA Business Council was launched in Cape Town and IBSA business summits were held simultaneously to the presidential summits in Brasilia 2006, Pretoria 2007, and New Delhi 2008.

Despite this flurry of activities, IBSA has remained weakly institutionalized and lacks a permanent organizational structure. It has no secretariat and its day-to-day business is carried out by the secretary in charge within the foreign ministry of the host country. In order to strengthen ties between member states, trilateral working groups have been built to foster cooperation in several sectors. The identified fields for cooperation cover a wide range of issue areas comprising agriculture, climate change, culture, defence, education, energy, health, information, society, science and technology, social issues, tourism, trade, and transport.[3] But typically for international institutions conforming to what we called 'shallow' multilateralism, cooperation in these low policy sectors is largely characterized by non-committal consultation rather than binding and precise agreements followed up by monitoring and evaluation of results. It therefore remains to be seen whether the large list of memoranda of understanding and cooperation agreements that have been signed so far within these issue areas will produce any tangible results in the near future. Perhaps the most important amongst them are those within the more crucial sectors of energy (Memorandum of Understanding on Bio-fuels), transport (Agreement on Merchant Shipping and Other Maritime Transport Matters) and trade (Action Plan on Trade Facilitation for Standards, Technical Regulations and Conformity Assessment).

In the Brasilia Declaration IBSA partners also call upon a large list of very general political objectives like respect for international law, strengthening the United Nations, prioritizing diplomatic means to maintain international peace and security, respecting the sovereignty of states, promoting social equity and inclusion, fighting hunger and poverty, and promoting health, social assistance, employment, education, human rights and environmental protection. Again, such declaratory politics and cooperation rhetoric perfectly coincide with 'shallow' multilateralism as does the emphasis placed on national sovereignty which stands for a concept of intergovernmental cooperation and signifies little inclination to sacrifice national policy-making autonomy for the sake of solving global border-crossing problems.

IBSA and the change of international norms and rules

While IBSA is in the first place a loose cooperative arrangement, conforming to the emerging 'shallow' multilateralism, a closer look at IBSA activities also corroborates our argument that one of its core objectives is changing the power equation in major global institutions. At the Third IBSA Summit, held in New Delhi in October 2008, IBSA members 'reiterated the need to make the structures of global governance more democratic, representative and legitimate in increasing the participation of developing countries in decision-making bodies of multilateral institutions'.[4] Framed in the rhetoric of democratizing international institutions, changing the power equation has thereby clear priority over the solution of collective action problems in the respective policy fields. In order to provide evidence for this claim, we will subsequently scrutinize IBSA's activities in several major international organizations and regimes including the UN, the Bretton Woods organizations and the non-proliferation regime.

UN reform

IBSA's objective of changing the rules of major international institutions in favour of its member countries is nowhere more striking than with regard to the reform of the United Nations. The UN and especially the Security Council, IBSA members argue, reflect the world after the Second World War, not that of today. Therefore a comprehensive reform is needed. In their Joint Declaration after the first presidential meeting the IBSA chiefs of state demand that the 'Security Council must be expanded to include developing countries from Africa, Asia and Latin America in both its permanent and non-permanent categories, so as to reflect contemporary realities and make it more democratic, legitimate, representative and responsive'.[5] Statements in subsequent summits were more circumspect but clearly reaffirmed the need for UN reform with the restructuring of the Security Council at the core.[6]

With a hint to their status as regional powers both India and Brazil claim one permanent seat for themselves. This discussion, building on their expanded power in a changing international system, underscores the power-political perspective of these rising powers which we have claimed is a major characteristic of 'shallow' multilateralism. Yet their argument that the inclusion of regional leaders would make the Security Council more democratic is more than ambiguous. While, on the one hand, the expansion of membership would certainly contribute to a stronger dispersal of power in international relations, on the other, despite IBSA declarations to the contrary, none of the three IBSA partners can claim strong support as representative of its region on this issue. Middle powers such as Argentina, Mexico, Venezuela, Pakistan, Nigeria or Egypt openly reject the idea that IBSA members from their region might speak on their behalf in the realm of security.

As a result of this opposition and facing the lack of support from within the African Union, South Africa decided to withdraw from the joint effort for the time being. Meanwhile India and Brazil went on to align themselves with two key actors from the North, namely Japan and Germany, to form the G4, thereby further pursuing their objective of a permanent seat on the Security Council. This is particularly problematic in the case of Brazil, because its ambitions for a permanent seat strain relations with Argentina (Soares de Lima 2005: 40), its most important strategic partner within the Common Market of the South (MERCOSUR), grouping Argentina, Brazil, Paraguay and Uruguay (MERCOSUR) and South America as a whole.

Reforming the IMF

Apart from the UN, IBSA has also lobbied strongly for reforming the two most influential international financial institutions, that is, the IMF and the World Bank. Both of them are seen as incarnates of what developing countries regard as an unjust, because highly inequitable, global economic order. In their view the IMF, in particular, with its weighted voting rights based on financial contribution and its sovereignty transcending behind-the-border interventions, is a bulwark of this order that in IBSA members' view needs urgent and fundamental reforms that would enhance their own position significantly. Therefore, they vocally call for a change of the voting system that would increase their voting power relative to the hitherto dominant developed countries of the global North. Yet, at the annual meeting of the WTO and IMF in Singapore in September 2006 India and Brazil opposed a reform widely agreed upon, that will increase the quota (and, hence, votes) of the four countries most underrepresented in these institutions, relative to their economic performance. This is particularly revealing because, with China, Mexico, South Korea and Turkey, all of the beneficiaries are countries from the South. But with only 1.8 per cent[7] the increase in their voting power was highly inadequate and temporarily even implied a relative loss for India and Brazil.[8] Therefore, much to the chagrin of India and Brazil, the reform was eventually adopted with some 90 per cent approval. Thus, in their Tshwane declaration from October 2007 IBSA leaders restated 'the need to provide a greater voice for and participation by developing countries in the WTO and IMF and expressed concern at the slow rate of progress that has been achieved so far'.[9] The global financial crisis has in their view dramatically increased the urgency for such reforms which were a main point of the agenda of the New Delhi summit of October 2008.[10]

Changing the international trade regime: IBSA and the WTO

Another good example to change the distribution of institutional power in its favour is IBSA members' negotiation strategy in WTO ministerials. Narlikar, for instance, shows that India (and more recently, one may add, Brazil as well) has persistently pursued at high costs what she calls a 'strict distributive strategy' (Narlikar 2006). Such a strategy operates with strong demands on others and concedes little or nothing to them. It is a strategy that views policy-making as a zero-sum game and, hence, seeks to split a constant pie. It strives for relative gains in order to change the institutional status quo. Such an attitude is strongly informed by notions of political realism and corroborates with what we have stated earlier about institutional power struggles under the aegis of 'shallow' multilateralism.

At the Cancun ministerial of the WTO in September 2003, India and its IBSA partners favoured an impasse in the negotiations over a compromise that would have expanded the pie and led to absolute gains for all. The outcome of the Cancun ministerial was thus – as Narlikar argues – 'beneficial to no one, least of all the developing countries, and hence can scarcely be regarded as a victory' (Narlikar 2006: 65). Instead of proposing, for instance, concrete tariff levels for certain products, Brazilian delegation leader and Foreign Minister Celso Amorim rather criticized the asymmetrical distribution of power within the present world trade order. This confrontational strategy was only abandoned a few months later when both India and Brazil were granted the status of official interlocutors together with the US, the EU and Australia within the so-called Five Interested Parties group (FIPS) or G5. Only under this novel institutional framework could a compromise solution on essential elements of an Agricultural Framework Agreement be reached by the end of July 2004 in Geneva that permitted the continuation of the Doha Round (Schirm 2005: 113 ff.).

Since 2004 India and Brazil have been negotiating the future of world trade talks with the US and the EU within the very exclusive G4 that at times was extended to a G6, which also comprised Australia and Japan. As is the case with the UN Security Council, here too exists a problem of representation. India and Brazil claim to speak on behalf of their regions and of the developing countries of the South within these negotiations. But as many least developed coutries (LDCs) are net importers of agrarian products they have no interest in cutting agrarian subsidies in the North that would eventually lead to increasing prices for the respective goods (Naidu 2006: 23).

Reviving third-worldism

Lobbying for changes of the institutional rules and the power distribution within international institutions as self-declared advocates of their regions and, in more general terms, the developing world as a whole, has also led to a flurry of coalition-building in which IBSA was at the forefront. One particular characteristic of this coalition-building is the conscious revitalization of age-honoured Third World institutions such as the G77 and the Non-Aligned Movement (NAM). Even though these older Southern alliances may have lost much of their previous relevance (Nafey 2005: 2 ff.), IBSA members continue to attend their meetings, as for the fourteenth summit of the NAM in September 2006 in Cuba, where Mbeki and Singh proceeded, subsequent to the first IBSA summit in Brazil. Compared to IBSA's narrow and rather pragmatic approach to international relations, these broad coalitions of highly diverse countries with widely differing political interests are surely not the most promising tool within the former's strategy. Since the Cold War is over and since all IBSA members engaged in market-opening reforms during the last years, South–South cooperation within these groups has also ceased to serve any ideological purposes. However, these Third-World coalitions may still serve IBSA as an institutional device to rally Southern countries that back their global goals. They can be enlisted to support the IBSA members' objective of gaining more influence in international relations and balancing the existing preponderance of the United States and other actors from the North (John de Sousa 2007: 2 ff.). Hence, its vocal role in these coalitions which make IBSA resemble the formers' *de facto* 'executive committee'.

Another, more concrete example of South–South cooperation with the objective of strengthening Southern bargaining power vis-à-vis the US and other developed countries of the global North is the Global System of Trade Preferences among Developing Countries (GSTP), established under the umbrella of G77. The GSTP came into effect in 1989 with a membership of 40 countries. Under its arrangements relating to tariffs, non-tariff barriers and direct trade, measures are negotiated on a product-by-product basis among developing countries (ESCWA 2004). The third round of negotiations launched in June 2004 in São Paulo should make up for the rather weak results of the first two rounds initiated in 1986 in

Brasilia and in 1992 in Teheran. As the Brazilian foreign minister Amorim pointed out in his inaugural speech to a special session at ministerial level:

> Today we have an additional point in the global economy. Trade among our countries represents a considerably high growth rate. Our economies are more open and have become a more important factor in the development strategy of our countries. The increase of South–South trade has been greatly influenced by regional integration agreements.[11]

A more recent, although most likely no more stable, coalition than the volatile G77 or NAM is G20, which under the leadership of India and Brazil first appeared during the WTO's Cancun ministerial in 2003. The main objective of this group of states since then has been to balance the position of the US and the EU in WTO ministerial meetings under the auspices of the Doha Round, which was once designated as a development round. The members of G20 demand better access for their agrarian products to the highly protected markets of the US, the EU and Japan, and seek to exclude the so-called Singapore issues[12] from further negotiations unless substantive progress has been reached with regard to the liberalization of agriculture (Fernandes de Oliveira 2006: 324 ff.).

Strengthening Southern interregionalism

The rationale behind IBSA's increased interest in Southern economic cooperation is thus to lend it more substance vis-à-vis relations with the North, thereby diminishing the still overwhelming economic dependence on developed countries. Fostering interregional relations between the regional organizations pertaining to the IBSA partners is part and parcel of this strategy. It is a counter-strategy to the fledgling interregional relations the Triad, as the globe's economic core regions consisting of North America, EU–Europe, and East Asia, has established through dialogue forums such as the Asia–Europe Meeting (ASEM), the Asia–Pacific Economic Cooperation (APEC) and the New Transatlantic Agenda (NTA). Compared to these interregional links, Southern countries have either established only weak interregional institutions of their own or rather preferred to establish direct interregional links with Northern countries.

It is thus noteworthy that in the area of trade, IBSA pursued some sort of proxy interregionalism. It is the regional equivalent to IBSA's role as some sort of a de facto 'executive committee' of global Third World coalitions. IBSA members have been spearheading preferential trade agreements, which are intended to be a first step towards the creation of a free trade area. Bilateral free trade agreements have been signed between India and MERCOSUR in January 2004 and between MERCOSUR and Southern Africa Customs Union (SACU) in December 2004. SACU and India also proclaimed the conclusion of a preferential trade agreement by the end of 2006 (CUTS 2006). Negotiations were eventually launched in Walvis Bay, Namibia, in February 2008, but have so far remained inconclusive.[13] That India has not brought in the whole of South Asia is testimony to the fragile regional economic cooperation of South Asia which despite the creation of the South Asian Free Trade Area (SAFTA) is still held hostage by Indian–Pakistani hostility.

Yet, with regard to the envisioned Trilateral Free Trade Agreement (T-FTA) between India, MERCOSUR and SACU the inclusion of the respective regional blocs is not only politically desired but also a necessity for Brazil and South Africa because both are already members of customs unions and therefore bound to maintain common external tariffs with their partners. In order to negotiate a free-trade agreement with other actors they would have to withdraw from MERCOSUR or SACU. Since both South Africa and Brazil view regional power bases in the form of integration schemes such as the Southern African Development Community (SADC) and the African Union (AU) or MERCOSUR and the Union of South American Nations (Unasur) as pivotal to their global ambitions (Miller 2005: 53; Hirst and Soares de Lima 2006: 29 ff.), this is unfeasible. However, IBSA members are not interested in a further strengthening of their regional organizations either. With regard to the weak institutional framework of MERCOSUR, SACU and SAARC, Flemes rightly indicates that IBSA members demand multilateral structures when it serves their interest to balance stronger actors but that they are far less disposed to accept stronger institutions if weaker actors' desire for deeper integration could limit their own freedom of action (Flemes 2007: 23).

The shallow institutional base of these quasi-interregional arrangements notwithstanding, economic studies on the possible outcomes of PTAs or FTAs amongst the IBSA members and their regional organizations show some promising results (ESCWA 2004, CUTS 2006). Given the still very low level of trade relations between the three countries, the potential for growth is considerable. On the other hand, there are several limitations for increased trade relations, at least in the short term. First of all, the long distances between the regions produce high transaction costs, especially because necessary air and shipping connections have so far hardly been established. A second problem is the lack of understanding of each other's trade potential and policies, and third, there is a lack of interest within the business circles of IBSA partners. Some of these issues have already been addressed within trilateral working groups and during the IBSA business summits. Perhaps the most striking problem is the lack of mutual benefits between the three economies, especially in the agricultural sector. In the wake of Indian Prime Minister Singh's visit to Brazil in September 2006 his Minister of State for Commerce, Jairam Ramesh, set off a diplomatic firestorm by telling a Brazilian journalist that the idea of natural allies 'is a little naïve' and that both countries were actually 'competitors'.[14] And finally it has to be borne in mind that the total trade with Southern countries will stay far below the total trade with the Triad countries. Notwithstanding a strong increase during recent years, its relative importance will remain rather weak.

Pay-offs

It would, however, be entirely wrong to belittle the results IBSA cooperation has achieved so far in its quest for a greater political role in international institutions.

Although IBSA may have made little progress with its agenda of reforming the UN and the Bretton Woods Institutions, the stature of Brazil and India in the WTO has markedly increased over the last few years. Here, India and Brazil managed to establish themselves successfully as exclusive interlocutors of their regions and the South with the most powerful actors in the world economy. This success is also reflected in the special relationships that the EU and the US have established with IBSA members. The EU launched strategic partnerships with India in November 2004, South Africa in October 2006, and Brazil in August 2007. In March 2006 US President Bush also announced a strategic partnership with India including, after long negotiations, a controversial nuclear pact between both countries which was eventually finalized in July 2007. Both Brazil and South Africa are considered as anchor countries within their regions by the US and during recent years both the Bush administration and the government of Barack Obama have repeatedly demonstrated the special importance they hold for Brazil within Latin America.

These special relations with major powers serve IBSA members' interests in two important ways. First, they underscore the recognition of their significantly increased power status by the US and the EU and thereby lend credence to their ambitions. And second, they enable IBSA states to advance their regional leadership and thereby to pursue their own national objectives. Brazil, for example, co-chaired, together with the US, the negotiations for a continental Free Trade Area of the Americas (FTAA) during its most crucial phase. As the strongest Latin American opponent of a free trade agreement with the US, it was not interested in a successful completion of the negotiations, thereby differing substantially from other states within the region. Nevertheless, Brazilian diplomacy skilfully managed to impose its own perspective of a 'FTAA light' and eventually brought down American plans of a comprehensive free trade agreement (Deblock and Turcotte 2005; Burges 2006).

In March 2006, however, the strategic partnership signed between India and the US put relations between IBSA members to the test. The agreement provides for a transfer of nuclear technologies from the US to India (Meier 2006). While the peaceful use of nuclear energy has always been considered as an important field of cooperation between IBSA members, differences stem from the divergent positions and the different status IBSA members hold within international non-proliferation regimes. Whereas both South Africa and Brazil abandoned their nuclear ambitions in the 1990s and signed the Non Proliferation Treaty (NPT), India not only refused to do so but even carried out tests on nuclear weapons in 1998, that is, two years after the Comprehensive Test Ban Treaty came into force. The positions taken by Brazil and South Africa within the Nuclear Supplier Group (NSG) were therefore of crucial importance. Since 2006 both countries successively chaired the multinational control body, which has to approve the transfer of nuclear technologies envisioned in the strategic partnership between the US and India. And both might have opposed the treaty because they perceived that India was ultimately rewarded for not signing the NPT while they complied with international expectations. But eventually they agreed, together with the other

NSG members, on a waiver for India in September 2008. One month later, in their Delhi Declaration IBSA members explicitly 'welcomed the consensus decision of the IAEA [International Atomic Energy Agency] Board of Governors to approve the India Specific Safeguards Agreement and the decision by the Nuclear Suppliers Group to adjust its guidelines to enable full civil nuclear cooperation between India and the international community'.[15] Both South Africa and Brazil have huge reserves of uranium and are prepared to sell them to India.[16]

The increased importance of India, Brazil and South Africa has also been recognized by the G8 members. Together with China and Mexico, the three IBSA partners have already been invited to attend G8 summits in the past, where they met their counterparts in so-called 'outreach meetings' under a G8+5 formula (Fues 2007: 17; Manz 2007: 35). As a result of the June 2007 summit in Germany this dialogue with major emerging economies is to be extended further. The Heiligendamm process aims at cooperation with emerging economies in the form of a topic-oriented dialogue. However, for the time being IBSA partners are determined not to assume the costs associated with their new role in global affairs. When discussions in Heiligendamm turned to the problem of global warming, Singh, da Silva and Mbeki declared that they will not accept binding greenhouse emission targets for their countries. Instead they pointed at the responsibility of the industrialized world and defended the emerging countries' right to development (Flemes 2007: 22).

Later the same month India and Brazil adopted a similar stance at a G4 meeting in Potsdam, when they were faced with demands by their counterparts to open their markets to industrial goods and services. Both countries went out of the trade talks and declared the G4 dead, once again referring to the above-mentioned distributive negotiation strategy, that Narlikar in the case of India had identified for other policy fields, such as non-proliferation (Narlikar 2006).

Conclusion

Our analysis has shown that legitimately or not, IBSA members pretend to speak for their regions and thus champion a regionalist claim. As (self-styled) advocates for their regions, their interactions adopt an interregional dimension. Yet, it also shows that it pursues a form of multilateralism that seeks to change the intra-institutional power equation. Multilateralism is thus reduced to a policy of institutional balancing and the formation of short-lived, shallow bargaining coalitions. It shows little interest in investing in the strengthening of institutions and pooling sovereignty in order to solve global problems. IBSA is primarily interested in rewriting the rules of the game in several crucial policy fields and institutional arenas.

Yet, in line with the characteristics of 'shallow' multilateralism, IBSA as such is most likely merely a quite fluid and temporary interregional coalition. Its capacity to become a 'multilateral utility' (Dent 2003, 2006) is curtailed by major divisions of interest. Given high transportation costs and the rather limited scope of mutual benefits between their economies on the one hand, and the outstanding importance of economic growth within the foreign policy strategy of these emerging powers on the other, IBSA members are most likely to remain competitors for market shares in the developed world. Further tensions may still result from differing stances in the area of non-proliferation where India increasingly acts like an established nuclear power. Other frictions may arise over relations with external actors. Some Brazilian analysts, for instance, argue that the alliance with India prejudices Brazil in the UN, because it attracts the opposition of China and Pakistan. With regard to the close relationship to China, they argue that Brazil only allied with the enemies of its friends, which will cause its relationship with this economically far more important partner to deteriorate. On the other hand occasional Brazilian calls for the admission of Russia and China exhibit the rather rhetorical function of IBSA's emphasis on democracy and human rights (Draper *et al.* 2004: 19 ff.) while at the same time underscoring the power-political considerations underlying this coalition. IBSA thus constitutes another shift towards a more power-driven order, even if embedded in an institutional context.

Notes

1 For categorizing IBSA as a form of interregionalism, see also Adelmann (2007).
2 Brasilia Declaration, 6 June 2003, http://www.ibsa-trilateral.org/brasil_declaration.htm
3 For an exploration of the potential for cooperation within the most promising sectors see Kumar (2006).
4 See the New Delhi Summit Declaration, http://meaindia.nic.in/pressrelease/2008/10/15pr02.html
5 First IBSA Meeting Joint Declaration, 13 September 2006, http://www.dfa.gov.za/docs/2006/ibsa0920a.htm
6 See the New Delhi Summit Declaration, http://meaindia.nic.in/pressrelease/2008/10/15pr02.html
7 *The Jakarta Post*, 18 September 2006, http://g8live.org/2008/03/27/imf-board-to-weigh-controversial-voting-reform-plan
8 In a second stage of reforms, India and Brazil's share were minimally increased in April 2008, http://www.thaindian.com/newsportal/business/india-gets-little-more-voting-power-in-imf_10043449.html
9 Tshwane India–Brazil–South Africa (IBSA) Summit declaration, 17 October 2007, http://www.info.gov.za/speeches/2007/07101810151001.htm
10 See the New Delhi Summit Declaration, http://meaindia.nic.in/pressrelease/2008/10/15pr02.html
11 Speech by Celso Amorin, 16 June 2004, http://www.unctadxi.org/templates/Page-6001.aspx
12 The Singapore issues were first introduced into the WTO agenda by the EU and other developed countries at the Singapore ministerial of the WTO in 1996 and include items such as procurement, trade facilitation, investment rules and competition policies.
13 See http://www.tralac.org/cgi-bin/giga.cgi?cmd=cause_dir_news_item&cause_id=1694&news_id=44823&cat_id=1073 and http://www.sacu.int/traden.php?include=about/traden/bilateral.html
14 *O Estado de Sao Paulo*, 30 August 2006.
15 New Delhi Summit Declaration, 15 October 2008.
16 http://www.thaindian.com/newsportal/uncategorized/brazil-south-africa-ready-to-sell-uranium-to-india_100107640.html

References

Abbott, K. W. and Snidal, D. (2000) 'Hard and Soft Law in International Governance', in *International Organization*, 54: 3, pp. 421–56.

Acharya, A. (2003/2004) 'Will Asia's Past be its Future?', in *International Security*, 28: 3, pp. 149–64.

Adelmann, M. (2007) SADC – An Actor in International Relations? The External Relations of the Southern African Development Community, University of Freiburg (Germany): PhD Dissertation.

Aggarwal, V. K., ed. (1998) *Institutional Designs for a Complex World: Bargaining, Linkages, and Nesting*, Ithaca: Cornell University Press.

Aggarwal, V. K. and Fogarty, E. A. (2004) 'Between Regionalism and Globalism: European Transregional and Interregional Trade Strategies', in V. K. Aggarwal and E. A. Fogerty, eds, *Europe's Trade Strategies Between Regionalism and Interregionalism*, London: Palgrave MacMillan, pp. 1–40.

Barnett, M. and Duvall, R. (2005) 'Power in International Politics', in *International Organization*, 59: 1, Winter, pp. 39–77.

Bersick, S. (2003) *Zur Politik der interregionalen Beziehungen: Das Beispiel des ASEM-Prozesses*, Baden-Baden: Nomos.

Burges, S. W. (2006) 'Without Sticks or Carrots: Brazilian Leadership in South America During the Cardoso Era, 1992–2003', in *Bulletin of Latin American Research*, 25: 1, 23–42.

CUTS (2006) *South–South Economic Cooperation: Exploring the IBSA Initiative*, Advocacy Document, Jaipur: CUTS Centre for International Trade, Economics and Environment.

Deblock, C. and Turcotte, S. F. (2005) 'Estados Unidos, Brasil y las negociaciones hemisféricas: el ALCA en modalidad bilateral', in *Foro Internacional*, XLV:1, pp. 5–34.

Dent, C. M. (2003) 'The Asia–Europe Meeting (ASEM) and Inter-Regionalism: Towards a Theory of 'Multilateral Utility'', in *Asian Survey*, 44: 2, pp. 213–36.

—— (2006) 'The Asia–Europe Meeting (ASEM) Process: Beyond the Triadic Political Economy?', in H. Hänggi, R. Roloff, and J. Rüland, eds, *International Relations in International Politics*, London: Routledge, pp. 113–30.

Doidge, M. (2004) 'East is East . . .' Inter- and Transregionalism and the EU–ASEAN Relationship, PhD Dissertation, University of Canterbury, Christchurch, 2004.

—— (2008) 'Regional Organizations as Actors in International Relations. Interregionalism and Asymmetric Dialogues', in J. Rüland, G. Schubert, G. Schucher and C. Storz, eds, *Asia–Europe Relations. Building Blocks for Global Governance?*, London: Routledge, pp. 32–54.

Draper, P., Mills, G. and White, L. (2004) *Much Ado About Something? Assessing the Potential of the India–Brazil–SA Forum*, SAIIA Report No. 46, Braamfontein: South African Institute of International Affairs.

ESCWA (2004) *Exploring Potential of South–South Agreements including Global System of Trade Preferences (GSTP)*, Report to the Forum on 'Multilateralism and Regionalism: The New Interface', a pre-event of the Eleventh Session of the UNCTAD XI, 8 June 2004 in São Paulo, Brazil.

Fernandes de Oliveira, M. (2006) 'Estratégias internacionais e diálogo Sul–Sul no governo Lula: alianças duradouras ou coalizões efêmeras?', in F. Villares, ed., *India, Brasil e Africa do Sul. Perspectivas e alianças*, São Paulo: Editora UNESP, pp. 313–33.

Flemes, D. (2007) *Emerging Middle Powers' Soft Balancing Strategy: State and*

Perspectives of the IBSA Dialogue Forum, GIGA Working Papers No. 57, Hamburg: German Institute of Global and Area Studies.

Forman, S. and Segaar, D. (2006) 'New Coalition for Global Governance: The Changing Dynamics of Multilateralism', in *Global Governance*, 12: 2, pp. 205–25.

Fues, T. (2007) 'Global Governance Beyond the G8: Reform Prospects for the Summit Architecture', in *Internationale Politik und Gesellschaft*, No. 2, pp. 11–24.

Hänggi, H. (2006) 'Interregionalism as A Multifacted Phenomenon: In Search of a Typology', in H. Hänggi, R. Roloff, and J. Rüland, eds, *International Relations in International Politics*, London: Routledge, pp. 31–62.

Hänggi, H., Roloff, R. and Rüland, J., eds (2006) *International Relations in International Politics*, London: Routledge.

He, K. and Feng, H. (2008) 'If Not Soft Balancing, Then What? Reconsidering Soft Balancing and US Policy Toward China', in *Security Studies*, 17, pp. 363–95.

Hirst, M. and Soares de Lima, M. R. (2006) 'Brazil as an Intermediate State and Regional Power: Action, Choice and Responsibilities', in *International Affairs*, 82: 1, 21–40.

Hurrell, A. (2004) 'Power, Institutions, and the Production of Inequality', in M. Barnett and R. Duvall, eds, *Power in Global Governance*, Cambridge: Cambridge University Press, pp. 33–59.

—— (2006) 'Hegemony, Liberalism and Global Order: What Space for Would-be Great Powers?', in *International Affairs*, 82: 1, pp. 1–19.

John de Sousa, S.-L. (2007) *India, Brasil, Sudáfrica (IBSA) ¿Un nuevo tipo de multilateralismo interregional del Sur?*, FRIDE Comentario, Madrid: Fundación para las Relaciones Internacionales y el Diálogo Exterior.

Kang, D. C. (2003) 'Getting Asia Wrong: The Need for New Analytic Frameworks', in *International Security*, 27: 4, pp. 57–85.

Keohane, R. O. (1986) 'Reciprocity in International Relations', in *International Organization*, 40: 1, Winter, pp. 1–27.

—— (1990) 'Multilateralism: An Agenda for Research', in *International Journal*, 45: 4, 731–64.

Kirste, K. and Maull, H. W. (1996) 'Zivilmacht und Rollentheorie', in *Zeitschrift für Internationale Beziehungen*, 3: 2, pp. 283–312.

Kuik, C.-C. (2008) 'The Essence of Hedging: Malaysia and Singapore's Response to a Rising China', in *Contemporary Southeast Asia*, 30: 2, pp. 159–85.

Kumar, N. (2006) 'Sectoral Co-operation within IBSA: Some Explorations in South–South Co-operation', in *Synopsis*, 8: 2, pp. 18–21.

Link, W. (1998) *Die Neuordnung der Weltpolitik. Grundprobleme globaler Politik an der Schwelle zum 21. Jahrhundert*, München: Becksche Reihe.

Loewen, H. (2004) *Theorie und Empirie transregionaler Kooperation am Beispiel des Asia–Europe Meeting (ASEM)*, Hamburg: Verlag Dr. Kovac.

—— (2005) 'Die multilaterale Leistungsbilanz des Asia–Europe Meeting (ASEM)', in *Südostasien aktuell*, 24: 1, pp. 20–40.

Manz, T. (2007) 'Allianzen und Gruppen im Global Governance-System – Multilateralismus zwischen partikularen Interessen und universellen Anforderungen', in *Internationale Politik und Gesellschaft*, No. 2, pp. 25–44.

Martens, J. (2003) *The Future of Multilateralism after Monterrey and Johannesburg*, Berlin: Friedrich Ebert Stiftung, Occasional Papers, No. 10.

—— (2007) *Multistakeholder Partnerships – Future Models of Multilateralism*, Berlin: Friedrich Ebert Stiftung, Occasional Papers, January, No. 29.

Maull, H. W. (1990) 'Germany and Japan: The New Civilian Powers', in *Foreign Affairs*, 69: 5, pp. 91–106.

—— (1992) 'Zivilmacht Bundesrepublik Deutschland. Vierzehn Thesen für eine neue deutsche Außenpolitik', in *Europa-Archiv*, October, pp. 269–78.

Mayntz, R. (2005) 'Governance Theory als fortentwickelte Steuerungstheorie?', in Gunnar Folke Schuppert, ed., *Governance-Forschung. Vergewisserung über Stand und Entwicklungslinien*, Baden-Baden: Nomos, pp. 11–20.

Meier, O. (2006) 'The US–India Nuclear Deal: The End of Universal Non-Proliferation Efforts?', in *Internationale Politik und Gesellschaft*, April, pp. 28–43.

Messner, D. and Nuscheler, F. (2006) 'Das Konzept Global Governance – Stand und Perspektiven', in Senghaas, D. and Roth, M., eds, *Global Governance für Entwicklung und Frieden: Perspektiven nach einem Jahrzehnt*, (Sonderband zum 20-jährigen Bestehen der Stiftung Entwicklung und Frieden), Bonn: Dietz, pp. 18–81.

Miller, D. (2005) 'South Africa and the IBSA Initiative: Constraints and Challenges', in *Africa Insight*, pp. 35, 52–7.

Nafey, A. (2005) 'IBSA Forum: The Rise of "New" Non-Alignment', in *India Quarterly*, 61: 1, pp. 1–78.

Naidu, S. (2006) 'IBSA: A Pragmatic Voice of the South or a Vending Machine of Competing and Diffused Interests?', in *Synopsis*, 8: 2, pp. 21–4.

Narlikar, A. (2006) 'Peculiar Chauvinism or Strategic Calculation? Explaining the Negotiating Strategy of a Rising India', in *International Affairs*, 82: 1, pp. 59–76.

Nolte, D. (2006) *Macht und Machthierarchien in den internationalen Beziehungen: Ein Analysekonzept für die Forschung über regionale Führungsmächte*, GIGA Working Papers No. 29, Hamburg: German Institute of Global and Area Studies.

Pape, R. A. (2005) 'Soft Balancing Against the United States', in *International Security*, 30: 1, pp. 7– 45.

Reinecke, W. H. (1998) *Global Public Policy. Governing without Government?*, Washington, DC: Brookings Institution Press.

Robles, A. C. Jr. (2008) *The Asia–Europe Meeting: The Theory and Practice of Interregionalism*, London: Routledge.

Roloff, R. (1998) 'Globalisierung, Regionalisierung und Gleichgewicht', in C. Masala and R. Roloff (Hrsg.), *Herausforderungen der Realpolitik. Beiträge zur Theoriedebatte in der internationalen Politik*, Köln: SH-Verlag, pp. 61–94.

—— (2001) *Europa, Amerika und Asien zwischen Globalisierung und Regionalisierung. Das Interregional Konzert und die ökonomische Dimension internationaler Politik*, Paderborn: Schoeningh.

—— (2006) 'Interregionalism in Theoretical Perspective: State of the Art', in H. Hänggi, R. Roloff, and J. Rüland, eds, *International Relations in International Politics*, London: Routledge, pp. 17–30.

Rüland, J. (1999) 'The Future of the ASEM Process: Who, How, Why and What?', in W. Stokhof and P. van der Velde, eds, *ASEM. The Asia–Europe Meeting: A Window of Opportunity*, London and New York: Paul Kegan International, pp. 126–51.

—— (2001) *ASEAN and the European Union: A Bumpy Interregional Relationship*, Bonn: Rheinische Friedrich-Wilhelms-Universität Bonn, Zentrum für Europäische Integrationsforschung, Discussion Paper, C 95.

—— (2006) 'Interregionalism: An Unfinished Agenda', in H. Hänggi, R. Roloff, and J. Rüland, eds, *International Relations in International Politics*, London: Routledge, pp. 295–313.

Rüland, J. and Storz, C. (2008) 'Interregionalism and Interregional Cooperation: The Case of Asia–Europe Relations', in J. Rüland, G. Schubert, G. Schucher and C. Storz, eds,

Asia–Europe Relations: Building Block or Stumbling Block for Global Governance?, London: Routledge, pp. 3–31.

Schirm, S. (2005) 'Führungsindikatoren und Erklärungsvariablen für die neue internationale Politik Brasiliens', in *Lateinamerika Analysen*, 11, pp. 107–30.

Sequeira, V. (2008) IBSA, International Relatitons Theories, and Changes in the Global Architecture, Paper presented at the Midwest Political Science Association Conference, Chicago, IL, 3 April.

Soares de Lima, M. R. (2005) 'A política externa brasileira e os desafios da cooperação Sul–Sul', in *Revista Brasileira de Política Internacional*, 48: 1, pp. 24–59.

Stamm, A. (2004) Schwellen- und Ankerländer als Akteure einer globalen Partnerschaft, Bonn: Deutsches Institut für Entwicklung, Discussion Paper No. 1.

University of Helsinki Network for European Studies (2006) ASEM in its Tenth Year. Looking Back, Looking Forward: An Evaluation of ASEM in its First Decade and an Exploration of its Future Possibilities. European Background Study, University of Helsinki, March.

Yeo, L. H. (2003) *Asia and Europe. The Development and Different Dimensions of ASEM*, London: Routledge.

10 MERCOSUR's relations with East Asian countries

A critical assessment[1]

Amalia Stuhldreher

Introduction

Since its creation in March 1991, MERCOSUR (Southern Common Market) has established the project of regional integration in Latin America which has reached the highest level of consolidation on the long list of integrative experiments carried out within the region. The fast progress made in its first implementation phase (until 1994) boosted it into the ground of an elected interlocutor for conducting commercial negotiations with the various actors in the global arena. Based on the decision to aim at creating a customs union, all member countries in 1994 made a commitment under the Ouro Preto Protocol (OPP)[2] to implement a common external trade policy.

However, the impasse that encircled MERCOSUR from 1998 triggered broad academic discussions and brought about repeated 'relaunching' attempts at political action level. The goal consistently aimed at joining forces to consolidate the regional integration process. Nonetheless, contrary to such good intentions, the bloc's internal dissension added to the crises the countries were undergoing and the decision by a potential full member country, Chile, to take on a more independent foreign trade policy, ended up increasingly debilitating the bloc while affecting its global position. In spite of this, and the concomitant 'devaluation' of MERCOSUR, although some observers did not hesitate to deem it a downright failure, for a long time MERCOSUR was taken into consideration as an influential interlocutor in hemispheric negotiations on the Free Trade Area of the Americas (FTAA), interregional negotiations with the European Union (EU), and global negotiations within the World Trade Organization (WTO), all of which were not exactly going through a dynamic spell during the last few years. Rather, they were dragging along the weight of their own failures. Additionally, the current global crisis poses the question about the further evolution of global commerce and its implications for MERCOSUR countries.[3] However, apart from the unfavourable international climate for trade liberalization movements, MERCOSUR itself is facing growing difficulties in terms of coordination of interest among its members related to its external agenda (INTAL 2009: 119).[4]

Beyond these negotiations, which have been regarded as the backbone of the bloc's external position, it is worth noting that, for a few years now, MERCOSUR has embarked on a series of negotiations with various regions and countries. Keeping in line with the widespread trend across Latin America to ascribe greater importance to East Asian countries, MERCOSUR laid bridges towards them. Some time later, however, it is thought that progress on this negotiation front gives no reason for elation. In view of these facts, the purpose of this chapter is to analyse the ongoing negotiation processes with East Asia in the light of some theoretical concepts within the discipline of international relations, upon which discussions may be conducted as to the entity of international actors of blocs such as the EU and MERCOSUR. The implicit intention of the analysis is not only to gather data regarding the particular current situation of the South American bloc concerning its relations with East Asian countries, but also to draw some conclusions as to the impact the negotiations with these countries may have on MERCOSUR's external agenda with a view to the future, while discussing the quality of MERCOSUR as an 'international actor'.

Theoretical reflections on the concept of 'international actor'

In order to consider MERCOSUR as an international actor, discussions should be embedded within current debates in the discipline of international relations. In theoretical terms, three alternative interpretative schemes are worth highlighting: the realistic approach puts forward that integration processes encompass strong power considerations, manifested in aspects such as national sovereignty, which is not easily relinquished in pursuit of a joint position. According to the interpretation of Classic Realism and Neorealism, cooperation initiatives between national states would only help to reach a temporary balance. Given the features of the international system – anarchical, decentralized, where force is a major and constant resort – an authentic integration among nations turns out to be an implausible prospect. The international structure constrains cooperation among states, which, as unitary and rational actors, become decisive driving forces of international relations (Morgenthau 1986). Thus, realists emphasize the central importance of the national states in, for instance, the cooperation in conceiving and implementing European joint foreign policy, even though it is acknowledged that, along with strong national 'trends of thought', there increasingly arise 'collective' elements that coexist in some dynamic balance with the former (Hill 1997). Within this approach, the political dynamics of regionalism are associated with forming alliances (Walt 1987) often linked to balance-of-power and economic competition dynamics in 'neomercantilist' terms (Roloff 2001).

Long opposed to the realist paradigm, two other theoretical approaches within the discipline of international relations are worth mentioning: liberal institutionalism and constructivism.

On the one hand, new-liberal institutionalism does not question the realistic premise which states that the international system is intrinsically anarchical. However, it emphasizes the feasibility of change through international institutions. Likewise, this approach conceptualizes such institutions as a reflection of power distribution within the international system, which is in turn a conditioning factor to its performance (Keohane and Martin 1995: 45). According to this approach, interests, strategies and political choices by the states become overt at the moment of creating specific institutions. It is in this instance that the question is posed as to how far international institutions – particularly subregional schemes – are capable of straining such national interests and identities. Instead, constructivism is centred in a role of compliance with rules and ideas in the surge of collective identities that would eventually lead to a consistent joint external position. Interstate cooperation is considered a social process that may lead to a new interpretation of political interests by the actors involved (Wendt 1992, 1994; Katzenstein 1996). Also, the effect of regulations is underscored, emphasizing their constitutive character in establishing new international relations (Klotz 1995): the surge of common regulations leads to a redefinition of national interests and gives way to the emergence of joint state identities. From this approach, the analysis of international relations is not merely reduced to its material factors (Adler 1991, 1997; Checkel 1998) based on such variables as culture, identity and perceptions, among others.

At the finest level of accuracy, in consideration of the strict conceptualization of the international role of blocs such as unified Europe, the work by Gunnar Sjöstedt on the 'actorness' criterion (Sjöstedt 1977) as well as the 'presence' criterion introduced by David Allen and Michael Smith (Allen and Smith 1991: 97–8) become key in this respect. According to Sjöstedt, an international actor constitutes an entity that meets three criteria: it is clearly delimited from other actors and its environment, is autonomous since it acts as its own lawmaker and makes decisions in an independent manner, and possesses certain structural prerequisites to operate at international level such as legal personality, a diplomatic corps, etc. Allen and Smith argue that the relevant point in this context is not the actor itself but, rather, its presence in the international arena. This 'presence' constitutes a feature in certain political areas which impacts on actions and expectations of participants, being either tangible or intangible in nature.

Seen as debate originally for consideration to the EU, the prevailing discussion in this context is the yet unfilled gap between the real capabilities of the EU and the expectations as to its activities (Hill 1993). This consideration is to some extent applicable to MERCOSUR. In an attempt to treat such a gap as relative, Christopher Hill interprets the European Union/European Commission (EU/EC) as a 'system of external relations'. This means that European nations constitute a sub-system as part of the international system as a whole. In turn, they make up a system (that is, not a single actor) which generates international relations (collective or individual in nature; of political or economic kind) rather than a clear-cut 'European foreign policy' as such (Hill 1993: 322). Given the existing gap between 'prescription' and 'reality' regarding the role of Europe, Allen and Smith point out that Western Europe should not be considered a fully developed actor susceptible of being compared with the national state model. In spite of this, Europe is believed to have a 'variable and multidimensional presence' in the international arena, acting in a relatively active manner in the various fields of international politics, which could be addressed as a 'variable geometry' (Allen and Smith 1991: 96–104).

In an eventual attempt to compare MERCOSUR and its role as an international actor, it is only fair to note that the situation of both blocs is clearly dissimilar. According to Sjöstedt's considerations on the concept of 'actorness' it is proven, however, that MERCOSUR has incipient elements which, if worked out in depth, could lay the foundations of its own possible consolidation as an international actor. Thus, as regards the criterion of constituting a clearly delimited entity as different from other actors and its environment, it may be assumed that its member states granted it international legal personality by signing the OPP on 17 December 1994. Such legal status is also acknowledged by third-party states which consider MERCOSUR as an entity separate from its members (Haller 2001: 285), which is clearly evidenced by the prolific agenda of negotiations the group is scheduled to follow.

While MERCOSUR possesses international legal personality, as is the case with any other international organization, such legal personality is only of secondary relevance (Cienfuegos 2001: 9). As regards autonomy and the capacity to make its own laws and decisions, it should be mentioned that MERCOSUR's institutional system, for being purely intergovernmental, actually determines that decision-making clearly depends upon the political will of its member states, given the lack of supranational elements that would grant some degree of independence to its bodies. On the contrary, as far as external autonomy is concerned, the bloc does not face any kind of restriction to its activities that exceeds the provisions of international law. With reference to the structural prerequisites for operating at international level, i.e. legal personality, as mentioned in previous paragraphs, the OPP explicitly stated such a feature, as opposed to the founding Treaty of Asunción. In practice, the major manifestation of MERCOSUR's international legal personality is the signing of international treaties. It is often used by the bloc and is governed by sections 8d and 14 of the OPP and supplementary sections 36, 40 and 42 of said protocol, internal regulations, and other unilateral acts by its institutions (Cienfuegos 2001: 2).

Sjöstedt also made reference to the capacity to have its own diplomatic agents. In this regard, it should be noted that both active and passive legation capacity was not precisely anticipated in the legal framework that gave origin to MERCOSUR, although it may be assumed on the grounds of the international legal status conferred by the OPP. MERCOSUR is neither a full member, nor does it have any lower status (e.g. as an observer) in other international organizations. Therefore, unlike other Latin American schemes such as the Andean Community (CAN – Comunidad Andina de Naciones) and the Caribbean Community (CARICOM), it did not take part in meetings held by other organizations (Cienfuegos 2001: 5).[5]

MERCOSUR's common foreign policy: modus operandi of its institutions

As already stated, despite the initial achievements by the bloc connected with favourable international conditions, mainly since 1998–9, increasing difficulties were seen at joint position level: as regards common external trade policy, the carefully planned common external tariff could not be implemented to the whole range of products. Besides, different priorities in foreign policies for the major partners, namely, Argentina and Brazil, became clearly visible, which consequently made it difficult to consolidate a consistent external position.[6]

According to the philosophy of the bloc, the group's foreign relations with other international legal persons are regulated in such a way that, when member states conduct bilateral or joint negotiations with third parties in matters within MERCOSUR's jurisdiction, this dimension is to be observed. When the bloc as such embarks upon direct negotiations, authority is divided between the Common Market Council (CMC) and the Common Market Group (CMG). The former represents the last instance in decision-making and the latter is in charge of the day-to-day formalities of the various processes. In practice, the chair of the Council holds the *pro tempore* presidency and takes over the representation of the bloc before the international community and must coordinate the position of MERCOSUR before the international bodies (Cienfuegos 2001: 7). In addition, special bodies called '*ad-hoc* groups' were created for operating support purposes. They do not report to any particular body; they gather only if necessary and are competent in specific issues. Among these is the 'External Relations-Ad-Hoc-Group'.[7] Similarly, the Technical Cooperation Committee was established under the CMG in charge of preparing agreements with international organizations and ensuring their fulfilment. It operates along with the CMG in its negotiations within this sphere. In addition, MERCOSUR Trade Commission (MTC) is responsible for following up on issues to do with intra-zone trade and with third-party countries. A step towards the consolidation of the bloc's external representation was given in 2003 when the Commission of Permanent Representatives of MERCOSUR was created under the Common Market Council.

External relations of MERCOSUR with regard to East Asia

In general terms, in spite of its broad agenda of external negotiations, the bloc has not been able to make any significant progress on the various negotiation fronts. More precisely, in the last few years, MERCOSUR's external agenda has been predominantly concerned about two issues which are not strictly related to the main subject of this paper: on the one hand, multilateral negotiations within the framework of the WTO, and on the other hand, Venezuela entering MERCOSUR trading bloc as a full member. However, the bloc has not been able to make progress in negotiations involving relevant matters, neither for the developed countries nor for their developing partners. In fact, multiple initiatives took place, such as negotiations launched with Morocco, Egypt, Canada, the Gulf Cooperation Council, Israel, Pakistan, Jordan and Turkey. In addition, the determination to negotiate a trilateral free trade area (MERCOSUR/India/SACU – Southern Africa Customs Union) was announced as part of the IBSA initiative (India, Brazil, South Africa). These negotiations, with a view to a fixed preference agreement between MERCOSUR and SACU reached an end, but the agreement remained unsigned.

There was a new rapprochement with Panama, the Dominican Republic, Central American countries and the Caribbean community (CARICOM). Nevertheless, a few agreements were eventually reached in recent years: first, the one with the Andean Community of Nations (ACN); second, the one with India; third, the one with SACU; and fourth, the one with Israel. Out of these four agreements only the first and second were enforced. With Jordan and Turkey only two Framework Agreements were concluded. In specific terms, the standoff in the negotiations with industrialized countries was imbued with a conflict of interests which prevented a great variety of related issues from being resolved. Likewise, negotiations with developing countries originated slightly ambitious agreements, both in terms of the range of goods covered and the negotiated tariff preferences (INTAL 2006: 79; and 2009: 119).

With reference to the specific relation between the bloc and East Asian countries, the balance is particularly modest. Beyond a shadow of a doubt, this region has gained importance in the last ten years in the eyes of decision-makers at the Foreign Offices of the Southern Cone. It is true as well that, as regards bilateral relations with those countries, each member of MERCOSUR has made individual progress, which, however, has not been promoted towards the level of joint decision-making. An emblematic comparison of the diplomatic activity by countries such as Argentina, Brazil and Chile (MERCOSUR member countries) with those of its Asian partners – in spite of the differences in the quantity of human and natural resources, etc. – has suggested a number of significant dissimilarities among them as regards their vision towards Asia–Pacific, the role assigned to the Asian region within the framework of external integration and international economic policy, the degree of knowledge about the counterparts, negotiation skills and strategies, and the coordination of policies and activities between the public and the private sectors (Moneta 2005: 198).

Focus has been channelled particularly towards the phenomenal growth of China as a global power which is already in the short term generating a series of winners and losers in Latin America and the Caribbean. Whether such a thing is a threat or an opportunity has triggered all sorts of differing opinions (Nogueira: 2007). In the case of MERCOSUR, there is no question as to the central role China plays as an importer of agricultural products, mineral products and fuels needed for their development process, which implied significant increases in South American exports during the last few years. Brazil is China's number one Latin American partner and bilateral trade practically tripled during 2000–06, a blessing for the indebted Brazilian economy and, especially, for soybean, steel and iron ore exporters, which account for two-thirds of overall Brazilian exports (Blázquez-Lidoy, Rodríguez and Santiso 2006: 35).[8] Moreover, in April 2009 China became Brazil's most important trade partner for the first time.[9] In addition to being an appealing market for the reception of Chinese investment (Oliva 2005: 216–18; Correa López and González García 2006; Oviedo 2005: 18), Brazil and China cooperated for a long time both in industrial and high-technology sectors (aerospace, satellite and telecommunications) under the 1995 'strategic partnership' agreement (Cesarin 2005: 30; Altemani de Olivera 2006; Oviedo 2005: 18–19).

In May 2009 the two countries subscribed to a joint action plan for the period 2010–14.[10]

Regardless of the above-mentioned figures, there are some additional strategic considerations at political-diplomatic level, especially for Brazil. The Sino-Brazilian relationship is marked by a similar view of the world that determines compatible perceptions about the world order, the South–South relations and the cooperation towards development. The activity by multilateral bodies is a key issue with regard to coincidences in the international sphere. China, one of the five permanent members of the United Nations Security Council, disclosed that the country may support Brazil's candidacy to enter the Council as a permanent member. Brazil endorsed China joining the WTO and recognized its 'market economy' status, a move which was copied by Argentina, Chile, Cuba and Venezuela.

As opposed to this positive perception, it is worth pointing out that the growing presence of China in the subcontinent also brings about different feelings of unease: as regards the implications as a competitor producer in third-party markets, especially in the manufactured products business line, its increasing competitiveness, comparative advantages in terms of allocation of production factors, production scale capabilities, and the strong presence of the Chinese government in fostering industrial activity, have already posed a serious threat to a great number of Latin American industrial business lines at all technological levels (Mesquita Moreira 2006; Schott 2006; Lora 2007). As has already been mentioned, even the intra-bloc trading dynamics were modified by the presence of China.[11] Despite the elation triggered by the reported agriculture and mining export records, one of the biggest concerns is the idea of a trading pattern that might reproduce the old Manila galleons' 'Silk Route' which clearly had negative consequences for local industrial development.[12] In this context, it was not really surprising that in August 2007 the Argentineans adopted restrictive measures against Chinese products, such as tyres, footwear, toys, textiles and clothing (*La Nación* 26 August 2007). Among non-traditional Chinese exports already causing worries is the automobile industry. At present, South American imports of Chinese vehicles do not pose serious competition for regional automobile industries. However, analysts underscore that this matter should not be underestimated, since Chinese exports have started to increase their market share in Brazil and Chile (Newsletter MERCOSUR ABC: 1 November 2006).

Beyond that, and considering the importance of foreign trade for the economies of MERCOSUR countries, it must be stated that the current global crisis presupposes great challenges to come. Even if the so-called 'traditional' trading pattern with China has not already been essentially modified, it is clear that the crisis has already affected evolution of MERCOSUR foreign trade.[13]

On a different note, the bloc as a whole lacks unity in action by the various members, which makes it difficult to build a relationship with China, since no consistent policy towards this country can possibly be adopted (Oviedo 2005: 2). In 1997, MERCOSUR–China Dialogue Meetings were set up. Since then, five meetings have been held between the parties,[14] intending to coordinate positions and deepen political dialogue and economic cooperation. Regardless of the above, in 2005 Charles Tang, a Chinese–Brazilian businessman, created by his own initiative the MERCOSUR–China and Asia–Pacific Chamber of Commerce. This is the first initiative of its kind aiming at fostering not only commercial but also social and cultural relations.

In the early stages, China had already manifested interest in signing a free trade agreement with MERCOSUR as a bloc. On the other hand, MERCOSUR made a proposal to the Chinese counterpart to make fixed tariff preferences flexible. However, two inconveniences showed up right away. First, an internal obstacle arose due to the MERCOSUR producers' strong fear of a virtual impossibility to compete with the giant-scale Asian production. Second, there was the fact that Paraguay maintained diplomatic relations with Taiwan and, by 2003, they had already signed a free trade agreement. In spite of this, the idea has not been totally discarded. From the conversations with Argentina and Brazil Foreign Offices' decision-makers, it is perceived that the subject should be addressed with some degree of flexibility since the possibility that Paraguay may change its position is not to be excluded. However, the current position has specific implications. In the eyes of some observers, it was precisely owing to internal inconsistency that MERCOSUR–China multilateral diplomacy was doomed to failure. Such a relation model is currently undergoing a critical moment as opposed to the boom of bilateral diplomacy (Oviedo 2005: 3, 8). Some analysts, however, have particularly underscored the indirect value inherent to the relationship between MERCOSUR and China in connection with the position on ongoing international trade negotiations. In this respect, Nogueira states that the trading relation with China is a strategic bond for the bloc, since the position of the Asian country favours the position of Argentina and Brazil in the discussion with the EU and the USA on the liberalization of trade, an ace the Argentinian and Brazilian governments would be holding within this framework (Nogueira 2004).

Similarly, Japan and South Korea are also counterparts with an interesting relationship potential for MERCOSUR countries, which, on an individual basis, especially since the 1990s, have endeavoured to strengthen relationships with these partners. Brazil represents a historically interesting case given the presence of a significantly large community of Japanese migrants' descendants. Even so, however, following the applicable general rule in Latin America, the relevance of the 'human dimension' in this bond contrasts with the relative insignificance of economic relations (Kagami 2002). Only after the 'lost decade' of the 1980s, have Latin American countries gained significance, still marginal, on Japan's external political agenda. When the Cold War ended, traditional US security policy aspects stopped being as determining as they had previously been. Meanwhile, Japan enhanced its image by introducing the nation as a partner, as it contributed with cooperation towards decreasing the economic and political instability in Latin America. With MERCOSUR countries in particular, dialogue was conducted on a regular basis since 1995. For Japan, this meant a more independent political course detached from the USA, although there was caution. Above all, the prospective Free Trade Area of the Americas (FTAA) worried the Japanese leaders.

However, in spite of the interests involved in Latin America, due to specific internal problems and the lack of a clearly shaped external policy, Japan is very unlikely to operate as a bridge between the subcontinent and East Asia (Franke 2004), which is proposed at diplomatic declarations level (Watanabe 2006). Nevertheless, the Japanese Chamber of Commerce and Industry (Japan–Argentina Joint Committee) and the Japan Economic Federation (Nippon-Keidanren, Japan–Brazil Economic Committee) asked the government of Japan to initiate negotiations with MERCOSUR to achieve an Economic Partnership Agreement between the two countries. Thus, according to JETRO (the official Japanese foreign trade organization) Buenos Aires authorities, the countries of the bloc and Chile would be included in the list of countries Japan expects to make agreements with by 2010 (Inaba 2004).[15] In 2006 MERCOSUR countries and Japan agreed upon the creation of a Working Group on Trade and Investment. Nevertheless, until June 2009 no significant progress was made on this front due to differences between the partners to define on which issues and under which conditions cooperation should focus.

Nonetheless, the Embassy of Japan in Argentina revealed data which show a dramatic increase in the number of Japanese visitors to MERCOSUR in the last few years, which took place concomitantly with the implementation of projects to promote tourism in MERCOSUR and with training of professionals of the bloc in Japan. The 2005 opening of the MERCOSUR Tourism Office in Tokyo is also worthy of mention (INTAL 2007).

With regard to bilateral relations with Korea, President Kim Dae-jung visited Brazil in 2001, which led to the creation of the 'Brazil–South Korea Special Alliance for the 21st Century',[16] an instrument that went farther in 2004 with the creation of 'Broad Cooperation Relation for Common Prosperity in the 21st Century'. Similarly, the Argentine and Korean governments immediately established the same cooperation mechanism. On this occasion, the real intention of Korean President Roh Moo-hynn was to replicate the model of the Chile–Korea agreement, by forcing a joint declaration that would commit Brazil and Argentina to initiate a serious negotiation aimed at signing a free trade agreement between Korea and MERCOSUR. The presidents of Argentina and Korea agreed upon the formal initiation of a feasibility and impact study in the event that the negotiation towards a free trade agreement was to be conducted. Such a study was officially completed by the end of 2007. However, such as with China, and notwithstanding the creation of a joint Working Group, progress in coordination of actions from the bloc with regard to Korea is not consistent with the potential ascribed to it. In this case, it should be noted that at the present time there are some differences that would make a joint position difficult: on the one hand, Argentina and Brazil agree on the fact that a free trade agreement with Korea would pose significant challenges to their local industries. On the other hand, Uruguay endorses the idea of a free trade agreement. Given Brazil's special weight within MERCOSUR it is difficult to assume that the bloc will engage in a negotiation like the one proposed by Korea. Rather both Argentina and Brazil suggested that the negotiation should be restricted to *general* trade and trade promotion.

According to some analysts, although it is too early to state that there is a real qualitative change in the relations between MERCOSUR and South Korea, there are some signs of change in mutual perception, where the real benefits of a closer relationship are glimpsed. In fact, economic studies reveal that the level of mutual benefits between the economies of the South American bloc and Korea is really high.[17] An antecedent which cannot pass unnoticed is the experience Korea and Chile have in negotiating a free trade agreement. After all, in the case of MERCOSUR–Korea, together with the different positions mentioned, some other serious, practical difficulties persist in the field of investment and trade (Woo 2004).[18] As Di Masi states, however, the main issue to elucidate is whether conditions are actually given for such dissimilar partners to initiate a long-term closer sustainable relationship process, amidst the need to generate a multi-dimensional vision of the rapprochement process beyond all economic issues (Di Masi 2006).[19] Yet, there is no really smooth mechanism of relations between the parties in spite of the dialogue with South Korea within the framework of MERCOSUR Committee of Permanent Representatives.

As regards bilateral links between MERCOSUR countries and the Association of Southeast Asian Nations (ASEAN), as mentioned previously, the relationship capacity is diverse in nature. Mairal states that ASEAN and MERCOSUR have only recently developed an interest in furthering a mutual relationship. It seems that both regions came to the same conclusion almost simultaneously that it is convenient to intensify their relations, or more precisely, that the evolution of a different scheme cannot be respectively overlooked, in spite of any difficulty that may arise during the development of the link between the economies of each region, such as difficulties in transportation, geographical distance and lack of mutual knowledge (Mairal 1996: 2). Particularly in the Southern Cone, it is acknowledged that ASEAN has proven diplomatic capacity and a potential to become one of the connecting threads of the set of Asia–Pacific integration agreements (Moneta 2005: 199).

Given the low level of economic interaction, it was only in 1995 that the design of a MERCOSUR–ASEAN dialogue was actually planned. In 1997, the then-president Carlos Menem encouraged the creation of a free trade area between both blocs. He was also seeking to establish a joint business council (*La Nación*, 2 April 1997). For a long time, however, the initiatives did not render any tangible results in spite of the discussion process that took place within the framework of the so-called integration forum between both regions. The aim was to exchange information mainly in the business area. In the beginning, deepening the bond with ASEAN raised remarkable interest among academics and government officials which faded away with time: the initiatives were limited to fostering trade and investment. Thus, for many the MERCOSUR years found it impossible to reach any institutional agreements, neither with ASEAN nor with any other Asia–Pacific association (Oviedo 2005: 4). In November 2008 the Ministers of both regions met for the first time in Brasilia in order to discuss some issues, such as the progress of global negotiation within the WTO, the international financial crisis and food security. They agreed upon the creation of a bilateral dialogue mechanism on trade and economic issues. On an individual basis, in March 2004 Singapore expressed its interest in launching negotiations aimed at signing a free trade agreement with MERCOSUR. However, MERCOSUR members only agreed upon the discussion of the Memorandum of Understanding on Trade and Investment with Singapore, which was concluded in September 2007. In October 2008 a Singaporean delegation visited MERCOSUR countries and proposed the initation of a feasibility and impact study. Moreover, in November 2008 the MERCOSUR–Singapore Consulting Group met for the first time in Brasilia and agreed upon further mechanisms to identify areas of cooperation.

Last but not least, it is worth mentioning that the MERCOSUR–India link was the only one that led to the signing of specific agreements within the spectrum of partner countries considered here: thus, in June 2003 a Framework Agreement was signed, which triggered negotiations between the parties aiming at the future establishment of a free trade area. In January 2004 the text of the so-called Fixed Preferences Agreement was signed, giving room to several rounds of negotiation (Zanchetta 2005: 141), although until March 2009 none of the resulting agreements have been in force since they had not been ratified by all the MERCOSUR members.

In precise terms, the Fixed Preferences Agreement consists of preferential coverage of 450 products made in MERCOSUR and 452 made in India, which may access the counterpart market with a tariff preference of 10 per cent, 20 per cent and 100 per cent.[20] Although this agreement has been described as important at diplomatic level ('a path-breaking pact of extreme importance': Amorim: 2005), it should not be overlooked that the products which bear a higher tariff are granted less tariff preference and only a few are granted 100 per cent. Among these, there are several on which there is a very low or zero tariff (Paladino 2005: 144).

For MERCOSUR particularly, it is estimated that in the future, India could become an interesting partner if, based on the rapid population growth, the nation liberalizes its strict restrictive policy in connection with agro-food imports. At present, except for soybean oil, India does not have to import any staple food product as a substitute. For this reason, the Fixed Preferences Agreement is not significant for the parties in the terms in which it was subscribed. Rather, expectations have been set on broadening the preferences during the following negotiation stage (De la Sota 2004: 4–5, 7). In this regard, although the situation is not expected to change dramatically (COMISEC 2007), the Foreign Offices of MERCOSUR countries are interested in making progress in this respect. Thus, in November 2006 the first negotiation round to expand and deepen trade negotiations took place.[21]

Conclusions

Within this framework, there arises the question of the impact on MERCOSUR's quality as an international actor, as progress on the external agenda in dealing with its East Asian partners is made. In comparative terms, not only is MERCOSUR clearly far from being as effective as the commercial diplomacy of the EU, exercised by the Commission, but also, it has a long way to go towards achieving the political-diplomatic coordination of the so-called EU 'second pillar'.

In principle, it is not due to legal-formal factors that the consolidation of MERCOSUR as an international actor becomes difficult to achieve. In Sjöstedt's terms, it may be said that MERCOSUR as an actor was, since its very origin, intuitively perceived as an autonomous entity, clearly delimited against other actors and its environment, designed with all the necessary structural conditions to act at an international level. According to Allen and Smith, the fast progress made by MERCOSUR, mainly within the first few years of its history, enabled the bloc to consolidate its 'presence' on the global scene. Hence, it may be concluded that, regardless of its intergovernmental character and novel nature, such 'presence' had an impact on the actions and expectations of the participants in the game of international politics, which made it possible for the bloc to position gradually at trade diplomacy level. Therefore, there is no doubt that recognition granted to the integration process around MERCOSUR encouraged numerous partners, among these, several East Asian countries, to try to strengthen ties with the South American bloc.

However, the dynamics that took over the definition of the external agenda within the bloc entailed a mortgage on its future development: The goals and methodology adopted in the negotiations varied according to the initiative, which would be completely logical. But rather, the problem lies in the fact that the criteria which determine the choices made are not clear enough. Thus, in some cases, a fixed preferences model is taken on (with or without product reciprocity), while in other cases, the choice tends to seek a free trade area agreement.

The analysis of the external negotiation agenda does not disclose the elements that guide the choices the bloc makes. While negotiations with industrialized countries have reached a virtually stagnant position, MERCOSUR seems to have embarked upon South–South agreements without applying selection criteria as far as economic factors are concerned. Similarly, many of the initiatives launched simply lacked continuity (INTAL 2006: 80). All of these cause an impression bordering on eclecticism which is often justified in terms of pragmatism. Since the concept of 'presence' involves elements of both a tangible and an intangible nature, and considering the potential attributed to a bloc that comprises an economy of huge potential such as that of Brazil, it is understood that the crises and the 'devaluation' of MERCOSUR in the last few years were not enough to completely deteriorate the bloc's external image. Sharp observers of the process have often had the feeling that the merits and achievements of the scheme were better recognized abroad than within the bloc. However, it is evident that for a while now, there has been a strong need for a future-oriented strategy to clearly define priorities around which the bloc's external negotiation agenda should revolve.

Even though there is awareness among decision-making circles in all MERCOSUR foreign offices as regards the implicit potential in the bond with East Asian countries, these partners are unlikely to emerge as an urgent priority for the bloc as such, since the accumulation of various negotiation fronts in the last few years caused a bottle-neck effect which is intended to be channelled as well as is possible.

The new international context presupposes remarkable challenges for the years to come, bearing in mind the relevance of foreign trade for the economy of MERCOSUR countries. Many international institutions have estimated reductions in the level of activity for the main developed economies and for the Latin American economies. Likewise, the political times prevailing in the region will possibly impact on MERCOSUR's external agenda, prioritizing such issues as physical and infrastructural integration in the South American space. This, however, should not be interpreted as a lack of interest towards the East Asian area but rather as the bloc's necessary reconciliation with its factual institutional weakness.

With reference to the future definition of MERCOSUR's external agenda with regard to other partners, in line with Moneta's statements and in spite of the current global crisis, it is foreseen that Asia–Pacific tends towards operating as a system, especially in the economic environment, around major actors such as China and Japan. Based on the network of subscribed agreements and those that may come up from ongoing negotiations, such integrative configurations that would also comprise ASEAN–India negotiations should be included in the definition of joint positions of the South American bloc, which means that Asia–Pacific would be perceived as a subregional scheme, overcoming the isolated perception by partners that has so far been predominant (Moneta 2006: 151–2). There is a clear need for a long-term comprehensive vision, hand-in-hand with access to strategic data to be integrated to the respective decision-making processes. On the other hand, there is an urge to develop broad dialogue and data networks with the various Asia–Pacific actors both of institutional and informal character (Moneta 2005: 199).

Finally, in generic terms and as a general action principle, it should be noted that it is imperative to avoid a merely symbolic policy across the entire spectrum of MERCOSUR external relations, including in this assumption the relations with East Asia. At an image level, which comes in as a fundamental factor in current international relations, the replication of fronts and the overlapping of negotiation processes of different importance and conducted at different speeds, in the long run may be interpreted by the counterparts as an attempt to offset its own lightness or insignificance, which in Allen and Smith's terms would stand for the scarce international presence of MERCOSUR as an actor. This may manifestly imply an even sharper weakening of its possibilities to establish itself as a consistent and operative entity.

Notes

1 I would like to thank Uziel Nogueira from INTAL (Institute for the Integration of Latin America and the Caribbean) for his warm willingness to share his viewpoints on the subject herein discussed. I extend my grateful acknowledgement to Ambassador Agustín Colombo Sierra, the Undersecretary for Latin American Politics of the Argentine Foreign Affairs Office, who kindly called on collaborators of his team to partake in a valuable discussion about some hypotheses included in this paper.

Especially, I would like to thank Pablo A. Grinspun, Felipe Alvárez de Toledo and Ma. Constanza Crespo, officials of the MERCOSUR's Economic and Commercial Affairs Office of said Ministry, for the information provided.

2 Ouro Preto Protocol (OPP). http://idatd.eclac.cl/controversias/Normativas/MERCOSUR/ Ingles/Protocol_of_Ouro_Preto.pdf (accessed 18 November 2009).

3 The impact of the international crisis on the real economy of these countries became particularly evident after the last quarter of 2008. Until then the effects had been mainly financial, with no impact on growth rates, which, in spite of the deceleration taking place in the last part of that year, were significant on average. The outlook for 2009 was not positive and reductions in the level of activity were forecast for some of the member countries. Regional trade, both intra- and extra-MERCOSUR, continued increasing during 2008. Nevertheless, intra-regional exports were still around 15 per cent of total export values (Lucángeli, Sanguinetti and Zamorano 2009: 15).

4 On the one hand, in September 2006 the Uruguayan President, Tabaré Vázquez, called for more flexibility in their external negotiation and proposed the incorporation of *bilaterality*, either within the framework of the joint negotiations or by allowing individual negotiations. On the other hand, Argentina has currently no great incentives facing new trade liberalization initiatives. Finally, Brazil has especially focused its efforts on getting results at the Doha Round.

5 In the last few years incipient efforts to strengthen joint diplomatic presence were seen; for instance, the November 2002 opening of the first-ever Joint Trade Promotion Office in the Capital City of Germany, the bloc's major European trade partner.

6 A clear example is Brazil's ambition to hold a permanent seat in the United Nations Security Council. Quite the contrary, Argentina looks forward to a temporary seat for Latin America. In this regard, international trade negotiations behaved as a catalyst given the necessity to arbitrate in the issue of disimilar agendas managed by the various members of the bloc. Some aspects remain pending such as are manifested by the long-lasting bilateral agreements which perforate the common external tariff (Bouzas and Fanelli 2001: 219). In spite of it all, a common standpoint was achieved to deal with the EU and the Free Trade Area of the Americas (FTAA). This did not occur when dealing with the Comunidad Andina de Naciones (CAN – the Andean Community) and Mexico in the beginning.

7 The ad hoc group dealing with foreign relations was created in 1995 from the merger of two pre-existent groups: one in charge of the relations between MERCOSUR and the WTO, and one in charge of the relations between MERCOSUR and LAIA (ALADI – Asociación Latinoamericana de Integración).

8 Some authors state that back in 2004 sales to China already accounted for half the highest export incomes Brazil had ever reached. Thus, China became a strong boost for the Brazilian GDP growth (Blázquez-Lidoy, Rodríguez and Santiso 2006: 36).

9 Until that time the bilateral trade betwen China and Brazil amounted to US$3,200 million while the trade between Brazil and the USA amounted to US$2,800 million. According to Brazilian official data, the bilateral trade betwwen Brazil and China topped US$6,400 million in 2008 which implies a growth rate of about 56 per cent compared to 2007 (*La Nación*, 20 May 2009). Compared to that, Argentine exports to China in 2006 amounted to US$46,569 million, which represented the fourth target following Brazil, Chile and USA. Argentine exports basically comprise oleaginous fruits, oil seeds, leather, fur skin, and steel and iron goods. Above all, however, the increase in oil shipping to China is noticeably significant, as it went from US$226 million in 2005 to US$906 million in 2006. Conversely, imports from China topped US$34,159 million in 2006. This particularly highlights that the average growth of Argentina's purchases from China between 2000 and 2006 reached 76.8 per cent, surpassing the growth of imports from Brazil (49 per cent) (*La Nación*, 27 February 2007).

10 The plan mentioned comprises many agreements related to different matters such as

financial cooperation or petroleum prospection by Petrobras and its Chinese partner SINOPEC (China Petroleum and Chemical Corp). It also includes a U$S10,000 million credit of the Chinese Development Bank to Petrobras (*La Nación*, 20 May 2009).

11 According to data provided by the Brazilian Foreign Trade Secretariat (Secex), in January 2007, sales from China into Brazil (US$791 million) surpassed the sales from Argentina to Brazil (US$672 million). A year before, in January 2006, Argentina had exported up to US$538 million into Brazil exceeding China's exports by a narrow margin (US$500) (*La Nación*, 27 February 2007).

12 An example of this is illustrated by the fact that 96 per cent of Argentina's exports into China in 2006 were made up of primary products, agricultural goods and fuels, while only 4 per cent were goods of industrial origin. Conversely, 97 per cent of Argentina's imports from China were manufactured goods: machinery and equipment, electrical and mechanical devices, chemicals, plastic, toys and footwear (*La Nación*, 27 February 2007).

13 According to official statistical data, in December 2008 Argentina's exports experienced the first reduction in the last six years (6 per cent compared to 2007) due to a reduction in commodity prices and to smaller sales, especially of soybean for China (*La Nación*, 22 December 2008).

14 After the First Meeting in Beijing, the Second Meeting was held in Brasilia in October 1998 where some cooperation proposals were outlined. Bilateral projects were differentiated from those projects to be carried out within MERCOSUR. In October 2000, in the Third Meeting held in Beijing, a Technical Cooperation Agreement was proposed. The Fourth Meeting took place in Montevideo in September 2003, and the Fifth, in Beijing in 2004. The MERCOSUR–China Liaison Group (Grupo de Enlace MERCOSUR China) was defined. A feasibility study on a potential trade agreement was agreed upon (Oviedo 2005: 6).

15 In July 2007 the House of Representatives of Chile approved the Free Trade Agreement (FTA) signed by this country and Japan. The agreement was then reviewed by the Chilean Senate Committees and voted on in plenary by the Higher House. As a matter of fact, Chile (associate member of MERCOSUR) was the first South American country to sign trade agreements with China, India, Japan and Korea. In June 2007 the Japanese Parliament ratified the agreement, which allowed a broad ratification of the Strategic Economic Association Agreement (SEAA) negotiated with Chile. The FTA will eliminate tariffs from almost all Japanese exports to Chile while 90.5 per cent of Chilean shipments will eventually pay zero tariffs throughout a ten-year period.

16 Based on this instrument, a few undertakings were started in areas such as information technology, biotechnology, space industry, electrical engineering, iron and steel industry and clean technologies (Di Masi 2006: 110).

17 MERCOSUR countries are interested in the openness of Korea's agricultural products market, which is highly protected by tariff and non-tariff barriers. On the other hand, Korean industrial products are highly competitive. For these reasons MERCOSUR's industrial sectors are reluctant about the idea of a broader agreement with the Korean counterpart.

18 It is worth mentioning (a) the existing high tariffs and non-tariff barriers, (b) commercial difficulties due to geographical distance and cultural differences, (c) different methods of payment, (d) incompatible international regulations, and (e) obstacles to investment such as lack of agreements to eradicate double taxation, the inflexibility of labour laws and the high banking costs (Woo 2004).

19 In this regard, the author underscores that one of the most important constraints in deepening bilateral relations is based on the recurrent crises the region has undergone. He cites the 1999 crisis in Brazil and the crisis in Argentina since 2001, which worried foreign investors. This resulted in projects being called off (Di Masi 2006: 104).

20 For further details about offers by MERCOSUR and India, refer to Paladino 2005: 143.

21 In New Delhi, the MERCOSUR delegation reaffirmed the proposal released in July

2006, which points at extending the range of preferences until it adds up to half the tariff nomenclature, establishing a general margin of at least 20 per cent. In addition, MERCOSUR suggested deepening the preferences that have already been negotiated. India submitted an additional list of requests for 626 other products. MERCOSUR submitted its own requests (for 2,099 other products).

References

Adler, E. (1991) 'Cognitive Evolution: A Dynamic Approach for the Study of International Relations and Their Progress', in E. Adler and B. Crawford, eds, *Progress in Post-War International Relations*, New York: Cambridge University Press, pp. 43–88.

—— (1997) 'Seizing the Middle Ground: Constructivism in World Politics', in *European Journal of International Relations*, Vol. 3, No. 3, pp. 319–63.

Allen, D. and Smith, M. (1991) 'Western Europe's Presence in the Contemporary International Arena', in M. Holland, ed., *The Future of European Political Cooperation – Essays on Theory and Practice*, Houndsmills: Macmillan, pp. 95–120.

Altemani de Olivera, H. (2006) 'China–Brasil: perspectivas de cooperación Sur–Sur', in *Nueva Sociedad*, No. 203, May–June, Caracas, pp. 138–47.

Amorim, C. (2005) *India, MERCOSUR, IBSA triangular trade alliance mooted – Signing of India–MERCOSUR Agreement Path breaking*, Press Information Bureau, Goverment of India, New Delhi, 21 March.

Blázquez-Lidoy, J., Rodríguez, J. and Santiso, J. (2006) '¿Angel o demonio? Los efectos del comercio chino en los países de América Latina', in *Revista CEPAL*, No. 90, December, pp. 17–43.

Bouzas, R. and Fanelli, J. M. (2001) *MERCOSUR: integración y crecimiento*, Fundación OSDE.

Cesarin, S. (2005) 'Ejes y estrategias del desarrollo económico chino: enfoques para América Latina y el Caribe', in S. Cesarin, C. Moneta, eds, *China y América Latina – Nuevos enfoques sobre cooperación y desarrollo. ¿Una nueva Ruta de la Seda?*, BID-INTAL, Buenos Aires, pp.3–48.

Checkel, J. (1998) 'The Constructivism Turn in International Theory', in *World Politics*, Vol. 50, pp. 324–48.

Cienfuegos, M. (2001) 'Las relaciones exteriores del Mercosur', in *Revista Cidob d'Afers Internacionals*, No. 54–5, November.

COMISEC (2007) 'Estado de Situación de las Negociaciones', in *Avances* III, Año 3, Presidencia de la República Oriental del Uruguay; Oficina de Planeameinto y Presupuesto; Comisión Sectorial para el MERCOSUR; Comisión Sectorial para el MERCOSUR, March, Communiqué COFCOR 1998.

Correa López, G. and González García, J. (2006) 'La inversión extranjera directa: China como competidor y socio estratégico', in *Nueva Sociedad*, No. 203, May–June, pp. 114–27.

De la Sota, M. (2004) *Acuerdo de Preferencias Arancelarias Fijas – MERCOSUR–India*. Dirección Nacional de Mercados, Secretaría de Agricultura, Ganadería, Pesca y Alimentación, Buenos Aires, 16 December.

Di Masi, J. (2006) 'Relaciones preferenciales MERCOSUR–Corea: Perspectivas de una idea en construcción', in *Revista HMMiC*, No. IV, pp. 101–12.

Franke, U. (2004) 'In weiter Ferne, so nah? Die Beziehungen zwischen Japan und Lateinamerika', in *KAS-Auslandsinformationen*, August, pp. 68–96.

Haller, A. (2001) *MERCOSUR – Rechtliche Würdigung der außenwirtschaftlichen*

Beziehungen und Vereinbarkeit mit dem Welthandelssystem, Aschendorff Rechtsverlag Münster, Verlag O. Schmidt, Köln, Schriften zum Außenwirtschaftsrecht; Bd. 7.

Hill, C. (1993) 'The Capability-Expectations Gap, or Conceptualizing Europe's International Role', in *Journal of Common Market Studies*, Vol. 31, No. 3, September, pp. 305–28.

—— (1997) 'The Actors Involved: National Perspectives', in E. Regelsberger, P. de Schoutheete de Tervarent and W. Wessels, eds, *Foreign Policy of the European Union. From EPC to CSPC and Beyond*, Boulder, London: Lynne Rienner Publishers, pp. 85–97.

Inaba, K. (2004) *La Dimensión Económica y Comercial de la relación Asia–América Latina:* Seminario El Asia–Pacífico y su proyección latinoamericana, Montevideo, 30 September.

INTAL (2003) Carta Mensual No. 87, October.

—— (2006) Informe MERCOSUR No. 11.

—— (2007) 'MERCOSUR–Japón: cooperación y evolución del turismo', in *Carta Mensual*, No. 128, March.

—— (2009) MERCOSUR Report No. 13. Buenos Aires, IDB-INTAL.

Kagami, M. (2002) 'Japan and Latin America', in K. Radtke, and W. Wiesebron, eds, *Japan, Europe, Latin America, and Their Strategic Partners*, Armonk, London, pp. 113–39.

Katzenstein, P. (1996) *The Culture of National Security. Norms and Identity in World Politics*, New York, Columbia University Press.

Keohane, R. and Martin, L. (1995) 'The Promise of Institutionalist Theory', in *International Security*, Vol. 19, No. 1, pp. 39–51.

Klotz, A. (1995) *Norms in International Relations – The Struggle Against Apartheid*, Ithaca, Cornell University Press.

Lora, E. (2007) *Should Latin America Fear China?*, IADB, Research Department, Working Paper Series, 531, February.

Lucángeli, J., Sanguinetti, M. and Zamorano, A. (2009) 'MERCOSUR: Consequences of the international financial crisis', in *CEI Journal, Foreign trade and integration*, No. 14, Ministry of Foreign Affairs, International Trade and Worship; Argentina, pp. 15–36.

Mairal, N. (1996) 'Diálogo MERCOSUR–ASEAN, el escenario inicial', in Boletín Informativo Techint No. 289, Unidad Analítica Asia Pacífico, MeyOSP, Secretaría de Industria, Comercio y Minería, Secretaría de Comercio Exterior, Buenos Aires, December.

Morgenthau, H. (1986) *Política entre las naciones. La lucha por el poder y la paz*, Buenos Aires, Grupo Editor Latinoamericano.

Mesquita Moreira, M. (2006) *Fear of China: Is There a Future for Manufacturing in Latin America?*, INTAL-ITD, Occasional Paper 36, Buenos Aires, April.

Moneta, C. (2005) 'China y el nuevo proceso de institucionalización de la integración en Asia–Pacífico: perspectivas para Argentina/MERCOSUR y América Latina', in *China y América Latina. Nuevos enfoques sobre cooperación y desarrollo. ¿Una nueva Ruta de la Seda?*, BID-INTAL, Buenos Aires, pp. 163–202.

—— (2006) 'Los escenarios de China en Asia–Pacífico. Reflexiones para el MERCOSUR', in *Nueva Sociedad*, No. 203, May–June, Caracas, pp. 148–59.

Newsletter MERCOSUR ABC, No. 145, 1 November 2006.

Nogueira, U. (2004) 'China, la gran carta para el MERCOSUR', in *Diario Clarín*, 27 June.

—— (2007) *China–Latin America Relations in the XXI Century: Partners or rivals?*, Working Paper Series, ICS No. 2007–5, Institute of China Studies, University of Malaya, Kuala Lumpur.

Oliva, C. (2005) 'Inversiones en América Latina: la inserción regional de China', in S. Cesarin, and C. Moneta, eds, *China y América Latina: Nuevos enfoques sobres cooperación y desarrollo. ¿Una nueva Ruta de la Seda?*, BID-INTAL, Buenos Aires, pp. 203–33.

Oviedo, E. (2005) *Crisis del multilateralismo y auge de la diplomacia bilateral en la relación MERCOSUR–China*, Ponencia presentada en la VI Reunión de la Red de Estudios de América Latina y el Caribe sobre Asia–Pacífico, BID/INTAL, 12 and 13 October, Buenos Aires: BID/INTAL.

Paladino, F. (2005) 'Impactos a análisis del Acuerdo: Asceso a mercados', in *Argentina–India: Un desafío y una oportunidad para la vinculación económica y comercial*, CARI/CEPAL/IICA, Morón, pp. 142–4.

Roloff, R. (2001) *Europa, America und Asien zwischen Globalisierung und Regionalisierung. Das interregionale Konzert und die ökonomische Dimension internationaler Politik*, Paderborn, Munich, Vienna, Zürich: Ferdinand Schöningh.

Schott, P. (2006) *The Relative Revealed Competitiveness of China's Exports to the United States vis à vis other Countries in Asia, the Caribbean, Latin America and the OECD*, INTAL-ITD Occasional Paper 39, July, Buenos Aires.

Sjöstedt, G. (1977) *The External Role of the European Union*, Westmead: Saxon House.

Walt, S. (1987) *The Origins of Alliances*, Ithaca, New York: Cornell UP.

Watanabe, M. (2006) *Asia y América Latina: El Papel de Japón*, Discurso del Ministro de la Embajada del Japón en la República Argentina en el XII encuentro de Estudiantes de Graduados en Relaciones Internacionales del Cono Sur 2006 por el CEERI, 10 November, Palacio San Martín, Buenos Aires.

Wendt, A. (1992) 'Anarchy is What States Make of it: The Social Construction of Power Politics', in *International Organization*, Vol. 46, No. 2, Spring, pp. 391–426.

—— (1994) 'Collective Identity Formation and the International State', in *American Political Science Review*, Vol. 88, No. 2, June, pp. 384–96.

Woo, J. (2004) *Resumen de la Relación Comercial e Inversión entre Corea y MERCOSUR: Ponencia realizada en el 'Seminario MERCOSUR–Corea*, organizado por el Ministerio de Relaciones Exteriores, Comercio Internacional y Culto de la Nación Argentina; Buenos Aires, Argentina, 4 June.

Zanchetta, M. E. (2005) 'Relación MERCOSUR–República de la India: Indtroducción', in *Argentina–India. Un desafío y una oportunidad para la vinculación económica y comercial*, CARI/CEPAL/IICA, Morón, pp. 141–2.

11 Trade bilateralism between Latin America and East Asia – notions on the interplay with the WTO

Howard Loewen

Introduction

Latin American and East Asian economies have grown substantially over the last decades based on the growth of foreign direct investment (FDI) and trade. Since the end of the nineties the governments in both regions have decided to put up a number of bilateral Free Trade Agreements (FTAs). This trend is another manifestation of a worldwide process of economic integration which currently encompasses 300 bilateral and regional free trade agreements. Seven years ago only 130 bilateral FTAs existed (*The Wall Street Journal*, 5 November 2007). Bilateral FTAs co-exist with regional integration schemes such as ASEAN (Association of Southeast Asian Nations), ASEAN+3 (ASEAN, China, South Korea and Japan), AFTA (ASEAN Free Trade Area) and EAS (East Asian Summit) on the Asian side, and MERCOSUR (Southern Common Market), Andean Community and LAIA (Latin American Integration Association) on the Latin American side. As the intraregional welfare gains in both regions increased, new interregional FTAs emerged as a means of securing access to new export markets. Currently there are nine FTAs in force, linking the two regions.

One common argument put forward against FTAs is that they endanger the multilateral World Trade System. Their diversity adds to the so-called noodle-bowl (Figure 11.1) of trade-distorting effects in general and overlapping agreements in particular. Does this interpretation also hold true for interregional FTAs? In order to answer this question we will take a look at the scope and WTO-relevant characteristics of the most important interregional FTAs between Latin America and East Asia. In this study, I will focus on FTAs linking the economies of China and Chile, Japan and Mexico, Japan and Chile, Singapore and Panama, and South Korea and Chile. It is argued here that the observed cases do not support the thesis that FTA interplay with the WTO is always of a disruptive nature. Examples for this synergetic interplay are, first, FTA elements that go beyond already existing WTO rules and, second, a significant record of FTA notification to the WTO. On the other hand, the mixture of different rules of origin may lessen the multilateral effectiveness of interregional FTAs.

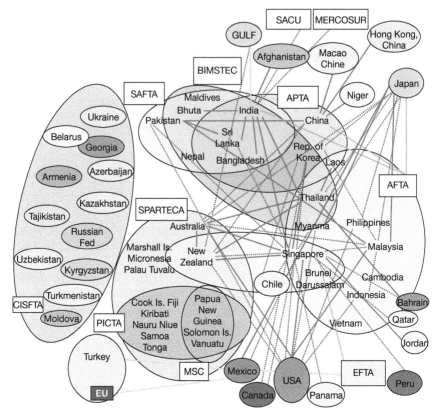

Figure 11.1 The noodle bowl of FTAs in the world
Source: APTIAD 2007.

Trade bilateralism

The expansion of bilateral Free Trade Agreements raises the question of how to conceptualize this phenomenon. Bilateralism in general may be conceived of as political and/or economic interactions between two states. Trade Bilateralism refers to trade policy or trade liberalization options that two states utilize by signing an agreement in order to optimize trade flow between their economies. The trade policy portfolio consists of unilateral, bilateral, minilateral and multilateral liberalization measures.

Unilateral trade liberalization occurs very rarely in the Asia–Pacific region. So far, only Singapore and Hong Kong decided to reduce trade barriers unilaterally. At present, all other states prefer to engage in bilateral trade agreements, which can be geographically concentrated (i.e. Singapore–Japan) or geographically dispersed (i.e. China–Chile). Minilateral Trade Agreements such as the North American Free Trade Agreement (NAFTA) and the Association of Southeast Asian Nations (ASEAN) may thus also be concentrated in one region or dispersed as in the case of the Free Trade Agreement of the Americas and the Trans Pacific Strategic Economic Partnership (Aggarwal 2006: 4). Multilateral liberalization can be located at the global level of trade policy and is governed by the World Trade Organization (WTO). Finally FTAs can be conceived of as international institutions. Their rules and regulations qualify them as 'persistent and connected set rules (formal and informal) that prescribe behavioural roles, constrain activity, and shape expectations' (Keohane 1989). They are therefore formal institutions negotiated by states in order to manage trade cooperation issues and problems.

Explaining Trade Bilateralism

Causes of Trade Bilateralism

In order to explain the emergence and the effects of bilateral Free Trade Agreements we will take a look at some explanations from the emergent literature on FTAs. Why do states decide to set up Free Trade Agreements? A first distinction can be made between economic and political variables: *Economic explanations* concentrate on the perceived economic benefits of FTAs (Lloyd 2002: 1284; Aggarwal 2006: 8–9).

According to these economic explanations, FTAs are more likely to be created if there is a match between two countries' industrial structure that would have an effect on the potential benefits of the bilateral agreement, producing an incentive for the states involved to come to an agreement. Similarly, FTAs are desirable from this perspective because they often trigger foreign direct investments and promise gains from trade, factor flows, greater competition in regional markets as well as from a harmonization of national economic policies and regulation.

Political explanations for the initiation of bilateral FTAs on the other hand do not just concentrate on the economic benefits for the states involved but look at a whole range of non-economic factors contributing to the decision to institute a FTA. Many liberals, for example, would look below the level of the nation-state and argue that special interest groups, especially industries or companies with exposure to trade development can strongly influence trade policy choices, steering policy away from the issues they would prefer the state to leave untouched while lobbying for agreements that satisfy their specific trade interests. Similarly, liberals might posit that a country's policy response will vary with its regime type. It may be hypothesized that democratic governments pursue a more liberal foreign economic policy than more authoritarian ones. Beyond regime type, the size and development status of a state might also influence its propensity to enter a FTA. Furthermore, trade policy choices might be determined by the preferences of interest groups, especially industries or companies with exposure to trade development. Last, liberals argue that the significant obstacles to building multilateral trade rules in the institutional context of the WTO as well as in regional arrangements like ASEAN, APEC and MERCOSUR stimulate the demand for bilateral trade institutions.

Scholars of a more realist persuasion deny that the absence of effective multilateral institutions is the reason for the increasing number of bilateral FTAs. For them the simple fact that it is easier for states to realize relative gains in a bilateral agreement is sufficient explanation, whatever the state of multilateral trade cooperation. Similarly, they see FTAs as a tool to reduce security threats.

Constructivist scholars, the last big group discussed here, approach the issue from a completely different angle. For them, the decision to create an FTA is not necessarily linked to tangible benefits for states or specific groups inside the state. It is much more the case that FTAs are currently being created because *that is what states do*. FTAs are in fashion, hence states generally feel obliged to engage in their creation, following an international norm. This tendency can be strengthened or contravened by domestic political traditions which favour less or more active government intervention, determining the openness or restrictiveness of trade policies.

Effects of Trade Bilateralism

More or less all WTO members take part in at least one of the 300 regional and bilateral free trade agreements. Sceptical arguments against FTAs generally start from this observation. It is argued that FTAs could 'threaten to fragment the multilateral trading system and to undermine its core principle of the most-favoured-nation (MFN) treatment' (Schott 2004: 7). Under this WTO agreement member countries are not allowed to discriminate between their trading partners. In short: 'MFN means that every time a country lowers a trade barrier or opens up a market, it has to do so for the same goods or services from all its trading partners – whether rich or poor, weak or strong' (WTO 2007). The most-favoured-nation treatment is laid down in the first article of the General Agreement on Tariffs and Trade (GATT), in Article 2 of the Agreement on Trade in Services (GATS) and in the Agreement on Trade-Related Aspects of Intellectual Property Rights (TRIPS). If countries set up a free trade agreement, a few exceptions may be granted. Under very strict conditions states may set up bilateral or regional rules that apply only to goods traded within the nations involved. These rules are defined in paragraphs 4 to 10 of Article XXIV of the General Agreement on Tariffs and Trade (GATT), the Enabling Clause, and Article V of the General Agreement on Trade in Services (GATS).

The effects of bilateral free trade agreements correlate with their institutional design and their interaction with other trade institutions a) on the global multilateral level (World Trade Organization) and on the regional level (other FTAs and minilateral institutions like ASEAN or APEC). These horizontal and vertical interactions are consequences of the increasing density of international institutions on the bilateral state-to-state level, the regional, the interregional and the global level of the global economic governance system (Young 1996).

Whether interregional free trade agreements are stepping stones or obstacles for the global trading system shall be answered by applying the criteria of *WTO notification*, *WTO-plus elements* (scope), the *rules of origin* and the *emergence of plurilateral FTAs* in the cases of China–Chile, Japan–Mexico, Japan–Chile, Singapore–Panama, and South Korea–Chile.

Trade relations between Latin America and East Asia

For a long time trade relations between Latin America and East Asia were the weakest link in the interactions between the world economic regions. In the late 1980s, however, many Latin American economies decided to unilaterally liberalize their trade policies. This had a significant effect on the interregional trade balance between Latin American and the East Asian economies. The successfully concluded Uruguay round of the General Agreement on Tariffs and Trade added momentum to this development as it eased the liberalization of developing countries' economies and their respective foreign economic policies.

In the last few years, increasing imports of commodities by East Asian states, especially China, have changed the dynamics of current trade relations between the two regions. Table 11.1 clearly shows that industrialized markets like the European Union and the United States have lost impact as Latin America's export destinations in the period between 1995 and 2006, while Asia has gained in importance. Moreover Table 11.2 shows that Latin America's imports from Asia considerably increased from 11.9 per cent to 19.5 per cent in the same period. This development can be explained primarily by the rising imports of Chinese products (from 1.2 per cent up to 6.8 per cent in 2005).

Table 11.1 Latin America's export destinations (in percentages)

	1995	2000	2001	2002	2003	2004	2005	2006
North America	46.0	58.8	57.8	58.1	56.0	54.1	52.9	48.2
EU	17.0	11.5	12.2	12.3	13.3	12.8	12.6	13.9
Latin America	20.7	18.5	17.7	15.9	16.2	18.0	18.2	19.0
Asia	9.8	5.5	5.8	6.8	8.3	8.5	8.9	10.9
Middle East	1.4	1.0	1.3	1.4	1.4	1.5	1.5	1.5

Source: IMF direction of trade statistics, http://www.imfstatistics.org/dot.

Table 11.2 Latin America's import origins (in percentages)

	1995	2000	2001	2002	2003	2004	2005	2006
North America	43.9	50.7	47.2	45.9	44.9	40.6	38.8	38.4
EU	19.1	14.0	14.9	14.7	15.0	14.4	14.4	14.3
Latin America	18.2	16.2	16.2	15.5	16.6	18.2	20.1	21.2
Asia	11.9	12.7	14.9	17.3	17.0	19.7	20.2	19.5
Middle East	1.1	0.8	0.8	0.7	0.7	0.9	1.1	0.8

Source: IMF direction of trade statistics, http://www.imfstatistics.org/dot.

Table 11.3 Bilateral FTAs between Latin America and East Asia

	Mexico	Peru	Chile	Panama	Nicaragua	El Salvador	Guatemala	Paraguay
China		Proposed (2006)	In force (2006) Scope					
India								
Japan	In force (2005) Scope		In force (2007) Scope					
Malaysia			Under negotiation (2007)					
Singapore	Under negotiation (2000)			In force (2006) Scope				
S Korea	Under negotiation (2006)		In force (2004) Scope					
Thailand		Under negotiation (2004)	Proposed (2006)					
Taiwan			Proposed (2006)	In force (2004)	In force (2006)	In force (2007)	In force (2006)	Under negotiation (2004)

Source: Asian Development Bank Database, Asia Regional Integration Center (www.aric.adb.org).

Note: For analytical reasons this study will only focus on the highlighted cases.

In order to manage the growing economic interdependence between the two regions, a number of interregional FTAs were set up (see Table 11.3).

WTO notification

The WTO notification status of the six interregional FTAs in question is laid out in Table 11.4 below. There are basically two types of notification, the Enabling Clause and the GATT/GATS provisions. Since the first criterion mainly provides for the mutual reduction in tariffs on trade in goods among developing countries as well as for developed countries to grant tariff reductions to developing countries, we will only consider the GATT/GATS provisions as relevant since the five interregional FTA cases presented here include industrialized and take-off countries, but no developing countries.

WTO legislation obliges its members to notify the organization of regional trade agreements, whether they are of bilateral or plurilateral nature. Since the year 2000 we can observe a significant trend towards notification under the General Agreement of Trade Art. XXIV (GATT Art. XXIV) and under the General Agreement on Trade in Services (GATS Art. V). In the case of East Asia, current studies imply that more than 53 per cent of concluded FTAs as of June 2007 were notified to the WTO. This rate is bound to rise since many agreements have just been concluded and the process of WTO notification has not yet been initiated (Table 11.4).

A short analysis of the WTO notification status of bilateral FTAs between Latin America and East Asia yields almost the same results as the one above on East Asian Free Trade accords. Of the five concluded interregional bilateral FTAs, three out of four notified under GATT Art. XXIV are also notified under GATS Art. V (Japan–Mexico; Singapore–Panama; South Korea–Chile). The China–Chile FTA has excluded GATS Art. V and the FTA between Japan–Chile has not been notified yet. Since Japan and Chile have notified all their bilateral FTAs so far, it can be expected that the rate of notified interregional FTAS might rise to 100 per cent in the observed cases. It seems as if interregional FTAs are as comprehensive and extending beyond preferences for some goods into services and regulatory issues as their regional counterparts.

Table 11.4 FTA growth in East Asia

	FTAs	*Concluded*	*Under negotiation*	*Proposed*
2000	7	3	1	3
2001	10	5	2	3
2002	14	6	4	4
2003	23	9	5	9
2004	42	14	16	12
2005	67	21	30	16
2006	96	31	42	23
2007	102	36	41	25

Source: Asian Development Bank Database, Asia Regional Integration Centre (www.aric.adb.org).

Table 11.5 WTO notification of bilateral FTAs between Latin America and East Asia

	China–Chile	Japan–Mexico	Japan–Chile	Singapore–Panama	South Korea–Chile
Notified year	2007	2005	No notification yet	2007	2004
GATT Art.	GATT Art. XXIV	GATT Art. XXIV GATS Art. V		GATT Art. XXIV GATS Art. V	GATT Art. XXIV GATS Art. V

Source: Asian Development Bank Database, Asia Regional Integration Center (www.aric.adb.org).

Scope of interregional FTAs: WTO-plus elements

Recent analyses of bilateral Free Trade Agreements in East Asia state that a large number of recent agreements go beyond the WTO framework (goods plus services) by including issues like intellectual property, labour etc. In order to identify 'WTO-plus elements' one can (a) identify the so-called 'Singapore-Issues' (trade facilitation, investment, government procurement, and competition policy). These issues were one part of the WTO Agenda prior to the WTO Ministerial Conference in Cancun in 2004, where they were taken from the agenda due to a lack of consensus. The highest possible WTO-plus contribution incorporates (b) goods, services, Singapore Issues and cooperation enhancement. The latter includes WTO-plus provisions such as labour standards, IT cooperation, small and medium enterprises (SMEs) and environmental issues (Kawai and Wignaraja 2007: 11).

Table 11.6 clearly shows that four out of five observed cases include WTO-plus elements, out of which two (Japan–Chile and South Korea–Chile) cover only Singapore issues and the other two cover Singapore issues and cooperation enhancement issues (Japan–Mexico and South Korea–Chile). The only FTA that stands out in this respect is China–Chile that is currently stuck on the level of goods. Since negotiations on agreement and services are ongoing, a final conclusion cannot be drawn on this bilateral process. Yet, it is quite obvious that WTO-plus provisions are dominant in interregional trade bilateralism between East Asia and Latin America.

Rules of Origin

Rules of Origin are criteria that define where a product was made and which goods will have preferential bilateral tariffs. Thereby they preclude trade deflection among member countries of an FTA. Foreign economic policies may discriminate between exporting countries by applying anti-dumping policies, countervailing duties, quotas and so on. Globalization and the emergence of international value- and product-chains increase the complexity of product processing in general. WTO

Table 11.6 Scope of interregional FTAs/WTO-plus elements

	China–Chile	Japan–Mexico	Japan–Chile	Singapore–Panama	South Korea–Chile
Goods	**Yes** 4 cooperation provisions on environment, e-commerce, information exchange, and SMEs. Ongoing negotiations on agreement on services and investment	No	No	No	No
Goods and services	No	No	No	No	No
WTO-plus elements					
Goods, services and Singapore issues	No	No	**Yes** Agreement has one cooperation provision on IPR issues	No	**Yes**
Goods, services, Singapore issues and cooperation enhancement*		**Yes**		**Yes**	

Source: Asian Development Bank Database, Asia Regional Integration Center (www.aric.adb.org).

Notes: * Cooperation enhancement: WTO-plus provisions such as labour standards, IT cooperation, SMEs and environmental issues.

member states have to ensure the transparency of their rules of orgin, that they do not have distorting, restricting or disruptive consequences for international trade relations, that they are managed in a homogeneous and reliable way and that they should give information about what exactly determines their origin (WTO 2007).

The rules of origin in East Asia show different characteristics and thus appear in different forms: (a) a change in tariff classification (CTC) rule defined at a detailed Harmonized System (HS) level; (b) a regional or local value content (VC) rule which means that a product must satisfy a minimum regional (or local) value in the exporting country or region of an FTA; and (c) a specific process (SP) rule which requires a specific production process for an item (Kawai and Wignaraja 2007: 12).

Table 11.7 shows that four out of five interregional FTAs between East Asia and Latin America have implemented a mixture of the three ROOs (Rules of Origin) rather than utilized a single regulation. Whereas only China and Chile use the Value-Added (VA) and/or change of tariff classification rules (CTC), the remaining FTAs (Japan–Mexico, Japan–Chile, Singapore–Panama, and South Korea–Chile) use a combination of all rules. This observation correlates with a trend in East Asia where 20 out of 30 FTAs use mixed ROOs. Based on company surveys Kawai and Wignaraja argue that the combination of ROOs increases the overlap density and thus complexity of the FTA network in the region (noodle bowl) by increasing the transaction costs (complex procedures to prove the country of origin; changes to production processes) of private business actors. About 64 per cent of the companies in question state that rules of origins should be harmonized in order to ensure stable business operations (Kawai and Wignaraja 2007: 12).

Table 11.7 Rules of Origin

	China–Chile	Japan–Mexico	Japan–Chile	Singapore–Panama	South Korea–Chile
Value-added (VA) rule only	No	No	No	No	No
VA and/or change of tariff classification rules (CTC)	**Yes**	No	No	No	No
VA and/or specific product rules (SP)	No	No	No	No	No
Combination of all rules (VA, CTC, SP etc.)	No	**Yes**	**Yes**	**Yes**	**Yes**

Source: Asian Development Bank Database, Asia Regional Integration Center (www.aric.adb.org).

Conclusion

This short analysis has revealed that interregional trade cooperation between Latin America is to a large extent consistent with WTO norms. By applying the criteria of *WTO notification, WTO-plus elements* (scope and the *rules of origin*) to the cases of interregional FTAs linking China and Chile, Japan and Mexico, Japan and Chile, Singapore and Panama and South Korea and Chile the following specific results were attained: almost all states in question have notified their bilateral agreements to the WTO. This trend correlates with the one in East Asia. Regarding the existence of WTO-plus elements we observed that four out of five interregional FTAs included such provisions. If these interregional FTAs are building blocks for the global trade regime governed by the WTO it remains to be seen. The obstructive nature of mixed rules of origin might harm trade flows and exacerbate the noodle bowl effect. Yet, the growing trend to plurilateral FTAs in regional (ASEAN+x) and in interregional terms (i.e. Trans-Pacific Strategic Economic Partnership) might be an indication of the degree to which states see some utitility in streamlining their different FTAs into more comprehensive, regional, interregional and even multilateral trade agreements.

References

Aggarwal, Vinod K. (2006) 'Bilateral Free Trade Agreements in the Asia–Pacific', in Aggarwal, Vinod K. and Urata, Shurijo, eds, *Bilateral Trade Agreements in the Asia–Pacific*, New York and London: Routledge, pp. 3–26.

Asia-Pacific Trade and Investment Agreement Database (2007), http://www.unescap.org/tid/aptiad/default.aspx

Asian Development Bank Database, Asia Regional Integration Center (www.aric.adb.org).

IMF Direction of Trade Statistics (www.imf.org).

Kawai, Masahiro and Wignaraja, Ganeshan (2007) ASEAN+3 or ASEAN+6: Which way forward?, ADB Discussion Paper No. 77.

Keohane, Robert O. (1989) 'Neoliberal Institutionalism: A Perspective on World Politics', in ibid. *International Institutions and State Power*, Boulder, CO: Westview, pp. 1–20.

Lloyd, Peter (2002) 'New bilateralism in the Asia–Pacific', in *The World Economy*, 25, pp. 1279–96.

Schott, Jeffrey J. (2004) *Free Trade Agreements*, Washington: Institute for International Economics.

WTO (2007) Understanding the WTO, Principles of the trading system (www.wto.org).

The Wall Street Journal (2007) 'Serious talks ensue on trade-distorting Asian FTAs', 5 November.

Young, Oran R. (1996) 'Institutional Linkages in International Society: Polar Perspective', *Global Governance*, 2, pp. 1–24.

12 Non-triadic interregionalism

The case of FEALAC

Gracia Abad

Introduction

Over the last decades, the rising importance of regions in the international context as a consequence of the emergence of many new regional projects and the establishment of different patterns of relations among regions has given rise to a broad literature on new regionalism and interregionalism.

Literature on interregionalism, though still scarce, tries to provide some theoretical insights into the patterns and features of relations among regions. Most of the studies have focused on the reasons for the emergence, development and maintenance of interregional dialogues and relations (including realist, institutional and constructivist arguments); the different types of interregional processes – inter- and transregional relations as well as a 'hybrid form'; the institutional setting and infrastructure on which the interregional processes may rely; and the nature and functions that these kinds of processes may fulfil.

Nonetheless, interregionalism theory has also attracted some criticism. It has frequently been accused of paying attention to those cases of interregionalism which take place within the triad, ignoring those which emerge outside.

According to some authors (Dosch 2005: 187, Rüland 2002), the latter would differ from the former in several aspects:

- The actors involved, which are not military or economic powers but medium powers at most.
- The volume of trade and investment exchanges among the participants is much lower.
- The lack of institutionalization, inherent to all the interregional processes, is even more acute.
- The spectrum of their cooperation: much broader in triadic interregional processes.

In this sense, the models and theoretical explanations developed by interregionalism theory would perfectly explain triadic interregionalism while their validity for cases of non-triadic interregionalism would still have to be proved. In this context, the application of functions usually attached to the interregional processes of the cases that take place outside the triad is of special interest. These functions, according to Rüland (2002), are balancing (including power balancing and institutional balancing), bandwagoning, institution-building, rationalizing, agenda-setting and identity-building.

Other authors conclude that some of them, especially balancing, are not as evident in non-triadic interregionalism (Olivet 2005: 12). Overall, further theoretical and theoretical-practical analyses are needed to clarify the characteristics and nature of non-triadic interregional processes.

Thus, first of all, this chapter will try to ascertain the roots of the differences between triadic and non-triadic interregional processes. Then, it will describe the case of FEALAC (Forum for East Asia–Latin America Cooperation), a prime example of non-triadic interregionalism. Finally, it will conclude that the interregionalism theory may also be applicable to the analysis of cooperation processes which emerge outside the Triad.

The regional-global dimension and the models of interregional relations

The different models of regionalism

All current regional cooperation processes, as long as they are cases of the so-called new regionalism, are attempts to handle the impact of globalization dynamics trying to take maximum advantage and/or to reduce to the minimum any negative effects. Helen Nesadurai (2003: 24) explains how every regional process can be considered as an outcome of, or as a response to, globalization. Similarly, Shaun Breslin and Richard Higgott explain how one of the main issues in the current debates on new regionalism is whether such a phenomenon may be seen as a defensive mechanism or as a way to secure access to global markets in order to be able to compete (Breslin and Higgott 2002: 339). Nesadurai suggests four different models which would constitute as many alternatives to articulate the regionalism-globalization relationship:

- open regionalism (neoliberal approach)
- open regionalism (foreign direct investment (FDI) model)
- resistance regionalism
- developmental regionalism.

Two of these approaches, open regionalism in its neoliberal version and resistance regionalism, have been extensively analysed by International Political Economy (IPE) literature over the last few years. The open regionalism approach considers regionalism as a way for national economies to participate in, and take advantage of, globalization dynamics and processes. In other words, it seeks to ensure the participation of a certain country in global activity. In contrast, resistance regionalism appears as a strategy developed, either by the state or by other economic actors, to resist the negative effects of globalization. Through regionalism, states and economic actors expect to be able to retain certain policy instruments and economic arrangements which they would lose if they confronted globalization individually. Nesadurai adds two other models for the explanation of the regionalism-globalization relationship: open regionalism in its FDI version and developmental regionalism.

In the case of the FDI version of open regionalism she emphasises how, even in a context of openness to the globalization process and its effects, governments may use regionalism to manipulate particular aspects of globalization so that they can favour the state, society or certain groups within it. (In the case of FDI, they would see the regional process as a way to attract FDI and thus take greater advantage of globalization.) The fourth type of regionalism regarding its relations with globalization is developmental regionalism. This category describes the employment of selective protection mechanisms or privileges for group member countries in order to allow the development of domestic industries and sectors until they are prepared to compete successfully in the global market. Thus, the features developed by each particular case of regionalism and the selected model depend very much on the states involved in the process and their specific national motivation.

The models of regionalism and their influence on the patterns of interregional relations: developmental interregionalism

While types of regionalism might appear as unimportant regarding the aims of this chapter, they are in fact not unimportant. On the contrary, as Björn Hettne rightly suggests 'regionalisation has structural consequences beyond and above the particular region' (Hettne 2005: 543–71) and so does regionalism; two different but related concepts in relation to which a broad range of literature already exists (Rosamond 2001, Breslin and Higgott 2003: 167–82, Kim 2004: 36–67).[1]

Thus, on the regional level, at least in some cases (those which are purely interregional processes and not transregional ones), interregionalism relies on regional groups as its obvious constituent parts. At the same time, interregionalism may well be considered an element in the sometimes complex political strategies of the regional formations involved (Hettne 2003: 40). Likewise, on the state level, both regional and interregional processes can be considered as elements in a broader strategy developed by the states to manage the globalization phenomenon and its consequences. This is to say that, as Tania Felicio suggests, states tend to respond to the 'complex interdependence of a globalizing world by delegating authority to levels of governance above, below and laterally' (Felicio 2006: 14). Similarly, Heiner Hänggi stresses how 'a "regional actor" is more often than not a framework for action of member states rather than an actor itself' (Hänggi 2006: 33).

Not surprisingly, those regional and interregional processes which entail certain similarities in terms of membership not only influence each other but to a certain extent also mirror each other. In other words, regionalization and globalization are dynamic processes which pose serious challenges (and often interesting opportunities as well) to individual countries. The latter responds to those pressures through a range of means, including regionalism, interregionalism and trans-regionalism. Hence, the patterns of interregional relations that states follow depend on the type of regional processes they belong to and, consequently, the way they prefer to handle the globalization phenomenon as well as their motivations and strategies. This is why – not surprisingly – we see more often than not that the reasons for different states to take part in regional and interregional processes are similar. Likewise, the dynamics they encourage in both sets of processes may be similar too. In this sense, following Heiner Hänggi, it might be possible even to 'classify interregional relations according to the types of regional actors involved' (Hänggi 2006: 33).

Therefore, we can see how the different characteristics of triadic and non-triadic interregional processes may well be rooted in the different strategies developed by the participant countries regarding globalization. Thus, while in cases of triadic interregionalism, we find that the vast majority of constituent countries uphold open regionalism strategies (with some elements of developmental regionalism at most) in cases of non-triadic interregionalism, developmental orientations are much clearer. Indeed, while in cases of triadic interregionalism, participant countries will use the process to take advantage of globalization, in the cases of non-triadic interregionalism, the process is another avenue in which to try to develop their developmental strategies. This is, of course, especially the case for those countries that belong to the non-triadic pole of a given non-triadic inter-regional process though, eventually, certain countries in the triadic bloc might expect to be able to follow some developmentalist strategies as well. In this sense, the functions of non-triadic interregionalism – especially from the perspective of the non-triadic pole – might also be called developmental interregionalism. While not very different from those of the triadic version, they have to be adjusted to the goals and motivations of developmental and even resistance regionalism, and their particular way of engaging with globalization dynamics. Therefore, while states also expect interregionalism to be a bridge between regionalism and multilateralism (Ocampo, 29 March 2001), as in the case of regionalism and multi-lateralism, what they expect from interregionalism differs slightly from the expectations of developed countries and members of the triad.

The case of FEALAC

The Forum for East Asia–Latin America Cooperation (FEALAC) is a good example for what has been explained earlier. One of the regions involved, Latin America, does not belong to the triad while the other, East Asia is the least powerful pole (at least in political and security terms) within it. This was especially so when FEALAC was created, just a couple of years after the unleashing of the Asian financial crisis. In this sense, many countries in Latin America, the non-triadic pole of the process, may be happy to follow developmental strategies through the interregional process. It goes without saying that the weaker among the East Asian participants may also find it interesting to take advantage of the process to pursue such kinds of strategies. At the same time, in a new global scenario characterized by an increasing web of interregional relations, the nonexistence of a link between two regions would translate into a loss of competitiveness for them as well as the situation of being in a worse position regarding globalization dynamics (Low 2006: 87).

Not surprisingly, in the Manila Action Plan of 2004, drafted on the occasion of the second ministerial meeting held in the capital of the Philippines, the members of FEALAC clearly stated that through the cooperation process they expected to achieve a more equal distribution of the benefits resulting from globalization as well as prevent the marginalization of any sector of human society (FEALAC, 31 January 2004). In this sense, apart from the geographical distance, the cultural differences or the lack of mutual knowledge, the existence of different patterns of integration, the lack of resources, the priority they had accorded to their relations with developed countries and/or regions, and the similarities between their comparative advantages are some of the factors which may explain the traditionally low level of the relationship between both regions (Wilhelmy 2005a: 190–7).

Thus, at the end of the 1990s, as the economies of both regions were getting more internationalized and diversified, the establishment of a forum with the characteristics of FEALAC – the only existing formal body of cooperation between East Asia and Latin America – was seen as a vehicle with which to take advantage of their opportunities and to face the common challenges resulting from globalization (The Ministry of Foreign Affairs of Japan, 21 February 2002). In fact, both regions have been facing similar internal and external challenges and may share experiences and develop a strategic partnership in order to handle successfully the dynamics associated with the globalization process (Soesastro 2002: 19).

In 1998 Singapore's Prime Minister Goh Chok Tong, inspired and encouraged by the establishment of ASEM (Asia–Europe Meeting) two years earlier, proposed to Chilean President Eduardo Frei the creation of a forum between Asia and Latin America with the name of East Asia–Latin America Forum (EALAF) (Kuak Jae-Sung 2004: 75). It would be 'a way to bridge the gap between East Asia and Latin America' (Jayakumar, 23 August 2005). While most of the Latin American governments initially did not react in a very enthusiastic way (Wilhelmy, 20 August 2007), the idea became a reality only one year later, in September 1999, with the emergence of a forum comprising 27 countries from both regions.

As in the case of ASEM, the purpose of the forum was to build on pre-existent bilateral as well as bi-regional (ASEAN–MERCOSUR) contacts (Low 2006: 85), to foster mutual exchanges and interactions so as to increase mutual knowledge, promote political dialogue and cooperation, strengthen political, economic and cultural ties between both regions as well as to create avenues for joint action in different areas. This was all formally stated on 30 March 2001, when EALAF held its First Ministerial Meeting in Santiago de Chile (initially planned for 2000) (Low 2006: 89). The meeting constituted the official launch of the forum (Kuak Jae-Sung 2004: 75) and the first of the three ministerial meetings which have been held so far.

On that occasion, the forum, following a Malaysian proposal, changed its name to FEALAC[2] (as it is currently named) and finalized its Framework Document (that the members had started to draft two years before in Singapore), which outlines the principles, goals, objectives and modalities of cooperation. Likewise, the forum also decided on the main organizational aspects that would characterize the process, as well as the level and frequency of the meetings. Once the forum was technically settled, in meeting after meeting the agenda reflected more and more clearly the interregional as well as developmental nature of the process. The third and most recent of these meetings, held at the Itamaraty Palace of Brasilia on 22–23 August 2007, was not an exception to this rule. During the course of the meeting and shedding some light on the likely future of the process, the participants seemed to come to terms with the reality of the limited achievements made for the forum so far and expressed the will to design a new cooperation agenda. However, the existence of the political will they claimed to promote (Xinhua, 24 August 2007) is, at least, doubtful. In fact, as we try to show in this chapter, the lack of such political will has been the main obstacle for the success of the process. In this sense, it is interesting to note, for instance, that most of the foreign ministers of the participant countries are not directly involved in the forum which is frequently left in the hands of high officials, working group coordinators and project managers. Foreign ministers limit themselves, at best, to participating in ministerial meetings every three years. Indeed, the very absence of summits is just another sign of the lack of such political will.

In any case, as mentioned before, the agenda as well as the main issues raised during the meeting were very much in line with the characteristics and evolution of the forum. In this sense, the participants stressed aspects such as poverty, hunger, exclusion, a widening gap between developed and developing countries, energy scarcity and environmental degradation, all of which make it difficult for many states to provide their populations with the most basic services (FEALAC 2007) and endanger the common aspiration to development; ultimately, the reason for them to participate in the forum.

To address these concerns, the representatives agreed to give special priority to the strengthening of trade and investment between both regions. At the same time, through a clear combination of the agenda-setting function of the process and the developmental strategies followed by its members and following the line they had already adopted on the course of the second ministerial meeting (BBC, 1 January 2004), they insisted on the convenience of an early and successful end of the Doha Round, in a sense favourable to poor and emerging countries (Portafolio, 27 August 2007). This approach was consistent with the aims of the United Nations Millennium Development Goals (MERCOSUR abc, 30 August 2007), which remain far from being achieved.

This trend does not seem likely to change in the near future as the agenda for the last Ministerial Meeting (April 2009) included topics such as the economic and financial crisis, and efforts to try to ensure a greater degree of social inclusion or aspects related to environmental protection and sustainable development, among the main issues to be considered by the participants in the meeting. Such orientation is consistent with the fact that many of the participants in FEALAC are also members of the G-20 which, under the leadership of Brazil and India, gathers a large number of emerging economies and international actors. Beyond that, the participants committed themselves to the promotion of integration, cooperation and multilateralism as well as to contributing to the strengthening of the United Nations' role, something which cannot be considered a surprise in any way if we take into account how frequently global issues make their way into the agendas of interregional processes.

Together with ministerial meetings there are, at least, four more levels of meetings. In this sense, we can see how the forum, in line with the usual structure of interregional processes, is organized on the basis of different structures and levels of meetings. They are as follows:

1   Two coordinators – One from each region. Appointed for three-year terms, it is their role to give continuity to the process. They are helped in their tasks by two assistant coordinators. Current coordinators, appointed in August 2007 in Brasilia, are Argentina and Japan which took the baton from Brazil and Korea, which, in turn, replaced Colombia and the Philippines, the first pair of coordinators.
2   Senior officials' meetings – They are held at least once a year to provide the forum with coordination and guidance. They also have to meet to prepare the ministerial meetings.
3   Foreign ministers' meetings – They take place every two years. They constitute the core of the forum. They focus on issues of common interest for both regions decided by consensus. Other sectorial ministerial meetings or summits may take place if the foreign ministers so decide.
4   Three working groups – They were created in 2001 as a way to facilitate work in different areas. They are focused on politics, culture and education; economy and society; science and technology, respectively. Each group has two co-presidents, one coming from each region. They have to come up with concrete proposals for cooperation in the areas covered by each of them. These proposals are prepared on the base of the different projects suggested by the participant countries. As they do not want to give the impression that they disregard the ideas of the different participants, most of the proposals are accepted. This, however, has a collateral effect, as long as it deepens the lack of focus inherent to the forum. These groups meet alternately in both regions in places decided by consensus.

It is interesting to note that the effort of the working group on economy and society which, in a meeting held in Quito in November 2008, stressed the importance of introducing measures in fields such as tourism, investments or small and medium enterprises, led towards trying to contribute towards the enhancement of socio-economic development levels in both regions.

The forum, after the inclusion of the Dominican Republic in 2007 (DR1.com, 29 August 2007), Guatemala and Nicaragua in 2004, and Costa Rica, Cuba and

El Salvador in 2001, currently has 33 participants – 15 on the East Asian side: Australia, Brunei, Cambodia, People's Republic of China, Indonesia, Japan, Korea, Laos, Malaysia, Myanmar, New Zealand, the Philippines, Singapore, Thailand and Vietnam; and 18 Latin American countries: Argentina, Bolivia, Brazil, Chile, Colombia, Costa Rica, Cuba, Ecuador, El Salvador, Nicaragua, Mexico, Guatemala, Panama, Paraguay, Peru, Uruguay, Venezuela and the Dominican Republic. The process might result in further expansion soon as Honduras and Mongolia were granted observer status in the context of the Senior Officials' Meeting held in April 2009 and their applications for full membership are very likely to be accepted by the 4th Ministerial Meeting which will be held in Tokyo. Likewise, Haiti, Surinam and Guyana attended the third ministerial meeting as guests and also expect to be given full member status soon (Xinhua, 24 August 2007). Finally, Brazil called for the admission of the rest of the Caribbean nations (MercoPress, 23 August 2007).

It appears that the United States and Canada are and will remain excluded from this membership by definition (Wilhelmy 2005a: 190–7). In this sense, the participation of Australia and New Zealand might seem contradictory; they are members thanks to Singaporean insistence and pressure and in spite of Malaysian opposition, which has always insisted on the non-Asian character of those countries and was already opposed to their inclusion in ASEM on the same basis.

Taking into account this membership, we can say that the forum constitutes a case of transregional relations (Olivet 2005) as long as the participant countries take part in the forum on an individual basis and not as a consequence of their membership in a regional process. This is not to say that the forum does not contribute to the strengthening of relations between MERCOSUR and ASEAN, two subregional or regional processes represented by many of their members in the forum, which in turn constitute a different and purely interregional process (Olivet 2005: 6). On the contrary, it does contribute.

It is also interesting to note that according to the rules of the forum, its members do not take part as 'countries' but as 'governments of sovereign states'. It seems obvious that we can find the explanation for this wording in Chinese interests to prevent any attempt to include Taiwan or Hong Kong in the forum (Wilhelmy 2005a: 190–7). In fact, this is actually the opposite of what happened in the case of APEC, where the participants do not take part as 'states' or 'governments' but as 'economies', in order to make it possible for Taiwan to participate.

Last but not least FEALAC is characterized by three important features, namely, first it mainly comprises developing countries, which, second, are at different levels of industrialization (hence, there are decisive industrialization gaps) and, third, the Asian members have a trade surplus vis-à-vis Latin America (Kuak Jae-Sung 2004: 79). If we have a look at the first two characteristics mentioned we can easily understand why most of the members of the forum are following regional and interregional developmental strategies.

At the same time, keeping in mind these characteristics, we can consider FEALAC the result of a diversification strategy aimed at enhancing the position of the participant countries in the North–South dialogues. This is especially evident if we take into account that FEALAC is the only process of cooperation between East Asia and Latin America where the United States does not take part. While it is unlikely that the process will become a priority either for East Asia or for Latin America, it is true that the dialogue plays a strategic role regarding other dimensions of the member states' external relations. As a result, the participant countries would try to be less peripheral and reduce their dependence. Thus, in political terms, they would strengthen their negotiation power vis-à-vis the US and the EU, an increase in bargaining power which would be even greater in relations with the United States, given the possibilities of 'triangulation' among the European Union, Latin America and East Asia opened by the existence of interregional processes between both shores of the Pacific (Montobbio 2004: 8). At the same time, in economic terms, they would attract investments (Wilhelmy 2005b) and gain better market access which, in turn, makes them less dependent as well. In other words, the involved actors would be clearly following a developmental interregionalism strategy and/or developing a case of developmental interregionalism.

FEALAC, as other processes of non-triadic interregionalism, is instrumental for its constituent countries to adjust to the globalization dynamics and the changes in the balance of power within the triad itself. Likewise, these processes may be used to gather support and gain legitimacy in order to thwart external pressures.

Now, in a sense, the formation of a group with enhanced bargaining power is a way of fulfilling balancing functions (Rüland 2002) as the aforementioned diversification strategy shows. Consequently, non-triadic interregional processes such as FEALAC also fulfil balancing and bandwagoning functions, although with certain peculiarities.

At this point, it seems also clear that the functions of identity-building, institution-building, agenda-setting and rationalizing are also performed by non-triadic interregionalism in general and FEALAC in particular. In this sense it is clear that both regions could put forward certain common points of view in multilateral and global fora. For instance, on behalf of FEALAC and its agenda-setter and rationalizer functions, the participant countries may try to include agenda issues related to the reform of the international financial architecture – a question of common concern. Likewise, they may also try to develop common postures regarding different issues of certain salience on the international agenda such as human rights, gender equility, environmental protection or the participation of civil society in development (Ocampo 2001).

In the same sense, there is no reason for saying that FEALAC would not be able to contribute to the strengthening of regional identities, both in Latin America and in East Asia. On the contrary, it probably does contribute, as the existence of a multiplicity of interregional processes may well force each of the participant regional groupings to adopt a consistent stance in them all.

In fact, the better they fulfil these other functions, the better they will fulfil the aforementioned ones of balancing and bandwagoning as well. In other words, in the case of non-triadic interregionalism, balancing and bandwagoning functions may be fulfilled although this will depend to a certain extent on the success of the rest of the functions.

While it is true, as some authors suggest, that FEALAC has not yet achieved much if compared with its original goals and objectives (Kuak Jae-Sung 2004: 76), we should remind ourselves that this is a common shortcoming – or at least a shortcoming commonly perceived – in all the interregional processes, regardless of whether or not they are triadic. This perception is mainly related to a lack of visibility and does not seem to correspond to the empirical fact that FEALAC's exchanges in all fields have increased over the last few years, with growth in trade as the most obvious example – currently it is more than three times the volume it was in 1998 when the forum was created (MercoPress, 23 August 2007).

Notes

1 As far as the distinction between regionalization and regionalism is concerned, there seems to be a certain degree of agreement among the different authors in the sense that regionalism refers to more normative and state-driven projects whereas regionalization is better used to designate more or less spontaneous and market-driven processes.
2 FOCALAE according to its Spanish acronym.

References

BBC Mundo.com (2004) *A. Latina y Asia se dan la mano*, 1 January. Available online at http://newsvote.bbc.co.uk/mpapps/pagetools/print/news.bbc.co.uk/hi/spanish/business/ (accessed 2 October 2006).

Breslin, S. and Higgott, R. (2002) 'Studying Regions: Learning from the Old, Constructing the New', in *New Political Economy*, Vol. 5, No. 3, pp. 333–52.

—— (2003) 'New Regionalism(s) in the Global Economy. Conceptual Understanding in Historical Perspective', in *Asia Europe Journal*, No. 1, pp. 167–82.

DR1.com (2007) *DR enters FEALAC*, 29 August. Available online at http://dr1.com/ trade/articles/303/1/DR-enters-FEALAC/Page1.html (accessed 11 September 2007).

Dosch, J. (2005) 'Southeast Asia and Latin America: A case of Peripheral Interregionalism', in Faust, Jörg; Mols, Manfred, and Won-Ho Kim, eds, *Latin America and East Asia – Attempts at Diversification*, Hamburg: LIT.

FEALAC (2007) *Brasilia Ministerial Declaration and Programme of Action*, III Foreign Ministers Meeting (FMM III), August. Available online at www.mofa.go.jp/region/ latin/fealac/dec0708.html (accessed 11 September 2007).

Felicio, Tania (2006) 'East Asia, the Missing Link in Multirregionalism', in Bersick, Sebastian; van der Velde, Paul and Stokhof, Win *Multiregionalism and Multilateralism*, Amsterdam: Amsterdam University Press.

FOCALAE (2004) *Plan de Acción de Manila*, Ministerial Meeting, Manila, 31 January. Available online at http://www.colombiainternacional.org/Doc%20PDF/AP-PlanDe Accion.pdf (accessed 25 September 2006).

Hänggi, Heiner (2006) 'Interregionalism as a multifaceted phenomenon', in Hänggi, Heiner; Roloff, Ralf and Rüland, Jürgen, *Interregionalism and Interregional Relations*, London: Routledge.

Hettne, Björn (2003) 'The New Regionalism Revisited', in Söderbaum, Fredrik and Shaw, Timothy, *Theories of New Regionalism*, London: Palgrave.

— (2005) 'Beyond the New Regionalism', in *New Political Economy*, Vol 10, No. 4, December, pp. 543–71.

Jayakumar, S. (2005) *Keynote address at the FEALAC Young Parlamentarians Forum*,

Ministry of Foreign Affairs, Singapore, 23 August. Available online at http://app.mfa. gov.sg/2006/press/view_print.asp?post_i=1421 (accessed 11 September 2007).

Kim, Samuel S. (2004) 'Regionalization and Regionalism in East Asia', in *Journal of East Asian Studies*, Vol. 4, No. 1, January–April, pp. 36–67.

Kuak Jae-Sung (2004) 'Galvanizing Inter-Pacific Relations: Korea's Role in Asia–Latin America Cooperation', in *East Asian Review*, Vol. 16, No. 4, Winter, pp. 63–80.

Low, Linda (2006) 'The Forum for East Asia – Latin America Cooperation (FEALAC): Embrionic interregionalism', in Hänggi, Heiner; Roloff, Ralf and Rüland, Jürgen, *Interregionalism and Interregional Relations*, London: Routledge.

MercoPress (2007) *Latinamerica and East Asia meet to boost trade ties*, 23 August. Available online at http://www.mercopress.com/vernoticia.do?id=11173&formato= html (accessed 11 September 2007).

Ministry of Foreign Affairs of Japan (2002) *Simposium for Intellectuals from East Asia and Latin America (SIEALA)*, 21 February. Available online at http://globalwarming. mofa.go.jp/region/latin/fealac/summary0202.html (accessed 15 September 2007).

MERCOSUR abc (2007) *FOCALAE: Argentina y Japón coordinarán Foro hasta 2010*, 30 August. Available online at www.mercosurabc.com.ar/nota.asp?IdNota=1241&Id Seccion=3 (accessed 11 September 2007).

Montobbio, Manuel (2004) *Triangulando la Triangulación: España/Europa – América Latina – Asia Pacífico*, Barcelona: CIDOB, December.

Nesadurai, Helen (2003) *Globalisation, Domestic Politics and Regionalism: the ASEAN Free Trade Area*, London: Routledge.

Ocampo, José Antonio (2001) *A New Economic Partnership between Asia–Pacific and Latin America in the Age of Globalization*, Luncheon Speech, First East Asia-Latin America Ministerial Meeting, Santiago, 29 March. Available online at http://www. cepal.org/prensa/noticias/discursossecretaria/1/6251/ForoAsiaPacifico-ING-mar29.pdf (accessed 26 July 2006).

Olivet, María Cecilia (2005) *Unravelling Interregionalism Theory: A Critical Analysis of the New Interregional Relations between Latin America and East Asia*, Paper presented at the VI Reunión de la Red de Estudios de América Latina y el Caribe sobre Asia–Pacífico. Available online at http://www.iadb.org/intal/aplicaciones/uploads/ponencias/ Foro_REDEALAP_2005_16_Olivet.pdf (accessed 20 July 2006).

Portafolio (2007) *America Latina busca más comercio e inversión*, Bogotá, 27 August. Available online at www.portafolio.com.co/port_secc_online/porta_inte_online/2007-08-27/ARTIC (accessed 11 September 2007).

Rosamond, Ben (2001) *Regional Integration in Europe and Asia*, Conference given at the Fourth ASEF University, January, Singapore.

Rüland, Jürgen (2002) *Interregionalism in International Relations*, Paper presented at the conference held at the Arnold-Begstraesser-Institute, Freiburg, Germany, on 31 January and 1 February. Available online at http://www.politik.uni-freiburg.de/pdf/Interreg Sum.pdf (accessed 20 September 2004).

Soesastro, Hadi (2002) 'El Nexo Asiático: APEC y ASEM', in *Estudios e informes del Pacífico*, No. 5, July.

Wilhelmy, Manfred (2005a) 'Chile, Latin America, and the Asia–Pacific Region', in *Revista de Ciencia Política (Santiago)*, Vol. 25, No. 2, pp. 190–7. Available online at http:// www.scielo.cl/scielo.php?pid=S0718-090X2005000200010&script=sci_arttext (accessed 5 September 2006).

—— (2005b) *East Asia, the Pacific and Latin America*, Speech at the Plenary Session I, PECC, The 16th General Meeting, Seoul.

—— (2007) *FOCALAE: Interrogantes hacia el futuro*, Conference given on the occasion of the III FEALAC Ministerial Meeting, organized by IPRI and Alexandre de Gusmao, 20 August. Available online at http://asiapacifico.bcn.cl/columnas/focalae-interrogantes-hacia-el-futuro (accessed 11 September 2007).

Xinhua (Chinese News Agency) (2007) *Argentina y Japón Coordinarán Foro de Cooperación AL–Asia del Este*, 24 August. Available online at www.spanish.sinhuanet.com/spanish/2007–8/24/conten_477476.htm (accessed 11 September 2007).

13 Interregionalism

A comparative analysis of ASEM and FEALAC

Charalambos Tsardanidis

Introduction

The decade following the end of the Cold War witnessed a remarkable increase in regional projects. New forms of often multi-layered interregional relations have appeared as a corollary of 'new regionalism'. Interregionalism refers on the one hand to the political/economic relationship between two regional more or less institutionalized cooperation schemes, and on the other hand to the process of building interactions and links between two separate regions.

Interregionalism theory emerged and differentiated itself from regional integration theory when scholars started to understand that regions were becoming actors in their own right. Regions exercised this status by developing their own external relations. Emergence of interregionalism could also be noted as a turning point in the study of regions and what it is that joins them together (Olivet 2005: 9).

Literature on interregionalism, though still scarce, tries to provide some analytical insights on the patterns and features of relations among regions. Despite the fact that this theory is still very much in a process of development, there are certain convergences between what scholars have written about it, as for the reasons of the emergence, development and maintenance of interregional dialogues and relations. Jürgen Rüland was one of the first to propose a research agenda on interregionalism and has described seven functions it performs: balancing and bandwagoning, institution-building, rationalizing, agenda-setting and controlling, identity-building, stabilizing and development (Rüland 2002a: 7).

However, most of the existing studies as Heiner Hänggi, Ralf Roloff and Jürgen Rüland observe, have so far failed to contribute to a better understanding of this new sub-field of international relations. 'Theoretical explanations, albeit rare, have been primarily deductive, at times even speculative, and mostly lacking sufficient empirical evidence' (Hänggi, Roloff and Rüland 2006: 7).

Following the description of different forms of interregionalism, the first part of the chapter develops a typology of comparing interregionalism; the second part compares the interregional relationship (a) of the EU member states with the East Asian Countries (ASEM), and (b) of the Southeast Asian Nations – ASEAN plus China, Japan, the Republic of Korea, Australia and New Zealand – with the Latin

America countries (FEALAC). The objective is to explore the similarities/common characteristics and differences in the process and development of these two arrangements of interregionalism.

A comparative analysis typology of interregionalism

The expanding network of interregional relations appears in a wide array of manifestations. In order to categorize existing interregional arrangements, three different forms of interregionalism can be distinguished:

(a) Relations between regional groupings/organizations which we could call **bilateral interregionalism** (Hänggi 2000: 3).[1] Clear examples are the relationships EU–ASEAN and EU–MERCOSUR and MERCOSUR–ASEAN (see Figure 13.1)

(b) **Transregional arrangements**. Membership in these rather heterogeneous arrangements is more diffuse than in traditional group-to-group dialogues; it does not necessarily coincide with regional groupings and may include member states from more than two regions. By the concept of transregionalism we refer to less institutionalized forms of relations between regions. There are two characteristics of transregional relations that are the most important:

First, transregionalism encompasses a broader set of actor relationships than simply those among states. Thus any connection across regions, including transnational networks of corporate production or of non-governmental organizations, that involves cooperation among any type of actors across two or more regions can in theory also be considered as a form of transregionalism (Aggarwal and Fogarty 2004: 5). Thus, the actors behind regional

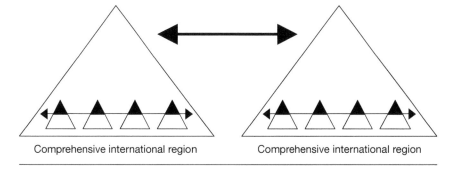

Comprehensive international region   Comprehensive international region

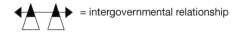 = intergovernmental relationship

Figure 13.1 Bilateral interregionalism

projects are no longer only states, but actually a large number of different types of institutions, organizations and movements. According to Christopher Dent, transregionalism implies the establishment of common 'spaces' between and across regions in which constituent agents (e.g. individuals, communities or organizations) operate and have close associative ties with each other (Dent 2003: 232).

Second, the membership of transregional processes is comprised of individual countries that may or may not be part of other regional groups, but if they are, they participate in an individual capacity and do not act on behalf of the regional group of which they are a part (Olivet 2005: 10). Examples of transregionalism are ASEM and FEALAC (see Figure 13.2).

(c) **Hybrid interregionalism**. Hybrid interregionalism could take three forms:

The first refers to relations between regional groupings and single states (e.g. EU–Russia, ASEAN–Australia) (see Figure 13.3).

The second type of hybrid inter-regionalism refers to the relationship between a formal regional group/organization and a 'constructed' regional group. The 'constructed' regional group is usually set up by countries that have been obliged to form a regional group in order to be able to cooperate with a formal regional group (Hänggi *et al.* 2006: 39). A clear example is the relations of the European Union (EU) with the African, Caribbean and Pacific Group of States (ACP countries) under the framework of the Cotonu Agreement, and the Euro-Mediterranean Partnership (EMP) (see Figure 13.4).

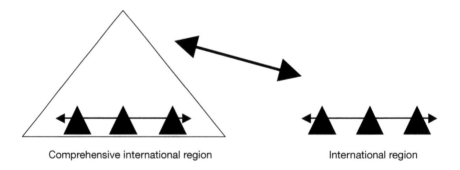

Comprehensive international region   International region

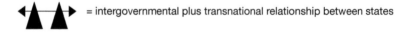   = intergovernmental plus transnational relationship between states

Figure 13.2 Transregionalism

The third type of hybrid interregionalism refers to the creation of institutional arrangement between major representatives of two or more regions which claim regional leadership. A clear example is IBSA, the trilateral, developmental initiative between India, Brazil and South Africa to promote South–South cooperation (see Figure 13.5).[2] Another example is the cooperation between Brazil, Russia, India and China (BRIC).

This chapter is based to a great extent on the systematic paradigm of Michael Schulz, Fredrik Söderbaum and Joakim Öjendal on how regionalism can be studied, conceptualized and understood (Schulz, Söderbaum and Öjendal

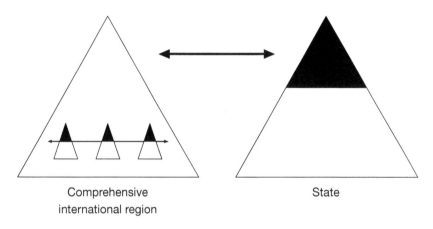

Comprehensive international region   State

Figure 13.3 Interregionalism single power relationship

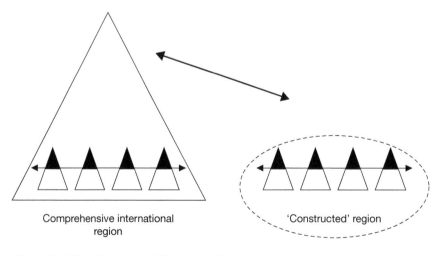

Comprehensive international region   'Constructed' region

Figure 13.4 Hybrid constructed interregionalism

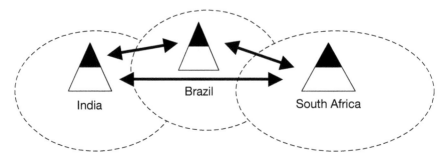

Figure 13.5 Hybrid interregionalism with leader states from different regions

2001: 234–76), and on the analytical tool of comparative analysis of inter-regionalism proposed by Hans Maull and Nuria Okfen (2006: 218–33). It attempts to develop a comparative analysis typology of interregionalism by looking at three key issues: the first one refers to the dynamics of interregionalism, the second to structural change, and the third to the preferred outcomes of inter-regionalism.

The dynamics of interregionalism

Michael Schulz, Frederick Söderbaum and Joakim Öjendal (2001: 250–6) pay attention to which actors and whose interests are the 'driving' (or impeding) force dominating the process of regionalism. Is it the states and their constituencies that push the process of regionalism and establish an agenda or is it the often neglected private economic forces and/or civil society? What is the relative strength and relationship between state, market, and (civil) society actors and how does this affect the dynamics from 'above' and the dynamics from 'below'? Exactly the same questions may be asked with regard to interregionalism.

Jürgen Rüland gives more emphasis on institution-building which he considers from two different perspectives. The first one relates to the 'creation of a new level of policy-making in a multi-layered international system and the creation of subsidiary institutions such as regular summits, ministerial and senior officials' rounds, business dialogues etc.' (Rüland 2006: 302). The second one stems from the fact that interregional dialogues create a need for unified positions and, hence, intensified consultation and coordination in order to carry out negotiations with a single voice, and in this way interregional relations may facilitate regional groupings to enhance institutionalization (Rüland 2001: 7) (see Figure 13.6). Julie Gilson pays more attention to cognitive institutionalization which goes beyond formal rules and structures to acknowledge institutions as social phe-nomena. Thus, 'cognitive institutionalization delineates the margins of the social script through which institutional participants communicate, and provides the basis upon which fixed and readily identifiable idea-sets for an institution's practices are founded'(Gilson 2001: 114).

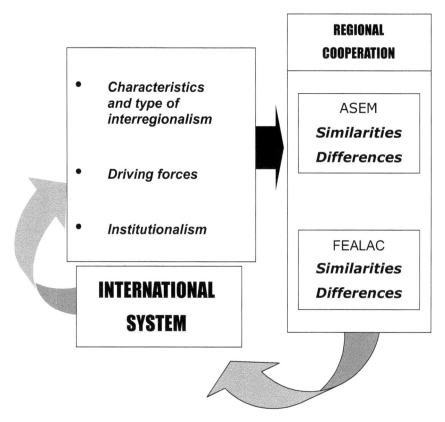

Figure 13.6 Comparative analysis typology of interregionalism: the dynamics criteria

The task at hand in the first key issue is to determine the characteristics of inter-regionalism; in other words, what type of interregionalism ASEM and FEALAC are, who the main actors – driving factors – are in the process of interregionalism and what kind of institution-building has been achieved.

Structural change or globalization versus interregionalisation

For some observers, interregionalism, as well as regionalism, is seen as an integral part of globalization, as one of its many manifestations. Interregionalism and globalization, are then seen as a seamless process, being an outlet of the same underlying phenomenon (Hettne 1999: 2). Other authors emphasize the distinc-tion between the two processes and view them almost as 'bouncing' towards one another – globalization being the challenge of economic and cultural homo-genization of the world, and interregionalism being a social and political reaction (Gamble 2001: 24). As Gilson points out, 'interregionalism may be seen as a response to changes in the structure of the global political economy and, especially since the events of 11 September 2001, as a means of tackling trans-border threats and challenges' (Gilson 2005: 321).

Regionalism and particularly 'open regionalism' can also be used as a stepping-stone towards more global or multilateral relations.[3] In deepening integration, and in proceeding with reform, new vested interests can be created through interregional liberalization as well. In that case interregional cooperation schemes could contribute to the balance of the international system as well as of the global governance structure. Furthermore, they may promote 'more balanced development in the world economy through increasing complementarity between remote or periphery areas' (Jyoung 2003: 61). Interregionalism in that case should be perceived as an externally focused, globally active variety. 'Globally active interregionalism is concerned with the expression of interregional cooperation on the global stage' (Doidge 2007: 242–3).

According to Rolf Roloff, globalization and regionalization pose two challenges to the nation states. They react to globalization either by strengthening regionalism or by launching interregional cooperation (Roloff 2006: 24). The regions participating in an interregional process aim to balance certain negative effects of globalization as well as balance expressions of power deriving from the emergence of certain international actors (other regions, countries or international institutions) that might affect their interests. In other words regional cooperation schemes are using interregional links in order to strengthen the bargaining power of regions vis-à-vis each other but also more generally in the international system. Thus, interregionalism offers an additional layer to multilevel governance which could facilitate the finding of solutions on a global scale in pre-discussing or even pre-negotiating issues to be taken up in a multilateral or global setting (Reiterer 2006: 241).

Jürgen Rüland distinguishes two forms of balancing: 'power balancing', if it has a military dimension and 'institutional balancing' if perceived disequilibria between regions are counterbalanced by interregional institution-building or the activation of existing interregional forums (Rüland 2006: 300). In this case, interregionalism might be considered as an 'internally' focused capacity building variety 'characterized by the way in which a weaker regional integration arrangement is gradually strengthened through involvement with a more advanced regional counterpart' (Doidge 2007: 242).

The structural change key issue refers to two questions:

- Political interregionalism versus economic globalization? In other words to what extent are interregional cooperation schemes in a new globalized world able to strengthen the balancing power of their participating regions in the international system as well as to balance a hegemonic power like the United States?
- From 'stumbling blocks' and 'stepping stones' to 'building blocks'? In other words, to what extent regional cooperation entities due to interregionalism are able to manage economic interdependence between themselves and to contribute to global governance? (See Figure 13.7.)

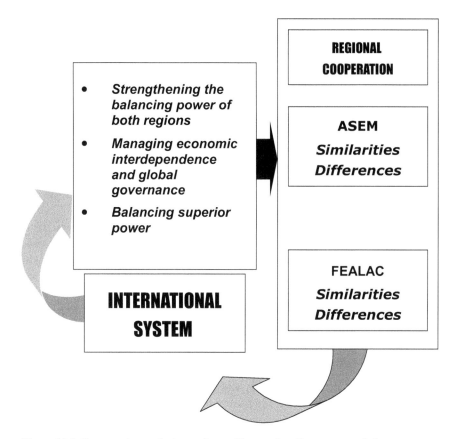

Figure 13.7 Comparative analysis typology of interregionalism: structural change
criteria

The preferred outcomes of interregionalism

This third key issue emphasizes mainly the values of peace and development. The
question is what does interregionalism arrangements mean for the promotion of
peace and development? More specifically, with regard to the fundamental value
of peace, in what way does interregionalism promote stability in the international
system, resolve forthcoming conflicts and deal with old animosities? One way to
investigate this is to try to assess whether regions are being transformed through
interregionalism from regional conflict formations and security complexes into
better functioning security communities by providing security.

With regard to development, both policymakers and theorists have emphasized
for decades the potential of new regionalism in stabilizing the international system
and promoting trade and economic development. However, strong criticism has
also been voiced against regionalist projects, for instance that they may reinforce
a narrow and particular type of regionalist economic regime which may largely

serve elitist interests and sacrifice social development concerns. It is therefore relevant to assess if, and in what way, interregional strategies and mechanisms actually contribute to genuine, new development.

Interregionalism may also contribute to spurring regional identity-building. As Julie Gilson observes, 'what is understood by "region" . . . will depend to a large extent upon how they [the participants of the interregional process] view themselves and each other within, and as a result of, the process of interaction' (Gilson 2002: 11). In the dialogue with another region, a region, therefore may enhance its own identity by talking and acting as a collective actor (Maull and Okfen 2006: 219). This process of identity-building may stipulate, especially in heterogeneous and newly formed regional groupings, regional identity-building. It may sharpen differences between self and other and thus help galvanize regional solidarity on the basis of shared norms and identifiable, aggregate interests and formulate goals and policies (Rüland 2002b: 10).

Another important aspect of interregionalism which has been neglected so far is its transformation. During the process of interregionalism some of the initial aims and priorities of the participating regions may change and in that case they will try to lead the interregional scheme to another direction from the initial one (see Figure 13.8).

Comparative analysis of ASEM and FEALAC

The dynamics criteria: ASEM and FEALAC

Both interregional groupings have by and large the same organizational mechanisms and a three-pillar agenda, comprising economic dialogue, political dialogue and other (socio-cultural) and more or less the same objectives moving beyond economic issues, while meanwhile being countries participating on their own individual basis. Thus, they have loose membership and a multidimensional approach, covering the full spectrum of relations between the two regions, and devoting equal weight to political, economic and cultural issues (Milliot 2004: 77). The choice of a multidimensional logic presents one major advantage and one major difficulty. It provides valuable flexibility by allowing participants to give more importance to trade, development or foreign policy depending on the circumstances. The difficulty lies with the obligation to have a proper overview of several logics of intervention unfolding simultaneously.

We can see that both are in line with the usual structure of interregional processes, although are organized on the base of different structures and levels of meetings. For example ASEM is holding biennial summit meetings, featuring Heads of State or Government, which give the overall political impetus to the ASEM process; meanwhile FEALAC has no comparable summit meetings. The absence of summits in FEALAC suggests that lower priority is attached by East Asian and Latin American governments to FEALAC than to other dialogues such as ASEM and APEC. It is in fact only a second-best device for strengthening mutual relations (Low 2006: 91). Senior Officials' meetings in ASEM are by far

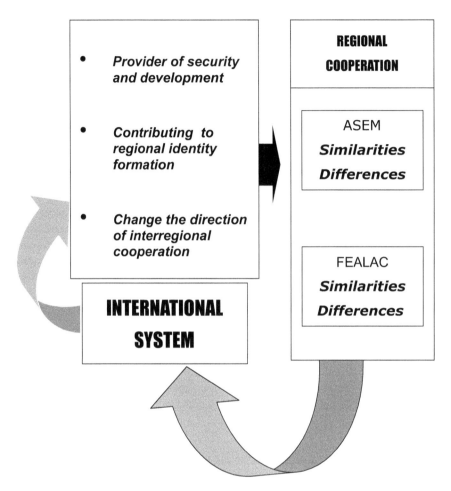

Figure 13.8 Comparative analysis typology of interregionalism: the preferred outcome criteria

more regular and more frequent than in FEALAC, meanwhile in FEALAC there is lack of a body or institution to implement actual cooperation programmes. In ASEM, this is the Asia–Europe Foundation (ASEF).

FEALAC uses, to a large extent, the 'ASEM way of promoting dialogue and cooperation. As far as FEALAC working principles, purpose and process are concerned, the work carried out within ASEM has largely served as a blueprint' (Hwee 2005: 48). ASEM and FEALAC could be considered as clear examples of transregionalism, although FEALAC should be regarded as 'peripheral' trans-regionalism. ASEM is an example of transregionalism because, seen from one angle, it comprises a large number of different types of institutions, organiza-tions and movements rather than simply transactions among those states, which constitute a 'bottom-up' cross-border process of interregionalism and from the other because ASEM is comprised of individual countries that are part of other regional groups and participate in ASEM in an individual capacity.

FEALAC could be considered as 'peripheral' transregionalism because it involves primarily lower-medium and small powers of the South which could not alter the main structural pillars of the international system. Meanwhile the volume of economic transactions, both in trade or Foreign Direct Investment (FDI) is insignificant.[4] One of the regions involved, Latin America, does not belong to the Triad while the other, East Asia is the least powerful pole within it, at least in political and security terms (Dosch 2005: 185). However, FEALAC is not the only interregional cooperation scheme between Asian and Latin American countries. MERCOSUR and ASEAN have developed close links and the first ASEAN–MERCOSUR Ministerial Meeting was held in Brasilia on 24 November 2008.[5]

Both regional groupings have also adopted a 'bottom-up' process of transregionalism by involving, parliamentarians, local authorities, the business community, organizations and professional groups from all participating states. All these are making proposals, mobilizing public opinion, using indirect strategies and organizing their own monitoring of interregional development. Consequently, FEALAC and ASEM mark, as David Milliot argues, the 'emergence of a multi-level governance, and creating a new transregional level between the regional and universal levels' (Milliot 2004: 86).

The EU is caught between the contradictions of trying to promote human rights and political and social change in ASEM, while trying to stabilize corrupted regimes. The ironic aspect of the imposition of Euro-thinking is that the introduction of democracy in some Asian counter-partners, could lead to political groups and parties gaining power through a popular election, which would be in direct opposition to EU interests.

Structural change or globalization versus interregionalisation: ASEM and FEALAC

Neither ASEM nor FEALAC can be regarded as having a substantial impact on the formulation of the international political and economic system. It seems, however, that both have been created to perform functions of institution-balancing: first, the regions can learn from each other's experiences in managing economic crises; second, ASEAN members wanted to extend the ASEAN+3 format to its external relations; third, Asia was seeing FEALAC as a device to protect and improve its access to the vital markets of South America; fourth, some member states of the EU, Latin American and Asian countries regarded ASEM and FEALAC as an attempt to balance strong US influence (Dosch 2005: 192). The contribution of ASEM and FEALAC to global governance in terms of institution-building, as well as regarding international monetary relations, has so far been negligible, despite the fact that both have managed to reduce barriers and obstacles to trade and FDI. Interregional cooperation schemes, however, like, ASEM, are not institutions meant to enhance global governance capacity directly. They are instruments primarily used for diplomacy, networking, information-sharing, gathering and confidence-building. To be able to contribute directly to global governance, the participating states must decide to use the process to define issues and problems, try to achieve consensus and come up with suggestions to resolve these problems (Fort 2004: 362).

As far as the management of economic interdependence is concerned, trade and FDI relationships within ASEM are much stronger than in FEALAC. The importance of Europe and Asia in the world economy, and the ongoing process of globalization, means that the prosperity of these two regions is inseparably linked. Asia's long record of dynamic growth, and rapid recovery from the crisis of 1997–8 (not ignoring the ongoing challenges of reform), makes it an essential trade partner for Europe. In 1992 trade flows between the EU and East Asia had for the first time overhauled the volume of transatlantic trade, thus making East Asia the most important regional trading partner from this time onwards (Dent 1999: 22). Since then Asian–European trade has become the most dynamic interregional trade in the global economy (Hilpert and Kecker 2008: 75). On the other hand, Europe's own weight in the international economy, as the largest single market, the largest source of FDI, and the largest global donor, in addition to its experiences in regional economic and monetary cooperation, makes it an essential partner for Asia.

The most constructive common agenda item for Asia and Europe in the ASEM process is to support multilateralism in general and the WTO in particular. ASEM is not a regional trade agreement, nor is there any need to turn it into one. With APEC becoming increasingly redundant on the one hand and the United States engaging in unilateralism on the other, ASEM can serve as a bulwark of the international trade order. The new challenges facing Asia–Europe relations in the context of globalization suggest that a particular emphasis should be placed on ASEM's potential to offer a forum for informal dialogue, and to use this forum for enhancing awareness and understanding between the two regions. FEALAC also (during the Third Foreign Ministers' Meeting which took place in Brasilia in August 2007) declared its intention to cooperate to bring the Doha Round negotiations of the WTO to a satisfactory term.[6] However, both ASEM and FEALAC have so far failed to reach a consensus in the WTO New Round, not to mention that they do not yet act as multilateral forums to develop embryonic WTO accords or as forces to counter American unilateralism. Rather than being a forum for new ideas for the WTO, ASEM appears to resemble an echo chamber for positions and disagreements articulated within the WTO (Robles 2008: 165). Therefore, it is still an open question whether issues such as the Doha Development Agenda could be considered in the ASEM and FEALAC frameworks as paradigms of multilateral utility theory or even as elements that could promote interregionalism between EU and East Asia on the one hand, and between Asia/Oceanica and Latin America on the other.

There is no doubt that the existing levels of trade and investment do not adequately reflect the true economic potential of each region. ASEM would therefore represent an opportunity to give a political impulse to economic cooperation. Both Asia and Europe have benefited tremendously from the economic liberalization of the past few decades. It is not certain, however, that the trend in favour of liberalization will continue automatically. In 1997 the Asian financial crisis raised the question about the free flow of goods and services, and the current global economic crisis could prompt an increase in protectionism, as governments in recession-hit countries emphasise boosting domestic jobs at the expense of free trade. In some developed economies there are signs of aggressive unilateralism, including frequent resource to anti-dumping charges. For this reason, the ASEM Foreign Ministers felt the need during their Ninth Meeting, which took place in Hanoi in May 2009, to declare that they reject protectionism, and all ASEM countries should 'enhance market access for the exports of developing countries, particularly in areas of their interest, and promote regional and interregional integration'.[7] Given the lengthy local and regional agendas of both Europe and East Asia, the ASEM process will have to sharpen its focus if it is to demonstrate tangible results. FEALAC also discussed the possibility of strengthening its role in contributing to member states' efforts to mitigate the negative impact of the global financial crisis on their respective real economies and thereby sustain economic development. However, it was decided to defer any practical decision on that issue until the fourth Foreign Ministers' Meeting due to be held in Tokyo in 2009.[8]

Intra-regional trade in East Asia and Latin America has increased in the last fifteen years and since 1995 has been at the level of 52 to 55 per cent (Reiterer 2009: 189). FEALAC members as a whole contribute about one-fifth of global trade. However, in recent years, as Howard Loewen points out, increasing imports of commodities by East Asian states, especially China, increased the dynamics of current trade relations between the two regions. Latin America's exports to Asia increased from 9.8 per cent of its total exports in 1995 to 10.9 per cent in 2006. Meanwhile Latin America's imports from Asia increased considerably from 11.9 per cent to 19.5 per cent in the same period as many Latin American economies considerably liberalized their trade policies (Loewen 2009: 74–5).

In terms of intra-FEALAC trade, East Asia accounts for 88 per cent, while Latin America accounts for only 8 per cent. Trans-Pacific regional trade between the East Asian and Latin American economies remains at a relatively low level of 4 per cent (Siddique 2004: 17). Without doubt the present economic relations do not reflect the potential for trade and investment that exists in an increasingly globalized world. This is particularly true when the tremendous progress made in reducing barriers to trade in both regions is taken into consideration (Hwee 2005: 46). Regarding FDI, Asian investment is mainly concentrated in the major Latin American economies, with Japan taking the lead and South Korea having caught up with huge investment projects, especially in its manufacturing industries. Even if Asian interests increased in absolute numbers, Asian firms did not participate as much as European and US firms in the Latin America FDI boom during the 1990s (Faust and Mols 2005: 10). The reasons why interregional FDI flows have lagged far behind the dynamic trends of total FDI flows in the two regions include not only the macroeconomic environment but also other economic and social factors. Lack of knowledge of companies in one region by the other, due to cultural, geographical and historical reasons, is one important factor. The scarcity of information, especially about recent trends in trade and FDI, regional integration and existing business opportunities in each other's regions is another important impediment to reciprocal trade and mutual investment (Kuwayama 2002: 28).

FEALAC member states have clearly stated, in the Manila Action Plan of 2004, that they expected to achieve a more equal distribution of the benefits resulting from globalization. Furthermore, FEALAC could be considered as the result of a diversification strategy aimed at enhancing the position of the participant countries in the North–South dialogues. Thus, while the EU and US developed interregional relations with East Asia, thereby looking to balance an existing situation, East Asia and Latin America approached each other in order to start participating in the modern international system and thus avoid being marginalized. Strategic decisions on how to diversify foreign policy are based on cost-benefit analysis considerations on the parts of the actors involved. At the same time, as Jörn Dosch has observed, peripheral interregionalism, like FEALAC, cannot necessarily be expected to generate international regimes or any other kind of measurable effectiveness (Dosch 2005: 186). However, FEALAC's political and economic weight, despite the promising signs and its importance for the future of East Asia and Latin American countries, is marginal in comparison to other interregional process. Definitely, as María Cecilia Olivet points out, '[it] cannot be regarded as a way to balance the structure of the international system or as a way to contribute to the construction of the global governance structure' (Olivet 2005: 17).

The preferred outcome criteria: ASEM and FEALAC

Neither of the interregional groupings are important for influencing global security developments and collective deterrence and were have so far been unable to become providers of security or to build up a collective regional identity. FEALAC has achieved very little compared to its ambitious visions, broad objectives and many good ideas. Although FEALAC, regarding political cooperation, could serve as an effective forum in exchanging views on security issues, all the gatherings of government officials have failed to advance beyond diplomatic rhetoric, and have not broken down the psychological and mental barriers that still divide the two sides of the Pacific (Jae-Sung 2004: 77). The main reasons are:

1   The wide geographical scope of FEALAC and the fact that many of its members are developing economies meant constraint on resources that can be used for various initiatives to step up cooperation between the two regions.
2   There is still a widespread information gap due in part to physical and cultural distance.
3   The internal dynamics and developments within the two regions also impact on the attention and interest that both regions accord to each other.

4   The FEALAC dialogue suffers from the incoherence and lack of actorness of the two loose regional entities (Hwee 2006: 3).
5   There is no definition of priorities. The approach taken is extremely decentralized. The projects are presented on a totally voluntary basis and lack coordination.
6   FEALAC needs more financial support, which is probably the main obstacle for enhancing the interaction, but also solidity, substance and the incentive to design and carry out projects that are not planned and executed on a multilateral level (Wilhelmy and Mann 2005: 42–3).
7   FEALAC lacks a clear regional institutionalization and representation on both sides of the Pacific (Mols 2005: 210).

ASEM political dimension remains symbolic and rhetorical. However, ASEM has been more successful discussing 'high politics' than FEALAC. Even in this, there have never been common positions or a compromise formula beyond a lowest common denominator, despite the fact that ASEM had explicitly included a political and security dimension from the beginning, thus enabling members, in principle, to bring up security issues. ASEM has made progress in the field of the promotion of a less militarized, softer security strategy, mainly in the definition of substantial principles which can be realized functionally (Kivimäki 2008: 67). The only significant traditional security issue which ASEM has been able to breach with some concrete results is the situation on the Korean peninsula, but even that has been characterized as fortuitous and circumstantial, rather than politically induced (Maull and Okfen 2006: 227). The EU has also failed to formulate a coherent and effective policy towards China and this failure has been reflected in ASEM performance. It seems, as Frank Umbach observes, 'the EU's security engagement with the Asia–Pacific region is still challenged by the overriding economic interests of its main member states, which often compromise the Union's long-term security interests in the region' (Umbach 2008: 115). However, Michael Reiterer is of the view that there has been 'a substantial political dialogue in ASEM, at all levels, based on one golden rule: the less you write about the political dialogue and the more you actually dialogue, the better the result!'(Reiterer 2002: 84).

Conclusions

By proposing a typology of comparing interregionalism this chapter has tried to examine the similarities and differences of two different forms of interregionalism: ASEM (transregionalism), and FEALAC (peripheral transregionalism). The analysis points at the need for more empirical comparative studies as a way of assessing the real value and impact of interregionalism. A fundamental question raised by Yeo Lay Hwee about ASEM but which also applies to FEALAC is the following: How do the member states themselves look at interregionalism? Do they see interregionalism as an instrument that can be used effectively to address issues of regional concern, global governance, and influence world politics? Or do they see it merely as an instrument to promote narrow self-interests? (Hwee 2003: 181).

Following the above typology we were able to find out some similarities and differences between the two interregional cooperations:

- Both ASEM and FEALAC have a three-pillar agenda, comprising economic dialogue, political dialogue and other (socio-cultural), and have loose membership where countries participate on their own individual basis. Both have norms such as non-interference, and decisions are made strictly by consensus.
- It is not only the states and their constituencies that push the process of interregionalism and establish an agenda, but also institutional bridges have flourished among Parliaments, economic actors and civil societies as well, more in the case of ASEM and less in FEALAC. All these actors are making proposals to mobilize public opinion, use indirect strategies and organize their own monitoring of the development of the interregional cooperation.
- Both have more or less the same organizational mechanisms. ASEM, however, is more institutionalized than FEALAC.
- The contribution of both to global governance in terms of institution-building does not have importance in influencing global security developments and collective deterrence.
- Neither has so far managed to reduce barriers and obstacles to trade and FDI, despite the fact that liberalization has been achieved to a certain extent. However, in ASEM, trade and FDI relationships are stronger than in FEALAC.
- Collective identity-building through interregionalism is minimal.
- Both forums are considered as vehicles for balancing the massive influence of the US in their region but are not able to function as a bridge between regionalism and multilateralism to be used on the parts of the partners for support on some WTO and UN issues, and consequently cannot be regarded as a way to balance the structure of the international system.
- In ASEM the EU uses interregional relations to export its values and concepts of good governance.
- Finally, whereas many of the ASEM and FEALAC interregional relations are conducted under the pretext of mutual benefits and win-win solutions, the distribution of these benefits seems to be a function of the relative power positions of the stronger region vis-à-vis its counterparts. As Helge Hveem has noticed, the dynamism in the contemporary interregional relations may probably be interpreted along two dimensions – the first is related to hegemony and sees interregional activism as an expression of the hegemon's strategy, and the second as a response to it by other actors (Hveem 2003: 97). The stronger the counterpart, the more concessions are given by the other (Söderbaum, Stalgren and Van Langenhove 2005: 377). This could explain how the EU negotiates with the relatively strong East Asian region and how the East Asian region negotiates with the relatively weak Latin American region.

Notes

1   Heiner Hänggi, after six years subdivided interregional relations into five types: (a) relations grouped around a regional organization/group and a third country, (b) group-to-group relations, (c) relations between a regional organization and a regional group, (d) relations between two regional groups, and (e) relations between a group of states from more than one region. Of the types only (b) to (d) are defined as interregional relations in the narrower sense (Hänggi 2006: 31–62).

2   The launching of the IBSA Dialogue Forum was formalized through the adoption of the 'Brasilia Declaration' in June 2006. The main objectives of the IBSA Dialogue Forum among others are: to promote South–South dialogue, cooperation and common positions on issues of international importance; to promote trade and investment opportunities between the three regions of which they are a part; and to promote international poverty alleviation and social development. The IBSA Dialogue Forum has regular consultations at Senior Official (Focal Point), Ministerial (Trilateral Joint Commission) and Heads of State and/or Government (Summit) levels, but also facilitates interaction amongst academics, businesses and other members of civil society.

3   Some analysts define 'open regionalism' in relation to official barriers against trade (protectionism) (Garnaut 1994: 273). Open regionalism means that policy is directed towards the elimination of obstacles to trade within a region, while at the same time doing nothing to raise external tariff barriers to the rest of the world (Gamble and Payne 1996: 251).

4   FEALAC members as a whole contribute only about one-fifth of global trade, and absorb about one-fifth of global FDI.

5   The Meeting held an in-depth discussion and exchange of views on various international issues of common interest in the spirit of South–South cooperation, including the WTO Doha Round and the international financial situation. It also considered developments in MERCOSUR and ASEAN as well as ways and means to enhance MERCOSUR–ASEAN cooperation in areas such as trade and investment, intellectual property, energy security, food security, agriculture, transportation, tourism, environment, people-to-people contacts, technical cooperation and other areas of mutual interest. See Press Statement First ASEAN–MERCOSUR Ministerial Meeting Brasilia, 24 November 2008, www.aseansec.org/22011.pdf (accessed 23 June 2009).

6   See for the Third FEALAC – III Foreign Ministers' Meeting (FMM III): Brasilia Ministerila Declaration and Programme of Action, Brasilia, 23 August 2007, http://www.focalae.org/user/office/View.asp (accessed 20 June 2009).

7   See Chair's Statement: The Ninth ASEM Foreign Ministers' Meeting, Ha Noi, 25–26 May 2009, http://www.aseminfoboard.org/Documents/ (accessed 20 June2009).

8   Coordinators' Report on the Ninth Senior Officials' Meeting (Ninth SOM) Forum for East Asia–Latin America Cooperation, Buenos Aires, 7–8 April 2009. See http://fealac.mofat.go.kr/newdata_eng/document/high/document_view.php?tbn=TP_high (accessed 20 June 2009).

References

Aggarwal, V. K. and Fogarty, E. A. (2004) 'Between Regionalism and Globalism: European Union Interregional Trade Strategies', in V. K. Aggarwal and E. A. Fogarty, eds, *EU Trade Strategies: Between Regionalism and Globalism*, Houndmills: Palgrave, pp. 1–40.
Dent, C. (2003) 'From interregionalism to transregionalism? Future challenges for ASEM', *Asia Europe Journal*, vol. 1, no. 2, pp. 223–35.

—— (1999) *The European Union and Asia – An Economic Relationship*, London: Routledge.

Doidge, M. (2007) 'Joined at the Hip: Regionalism and Interregionalism', *Journal of European Integration*, vol. 29, no. 2, pp. 229–48.

Dosch, J. (2005) 'Southeast Asia and Latin America: A Case of Peripheral Regionalism', in J. Faust, M. Mols and W. H. Kim, eds, *Latin America and East Asia – Attempts at Diversification*, Münster: Lit/ KIEP, pp. 183–96.

Faust, J. and Mols, M. (2005) 'Latin America and East Asia: Defining the Research Agenda', in J. Faust, M. Mols and W. H. Kim, eds, *Latin America and East Asia – Attempts at Diversification*, Münster: Lit/ KIEP, pp. 1–13.

Fort, B. (2004) 'ASEM's Role for Co-operation on Security in Asia and Europe', *Asia Europe Journal*, vol. 2, no. 3, pp. 355–63.

Gamble, A. (2001) 'Regional Blocs, World Order and the New Medievalism', in M. Telo, ed., *European Union and New Regionalism. Regional Actors and Global Governance in a Post-hegemonic Era*, Aldershot: Ashgate, pp. 21–38.

Gamble, A. and Payne, A. (1996) 'Conclusion: The New Regionalism', in A. Gamble and A. Payne, eds, *Regionalism and World Order*, London: MacMillan Press, pp. 247–64.

Garnaut, R. (1994) 'Open Regionalism: Its Analytic Basis and Relevance to the International System', *Journal of Asian Economics*, vol. 5, no. 2, pp. 273–90.

Gilson, J. (2005) 'New Interregionalism? The EU and East Asia', *Journal of European Integration*, vol. 27, no. 3, pp. 307–26.

—— (2002) *Asia Meets Europe. Interregionalism and the Asia–Europe Meeting*, Cheltenham: Edward Elgar.

—— (2001) 'Europe–Asia: The Formal Politics of Mutual Definition', in P. W. Preston and J. Gilson, eds, *The European Union and East Asia*, Cheltenham: Edward Elgar, pp. 109–24.

Hänggi, H. (2006) 'Interregionalism as a Multifaceted Phenomenon: In Search of a Typology', in H. Hänggi, R. Roloff and J. Rüland, eds, *Interregionalism and International Relations*, London: Routledge, pp. 31–62.

—— (2000) 'Interregionalism: Empirical and Theoretical Perspectives', Paper prepared for the Workshop *Dollars, Democracy and Trade: External Influence on Economic Integration in the Americas*, Los Angeles, CA, 18 May, pp. 1–14.

Hänggi, H., Roloff, R. and Rüland, J. (2006) 'Interregionalism: A New Phenomenon in International Relations', in H. Hänggi, R. Roloff and J. Rüland, eds, *Interregionalism and International Relations*, London: Routledge, pp. 3–14.

Hettne, B. (1999) 'Globalisation and the New Regionalism: The Second Great Transformation', in B. Hettne, A. Inotal and O. Sunkel, eds, *Globalism and the New Regionalism*, Houndmills: Macmillan Press, pp. 1–24.

Hilpert, H. G. and Kecker, K. J. (2008) 'Interregional Trade and Investment Between Asia and Europe', in J. Rüland, G. Schubert, G. Schucher and C. Storz, eds, *Asian European Relations. Building Blocks for Global Governance?*, London: Routledge, pp. 73–94.

Hveem, H. (2003) 'The Regional Project in Global Governance', in F. Söderbaum and T. M. Shaw, eds, *Theories of New Regionalism: A Palgrave Reader*, Houndmills: Palgrave, pp. 81–98.

Hwee, Y. L. (2006) 'ASEAN Integration and Inter-Regionalism – Playing Catch-up in FEALAC', Paper presented at the workshop *Interregional Relations Between East Asia and Latin America*, Department of East Asian Studies, University of Leeds, 9 November.

—— (2005) 'The Forum for East Asia and Latin America Cooperation (FEALAC) – Taking a Long View', in *The Encounter of Two Continents. Cross-Pacific Economic Integration Workshop*, Singapore: Konrad-Adenauer – Stiftung, pp. 45–52.

—— (2003) *Asia and Europe. The Development and Different Dimensions of ASEM*, London: Routledge.

Jae-Sung, K. (2004) 'Galvanizing Inter-Pacific Relations: Korea's Role in Asia–Latin America Cooperation', *East-Asian Review*, vol. 16, no. 4, pp. 63–80.

Jyoung, T. H (2003) 'Economic Relations between Korea and Latin America', in P. H. Smith, K. Horisaka and S. Nishijima, eds, *East Asia and Latin America: The Unlikely Alliance*, Lanham: Rowman and Littlefield, pp. 58–71.

Kivimäki, T. (2008) 'ASEM. Multilaralism, and the Security Agenda', in B. Gaens, ed., *Europe–Asia Interregional Relations: A Decade of ASEM*, Aldershot: Ashgate, pp. 49–68.

Kuwayama, M. (2002) 'Search for a New Partnership in Trade and Investment Between Latin America and the Asia Pacific', Paper presented At *the PECC Trade Forum*, Lima, 17–19 May.

Loewen. L. (2009) ' WTO Compatibility and Rules of Origin – Assessing Bilateral Trade Agreements between Latin America and East Asia', *Journal of Current Southeast Asian Affairs*, vol. 28, no. 1, pp. 69–81.

Low, L. (2006) 'The Forum for East Asia–Latin America Cooperation (FEALAC): Embryonic Interregionalism', in H. Hänggi, R. Roloff and J. Rüland, eds, *Interregionalism and International Relations*, London: Routledge, pp. 85–96.

Maull, H. W. and Okfen, N. (2006) 'Comparing Interregionalism. The Asia–Pacific Economic Cooperation (APEC) and the Asia–Europe Meeting (ASEM)', in H. Hänggi, R. Roloff and J. Rüland, eds, *Interregionalism and International Relations*, London: Routledge, pp. 217–33.

Milliot, D. (2004) 'ASEM – A Catalyst for Dialogue and Cooperation: The Case of FEALAC', in W. A. L. Stokhof, P. van der Velde and L. Hwee Yeo, eds, *The Eurasian Space – Far More Than Two Continents*, Singapore: International Institute for Asian Studies/Institute of Southeast Asian Studies.

Mols, M. (2005) 'Latin America and East Asia: Between Bilateralism and Inter-regionalism?' in J. Faust, M. Mols and W. H. Kim, eds, *Latin America and East Asia –Attempts at Diversification*, Münster: Lit/ KIEP, pp. 197–211.

Olivet, M. C. (2005) 'Unravelling Interregionalism Theory: A Critical Analysis of the New Interregional Relations Between Latin America and East Asia', Paper presented at *The VI Conference of REDEALAP*, Buenos Aires, 12–13 December.

Reiterer, M. (2009) 'Asia–Europe Meeting (ASEM): Fostering a Multpolar World Order Through Interregional Cooperation', *Asia Europe Journal*, vol. 7, no. 1, pp. 179–96.

—— (2006) 'Interregionalism as a New Diplomatic Tool: The EU and East Asia', *European Foreign Affairs Review*, vol. 11, no. 2, pp. 223–43.

—— (2002) *Asia–Europe. Do They Meet?Reflections on the Asia–Europe Meeting (ASEM)*, Singapore: Asia–Europe Foundation.

Robles, A. (2008), *The Asia–Europe Meeting – The Theory and Practice of Interregionalism*, London: Routledge.

Roloff, R. (2006) 'Interregionalism in Theoretical Perspective', in H. Hänggi, R. Roloff and J. Rüland, eds, *Interregionalism and International Relations*, London: Routledge, pp. 18–30.

Rüland, J. (2006) 'Interregionalism. An Unfinished Agenda', in H. Hänggi, R. Roloff and J. Rüland, eds, *Interregionalism and International Relations*, London: Routledge, pp. 295–315.

—— (2002a) 'Conference Summary', *Conference Interregionalism in International Relations*, Arnold-Bergstaesser-Institute, Freiburg, Germany, 31 January and 1 February, pp. 1–15.

—— (2002b) 'Inter- and Transregionalism: Remarks on the State of the Art of a New Research Agenda', Paper presented at the *Workshop on Asia–Pacific Studies in Australia and Europe: A Research Agenda for the Future*, Australian National University, 5–6 July, pp. 1–10.

—— (2001) *ASEAN and the European Union: A Bumpy Interregional Relationship*, ZEI Discussion Paper C95, Zentrum für Europäische Integrationsforschung, Centre for European Integration Studies, Rheinische Friedrich Wilhelms-Universität Bonn.

Schulz, M., Söderbaum, F. and Öjendal, J. (2001) 'Key issues in the New Regionalism: Comparisons from Asia, Africa and the Middle East', in S. Hettne, A. Inotai and O. Sunkel, eds, *Comparing Regionalisms – Implications for Global Development*, London: Palgrave, pp. 234–76.

Siddique, S. (2004) 'Executive Summary of Study on Trans-Pacific Trade and Investments: Overcoming Obstacles and Impediments', in *Cross-Pacific Economic Integration*, Singapore: Konrad-Adenauer – Stiftung, pp. 17–20.

Söderbaum, F., Stalgren, P. and Langenhove, L. Van (2005) 'The EU as a Global Actor and the Dynamics of Interregionalism: A Comparative Analysis', *Journal of European Integration*, vol. 27, no. 3, pp. 365–80.

Umbach, F. (2008) 'Asian–European Relations – More Security Through Inter- and Transregional Relations?', in J. Rüland, G. Schubert, G. Schucher and C. Storz, eds, *Asian European Relations – Building Blocks for Global Governance?*, London: Routledge, pp. 114–42.

Wilhelmy, M. and Mann, S. (2005) 'Multilateral Co-operation Between Latin America and East Asia', in J. Faust, M. Mols and W. H. Kim, eds, *Latin America and East Asia – Attempts at Diversification*, Münster: Lit/KIEP, pp. 29–44.

Index

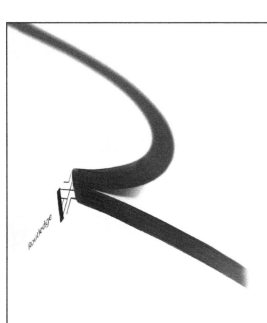